DISCIPLES
OF
DESTRUCTION

DISCIPLES
OF
DESTRUCTION

Charles W. Sutherland

Prometheus Books
Buffalo, New York

To my friends, whose beliefs I may not
share but whose affection I cherish
and
to my mother, whose compassion has always
triumphed over the allures of dogma

Library of Congress Card Catalog No. 86-42915
ISBN : 0-87975-349-8

Contents

Preface

For someone who is not a scholar to embark upon a project of this nature and scope could seem arrogant. I began the scribbling that became this book merely to clarify my thoughts, not to publicize them. It all started with observations and ideas I dashed down on notepads and napkins while sitting idle in hotels and airports around the world. During years abroad in studies, business, politics or travel in almost all of the countries discussed herein, the inconsistencies of human behavior I witnessed often appalled me. Privately people profess rationality and compassion; publicly they not only countenance violence and repression but seek to justify them morally.

A number of people belonging to the creeds criticized in this book, some in high places manipulating the machinery of civilization, have with time become my friends; such is the nature of human gregariousness. On occasion, they share many of the ideas presented here; at times they can even be the strongest critics of their own creeds, but not always publicly. My original labors were an attempt to reconcile what my heart wanted to feel with what my mind was compelled to conclude. Years of energetic discussion transformed this difficulty into a project: to publicly articulate the opinions set down here because others who shared them were not willing to do so.

To formulate sound ideas on such a sprawling subject as the relationship of religion and civilization, even when fortified by the knowledge of people privy to world secrets, is not an easy task for the novice author. To make such ideas suitable for dissemination to a wider readership required considerable historical research, taking me back to my days as a student of philosophy; it also required the willingness to recognize my own severe limitations, due to time constraints imposed by professional responsibilities and to the undeniable fact that erudition is not this author's forte. For all of these reasons the reader may unfortunately suffer. But of "those to whom much is given, much is expected." The opportunity to travel the world and analyze the beliefs and myths that cause so much daily suffering gradually became a responsibility to express the understanding formed in such fortunate circumstances. This took precedence over criticisms the author will undoubtedly face, both from people more knowledgeable and from ideologues, whether political or religious.

My ability to undertake this authorship is largely due to others, friends who provided inspiration and assistance. I would specifically like to thank Janet Donovan, who prodded me to publish what probably would have remained only reflections for personal edification; my publisher, Paul Kurtz, who had the courage to print what others would not; and my editor, Reg Gilbert, whose intelligence, broad perspectives, conscientious efforts, unrelenting criticisms and, ultimately, friendship, have helped give this book whatever worthwhile may be contained herein. Others to thank include those who have reviewed chapters, provided criticism of ideas, or assisted in research, proofreading, typing and/or carrying the burden of my professional responsibilities while I was busy writing "the book." They include Lisa Kelly, Marie Traylor, Gloria Hardy, Cathy Metta, Davie Crockett, Ronald Gunville, Arthur Davis, and others. To those who have reviewed various drafts but whose names cannot be mentioned, I am in debt. Despite the prodigious efforts of all who have helped, however, any errors contained herein, either of historical fact or political judgment, are of course my responsibility alone.

DISCIPLES
OF
DESTRUCTION

It is convenient that there be gods, and, as it is
convenient, let us believe there are.

—Ovid

It is something to have smelt the mystic rose,
although it break and leave the thorny rods;
it is something to have hungered, as those must hunger
who have once ate the bread of gods.

—G. K. Chesterton

Man's future is based upon his ability to think, not his capacity to believe.
—Semyaze

Introduction

We in the West are accustomed to taking pride in what we term our Judeo-Christian heritage. It has led us, we believe, to the time we now enjoy as the apex of human civilization. We act, on the whole, rationally and compassionately, we think. Despite the advent of the nuclear age, we foresee a future of tolerance and decreasing human misery.

There is much truth in these beliefs, but here and there, in the broadcasts of certain religious television and radio stations, in the posturing of armies in the birthplace of civilization, in the prevalence of terrorist acts, in the proclamation of "people's republics," lie disquieting signs of another future. All are remnants of another time, one also blessed by the Judeo-Christian ethic, when humanity was hardly rational, hardly compassionate, and hardly able to foresee a future when either rationality or compassion would hold sway.

Acclaimed as a tradition of morality, the Judeo-Christian ethic is in fact predominantly a legacy of intellectual nihilism, psychological repression, violence and war. The ethical basis of Judaism and Christianity is revered in the West, as all that is one's own is usually revered, but its characteristics are in the main quite the opposite of those touted, and both its own manifestations and its influence on the other two principal creeds of the world, Islam and Marxism, have served more to promulgate the pernicious than to extend civilization. Ever since it repudiated the rational constructions of the ancient Greeks and adopted in their place the myths of the Hebrews and Christians, Western society has struggled merely to regain an enlightenment already achieved: the supremacy of reason. The most powerful foes of this advance have been the emissaries of the divine, and it is they who are the subject of this book.

The myths invented by humanity have often inspired war, created pain and added imaginary sufferings to real ones, but not until Judeo-Christian myths were transformed into theology were metaphysical fear, guilt and intolerance given the power to outlive their cultural origins. Once ensconced in the citadel of monotheism and given immortality via doctrine and text, these pernicious concepts could be freely inflicted on the world's uneducated and helpless, both in the psychological realm, with the repression of independent thinking, and in the physical arena, with intolerance, inquisition and the divine sanctioning of war.

Religion was born when man's ignorance was overwhelming; it was a primitive attempt to organize human conduct and provide an antidote to metaphysical fear. Unfortunately, it merely replaced one fear with another; as for social organization, its techniques were rooted in the psychology of barbarism. While often serving the role of a secular constitution in providing social order and cohesion, religion created a ruling class of high priests who eventually became theologians. As societies emerged, the tribal chiefs became secular rulers, but they continued to rely upon the hierophants of the occult. A symbiotic relationship developed between these two halves of authority, the secular potentates and the dictatorial arbiters of the divine. These twins formed the ruling class which has characterized most of Western history. But, absent scientific knowledge, universal education, and a concept of human rights, their authority was based on fear, the progenitor of power.

Four creeds dominate the actions of more than three-fourths of the world's population: Judaism, Christianity, Islam and Marxism.

While accounting for only fifteen million people today, less than one-half of one percent of the world's believers, Judaism was seminal to the other three creeds, each of which, in greater or lesser degree, evolved from this ancient Hebrew cult. The Judaic religion is based on the fable of Abraham, whose existence is unlikely but who is said to have communicated with a storm god called Yahweh while in the sun-baked deserts of Palestine more than three thousand years ago. During this mythical conversation, Yahweh is said to have made a covenant with this desert nomad. Abraham was told he could seize all of his neighbors' territories and kill those who dwelled there. Incredibly, a number of those who consider themselves Abraham's twentieth-century descendants seriously believe they are divinely entitled to own several thousand square miles of real estate in the Middle East, and have set up a military nation, Israel, to claim it. That nation now has nuclear bombs, and a growing number of fundamentalists with few compunctions about using them.

The second religion treated in this book is Christianity. It has nearly one billion believers, and is based on the myth that many thousands of years ago a man and a woman named Adam and Eve ate the wrong piece of fruit and thereby condemned mankind to physical pain while alive and eternal fires when dead. To atone for this loathsome act of eating apples, millennia later another man, named Christ, when crucified by the imperial empire of ancient Rome for inciting insurrection, was said to have died to provide an opportunity to escape the fiery future prescribed as just punishment for this ancient agricultural transgression. The cross on which he died, itself a symbol of Roman persecution, was used to justify seizing political power in the Western world and retaining it for fifteen centuries. When the principal church that resulted from this ancient fairy tale lost its military power in the nineteenth century, the responsibility for defending these fables was passed on to the most powerful nation on earth, the United States. This successor has nuclear weapons and an ever-expanding congregation of Christian fundamentalists who advocate their use.

The third world religion is Islam, with just under a billion devotees. This religion is based on a book called the Koran, inspired by an illiterate, seventh-century nomad whose given name his followers do not even know, so he is called by an honorific title, Muhammad, meaning "highly praised." Unrestricted by any specific covenant, Muhammad's ambitions compelled him to claim that his god, called Allah, told him to plunder every nation in the known world. It did not matter that the final writing of the Koran waited until conquests were completed and a class to rule over the spoils largely consolidated, or that the final version of this allegedly divinely inspired document was only agreed upon through political negotiation. Some of this creed's disciples, those in modern Pakistan, will soon have the nuclear bomb, and the Islamic world has its own resurgence of religious fundamentalists.

The fourth creed treated here is Marxism, which controls over one and a half billion human beings. This creed was created by an impoverished nineteenth-century German intellectual named Karl Marx, whose emotional disposition and financial sagacity were largely obtained by spending almost all of his life borrowing money from friends and supervising the bankruptcy of most of the organizations he headed. Never successful in achieving his own economic well-being, Marx became adept as a financial leech and codified the skill into a system of metaphysics. To help his disciples be more effective than he had been, Marx made violence an integral component of his system of parasitism. Borrowing the worst features of Judaism and Christianity, Marx and his disciples posited a secular eschatology allegedly determined by scientific inquiry, a utopia of human economic equality to be realized at the price of the blood and treasure of those who did not accept this aberrant form of philosophical nonsense. Once empirical reality relegated Marx's economic theories to the garbage dump of history, his principal disciples, the leaders of the Soviet Union, created a new deity to whom truth could be sacrificed: the largest military establishment in the history of the world, complete with nuclear weapons.

These are the four creeds which dominate human behavior, making it quite probable that if there is intelligent life in the universe it must be on other planets. It is frightening that side by side with the geometric advance of nuclear technology, each of these creeds has been generating ever more numerous fundamentalists who reassert the scriptural truths of their original myths. If the acts of the creators of these myths are any guide, this confluence of developments in human affairs is to be feared.

Most people profess to be opposed to war. Yet the history of the human race is the history of war, usually sanctified by some deity. In *The Lessons of History,* Will and Ariel Durant note that, "In the last 3,421 years of recorded history, only 268 have seen no war. We have acknowledged war as at present the ultimate form of competition and natural selection in the human species." The incidence of war has not been reduced by economic systems, political democracy, the rise of what we optimistically refer to as civilization, or religion. Disappointingly, religion has clearly been a catalyst of war rather than an impediment to it. Indeed, Judaism and Islam were created for the express purpose of conquest, and the creed of Christianity (as distinct from its original principles) was immediately used for the purpose of justifying imperialism, a tradition it embellished in rationales for commercial colonialism and passed on to others in the form of colonialism's alleged inverse, Marxism.

Heraclitus proclaimed, *Polemos pater panton,*—war, or competition, is the father of all things. It has in fact been the parent of inventions, the basis for many institutions, the creator of technologies, the ultimate source of the state. History, like newspapers, records the dramatic episodes of human affairs. The underlying goodness in many people, the unheralded acts of kindness and even nobility, these historical facts frequently go unrecorded. How many more wars may have occurred had good and courageous people—some of them priests no doubt—not prevented them can only be a matter of speculation. What we do know is that war is one of history's constants. Furthermore, war has always been legitimized by religion, which traditionally provided doers of violence with a sense of moral purpose. One of the earliest extant writings of Western culture, the Old Testament, documents religion's calls to arms. Papal bulls of the nineteenth century, and Christian televangelist, Zionist, Islamic, and Marxist diatribes issued even today show that this was no passing barbarism.

Given religion's professed emphasis on the moral and the good, why has this been the case? In antiquity hardly anyone doubted the validity of omens. People have always invented myths as a framework of reference by which they attempt to organize their attitudes toward the world. Historically, we discover that beliefs not based upon empirical observation are usually a barometer of the dominant fears and passions of those who invent them. Since most religious beliefs have no basis in physical reality, the believer must continually prove that his or her creed is valid. This is usually achieved by proselytizing or militarily conquering others. Only by being able to point to others as sharing a belief system are the true believers able to demonstrate some empirical basis for their own myths.

Not having telescopes with which to understand the universe, our ancient ancestors created a theological cosmos that was a mirror reflecting their fears, one in which the entire spectrum of human emotion was projected into another world. Since man was unable to control the physical forces that governed his daily life, the elements of the universe were viewed as participants in a grand conspiracy to make him happy or sad. The notion that the universe might be cold and indifferent to human desires is one from which most people shrink, and to which very few ever wholly accommodate themselves. It is difficult to accept the idea that not only are our desires usually unsatisfied by hope, but that indeed our needs can go unfulfilled by even the most strenuous effort. It was accordingly easier for the ancients to invent sin than to develop science; man created prayer and guilt, and their constant companion, self-righteousness. The logical consequence of this psychology was that man attributed to sinfulness that which was quite adequately explained by ignorance or stupidity.

Unable to control the storms of the heavens, man fell down to worship those powers he thought governed them; he has remained kneeling ever since. But with his eyes turned to the heavens to placate his self-flagellating thirst for worship, man turned his attention away from thought and from the material means to improve his earthly existence. Deafened by the cacophony of their own incantations, many of those in a position to help could not hear the cries of those who suffered, the woebegone needing compassion more than prayers.

The myths man has invented over the centuries have brought him more harm than good. Napoleon once said that religion keeps the poor from murdering the rich. It is certainly true that the poor have only rarely come to realize that the ruling classes oppressing them are composed of both secular exploiters and religious charlatans, the sophistry of the latter indispensable to the power of the former. As Voltaire said, human happiness can be achieved only when the last king is strangled by the entrails of the last priest.

The world's religions have always served as a central component of a society's ability to legitimate war, to justify it as a necessary element of human conduct. The cosmic mirror created by the ancient high priests taught man that humanity is a microcosm of an eternal battle between good and evil. Only gradually does the march of education inform humanity that this battle is being waged not in the cosmos, but only in the self, that "the kingdom of God is within you."

Born with a hunger for knowledge and understanding, primitive man came to develop the power of thought. But he had to discipline the impulse to believe, the impulse to create deities instead of science. The gods of the Greeks were patterned after man, used to assist human understanding. The oriental deities created east of Greece, however, were endowed with the disposition of the tyrant; their character was to limit rationality and to control thought. From the storm god, Yahweh, came Judaism and its principal sects, Christianity and Marxism. The Greeks and Romans both had gods of war, but they were not dominant; Yahweh however was supreme and remained so. While Mars provided the rationale to conquer, powerful Venus was the counterpoint of love; there was no deity of love in the Hebrew pantheon of one. Prometheus, whose name means "forethought," was punished by Zeus for seeking to help mortals by bringing them fire, but the Olympian pantheon gradually sided with him. In the oriental construct, meanwhile, when Adam and Eve of the Hebrew tradition sought knowledge, they were banned from paradise for blasphemy; the disciples of Yahweh ratified this decision, making it into a theology that glorified ignorance and irrationality.

The Hebrew-Christian god was the personification of man's fears more than his hopes, fears manifested in intolerance and in aggression. Unlike the mythology of the gods of the Greeks, the theology built around the Hebrew-Christian god inspired men to sacrifice fellow humans in a contest for divine favor. Religious sanction for the impulse to kill was no longer limited to ritual sacrifice and the exercise of justice; it was expanded into war and imperialism.

The long battle to liberate the mind from the tyranny of fear continues, as slowly knowledge replaces myth. In our age, however, the slow process of slaying the dragons of mythology is not keeping step with the geometric pace of nuclear weapons development and deployment. In our century, the proliferation of nuclear weapons accelerates in the context of an equally explosive growth of religious fundamentalism, manifest in the increasing numbers and influence of the militant Christians, the Zionist Jews, the orthodox Muslims and the frustrated Marxists, all busy pressuring or inspiring their symbiotic twins, the rulers of the world's nations. Somewhere, the ancient gods of war are laughing.

Part One

THE THEOLOGY OF CONQUEST

And when the Lord thy God shall have . . . given thee great and goodly cities, which thou didst not build, Houses full of riches, which thou didst not set up, cisterns which thou didst not dig, vineyards and oliveyards thou didst not plant, and thou shall have eaten and be full: take heed diligently lest thou forget the Lord.

—Deuteronomy 6:10–13

Of those cities that shalt be given thee, thou shalt suffer none at all to live: but shalt kill them with the edge of the sword . . . as the Lord thy God hath commanded thee.

—Deuteronomy 20:15–17

Thy right hand, O Lord, is become glorious in power: thy right hand, O Lord, hath dashed in pieces the enemy.

—Exodus 15:6

I

Abraham: Fabled Figure of Unity

I n the eyes of religious Jews, the central theme of Jewish belief, Jewish claims of being the "Chosen People" of God, and Jewish claims to specific geography in the Middle East all stem from the "covenant" (contract) entered into between God and the Jewish people. This covenant is the cornerstone of orthodox Jewish belief and conduct. The first mention of the covenant is in Genesis 15:18, when God promised to give the territory of Canaan to the descendants of Abraham:

> In the same day the Lord made a covenant with Abram [Abraham], saying, Unto thy seed have I given this land, from the river of Egypt unto the great river, the river Euphrates . . .

Although God apparently had a detailed knowledge of geography, he did not show much diplomatic ability. God apparently neglected to discuss the covenant with the people of Canaan, who refused to be convinced that a god had entered into such an unlikely arrangement. Nevertheless, to fulfill God's will (and, of course, their own desires) the Hebrews one day would take Canaan by force of arms and, according to the Book of Joshua, they slaughtered its people by the thousands. Joshua destroyed the town of Ai so completely that "few traces of it are to be found," according to one Judaic scholar, who says that "Joshua subjected it to what was known during the Second World War as the 'scorched earth policy'."[1]

The surviving Canaanites apparently did not continue to physically contest this supposedly divine agreement, although one doubts they were ever provided a copy with God's signature. As in divine agreements in other religions, the signature of God on Abraham's covenant was forged— penned in by the believers with the blood of the vanquished. As centuries passed, this covenant was "ratified" continuously, in scripture and by force of arms. Since Abraham's covenant with God is one of Judaism's most important foundation stones, we must investigate further the legend of Abraham itself.

The legend of Abraham was written centuries after the man it concerned supposedly lived. Apart from Old Testament legends, probably written in the time of Moses, there is no evidence that he actually existed.[2] The historical books of the Old Testament were mostly compiled after the captivity of the Jews in the sixth century BCE (before the Christian era), and the writers "were innovators to a much greater extent than appears in the Bible when read unhistorically."[3] In all likelihood the legend of Abraham was created in the time of Moses in order to create a Hebrew "tradition" that could unite an enslaved Hebrew people, and in which Moses could become a principal player. (Centuries later Muhammad also accepted Abraham as the founder of the Muslim religion;[4] Abraham is not only referred to in the Koran but is part of the history of Islam's sacred shrine in Mecca, where it is claimed he once stood.[5]

Unlike modern American politicians who like to claim that they rose to prominence from small-town obscurity, the Hebrew politicians liked to claim that they and their ancestors were born and reared in the important cities. Ancient leaders generally claimed to be favored by the gods, or, at a minimum, maintained some pretense of actual or pseudo patrician origins (democratic "success stories" were not appreciated in those days). Accordingly the legend places Abraham in Ur, which would have been the contemporary equivalent of New York.

In Genesis 11:31 it appears that Abraham, the towering figure on whom all Jewish tradition is based, was born in Ur as Abram (he changed his name at God's command during the making of the covenant). Scholarly opinion varies as to the date of his birth, but it is generally accepted as being between 2100 and 1700 BCE. Ur is a well-known city near the Chaldees, presently about 120 miles from the Persian Gulf. Abram (Abraham) was apparently a citizen of a great city and ancient civilization, and his father, Terah, may have been an important person in the city. The question is—why did they leave Ur?

The reason may be that the conquest of Ur by Hammurabi introduced religious practices unacceptable to Abram's father. Ur was the center of worship of the moon god, Sin (not associated with the word meaning moral evil), whose temple was high on the top of a mount called Ziggurat, located above hundreds of stone stairs. In this temple, called the "House of Great Light," the people gathered to perform their rituals, one of which was human sacrifice: killing the first-born male. At the burial ceremony of a reigning king, human sacrifice was performed on a grand scale so that the king could go to his rest surrounded by his women, soldiers, attendants and courtiers—all slaughtered for the occasion. Since Abram clearly believed in the practice of sacrificing the first-born (Genesis 22), he and his father, Terah, may have been part of this moon-god cult. When Hammurabi conquered Ur, he introduced the cult of sun worship, which may have led Terah and Abram to leave. Apart from the gods of the sun and moon, there were numerous other gods common to ancient Middle East peoples, associated variously with food, weather, crops, and even landscape. Human nature being what it is, occasionally some of the area's people believed (or hoped) that one of these gods was superior to the others.

At some point Terah and Abram left Ur, travelling northward to a place called Haran, where they settled. When Terah died Abraham took his relatives, including his wife, Sarah, and his nephew Lot, and traveled to the territory of Canaan.

It is at this time that Abram and his followers received the name of *habiru*, a word attached to them by peoples in the Middle East which in both Hebrew and Greek means "one who crosses (from place to place), a transient, a nomad." Among those hostile to them, the term came to imply "plunderer, brigand," people without a settled home who lived by their wits, selling their services or whatever goods they could carry, soldiers of fortune, traders who made quick deals or fighters who fought quick battles.[6] Indeed, *habiru* was a general term used to describe nomads of the area, both Semitic and non-Semitic. The "Hebrews" of Jewish tradition, however, did not come into existence as a group at least until Moses organized the slaves of Egypt.

Somewhere during the journey to Canaan, so the legend goes, the herdsmen of Lot and Abram began to quarrel over water supplies. The group separated. Lot went eastward to the green pastures of the Jordan plains. Abram went to Hebron, which lay in a fertile valley. There he set up a tent camp, dug wells, and received the hospitality of the people who lived in the area. Abram was the patriarch of his followers, relatives and servants, all of whom submitted to his authority.

Eventually Abram and Sarah had a son, whom they named Isaac, "laughter." With the birth of Isaac, Sarah grew jealous of Abram's slave wife, Hagan, and Hagan's son, Ishmael, lest Abram's inheritance not go to her own son. She persuaded Abram to send them into the wilderness, thereby making Hagan and Ishmael the first recorded Palestinian refugees. They almost died wandering through rough, rocky wasteland without water and amidst wild animals, but Hagan found a well and they were helped by friendly people. Years later, so the legend goes, Ishmael would become the leader of a nomadic tribe whose descendants today are said to be the pure Arabs—the *Bedaween* (Bedouin) desert dwellers, "wild-ass men" (Genesis 16:11-12). So while the Arabs are said to be descendants of Ishmael, the Jews are alleged to have descended from Isaac, his half brother, which would partially explain why Jews and Arabs have always been so hostile to each other: sibling rivalry.

According to the legend, one day Abram decided to slaughter his first-born child in sacrifice to the god he worshipped, a tradition also practiced in Canaan. Isaac was chagrined: Ishmael had been sent away too soon, leaving Isaac as the only available candidate for sacrifice, even though he was not the first born! Abram built an altar, laid Isaac upon it and pre-pared to slay him. But, just as he was about to plunge the sacrificial knife into his son, Abram's hand was stayed. God revealed to him that there was a better way to worship than by human sacrifice (a view no doubt shared by Isaac).

To the authors of Abraham legend is credited what many consider one of the great advances of Western civilization—postulating a deity above, not merely more powerful than, all other gods. This was a revolutionary idea: a leader above all leaders, an ethical system in embryo, and an exceedingly simple view of the cosmos all in one. Unlike the moon god, the thunder god and the lightning god, all of whom could be characterized in some way, this new god of the mind's creation was too holy to be described, and so was called simply "I am who am," *Yahweh* in Hebrew, but never-theless attributes were assigned to this god year after year, century after century, depending upon the psychological disposition and physical plight of the leading believers and their followers.

From the outset, two of this god's characteristics were anger and vengeance; he was a god of war. Over the centuries the quality of "just" was ascribed to him, reflecting human society's gradual ethical develop-ment. Still later the quality of love was attached to Yahweh, so that by the time Christ arrived, more than a thousand years after the creation of Yahweh, he would refer to this deity as "the God of love"; by then the Hebrew prophets had extended the idea of social justice far enough to call it love. It was only natural that this idea entrench itself in the realm of the supernatural in a more fixed way. Christ's god was nonetheless still called "the Father Almighty," signifying his continuing personification as mascu-line, omnipotent power.

Yahweh's original character was less complex. Abram's legendary covenant with God was simple: in return for Abram's acceptance of Yahweh as his only god and as the deity of his people, Abram would receive a divine right to the territory of Canaan. Why a god should want or need to enter into such an agreement is not explained, but there are reasons why Abram—that is, the authors of the Abraham legend—may have wanted to do so. A leader naturally wishes to unify the people under his rule. It is easiest for a people to coalesce around a single system of belief; social cohesion is more difficult if a people worship various gods, or worship the same gods with varying emphases. The unification of a people serves rulers well. One can speculate on the advantages to Abraham of asserting the existence of a single god, one for whom, of course, he was the main spokesman. In a polytheistic system, there are priests (spokesmen) for many gods. One may be more powerful than others, but in the making of political decisions, and the securing of divine guidance to inform them, a system of many gods, of whatever relative importance, allows also for many voices in the earthly representation of their advice. As a result, primitive polytheistic societies (in definite contrast to more developed ones, such as the Egyptian) generally tended to oligarchy rather than monarchy. Rather than invoking the purported instructions of many gods, as was traditional up to that time, it would be simpler for the purpose of seizing the land of Canaan to have one god to whom one could attribute divine commands. The authors of the legend of Abraham can thus be credited with harnessing theism to the cart of militarism in an entirely new way, fundamentally differently than the theocracy of Egypt which was the model of the day, and in a way that would prove, over the run of succeeding millennia, to be far more effective.

Abram's contract with God is described in Genesis 17:7:

> And I will establish my covenant between me and thee and thy seed after thee . . . to be a god unto thee, and to thy seed after thee.

Because of his new relationship with God, Abram changed his name to Abraham, to reflect his new identity. He put his signature on this agreement (the Hebrew term is *b'rith,* meaning "covenant") by agreeing to the rite of circumcision, as prescribed in Genesis 17:10:

> This is my covenant, which ye shall keep . . . Every man child among you shall be circumcised.

The ritual of circumcision became the outward manifestation (and reminder) of every male Jew's covenant with Yahweh. Female Jews had no similar outward sign, because the Hebrews were a male-dominated society. (In the twentieth century this would change somewhat, as women became more socially liberated; a very few are even in the process of becoming rabbis.)

Circumcision is the removal of the foreskin of the penis, a loss which does not interfere with the sex act, and many believe that it adds to overall hygiene. Circumcision has its origins in prehistoric antiquity, and was adopted by the Hebrews. It was practiced by the Egyptians, as well as by the Canaanites who were under the domination of the Egyptians during Abraham's era.

Jews began to use the mark of circumcision to distinguish themselves from others, particularly the Philistines and Babylonians. This mark of separation came to be viewed as legal evidence that the Promised Land was Jewish by divine agreement and would always belong to Jews. However, circumcision was a "borrowed" symbol, not unique to the Hebrews. Some scholars say that Moses gave the Jews the law of circumcision, and, if so, "he was no Jew, but an Egyptian."[7] The legend of Abraham, like most legends, was probably continually embellished in succeeding centuries.

It must be admitted that circumcision is an improvement over Abraham's former practice, the Canaanite custom of killing the first-born child. Had he maintained the "first-born" custom it would undoubtedly have been more difficult to propagate the Jewish people. Why Abraham chose circumcision as the outward expression of the pact with his god is not really known—or even if he actually did. The legends of Abraham were written during the era of Moses. It is fair to say that those who finally recorded them on paper stressed certain elements in accordance with contemporary realities. A people seeking nationhood would only naturally look at historical accounts to support that ambition. Did Abraham adopt the rite of circumcision as the outward sign of his compact with his god? Or did Abraham's people and time occasionally practice circumcision, only later to have it interpreted as such a sign? Or was it a tradition created entirely in the era of Moses so that Moses could inspire his constituency of slaves by informing them that they had a long history in a land far away from Egypt? We will never know.

The issue is important because the rewriting or editing of history is perhaps the first impulse of those hoping to use that history to their own ends, be they for good or evil. This is often how "tradition" is born, a strong reason for questioning it as a basis for contemporary belief and action.

The original celebration of Abraham's covenant with God was barbaric. First Abraham was instructed by God to kill several animals: "Take me a cow of three years old, and a she-goat of three years, and a ram of three years, a turtle also and a pigeon. And he took all these, and divided them in the midst, and laid the two pieces of each one against the other; but the birds he divided not" (Genesis 15). God represented himself as a fire burning between the body parts and Abraham then walked between them. In this fashion the two walked together in the body of the sacrifice and were bound together as "one." This pagan act is the original basis for the Hebrew claim to being the earth's Chosen People and to be entitled forever to hundreds of square miles of territory in the Middle East.

Genesis also describes the result: "That day God made a covenant with Abram, saying: To thy seed will I give this land, from the river of Egypt even to the great river Euphrates. The Cineans and Cenezites, the Cedmonites. And the Hethites, and the Pherezite, the Raphaim also. And the Amorrhites, and the Chanaanites, and the Gergesites, and the Jebusites." With this barbaric animal ceremony the covenant was said to have been created, and the theological justification for Hebrew uniqueness—and rule—established. Judaism and its Christian and Islamic descendants were thus born in a superstitious ceremony ratifying imperial ambition—a heritage which they all would embellish to the fullest. Viewed objectively, the Hebrew covenant with Yahweh is difficult to differentiate from the contract between Dr. Faustus and Mephistopheles centuries later, except as a matter of theological taste. In both cases mortals sought earthly power by making a pact with the supernatural.

Abraham had become an old man by this time, "ninety years old and nine, when he was circumcised," according to Genesis 17:24. Nearing the end of his life, he faced the problem of perpetuating his life's work. Given his age, modern psychologists would probably tell us, Abraham might have reflected on his situation and wondered what he had done of any lasting value. When he died, who would be the leader of his tribe? Would it disperse after he had spent most of his life holding it together? To solve both problems Abraham decided to create for his people some binding political organization with an objective to pursue. Moses faced nearly the identical task; perhaps he was a model used by the authors of the Abraham legend.

Acquiring political power over all of the people in the area could be an effective strategy, although an ambitious one. But since the neighboring tribes had been reasonably friendly, so the Bible tells us, Abraham could not single out any particular one to attack. That would be transparent as self-aggrandizement. If he were going to claim to have a mandate from Yahweh, Abraham had to claim a divine right to rule *all* his neighbors. This would serve the dual purpose of providing social and political cohesion to his tribe, and would also mitigate his own frustrations. He could bequeath a legacy to his followers. The plan had the additional advantage of leaving Abraham out of the fighting, because he would die of old age before it began. Moses would be in much the same position.

Since much of the Old Testament is myth and legend written decades or centuries after the events, any psychological analysis is speculative at best, an attempt to interpret unverifiable myth. The inability to separate fact and myth also prevents the formulation of any credible theology—yet on the skimpy legend of Abraham Judeo-Christian theology is based. It would be used over the centuries to justify killing millions of people. Compared to the centuries of divinely sanctioned slaughter that were to follow, ritual killing of the first-born male would seem like naive child's play.

The singular contribution of the authors of the Abraham legend was the revolutionary transformation of man's attitude toward the gods. Before Abraham, the gods and their periodic displays of anger were viewed with fear; after Abraham, fear of the divine was transformed into cooperation with it in a revolutionary partnership by which one god was supreme and directed his anger *only against the enemies* of Abraham's people—so long as they obeyed his commands. The first enemies were those inhabiting the land Abraham sought to acquire. When his nomadic kinsmen from the steppe came into contact with the urban populations of Palestine, the superior level of civilization could not have failed to make them envious. How to acquire these urban benefits for themselves? And since force seemed likely to be necessary, how to create a rationale for it? Thus, the mythical Abraham began the movement toward monotheism, whether for theological or political purposes. The powers of the storm god, Yahweh, were embellished, and Abraham could promulgate his god as more powerful than any other, so powerful that no other gods could be worshipped in any way, so powerful that he could only be described as "I am who am." As specious or as substantive as Abraham's tale may sound, the "covenant" attributed to him is the origin of the Jewish claim to being earth's Chosen People, and the Jewish claim to ownership of property in Palestine. All Jewish history and most Jewish military exploits stem from those primitive assertions.

The legend of Abraham, and its expanded legacy, should be put into perspective. Antiquity was characterized by both polytheism, belief in many gods, and henotheism, loyalty to one god above many. The myths of these gods satisfied the soul by reducing unbounded metaphysical fears to coherent if not controllable dimensions, and provided social solace by allowing people to perform their daily chores, and even to progress, believing they had fraternal friends in the skies. But the tribal leaders, like politicians of any era, were not satisfied. Abraham (or Moses) in particular had larger ambitions, requiring a unique god. He needed a "constitutional" framework to organize his people, and a set of rationales to justify his intentions. Belief in a unitary figure above was a psychic sanctuary where conduct would be dictated and choices clearly provided. This was preferable to the uncertain world of competing gods, whose reasons for blessing earthly efforts were complex, and subject to the activities of other gods. Middle Eastern cosmology before Abraham added up to little more than the uncertainties of the cycles of Fate, which in Greek mythology ruled both gods and men.

Such a system does not create certainty out of the chaos, which, after all, is touted today as the chief benefit of religious feeling. One can see the attraction of monotheism, and understand its celebration as an advance in religious understanding and therefore of civilization itself. It was not. Unlike the ancient Greeks, who viewed the unknown as a series of unexplored possibilities, the Hebrews managed to suspend the anxiety of the indefinite rather than come to grips with it. In this sense, monotheism is an escape from reality.

Hebrew monotheism, and the regimentation it required, was far more coherent than its polytheistic forebears. Monotheism provided a simpler picture of the supernatural world, and both more imperative and more easily understood direction from it. Hebrew monotheism provided psychic certitude by creating rules for living given out by a stern god, and therefore permitted a confidence in dealing with all aspects of life: social relationships, political affairs, and the needs of security such as food, shelter and protection from one's enemies.

A psychological *cul-de-sac* in primitive thought caused the detour to the Hebrew variety of monotheism (with their more advanced systems of thought, the Greeks and Romans could presumably have done better) and it was political ambition which inspired its peculiarly regressive application to the social order. Lacking effective means to motivate his flock, that is, the means to implement his imperial ambitions, Abraham (or Moses, acting through the figure of Abraham) ascribed both his objectives and the methods to achieve them to an unchallengeable deity. Seizing neighboring lands would provide a source of security and riches, but even the primitive morality of the time required an ethical justification for such imperial self-aggrandizement. Yahweh was Abraham's *deus ex machina,* about to become real. The fateful and ultimately irrevocable transition from mythology to theology began.

With the move from a regime of many gods to that of only one, generalized belief became focused faith; intolerance and aggression became more incontrovertibly sacred. The many gods had required respect, but God was said to command obedience. Polytheistic belief had been a psychological outlet with limited repercussions; monotheistic faith, however, demanded exclusion of other beliefs and contempt in the face of them. The Hebrew people did not simply become aware that there was only one god. That would be only good news that needed spreading. They became at the same time aware of another fact: he had chosen *them* as his special people. The accompanying view of neighboring peoples with different beliefs necessarily edged toward contempt. Aggression would soon follow.

Though his name was too sacred to mention, Yahweh was no less anthropomorphic than his predecessors, merely less positively so. It would be a long time before Yahweh became a god of love, even of justice, and he had none of the useful interests in the harvest and other life-sustaining elements of human activity which, even in a religious context, could serve people's material interests quite well. Instead Yahweh was a god of vengeance and interested most in compelling reverent obedience and loyalty. Yahweh had none of the gentile characteristics of the West, as some of the Greek gods and goddesses did; he was an oriental despot.

Far from a supposed intellectual advance, the creation of this new kind of deity was an exercise in intellectual and social regression—powers of independent reasoning were surrendered, and solving the practical problems of the day took second place to fulfilling the exacting requirements of a watchful and wrathful overlord. Submission to a powerful divinity in the skies severed humanity from earth and directed its attention to the nebulous realm of the celestial, in honor of which centuries would be spent in prostrate adoration.

By providing rules of social conduct, the new faith harnessed rather than diluted the impulses which caused crime and other behavioral excesses, redirecting them from kinsmen to people left out of this revolutionary covenant with the divine. It provided legitimization of violence on a grand scale. Monotheism gave good credentials to Abraham's (or Moses') pursuits, the limited imperial objectives of seizing Canaan. When later embellished by the Christians to encompass salvation of all the world's souls, Yahweh's mandate to conquer would endow succeeding millennia of ruling classes with inestimably strengthened celestial approval.

The Greeks did not believe that the gods created the universe; they believed the universe had created the gods. In the Greek cosmology, when the gods had finished their internecine contest for supremacy and the order of the world was stable, earth became a place of comfort and security and was therefore ready to be occupied by mankind. But the Hellenic people who dwelled along the sunny shores of the Aegean had more reason for such optimism than the Hebrews living in the sun-baked sands and cold desert nights of Palestine. The Hebrew people lived in fear, not in hope, and their god was a creation of that anxiety.

The Greeks thought they were ruled by gods, but these gods did not have complete license, due both to their multiplicity and to the fact of their place in the universe, subordinate to Fate. Each had a wide range of human qualities, and each a particular virtue, and vice, which appealed to the people. Although the deities fought each other, their contests were psychologically instructive to mortals, for whose allegiance they also contended. The whole of humanity, its strengths, weaknesses and aspirations was replicated in the polytheistic world. It had its implicit sense of right and wrong, told not in absolutes but in the story of the gods.

Polytheistic morality, just as humanity's is fated always to be, was mediated by events. The gods, that is, their actions and the virtues and vices which informed them, were subject to critique; the lessons of their stories were subject to interpretation. So too, of course, is the Bible, Old Testament and New. But in the Bible, interpretations are circumscribed. The meanings of tales and parables exist in frameworks, the Ten Commandments and the laws of Deuteronomy, or the rules for attaining the afterlife come from the mouth of the Son of God. As a result they tend more to define human action than to draw wisdom from it—monotheism, finally, is more received than lived. As such, its potential to "do" good on earth is great, but equally its potential to do evil. The evil committed or abetted by monotheistic belief has in fact been great, monstrous, war its supreme, widespread and indefatigable vehicle. The good, perhaps, has been only less dramatic. But of the good we have only some features of the id and evidence of charity. These achievements are difficult to quantify or to measure against that which they overcame, while the heaps of bodies after combat and pillage speak for themselves. Nonetheless, surely it is safe to say that the record of monotheistic religion hardly reflects its billing as a leap up the ladder of civilized advance.

Unlike the Greek gods, created as vehicles for man's understanding of his own personality, the Hebrew god was not created to impart wisdom, but to be the personification of the frustrations and terrestrial ambitions of his creators. The Hebrew tradition, passed on to the Christians and Western civilization, created a god in whom was invested all the attributes needed to channel psychological fears into repression and a great deal of political ambition into aggression. The new god of the Hebrews was first and foremost the scornful supreme commander of the military forces of the Chosen. From that day until the rise of Marxism, authoritarian regimes tasted of monotheism and found it invigorating.

In the story of the God of Abraham tyranny took its first lasting ideological form. Although the imperial ambitions of the Hebrews were limited, those of their successors were not. The Hebrews did not invent mathematics or engineering, like the Chinese, Indians or Egyptians, nor did they conceive a system of thought like the Greeks. The primary legacy left to mankind by the authors of the Abraham legend was a theology of conquest. Of the "advances" it represented long term, the most important was that it was written down. This extended its power fantastically, enabling it to shape Christian and Muslim ideas. Their imperial objectives would not be limited to so small an area as Canaan.

The bread of deceit is sweet to a man; but afterwards his mouth shall be filled with gravel.

—Proverbs 20:17

II

Jacob: Founding a Faith on Fraud

To perpetuate his patriarchal family and the covenant that would assure it, the legend has it, Abraham realized that his son Isaac had to be married and have children. He forbade Isaac to marry a Canaanite. He considered them foreigners who worshipped idols. So Abraham sent his servant, Elieza, with ten camels laden with gifts back to his adopted hometown of Haran; many of his kinsmen still lived there. Elieza met a girl named Rebekah at a watering hole and showed her several objects—a ring and two bracelets of gold. Recognizing them as betrothal gifts, Rebekah rushed to tell her family, who, apparently without asking any questions, extended Eastern hospitality to Elieza and allowed him to board his animals and spend the night. Elieza explained his mission and the family accepted the gifts; he left the next morning with Rebekah and her nurse, Deborah. According to custom, Rebekah had no voice in the matter (quite unlike modern Israeli women) and left on a journey of many miles to spend her life with an older man she had met only the day before.

Isaac and Rebekah had twins: Esau, a "physical" man and skillful hunter who was the first born and therefore entitled to the blessing and birthright of his father; and Jacob, a quiet, introspective fellow who was a shepherd with much time to reflect upon his life's ambitions.

One day Isaac sent Esau to get some "savory meat" (venison), after which he would bestow his blessing upon him. Rebekah, conspiring with Jacob, put pieces of kidskin on Jacob's arms and body so that Isaac, nearly blind, would believe these were the hairy arms of his first-born. Completely deceived, Isaac bestowed his blessing on Jacob by mistake. Esau was furious when he learned of the deception (Genesis 27) and Jacob fled for his life back to Haran.

At the well of Padanaram, Jacob met a young girl named Rachel, with whom he fell in love. Having no money, Jacob promised her father, Laban, that he would make up the dowry by working for him for seven years without pay. Laban agreed, and after seven years a marriage ceremony was performed. Jacob removed the veil from his bride's face to pledge his lifelong commitment—and discovered Rachel's older sister Leah! Laban explained that according to Eastern custom the first-born girl had to be married first. He demanded that Jacob accept Leah as his wife. Jacob refused to go along with this deceit, apparently only approving of deception when he could benefit from it. Instead, Jacob bargained with Laban to allow him to have Rachel if he worked seven more years. When all was added up, Rachel cost far more than the ordinary dowry, although we are told that Jacob regularly cheated Laban in his work for him as a shepherd.

Jacob had many children and his numerous offspring changed the Hebrew people from a family to a group of tribes. According to Genesis 35, "Now the sons of Jacob were twelve. The sons of Leah: Reuben the first born, and Simeon, and Levi, and Juda, and Issachar, and Zabulon. The sons of Rachel: Joseph and Benjamin. The sons of Bala, Rachel's handmaid: Dan and Nephtali. The sons of Zelpha, Leah's handmaid: Gad and Aser: these are the sons of Jacob, that were born to him in Mesopotamia of Syria." Leah had at least one daughter, Dina, presumably from Jacob. In general, daughters were not regarded as worth mentioning in the Bible. Together these offspring of Jacob and their families became the Twelve Tribes of Israel, some of whose descendants would claim to have inherited Canaan.

To keep things in perspective, it should be mentioned that there were many nomadic tribes moving around this area of the world in this period. The Hebrew tribes allegedly descended from Abraham's various offspring were moving everywhere in the Middle East. The story of the Bible focuses on particular people, but that is because it is a story by authors who had an objective: creating a national history and an ethnic ideology. Fact and fable are interwoven in the Bible, and much of it was written hundreds of years after the events. By the time the authors wrote their accounts, the Bible was a highly edited view of history which drew on "facts" passed on by word of mouth for generations and on hopes converted into beliefs. The story of Exodus asserts that there was only one group of Hebrews, which contradicts the conclusion from the legend of Abraham that there were innumerable other tribes and groups of Hebrews migrating from one place to another in the Middle East. The editors of the text overlooked this detail when weaving the Hebrew tradition needed to support the tale of Moses' forging of the Hebrew nation.

Upset that he had to work another seven years to obtain his beloved Rachel, Jacob compensated by stealing Laban's best animals for his own flocks. Then, when Laban went on a journey, Jacob gathered his wives and possessions and went southward. Jacob took with him Laban's sacred household teraphim—terra cotta images of the goddess of fertility, Astarte, who people believed protected the crops. Yahweh was apparently not the sole object of Jacob's beliefs. Jacob may have had little allegiance to Abraham's only god. Laban pursued Jacob, caught up with him, and reprimanded him for being deceitful. Jacob returned the compliment and reproved Laban for his twenty years of deception. All was resolved by agreeing to forget the past.

Jacob, as the legend goes, continued on his journey and at one point encountered Esau, whom he pacified with apologies and gifts. Jacob's tribes later moved southward into Canaan, while others stayed behind and became the Syrians whom we will meet later as enemies of Israel. (Note that all of these people allegedly came from the same family.)

During this journey, Jacob was gripped by internal doubts regarding his life and conduct. The Bible says an "angel" gripped him. He wrestled with the angel (his thoughts) all night and by morning had "won" the battle! He had "striven with God and with men and hast prevailed." This is a bizarre passage in Genesis—the angel, God's representative, lost the struggle. Jacob would not permit him to leave ("I will not let thee go, except thou bless me!") At light of dawn Jacob's "angel" instructed him to change his name to Israel, Hebrew for "he who strives with the lord" (Genesis 32:24-30).

God must have been surprised that Jacob defeated even his own messenger (and, by implication, God himself), and then demanded to be blessed for his conduct and goals. It does tell us something about Biblical arrogance that Jacob competed with God and won, and the name "Israel" itself means exactly that. "Thy name shall not be called Jacob, but Israel: for if thou hast been strong against God, how much more shalt thou prevail against men?" (Genesis 32:28). Of such beliefs is bred fanaticism.

The resettlement in Canaan did not go without incident. Jacob's sons in particular caused many problems. Two, Simeon and Levi (sons by Leah), slaughtered the men of Shechem; Reuben (also by Leah) slept with Bala, Rachel's handmaid and Jacob's concubine, thereby causing some complicated family problems; and Joseph (a son of Rachel) was sold into slavery to the Ishmaelites by his half-brothers, born of Leah. In general, it must be observed, Jacob and his family were characterized by promiscuity, incest and treachery.

When famine came to Canaan, as it had in Abraham's time, Jacob sent his sons to purchase food from the granaries of the pharaoh, then went to Egypt himself. The family never returned to Canaan, but settled in the region of Joshen. As Moshe Dayan, the late Israeli general, observes in his *Living with the Bible*, it was an "unpardonable sin" that the children of Israel should forsake their land, particularly Jacob, the man after whom Israel was named.[1] Dayan does not address the larger question: the ancestors having forsaken their land, how could the descendants return centuries later to claim it on religious or any other grounds? More to the point: How can contemporary Israelis take this claim seriously enough to assert the right to possession of "biblical Judea and Samaria"—and do so by forced relocation of peoples resident there for millennia?

In summary, the legacy of Jacob is that he conspired to gain his father's blessing by deception; he spent much of his life stealing from his father-in-law; he conceived sons noted for murder, debauchery, and selling a brother into slavery; and he fled Canaan, violating the covenant of Abraham and forfeiting any Hebrew claim to being the "Chosen People." Judaism and Christianity trace their lineage from Jacob, the illegitimate heir, and his successors.

The pattern established through the time of Jacob was hardened into tradition; through scripture and canonization it became sacred. The Old Testament is an ideological statement of a people seeking nationhood and attempting to justify it theologically. The deceit illustrated in these Old Testament Scriptures, however, while offensive to a twentieth-century mentality, was apparently acceptable behavior and even regarded as divinely inspired. How a modern mind could subscribe to such tripe in any form, much less as "holy," is a mystery of psychology.

From Jacob and his various descendants, the Twelve Tribes of Israel were born. According to the legend some would return to Canaan centuries later, under the leadership of Moses, to militarily persuade the local people that the Hebrews were the divinely invested owners of the land despite an absence of hundreds of years. The Canaanites naturally had difficulty accepting this notion; when they struggled to keep their land, they were slaughtered. Among the victims were other tribes of Hebrews, unfortunates left unprotected despite the fact that the editors of scriptural text had accidentally left them in the covenant's fine print.

God is a Man of War.

—The Song of Moses

We have made a covenant with death, and with hell are we at agreement.

—Isaiah 28:15

III

Moses: In Search of a Constituency

T he story of Moses begins with the severe persecution of the slaves in Egypt under Pharaoh Ramses II, sometime during the second millennium B.C.E. Moses is alleged to have led these slaves out of Egypt, and from this time commenced the period of conquest which led to the formation of specifically Hebrew states.

The conquest began with Moses' reaffirmation of Abraham's supposed covenant between Yahweh and the Hebrew people, which had been discarded by Isaac's sons, Esau and Jacob, and subsequently abandoned by the Hebrews. A Hebrew ideology was developed by biblical authors around this body of Egyptian slaves, even though "all the evidence . . . would seem to indicate quite definitely that there were Hebrews in Palestine, particularly in Northern Palestine . . . and that only a comparatively small group ever went to Egypt."[1]

Ramses II seems to have been preoccupied with constructing monuments and buildings, and the Hebrews, among others, were part of the pool of slaves used to construct them. They were growing in numbers despite the conditions they lived under; the pharaoh feared their potential power. He kept them in slavery principally as brickmakers, and (according to Exodus) had male Hebrew babies put to death. Old Testament legend has it that one Hebrew mother reacted by putting her newborn son into a basket and floating it onto the Nile River. The infant was discovered (some biblical scholars say) by Hatshepsut, daughter of the pharaoh, and he was eventually elevated to power.

The boy was Moses. He was raised in the Egyptian court, taught to read and write and made a member of the Egyptian ruling class. Some scholars believe that Moses was an Egyptian but it is difficult to distinguish historical fact from legend here.

When he was a young man Moses interfered with the beating of a Hebrew slave by an Egyptian slave-master. He killed the Egyptian and buried the body in the sand. Sometime later, so the account goes, Moses encountered two Hebrews fighting. When he tried to separate them, one said, "Who made thee a prince and a judge over us? Intendest thou to kill me, as thou killest the Egyptian?" (Exodus 2:13–14). Surprised to learn that his deed was known to others and would eventually be learned by the pharaoh, Moses fled into the desert. He stopped by a well to rest, met a lovely girl whom he married, and settled down for the next few years tending his father-in-law's sheep. The girl and her father, Jethis, were Midianites, a desert people who raised sheep and camels and wandered and traded along the Euphrates and the Nile rivers. As was the custom of most desert people, Moses was accorded hospitality and courtesy.

For decades Moses lived happily. Then, when he was supposedly almost eighty years old, twice the age of the average lifespan in this period, Moses received the idea to return to Egypt to help the Hebrews escape. Exodus 3 says that an angel appeared to him "in the midst of a bush" that "burned with fire" yet "was not consumed," and that the voice of God called out his name from the bush and told him, "I will send thee unto pharaoh, that thou mayest bring forth my people the children of Israel out of Egypt."

It is of course strange that Yahweh would wait until Moses was eighty years old to send him on a mission of this nature. It is more likely that Moses was somehow ostracized from the centers of Egyptian power, possibly because he had killed a man. As a result he might have sought power by unusual means. The slaves in Egypt were a potential constituency; leading them in revolt could lead to political power. Moses recognized the opportunity when it appeared. Exodus 2:23: "And it came to pass in the process of time, that the king of Egypt died." Meneptah, a weak leader, succeeded Ramses II, and during his reign Egypt and its territories were boiling with plague, dissension and economic collapse. Moses saw and seized the opportunity to aid the slaves in escaping from Egypt. Whatever the impetus or motivation, Moses left his cattle and camels and returned with his wife and sons to Egypt.

There were many Hebrew tribes roaming the area, but the politician in Moses may have seen an opportunity to rule a tribe easily—it was in obvious need of leadership. To develop contacts with any of the other

Hebrew tribes already in or near Canaan, and to attempt to persuade them that he was chosen by God to lead them would have been folly. It would have been difficult to offer them "the Promised Land" they were already living on!

Once a political base was established with the group of oppressed, expatriate Hebrews, Moses could gather other Hebrew tribes into his constituency, both by assimilation and by military conquest. The first step on the path to political power led to Egypt.

For Moses there were two central issues in any attempt to free the slaves from bondage in Egypt. The first was the problem of actually freeing them from the pharoah; the second was where to take them once they were released.

The number of slaves involved is in dispute. Exodus 12:37 says "about six hundred thousand men on foot besides the dependents," while Numbers 20–46 actually provides a numerical count by tribe, adding up to somewhere around six hundred thousand in total. How a census was taken is not known. Exodus 1:15, by contrast, seems to indicate that there were so few slaves that only two midwives were needed. The geography across which the Hebrews would have to travel was arid and largely barren, and even with modern irrigation could not have supported a large number of people, probably only a few thousand.[2] Given the contemporary size of populations in the region, it is probable that the figures were hugely exaggerated.

Regardless of the number involved, Moses would have to provide his future rebels some plausible reason for the success of a revolt against the oldest and most powerful state in the known world, and further, to propose a place to go once success had been achieved—that is, a solution to the problem which had long helped keep Egyptian slaves in their place, desert in every direction from Egypt. The power and favoritism of Yahweh was the reason revolt could succeed. The Land of Canaan was a place to which the slaves could flee. The covenant with Yahweh, legitimated perhaps even then by its supposed roots in the time and bloodline of Abraham, granted both.

In exchange for worshipping only him, according to Deuteronomy 6, Yahweh would bequeath to the Hebrews certain riches and territories:

And when the Lord thy god shall have . . . given thee great and goodly cities, [the Promised Land] which thou didst not build, Houses full of riches, which thou didst not set up, cisterns which thou didst not dig, vineyards and oliveyards which thou didst not plant, and thou shall have eaten and be full: take heed diligently lest thou forget the Lord.

If ever there was a motivation to throw off bondage, this must be one!
The passage continues,

> and do that which is pleasing and good in the sight of the Lord, that it
> may be well with thee: and going in thou mayest possess the goodly land,
> concerning which the Lord swore to thy fathers, that he would destroy all
> thy enemies before thee, as he hath spoken.

Not only did the Hebrews have a reason to challenge the power of the
pharoah, they also had a divine license to steal. Yahweh—who could be
better equipped for the job—would help them destroy those who opposed
them. This opposition included the inhabitants of the territories to be
conquered, even when they were fellow Hebrews. Moses had solved his
problem—how to inspire the slaves. In so doing, he (or later biblical
authors) attributed to Yahweh a covenant with Jacob's descendants man-
dating worship of Yahweh alone, or the forfeit of his largesse.

Moses' followers never took the condition as seriously as the reward.
They frequently lost interest in Yahweh and reverted to worshipping other
gods, including idols; rarely, however, was the divinely granted right to
Canaan forgotten.

The covenant between Yahweh and the Hebrews was one by which
military aggression was given theological legitimacy. It was not merely
Realpolitik, it was divinepolitik. It is questionable whether Moses inspired
his new constituency with all of these divine claims, or whether authors
writing centuries later clothed his imperialism in theological garb in order
to create a more powerfully binding tradition.

Armed with divine weapons, so the story goes, Moses sought to free
the slaves in Egypt from bondage. Moses met with the pharaoh several
times over the months and would say to him, "Let my people go," explaining that evil from God would fall upon him if he did not. Egypt was in fact
the victim of numerous plagues during this period. Exodus records them
as occurring successively as the pharaoh repeatedly refused to free the
slaves, but natural causes, even examined three millennia later, provide the
likely explanation: the waters of the Nile were receding during these years.
Polluted water resulted and the consequences were predictable: "Thousands of frogs [fled onto the land], armies of flies and mosquitoes . . .
infested cattle and flocks with disease; children and animals suffered from
boils covering their bodies from head to foot—a common occurrence;
heavy hail storms destroyed crops. Millions of locusts . . . devoured every
leaf and blade and lay ankle deep."[3] There were also blinding sandstorms
lasting two or three days. Finally some dreadful epidemic arrived. The
pharoah apparently saw these developments as natural disasters, not divine
interventions, and so remained intractable.

With the final attack of epidemic, however, the pharaoh probably had enough on his hands without a slave revolt. The slaves were a political threat, so he said good riddance to them. The slaves themselves were no doubt victims and carriers of diseases because of the poor sanitation accompanying their poverty; although the pharaoh could not be sure his troubles would end by allowing them time to leave, it wouldn't hurt to try. He told Moses to take the slaves and go.

Naturally the account of the epidemic in Exodus is a bit skewed. The final plague is recorded as the death of all Egyptian first-born sons. God would send an angel of death to carry out the executions and he told Moses that the slaves could protect themselves from his minion by putting a mark in lamb's blood over their front doors. This would be the signal for it to "pass over" the houses of God's Chosen People. (It is not known why God would need a signal to identify his Chosen People, particularly since he was already so involved in tactical details.)

Like other ancient peoples, the Egyptians had long believed that they could escape their misfortunes by putting them on the head of a slain animal; hence the term "scapegoat." The sacrificial lamb served this function in the current time of troubles too. The blood of the lamb was sprinkled at the entry way of each tent to prevent evil spirits and pestilence from entering. The Hebrews turned this festival into the Feast of the Passover, a celebration of deliverance from Egyptian bondage. Centuries after the Romans killed him, Christ would be declared the sacrificial lamb (Lamb of God), transforming the Passover celebration, for Christians, into the Feast of the Redemption. Christ delivered all men from the bondage of sin by taking it on his head like the traditional scapegoat.

Many slaves chose to remain in Egypt, but many left at once and were joined by a "mixed multitude" of other people (Exodus 12:38) who wished to leave Egypt as well, with or without the knowledge and consent of the pharaoh. Thus the constituency of Moses was not only Hebrew—if such a distinction among the slaves existed at all up to this time.

For some reason, perhaps out of treachery or the realization that his construction projects would be crippled without a pool of slave labor, the pharaoh and his chariots pursued the people of the Exodus and caught up with them by the sea at "Pihahinoth . . . over against Badzephon" (Exodus 14:2). They would soon wish they hadn't, the Old Testament says.

This stretch of water was the Sea of Reeds or the Reed Sea, not to be confused with the Red Sea. The actual crossing place is unknown but was probably at the southern end of Bitter Lake, north of the Gulf of Suez. According to Exodus 15, a "strong and burning wind blowing all the night" came from the southeast, which would push the waters northwest to provide a ford shallow enough to cross. The pursuing Egyptian chariots became stuck in the mud. When the dawn came and the wind shifted, the returning waters flooded them "and now the morning waters was come, and behold the Lord . . . overthrew the wheels of the chariots, and they were carried into the deep." In Catholic grammar school it is taught that Moses parted the water of the "Red Sea" with his staff. In fact, the Scriptures simply say that the Reed Sea's water was parted. Speculation and fabrication by ancient authors is not enough it seems. Legend apparently has to be embroidered by modern interpreters too.

Throughout the journey the Hebrews—for it is only with the Exodus that such a people can truly be identified—grumbled about the lack of water, shortage of food, unfriendly tribes, hot desert days and cold desert nights. When they were hungry they frequently ate manna, which is taught as having come from the heavens; in fact it is a sticky, honey-like juice, derived from the secretion of insects on tarfa and tamarisk trees, which cakes into a white-scaled sugary substance. Manna was boiled and strained and eaten with unleavened bread. The Hebrews also ate birds supposedly sent from God in answer to their prayers; in fact, the birds were quail which flew with the prevailing winds in flocks across the Mediterranean and onto the Sinai, falling exhausted to the ground as soon as they reached land. The Hebrews were able to capture them while they were in an exhausted condition and eat them.

En route to Rephidim the congregation was attacked by the Amalekites. According to legend and to writers on the Bible, including Moshe Dayan, this was Moses' first military encounter.[4] If so, the first battle fought by these Hebrews was against a people identified in the legend of Abraham as other Hebrews, an auspicious beginning! They were not just any fellow Hebrews. The Amalekites were the "legitimate" Hebrews of the legend of Abraham, the descendants of Isaac's first-born, Esau, who had settled in Edom, south of the Dead Sea. (Two millennia later, when the state of Israel was brought into existence, some of the first battles fought by the Israeli army were also against their own. In June 1948, one month after the new country was established, the terrorist Irgun organization—headed by Menachem Begin, later to become prime minister—refused to submit to the authority of the newly formed government headed by Ben Gurion. The first prime minister of Israel ordered the Israeli army to attack the Irgun.)

The Amalekites, spread across the entire face of the Sinai Peninsula and with trained fighting men on camels, apparently attacked the congregation of Moses because they wanted to retain control of their water wells, valley grazing grounds and groves of date palms—all coveted by the group led by Moses.

Strange to say, neither tribe fell into any discussion of Yahweh's covenant with Abraham. If the covenant was to maintain any validity, both groups surely had a mutual right to the area of Canaan. It was not to be: the covenant was an instrument of opportunism, not a sacred contract. Moses accordingly called upon Joshua, the son of Nun, to mobilize able men to fight the Amalekites for the water supplies. The battle was joined, and the people of Moses were victorious. The rightful heirs to Abraham's compact with God were suddenly disinherited. Political and military power rather than ancestry interpreted the terms of the divine covenant.

Conceived by Abraham (so it is written), the theology of imperialism was finally animated by Moses. Military might determined that Moses would lay the foundation for the Hebrew faith. It did not matter what legal or territorial rights others had to the land of Canaan. Moses and his group of Hebrews were coming to take it by force of arms. Thus the foundation of Judaism is based on the military destruction even of legitimate heirs. This is an historical detail conveniently ignored by contemporary religious zealots who have not studied the Bible with care.

Moses played two critical roles. The first was as deliverer of a Hebrew tribe from bondage in Egypt; the second was that of law-giver. Moses is credited by later authors with providing the Torah (the first five books of the Old Testament, often called the Pentateuch). Over the centuries it was adopted by the other Hebrew tribes and peoples. The pillars of the Torah, described in Exodus, are the Ten Commandments, also called the Decalogue:

> And Moses came and called for the elders of the people, and laid before their faces all these words which the Lord commanded him, and all the people answered together, and said, "All that the Lord hath spoken we will do."

This quotation from Exodus 19 refers to the occasion during the Exodus when Moses went to the top of a mountain and received God's commandments for his Chosen People. The patriarch returned with verbal instructions on worship and such matters as how to fashion a tabernacle— and also with stone tablets carved with inviolable commands for basic ethical conduct.

While Moses was away his followers grew impatient for his return and may even have feared that he had died. They persuaded his brother Aaron to melt down everyone's gold jewelry and make a golden calf to worship. Again the covenant was forgotten, if it even existed at this time. When Moses finally came down from the mountain and saw his people worshipping a golden idol, according to Exodus, he smashed the two tablets on the ground and asked, "If any man be on the Lord's side let him join with me."

Exodus 33 recounts that "all the sons of Levi gathered themselves together unto him," and that Moses declared, "Thus saith the Lord God of Israel: put every man his sword upon his thigh: go, and return from gate to gate through the midst of the camp, and let every man kill his brother, and friend and neighbor." They carried out his wishes with a vengeance: "The Sons of Levi did according to the words of Moses, and there were slain that day about three and twenty thousand men."

Since the stone tablets lay smashed on the ground, one must assume that the Fifth Commandment, "Thou shalt not kill," was not yet technically in effect. Religious leaders often have the remarkable ability to conveniently forget that which is not presently useful to them. This incident may be the first instance in Judeo-Christian history of internecine slaughter commanded by religious authorities. It would not be the last.

Moses took two new stone tablets and went back up the mountain for another forty days. When he returned they were inscribed with "all the words that were in the first tablets." Why God would need forty days to do this is not discussed; if Moses himself chiseled the stone, however, it is understandable. Moses was a skillful politician and psychologist. It would have been sensible for him to have created a moral code for his followers. Moses knew that to develop political and social cohesion among them he would have to lay down some rules; even then it would require persuasion and punishment (as we have seen) to compel the people to obey them. The only way they would ever survive as a society was to have an established code of conduct. They were journeying hungry and thirsty to a strange land, and anticipated violent physical opposition from the people of Canaan, to whom Yahweh had not yet disclosed his covenant with the Hebrews. Moses knew what he was doing. All of these activities would require a sense of moral purpose, and a set of laws to control erratic behavior.

Mingling now with other tribes, either as friends or as military conquerors (over such tribes as the Amalekites), Moses seized the opportunity and sought to make himself the head of everyone as chief shaman, or *kahin*. He endeavored to organize his followers into a confederacy, collecting the laws and customs of the various groups and organizing them into one confederate code. His followers, organized for the purpose of rebellion, did not lose that inclination in the desert. Largely in reaction to their experiences as slaves in Egypt, they cultivated an anti-establishment psychology that can be fairly identified to this day. It is plausible that this made it difficult for Moses to maintain leadership and control, as demonstrated time and again in the biblical account. Yahweh was again the

solution to Moses' dilemma. He could write down the framework for
social control for all to see. So Moses went to the top of a mountain to
write down God's pronouncements. Religious legend says the mountain
ascended by Moses was Mount Sinai, but this is unlikely since at the time
it was controlled by the Egyptians as a prime source of mineral wealth
(copper and turquoise).[5]

Moses is revered as the Law-Giver of the Hebrew faith. Yet it is
impossible to say which laws can be attributed to Moses, and unlikely that
any law in its present form can be traced back to him.[6] Even the reconstruction of the original form or wording of the Ten Commandments is
highly speculative,[7] and the arrangement of the Decalogue in Exodus 20 is
different in different versions of the Bible. Nevertheless, none of this has
deterred either Jews or Christians, down to the present day, from accepting these legends and laws as God's word delivered through Moses—
and as the legitimate basis of Judeo-Christian law. That Moses was the
first to break these laws, and in no little way, should be even more
disturbing.

Although the myth of Moses maintains that he was a Hebrew, who through
circuitous circumstances ended up as an Egyptian prince, there is evidence
to suggest that he was an Egyptian who mobilized the Egyptian slaves
solely for his own purposes. This would partially explain his adopting the
custom of circumcision, which was practiced in Egypt and viewed there
as a mark of superiority.[8] Those who were not circumcised were often
treated with contempt.

For Moses, circumcision became the outward sign of the Jew. Moses
may have wished to make the Hebrews "at least the equals of the Egyptians." More importantly, he might have thought that the mark of circumcision would help assure a political and social isolation of the Hebrews,
discouraging them from "mingling with the other foreign peoples they
would meet during their wanderings."[9] Circumcision, it might be said, was
a shibboleth.

Later Jewish teachings were compelled to denigrate the notion that
circumcision originated with the Egyptians, to whom the Jews were
hostile. "To admit that circumcision was an Egyptian custom introduced
by Moses would be almost to recognize that the religion handed down to
them from Moses was also Egyptian . . . therefore the truth about circumcision had also to be contradicted."[10] Today this would be called
disinformation.

There may have been reasons apart from social-political psychology
which argued in favor of circumcision. Perhaps it was a way for men to
symbolically emasculate themselves, showing their dependence upon God.

According to Sigmund Freud, "Circumcision is the symbolical substitute for castration . . . and whosoever accepted this symbol showed by so doing that he was ready to submit to the Father's will, although it was at the cost of a painful sacrifice."[11] (Women were regarded as being dependent upon everyone and therefore had no need of such a symbol.) Edward Gifford says the practice was originally an imitation of menstruation—the boys were even dressed up in girls' clothes for the occasion.[12] For whatever reason, Moses is credited with reintroducing circumcision into the Hebrew faith as the external sign of the covenant.

It must be observed that the relationship between Moses and Yahweh is not the only historical occurrence of a god imparting divine instructions to mortals and, going further, giving these instructions to a particular group of mortals whose political ends were coincidentally served by these divine commands. The god Thoth gave laws to Mens for Egypt, the god Shamash gave Hammurabi a code for Babylonia, the divine nymph Egeria gave laws for Rome to Numa Pompilius; these are only some examples. This approach to creating law is common in history as a road to political and religious power, particularly as a method for legitimizing such power. Moses, building on the legend of Abraham, refined the technique into a coherent theology of imperialism.

Cry, "Havoc," and let slip the dogs of war.

—Shakespeare, *Julius Caesar*

IV

The Rules of War

T he divine jurisprudence of the Hebrews placed the highest priority on military affairs. The Mosaic laws on war are described in Deuteronomy 20, and they are not pretty. One declares that should the Hebrews desire to seize a city other than those in the Promised Land, they should first give the inhabitants an opportunity to surrender peacefully:

> If they receive it, and open the gates to thee, all of the people that are therein, shall be saved, and shall serve thee by paying tribute. If the city does not surrender and pay tribute, then thou shalt besiege it. And when the Lord thy God shall deliver it into thy hands, thou shalt slay all that are therein of the male sex, with the edge of the sword. Excepting women and children, cattle and other things that are in the city. And thou shalt divide all the prey to the army and thou shalt eat the spoils of thy enemies, which the Lord thy God shall give thee. So shalt thou do to all cities that are at a great distance from thee, and are not of these cities which thou shalt receive in possession.

There is nothing ambiguous about instructions on how to wage war. Why the Hebrews should have to conquer other territories in addition to the Promised Land is, in itself, a question . . . or an answer: theology here is indisputably just a codification of contemporary imperialist practice.

The "merciful" sparing of women and children, it should be noted, applied only to cities that were seized outside the land of Canaan. Those living in the Promised Land were not to fare as well:

> But of these cities that shall be given thee, thou shalt suffer none at all to live: but shalt kill them with the edge of the sword, to wit, the Hethite, and the Amorhite, and the Canaanite, the Pherezite, and the Hevite, and the Jebusite, as the Lord thy God hath commanded thee.

There is only one reasonable interpretation of such unmitigated barbarity: Hebrew theologians wanted title to land free and clear. None of the dispossessed could be left alive, lest they someday lay claim to their property. Those unfortunate enough to be dwelling in the land of Canaan were all to be slaughtered—on direct orders from Yahweh as received by Moses. The theology of imperialism now had "canon laws" of conduct, detailed in Deuteronomy. These laws came to permeate the attitudes of the descendants of the Hebrews, and eventually of both the Jews and the Christians down to the present day. As divine laws, they were by definition seen to be "just." Religious justice has always been far less compassionate than human justice.

Nonetheless, many Jews and Christians believe in the literal interpretation of the Bible even today. Believers who reject literal in favor of allegorical interpretations regard these laws as conveying the spirit of God's intentions, and contend that this spirit has changed with human evolution over the centuries. A bizarre analysis.

After forty years of wandering in the desert, the Hebrews finally reached the river Jordan. The land of Canaan (the Promised Land) was near at hand. Why this journey took forty years remains a mystery, for to look at a map it should not have taken more than a few months. It was probably due to military strategy. During much of the journey Moses sent out spies to survey the land and the strengths of the various peoples. There was much to survey, for during this era there was much change. Barbarian invasions were putting pressure on Greece and southeastern Europe generally. From this pressure raiding parties from Greece, Crete, and other areas spread out across the Aegean west, south and east, invading Asia Minor (the Trojan War may have been part of this invasion) and making assaults in every direction. One consequence of the resultant chaos in Asia Minor was that a native people, the Phrygians, rose to power and delivered a fatal blow to the Hittite Empire, which had already been badly debilitated in a great war against Ramses II of Egypt. The Hittites became weak and vulnerable, and must have appeared to the spies of Moses as just a small tribe. Egypt too was experiencing political instability, due to recurrent plagues of locusts, hailstorms, disease and boils on the bodies of animals and children. If an assault were to be made on the land of Canaan, now was a propitious time to do it.

Equally important, a new generation of Hebrews had supplanted those who had fled Egypt forty years before; it had not known slavery in Egypt and wanted to stop wandering and settle down. Moses' congregation was also growing larger, making it more difficult to continue wandering—but making it easier to develop a formidable army.

Moses' spies of choice were the twelve "heads of the children of Israel," namely the leaders of tribes. According to Numbers 13, in addition to ascertaining the military strength and attitude of the inhabitants, the spies were to learn the details of the territory itself:

> Whether it be good or bad . . . fat or lean, whether there be wood therein, or not. And be ye of courage and bring back the fruits of the land.

The spies returned, bringing figs, pomegranates, grapes—and information. They told Moses the "land wither thou sent us floweth with milk and honey."

The twelve leaders who had gone to reconnoiter now sat down with Moses to discuss strategy. All but two were afraid to launch an attack, fearing defeat from the Amalekites, Hittites, Jebusites, Amorites, Canaanites, and above all, "the sons of Anak" (*anak* is the Hebrew word for giant), whom they found dwelling in Hebron. Two of the leaders had no qualms, however: Joshua, the son of Nun, and Caleb, the son of Jephunneh. They urged Moses, it is recounted in Numbers 13:20, to "let us go at once and possess [the land], for we are well able to overcome it."

It is interesting to observe that Joshua and Caleb were some of the last remaining leaders from the original group that fled Egypt. The ten leaders of the new generation were all reluctant to fight. The older men wanted to attack immediately. It is not uncommon in history to have the old send the young into battle; that is probably why foot soldiers are called children ("infantry" is derived from "infant"). Older men often seek a final orgasm of power; after all, it doesn't cost them anything—they are too old to have to fight themselves.

Moses, being one of the older men, agreed with Joshua and Caleb and the Hebrews attempted a direct entry into Canaan. They were repulsed from the hills around the Sinai border by the Canaanite king of Arad in the northern Negev acting in concert together with the Amalekites (the Hebrew tribe whom they had previously defeated). The Hebrews lost and their enemies took some of them prisoner.

Obviously a new approach was needed. Rather than attack the fortified border cities where the people were armed and accustomed to fighting off invaders, the Hebrews made a long, tortuous journey around the strong cities and towns and arrived at the stream of Arnon, which separated the people of Moab in the north from the land of the Amorites. Wanting to bypass even these places in order to go deeper into Canaan by a less-protected route, Moses requested of the Amorite king, Sihon, "free passage" through his lands. Sihon, perhaps thinking it was a ploy, attacked instead.

By now the Hebrews had developed basic military skills. Defense being less costly than offense, they located their forces in strategic positions around Jahaz and awaited the assault. When it came, the Hebrews withstood the attack, routed the Amorites and took control of the Amorite kingdom from the Arnon north to the river Jabbok.

Since theological zeal was now fortified with military confidence, the Hebrews attacked the kingdom of Bashon and wiped out the king and his people, taking possession of that territory as well. The land of Canaan was in sight. The Hebrew conquests had begun.

At this point Moses had to bow out. He was forbidden by Yahweh, so it is said, from ever entering the Promised Land, as punishment for breaking the first tablets of the Ten Commandments. In any case Moses was now 120 years old, according to the Old Testament; he would hardly have been in shape for the long military campaign required to conquer Canaan. So Joshua took command as Moses bade his people farewell on the plain of Moab and climbed Mount Nebo. From there he could see the Promised Land he would never set foot upon.

Moses' burial place is unknown, although there is a traditional site. His place in history has been assured: a fugitive at birth for being Hebrew (so it is said); a fugitive as a young man for killing an Egyptian; a husband and father for fifty years; a law-giver; a politician; a governor of his people and the founder of a nation.

Divine excuses aside, the real reason why Moses may not have wanted to lead the Hebrew people into the so-called Promised Land is that he probably did not really have faith in the alleged covenant. Perhaps he simply had no stomach for purchasing a land of milk and honey at the cost of flooding it with blood. Had he believed in the prophecy of the covenant, however, Moses would surely have taken the Hebrews directly to the Promised Land, confident of Yahweh's assistance when they arrived. Instead he dragged the Hebrews around the hot desert for forty years, two generations.

It was not the conduct of a man confident of the destiny of his people. When Moses tried to play out his hand by attacking the Canaanites soon after the departure from Egypt, the defeat was decisive. It was a stunning setback for actions supposedly sanctioned by the Almighty, and, of course, for Moses' politics too. Expressed in democratic language, the Promised Land was a campaign promise difficult to fulfill. Given the historical fact that the Hebrews occupied their prophesied home for only a small percentage of the next two thousand years, Yahweh certainly has not kept his part of the divine "covenant."

It is possible that Moses' abandonment of his people gave birth to the first hopes of the coming of a messiah. Without Moses, the Hebrews were on their own. As Sigmund Freud observes in *Moses and Monotheism*, "Sometimes, it is true, we hear of a people adopting another god, but never of a god choosing a new people. Perhaps we approach an understanding of this unique happening when we reflect on the connection between Moses and the Jewish people. Moses had stooped to the Jews, had made them kin people; they were *his* 'chosen people' "[1] (emphasis added). Moses had told the Hebrews that they were the Chosen People only to fulfill his own political ambitions; they were an unorganized constituency in obvious need of a leader. That painful truth became evident when he was gone, remaining so for a thousand years, until Ezra and Nehemiah revived the terms of the covenant and rendered it into scripture to suit *their* own political purposes.

For the moment, however, while they still seriously believed that they were the Chosen People, the Hebrews attacked the inhabitants of Canaan. "And it is the proof of a special physical fitness in the mass which had become the Jewish people that it could bring forth so many persons who were ready to take upon themselves the burden of the Mosaic religion for the reward of believing that their people was a chosen one and perhaps for other benefits of a similar order."[2] The concept of being the Chosen People was emotionally gratifying and ego-satisfying for these primitive Hebrew wanderers. To be politically effective, however, the idea had to develop an historical tradition to which believers could retreat and seek both psychological solace and real-world inspiration. The importance of some historical events had to be elevated above others; the motivations of certain historical figures had to be divined; the significance of the past for those living in the present had to be conceived. None of this could be done objectively. Scholarship *per se* was unknown in these times, so that the ignorance, prejudices, and of course the personal and political needs of the interpreters all necessarily had great impact on their work.

"The religion of Moses exercised influence on the Jewish people only when it had become a tradition," Freud asserts.[3] This tradition was no received thing. It declined soon after Moses passed away, not to return securely for nearly a millennium.

What we know today as the tradition of the Jews was a creation of man, of ancient authors with limitations and personal quirks and attitudes aplenty. The Hebrew covenant with God, important as it may have been to Moses and his followers, was forgotten for centuries after the death of Moses.

Whence then its revival? Dimly recalled history became the tradition of a people only through concerted intellectual effort (one could easily call it propaganda) by certain spiritual (read also political) leaders. Why they chose to create this tradition and its particulars we can only speculate, but not without some basis: its contemporary use is less obscure than the nature of its authors. Clearly the tradition of the covenant in the time of Moses and later was used both as a device to further social cohesion and as a justification for war. This latter historical fact seems to have been overlooked by many modern believers, Jewish and Christian.

Sometime "forty years" after the night of the Exodus from Egypt, the original Passover, the Hebrews crossed the Jordan River and entered into the so-called Promised Land. They crossed from the deserts of Moab on the east bank of the Jordan over to the Jericho plains on the river's west bank, setting up their camp at Gilgal. It was about 1400 B.C.E. Canaan had changed greatly since the time of Abraham. Yahweh had neglected to tell Moses that the people of Canaan had developed military defenses in the interim. During the intervening hundreds of years many other nations and peoples had invaded and settled in the area, creating walled towns and fortified cities where small villages and towns once stood.

Along the coast from Gaza to Askelon lived a strong race of people originally from the island of Crete. They were called the Pulasti or Philistines, sea voyagers driven by Ramses II from previous settlements in the Nile delta. The Philistines carried shields and heavy broadswords and wore armor, a fearsome ensemble in those days.

By the time of Moses the Philistines had dwelled so long in the territory that Canaan had been renamed after them: Palestine, the land of the Philistines. These people of Canaan were idol worshippers, and many Hebrews settled peacefully in the area and intermarried with them, generally relinquishing belief in Yahweh in the process.

Trees of all kinds were in abundance for building homes and fashioning the implements of farming. The Canaanites also excelled as artisans and traders, selling spices, musical instruments and metal weapons to Egypt in exchange for gold and silver ornaments, pottery, and scarabs (stone or ceramic beetles used as talismans or fertility symbols). Canaanite culture was apparently advanced as well; hundreds of examples of correspondence with Babylonia on sun-baked, cuneiform-inscribed tablets were discovered in 1887 at Tell-el-Amarna.

The climate too was favorable. There was sufficient rainfall to permit both agriculture and pasturing for sheep and cattle. The people of Canaan were able to grow wheat, barley, and fruit, and to maintain hillside vineyards. Olive orchards produced the precious oil for cooking, lighting and washing. Moses' spies had not exaggerated. Canaan truly was a "land of milk and honey."

The conquest of Canaan by the Hebrews was probably not the dramatic single-battle event described in the Joshua, but more likely successive attacks on one tribe at a time as described in the Judges. The famed Tell-el-Amarna letters describe some of the movements of the Hebrew invaders at this time. They include letters between the Egyptian pharaohs and their officials in Palestine complaining of Hebrew "treachery," nomadic settling which forced the slow withdrawal of Egyptians (similar to today's Israeli settlements on the West Bank and elsewhere) and the occasional military seizure of the pharaoh's cities.

With the Ark of the Covenant at their head, believed to be literally a device of divine protection, and carrying swords, shields, bows and arrows and other weapons (in the event that God helped only those who helped themselves), the Hebrews began their conquest of Canaan by marching on Jericho.

Hebrew spies got the lay of the land and critical refuge from a local prostitute named Rahab; soon Joshua laid siege to the walled city. Rams' horns carried by priests were blown with great energy signalling the advance. Strategic fires were set along the walls and waves of soldiers stormed the defenses. The walls fell and the Hebrews slaughtered the inhabitants, excepting Rahab and her kin, and then burned the city to the ground. Not all was lost to destruction, however. "But whatsoever gold or silver there shall be, or vessels of brass and iron, let it be consecrated to the Lord, laid up in his treasures," are the instructions recorded in Joshua 6:19. Theft was consecration; pillage was divine.

The Hebrews then dedicated this first conquest in Canaan to Yahweh as the beginning of the fulfillment of the covenant. God must have been proud.

The next city on the agenda was Ai, a few miles to the east of Jericho. The first Hebrew assault was repulsed when the warriors of Ai came out of their walled city to meet the attackers head on. The Hebrews were pushed back and then fled. Joshua was apparently concerned that this would cause a morale problem among his men ("The hearts of the people melted, and became as water"—Joshua 7:5), so he devised a strategy to assure the complete destruction of Ai.

A small Hebrew force attacked the city, then retreated "as if they were beaten," luring the soldiers of Ai in pursuit. Meanwhile the bulk of the Hebrew armies laid in wait on the other side of the city. With Ai virtually undefended, the Hebrew force stormed the city and set it on fire. Seeing their home aflame, the soldiers of Ai returned to beat back the attack, but found themselves caught between the two Hebrew forces, pummelled from both front and rear. They were wiped out.

The city and its inhabitants were destroyed so completely that few traces of it are to be found. Hebrew gratitude was appropriately expressed to Yahweh, who, to any objective observer, was now obviously a god of war. The Hebrews proudly maintained that attitude, as evidenced in the Song of Moses ("God is a Man of War"). It would be centuries before *shalom* (peace) entered the Hebrew political lexicon, not until about 500 B.C.E. By then the Hebrews were the victims of conquest rather than its perpetrators; peace was finally to their benefit.

The Hebrews went on to seize the cities, towns, and land of Canaan. To the Hebrews, slaughter was the rule of law, the operational details required to fulfill the covenant. It would continue until they had decimated the inhabitants of Canaan and ruled it unchallenged. Granted the divine bequest, however, the correspondent obligations would be put on hold. By 1250 B.C.E., many Hebrews had reverted to idol worship . . . until the "covenant" was needed yet again, to justify more killing to acquire or protect territory.

That time came around 1150 B.C.E. A man named Gideon rose up to destroy the idols and revive the exclusive worship of Yahweh. It is hardly coincidental that he wished to organize an attack on the Midianites and their friends the Amalekites (who were, we must again recall, also Hebrews). Otherwise, Yahweh would probably have remained just another god among the multitude of gods.

Examined with these events in mind, Hebrew history clearly demonstrates that Yahweh and the "covenant" were originally political concepts masquerading as theology. Yahweh's significance as a god above all others was invented by Abraham, or his biographers, because he wanted a god more powerful than the gods of his neighbors. The covenant was invented by the authors of the Abraham legend to justify his claim to real estate that did not belong to him. Some Jews and fundamentalist Christians assert this logic even today. It all had little to do with theology, everything to do with rationalizations for waging war.

One thing that Abraham, Moses, Joshua, Gideon and others down to the current leaders of Israel all seem to have known, and it appears to have been equally well understood by Christian popes and emperors, Islamic mullahs, and Communist party chairmen, is that wars paraded as moral crusades have greater appeal to the general population. To invent approving gods and justifying goals, to paint political plans with the whitewash of moral purpose, will always help generate wider popular support. Hebrew authors have done this so well that several million believers around the world actually accept Hebrew political legend as holy history. As any scholar will tell us, most of it is not history; and as any sensitive human being can discern, even less of it is holy.

Theologians argue that no matter how or why the concept of one god

entered the mind of Abraham, it was a divine way of introducing monotheism to the human race. Any disinterested historian can observe that the
original imperialist use of monotheistic ideology—brutally embellished
through the end of the nineteenth century at least—was an unnecessarily
bloody way to inspire the spiritual and intellectual evolution of humankind.

In every age the soul of the Jew has been torn between the resolve to make his way in a hostile world, and his hunger for the goods of the mind. A Jewish merchant is a dead scholar; he envies and generously honors the man who, escaping the fever of wealth, pursues in peace the love of learning and the mirage of wisdom.

—Will Durant, *The Age of Faith*

V

Mythology Merges into History

The number of Jews in the world is not large compared to the adherents of other religious denominations. Among the populations of believers (or those controlled by their respective priestly authorities, since one can never know how many believers are sincere), there are today more than nine hundred million Muslims, as many Christians, and one and a half billion souls under the sway of Marxist theology . . . but only an estimated fifteen million Jews.

Although the world's Jewish population is small—a minuscule one half of one percent of the worldwide religious brethren—its influence has been disproportionately large. Jews have become a central part of Western culture, which has completely dominated earth's history until relatively recent times. Because many Jews believe that they are the Chosen People and must accordingly suffer persecution, their theological frame of reference can enable them to persuade themselves (and sometimes non-Jews as well) that they are the earth's principal martyrs.

Jews have in fact been persecuted for a length of time unrivalled in history and to a degree comparable only to a very few peoples. Owing to its psychology, the Jewish faith has proven resourceful and enduring. Judaism exists today as a vital religion which has emerged intact from thousands of years of persecution and conquest. Judaism was the main factor in shaping the Christian and Moslem religions; the three together constitute the major religions of our time. Judaism also shaped Marxist attitudes, notably its contumacy (Karl Marx was Jewish, as were many of the founders of the Russian Revolution), but more importantly through its influence on Christianity, whence, through Hegel, Marxism arose.

The Old Testament is the principal source of information regarding early Judaic history, but how much is historical fact and how much legend is not always possible to know. The preceding descriptions depict events and people known from the Old Testament and corroborated by very few, if any, other documents; henceforth the Old Testament is supplemented by other historical documents.

Let us go back for a moment and develop an overview. The Hebrew cosmology is related in Genesis: the world was created in six days and on the seventh day God rested, thereby introducing the practice of the Sabbath. Jewish chronology situates the origin of the world at 3761 B.C.E. The world was created by God *ex nihilo*, neither from himself nor from any pre-existing matter. Man was created from clay, and woman from the rib of the man. Above the stars was heaven, with its heavenly ocean that was the sky, and beneath the stars was the earth. The world view of the Bible is entirely in keeping with the view of the ancient oriental world.

Like all primitive religions, pre-Judaism had many gods, but Yahweh came to be regarded as the most powerful, or at least the most popular. Although Yahweh was God, he created a number of powers subject to him but far superior to men. These are the angels, the seraphim and the cherubim, one of whom guards the gates of Paradise with a flaming sword. Certain realms of nature are in the domain of the elite archangels. Michael is the protector of the Jews, Gabriel the proclaimer of divine revelation and the ruler of fire, Uriel the ruler of the stars and weather, and Raphael the miracle-working physician. As the executor of Yahweh's will, an angel is said to have destroyed 70,000 men through a plague (II Samuel 24), and in one night an angel killed 185,000 men in the camp of Assyrians (II Kings 19). The angels at this time were not noted for performing acts of kindness such as saving drowning children—this came in later centuries, particularly in the Christian era.

Judaic cosmology lacks Christianity's eternal conflict between Good and Evil, but it does incorporate a sense of wrathful power and dominance by Yahweh over evil forces, particularly those who were the enemies of the Hebrews. While Judaic cosmology does not give evidence of an acceptance of war and conflict as a part of the ordered way of the universe, the doctrines of angelology and the intervention of Yahweh on behalf of his Chosen People demonstrate a *Weltanschauung* which incorporates violent action as a necessary way of life on earth, and of deliverance, legitimated by a covenant between Yahweh and the Hebrews. This is evident when we examine a brief history of the Jewish people and study certain of Judaism's scriptural exhortations.

If we were required to put an historical date to the beginning of Judaism it would be at Moses' deliverance of the Hebrews from Egyptian slavery, and the subsequent covenant between Yahweh and the Hebrews at Mount Sinai, or wherever it may have been, approximately 1450 to 1400 B.C.E.

The Hebrew covenant with God was a unilateral agreement. Because they were chosen by God, the Hebrews were bound to obey his Law as laid down in the Torah (Exodus 19:5-7; 34:10). In return they were guaranteed freedom, security, and the right to seize the land that could provide them with prosperity. Disobedience was supposedly punished by misfortune, poverty, oppression and exile.

The proscriptive elements of this agreement, described in Exodus, are said to have been revealed to Moses around 1450 B.C.E., but the law itself was not officially adopted by the Hebrews until 444 B.C.E., at the initiative of Ezra, revered as the restorer and last author of the Torah.[1] To any objective observer, it must seem strange that ten centuries elapsed before the most essential basis of all Hebrew belief was officially adopted and promulgated. There is a non-theological explanation, however: the Torah (as we will see later) was adopted in circumstances when the Hebrews, once again, had need of being organized into a politically and socially cohesive society.

The harsh reality of war is an intricate part of the Jewish experience, which (the Hebrews believed) validates the divine favor of Yahweh for his Chosen People. This is not to say that the Jews did not suffer defeats and persecutions; the blame for such events was always interpreted as the result of some transgression.

The Hebrews were a military people. They believed in the powers of Yahweh; all that happened, happened by his will. If pharaoh's heart was embittered towards the Hebrews, God hardened it. If Israel conquered in battle, it was through the power of the Lord. "The Lord is mighty in battle" (Psalms 24:8), and David battles Goliath "in the name of the Lord of Hosts, the God of the Army of Israel which you have defied" (I Samuel 17:45).

Deuteronomy 20 declares that before engaging in battle, the priest shall exclaim:

Hear, O Israel, this day you are joining battle with the enemy, do not lose heart or be afraid, or give way to panic in the face of them; for the Lord your God will go with you to fight your enemy for you and give you the victory.

Yahweh's role was to militarily deliver his Chosen People, and to punish them harshly when they failed Him. Clearly Yahweh was regarded as a militant god. One of the most common praises of the Lord is that he delivered his people from bondage. In Exodus 15 this is evaluated as quite particularly a military deliverance:

> The Lord is a man of war: the Lord is his name. The Chariots of Pharaoh and the army he has cast into the sea . . .

> Thy right hand, O Lord, is become glorious in power: thy right hand, O Lord, hath dashed in pieces the enemy.

Such praises of Yahweh were sung constantly, and the force of all victories in battle was attributed to his providence, while all defeats were ascribed to some infraction by the Chosen. (One will notice in all religions an ideology in strict contrast to normal human behavior: in the secular world, humans are quick to accept credit but seek elsewhere to place the blame; in the realm of theology, the gods receive all credit, and the humans accept all blame.)

After the death of Moses, the Hebrews expanded their control of Canaan for three centuries, culminating in the crowning of Saul as the first Jewish king of what was called Israel. Throughout this period of conflict, the Hebrew people were confident in the governance of Yahweh over their affairs:

> When you go forth to war against your enemies, and see horses and chariots and an army larger than your own, you shall not be afraid of them; for the Lord your God is with you up out of the Land of Egypt . . . for the Lord your God is he that goes with you to fight for you against your enemies, to give you victory.[2]

This is the period of the classic "Joshuaic" wars, in which the Hebrews reaped the fruits of military victory due to their faith in, and (they believed) the intervention of, Yahweh. Joshua describes these events. It was probably not the work of a single author, and was written from the viewpoint of the so-called Deuteronomic law code (Deuteronomy 4:44 to 30:20), which was incorporated bodily at the beginning of the work. The authors sought to demonstrate that this principal focus of Deuteronomy— that Israel's success and well-being is contingent upon obedience to the law of God—had actually been proven by historical fact, that with divine assistance the Hebrews had successfully conquered and slaughtered the inhabitants of Palestine as promised by God.

This rationale for military and political behavior is hardly a dead letter. Belief in the divine sanction of political acts is held by some Jews today, notably the most militant Zionists, and some international defenders of the contemporary state of Israel. Although Zionism began as a relatively secular movement, many contemporary Zionists use the biblical mandates of the covenant as rationales for their actions, however repugnant they may be in the context of human rights as they are currently conceived.

After the era of the "Joshuaic wars," an organized state with a standing army came into being. Beginning with Saul there were no more imperialist "holy wars" of the Joshua type until the twentieth century. This is not to say that the god of the Hebrews was not seen as playing a role in the survival of the state. In the seventh century B.C.E., Assyria's King Sennacherib attacked the fortified cities of Judah (the southern half of the lands occupied by the Hebrews). He then sent a great army against Hezeki'ah in Jerusalem. Hezeki'ah was worried, but the prophet Isaiah answered him:

> Thus says the Lord: Do not be afraid because of the words that you heard, with which the servants of the King of Assyria have reviled me. Behold, I will put a spirit in him, so that he shall hear a rumor and return to his own land; and I will make him fall by the sword in his own land.[3]

As victory was attributed to God, so defeat, persecution and exile has been blamed by Jews on themselves. The vocation to suffering is one of the greatest characteristics of the Judaic mindset, and the acceptance of sufferings is one of the prime concerns of rabbinic discourse. In the Beth Ha Furoth in Tel Aviv, one of the most important museums in Israel, there is an inscription on the wall: "Sometimes the gates of prayer are open, sometimes they are closed. The gates of penitence are always open."

Suffering and penitence are a consistent theme in Judaic thought. The Judaic sense of suffering is essential to Judaic psychology and was passed on to the Christians who made it into a doctrine of faith. It differs from other notions of suffering, for example that of the Buddhists, in two respects. First, some Jews believe their suffering is the result of their failure to worship Yahweh alone as the one true God; since Jewish suffering thus resulted from conscious acts, it carries with it a feeling of guilt which also permeates Jewish psychology. The Buddhist concept of suffering, by contrast, portrays it as necessary to purify oneself; one suffers through human desires in order to achieve the spiritual tranquility of the state of nirvana.

Secondly, some Jews developed their attitude toward life in reaction to particular events, namely wars which they lost as a consequence (so it is written) of their failure at times to worship Yahweh alone. They must atone, some Jews have therefore concluded, by prosecuting other wars under the banner of Yahweh. The Buddhists developed their attitude toward life by observing suffering and concluding that God must have intended it for the purpose of purification. Thus, the Buddhist sense of suffering carries no guilt, while Jewish belief (later amplified in Christian theology) is accompanied by guilt expressed socially and politically as well as inwardly.

This guilt traces its existence to numerous possible sources: the usual primitive guilt of most primal religions, associated with fear of angering the gods; the guilt of continually violating Mosaic law; the collective guilt of repeated abandonment of Yahweh, until political circumstances suited a reinvention or reaffirmation of Yahweh and the "covenant"; and guilt, some say, by rebellious Hebrews who grew tired of Moses' temper tantrums and beliefs and killed him.[4] Guilt became one of the primary components of the Jewish psychology.

The obsession with guilt was so strong in Hebrew psychology that when Judaism later fragmented and Christianity was born, St. Paul attempted to provide a rational explanation of the feeling of guilt and attributed it to a primeval source, calling it "original sin." He then made original sin into a doctrine of his new faith and into the quintessential component of the Christian religion. (As we will see later, Christians seldom miss an opportunity to create a doctrine.) Thus did guilt become the basis of both religions, Christianity and Judaism, afflicting its inheritors down to the present day.

The psychology of guilt is central to Judaic teachings, but the psychology of fear—integral to that guilt, as we have seen—is almost as strong and is also contained in Scripture:

> The Lord shall scatter thee among all people, from the farthest parts of the earth to the ends thereof . . . Neither shalt thou be quiet, even in those nations, nor shall there be any rest for the sole of thy foot. For the Lord will give thee a fearful heart, and languishing eyes, and a soul consumed with pensiveness: and thy life shall be as it were hanging before thee. Thou shalt fear night and day, neither shalt thou trust thy life. In the morning thou shalt say: Who will grant me evening? and at evening: Who will grant me morning? for the fearfulness of thy heart, wherein thou shalt be terrified, and for those things which thou shalt see with thy eyes.[5]

In the tenth century B.C.E. Israel divided into two kingdoms, called Israel and Judah, in a dispute over the line of succession after the death of Solomon. In II Chronicles 16 there is recounted an alliance between Judah and Syria against Israel. This action, a reliance upon political and military resources over the will of God, resulted in a vision by the prophet Hanani, told to the king of Judah, in which the breach of faith is cited as the cause of destruction and misery:

You relied on the King of Syria, and did not rely on the Lord your
God . . . Were not the Ethiopians and Libyans a huge army with exceedingly many chariots and horsemen? Yet, because you relied upon the
Lord He gave them into your hand . . . You have done foolishly in this
for from now on you will have wars. (emphasis added)

And so it was. According to the Old Testament, the Jews will continue to
have wars, and Armageddon will eventually come. Despite the tradition of
reliance on God for military success, modern Israeli military dependence
on Yahweh has usually been supplanted by reliance on worldwide Jewish
wealth, and on Jewish political influence in Washington. When Israel encountered resistance in the invasion of Lebanon in 1983, Israel spokes-
persons appealed to foreign Jews, and to the Pentagon, for political and
economic support in their "crisis." Yahweh's name was not generally
invoked.

In 722 B.C.E. the Assyrians conquered the northern kingdom of Israel,
and Judah, the smaller of the two Jewish states, remained to preserve the
traditions only because of its comparative insignificance. In 586 B.C.E. the
Babylonian Nebuchadnezzar attacked Judah and destroyed the Temple of
Solomon after the fall of Jerusalem. The destruction of the Temple is one
of the most important events in Jewish history and psychology. In Jewish
wedding ceremonies today, the groom symbolically crushes under his heel
the glass from which the marrying couple have drunk, as the rabbi ad-
monishes them "on this, the happiest day of your life, to remember the
destruction of the Temple." That this sad remembrance should be in a
joyful wedding ceremony is revealing.

It was the tribe of Judah (descended from the fourth son of Jacob and
Leah) which controlled Jerusalem and the Temple when it was destroyed
by Nebuchadnezzar. It is from this tribe of Judah, which was prominent
among the Hebrew tribes, that the term "Jew" arose.

The destruction of the Temple of Solomon was a critical point in the
development of Jewish beliefs—and in the worldwide reception of Jews.
They fled in every direction, resulting in the creation of the "Diaspora,"
from the Greek word *diaspeirein,* meaning "to disperse" or "scatter."

There were two alternatives open to emigrating Jews: to reject their
belief in Yahweh and his covenant, or to put events in the context of the
covenant, accordingly blaming themselves for their adversity. The second
option seems to have held sway. To do this required a certain amount of
intellectual gymnastics, requiring orthodox Jewish society to stress certain
elements of their faith with a vehemence previously unknown. Individual
Jewish families, now in relative isolation in foreign lands, sought to maintain their identity much as many of history's refugees have; unlike many

other foreign peoples who were the victims of conquerors, however, the Jews shared a religious disposition which was passionate. It inspired them to subordinate their individual desires to their religious hopes; personal protection for themselves and their families took second place to theological fervor, particularly since so many lands were willingly providing them with the liberty of refuge and the right to pursue the objects of their happiness, whether religious or economic.

This ideology of nationhood ultimately enabled religious Jews to strengthen the orthodox Jewish notion that survival was based upon Jewish society as a whole, not upon individual happiness, regardless of the land lived in, or how small its Jewish community. One encyclopedia summarizes the impact of this development simply: "To this day, orthodox Jewish ethics has remained in its essence national rather than individual."[6] The Jewish people, lacking the common characteristics of nationhood—territory, state and language—responded to dispossession by intensifying their belief in being the Chosen People. This required that they live always as communities separate from host societies.

The refusal to assimilate into other societies caused them to lead an unnatural existence, leading them, according to Salo Baron, "to their characteristic polarity in action and thought."[7] They were required to lead two lives: a functional life in their host society, and an intellectual and spiritual life in their own Jewish community. To non-Jewish fellow citizens, this separate existence was often viewed suspiciously, or at least as a form of ingratitude. From these sentiments anti-Semitism was not long aborning.

In exile the Jews found able leaders, such as Ezekiel and Deutero-Isaiah, to provide them intellectual guidance among the new perplexities of life. A transcendent and holy God, they taught, had chosen the people of Israel as his holy nation, for reasons known only to him. Through a life of holiness and, if necessary, of great suffering, this people was to continue to make known the name of God until the end of days, when all nations would recognize their error and worship the one God. In the meantime, the Jews were to keep aloof from the people of their host countries, lest they be contaminated by unholiness. The life thus demanded of the Jews was necessarily artificial and, to Jewish youth, must often have seemed schizophrenic, since they were raised in countries to which they were able (or allowed) to develop only partial political loyalty and limited intellectual empathy. To the non-Jews of these countries, in logical (if inhumane and often inaccurate) consequence, the Jews were frequently regarded as untrustworthy and disloyal citizens whose allegiance was to a foreign "nation" instead of to the country which provided for them.

Theologically, the center of Judaism remained in Palestine, although the Jews of the Diaspora far outnumbered the Jews who had stayed in the homeland. Nationally and emotionally disruptive though the Exile was, many Jews of the Diaspora saw benefits in a widespread creed which offered them brotherly reception in communities of their co-believers all over the world. Psychologically this was also an acceptance of the undeniable.

In 537 B.C.E., however, the Persians under Cyrus wrested control of Palestine from Babylonia and invited the Jews to return; many did so, prospering enough to soon rebuild the Temple.

Originally, as we have seen, the Hebrews and their neighboring tribes worshipped many gods, of whom Yahweh was one, although it was generally decided that Yahweh favored the children of Israel. With the covenant, Yahweh became the principal god of the Hebrews. The experiences of the fall of Jerusalem and the subsequent Exile led the Israelites to further define their view of their relationship with Yahweh. Now they focused even more on the issue of Yahweh as their only god and on the commandment, "Thou shalt have no other gods but me." Past persecutions were now attributed to the worship of other gods. To prevent a recurrence of these disasters, Jewish theologians made it even more sinful to worship other gods. Jeremiah and Ezekiel, two prophets, were the most effective in emphasizing this notion. In Jeremiah 7, God is irritated:

Seest Thou . . . the children gather wood, the fathers kindle fire, the women knead their dough to make bread for the queen of heaven and to pour out offerings of libation onto other gods, that they may provoke me to anger.

And in Ezekiel 7 we find him petulant:

Therefore I will also deal with them in my wrath: my eyes shall not spare them, neither will I show mercy: and when they shall cry to my ears with a loud voice, I will not hear them.

This harsh passage epitomizes an ideology which enabled the Israelites to coalesce under one God, develop a nationalistic fervor to preserve themselves, and destroy the gentiles who believed in many gods. Thus, through the power of the pen, Jeremiah and Ezekiel reaffirmed traditional Hebrew monotheism, which sanctioned irrational and endemic guilt and required the maintenance of a fierce nationalism among the Chosen People to attenuate it. This has motivated much Jewish conduct throughout history.

This ideology made a critical demand on the Jews. To preserve Jewish identity, non-Jews were excluded socially and fraternizing was prohibited generally. After the Return, this effort was largely at the direction of a man called Ezra, often alleged to be the actual author of Mosaic Law. Ezra's desire to exclude "aliens" from mixing in with Jewish society was designed to protect the purity of the Jewish people. It was also evidence of a notion of Judaic superiority both moral and cultural. This tenet influenced Jewish conduct for centuries, and remains an important part of Jewish psychology today.

It was an ideology that gained wide acceptance throughout the Diaspora. The fear and dislike among non-Jews generated by this behavior are a part of the original basis for anti-Semitism. Apion asked how the Jews, whose cult had not images, could be legitimate citizens of Alexandria when they repudiated the city's gods. Seneca regarded the repose of the Jewish Sabbath as congenital idleness. Tacitus accused the Jews of fostering disloyalty toward the state. Kosher food laws were regarded as bizarre; the observance of circumcision was deemed "unnatural"; moral self-righteousness was frequently viewed as superstitious or hypocritical; any concern with financial survival was often seen as miserliness; preoccupation with ethnic identity often created the impression of a secret society in league with Satan. During the European black plague of the fourteenth century, as millions died, Jews were alleged to have remained unaffected—perhaps they were its cause, some charged. It is not reliably known whether Jews suffered less than others from the dread disease, but if so it was likely due to their diet, hygiene and sequestered living quarters. Name the evil and the Jews were often blamed and persecuted for it. All of these issues conspired to create a feeling of fear and hostility toward Jews which created anti-Semitism, which fed on itself to accelerate that hostility until six million Jews lay in embers.

When Christianity emerged, its adherents seized upon "strange" Jewish behavior and taught that the Jews were a pariah people—even that they had killed Christ! Paul wanted Roman converts, and accordingly could hardly accuse Rome of killing the central figure of his religion. This virulent racism was not simply occasionally present, but hardened into canon, the New Testament's "perfidious Jew." Since Jews were inhabitants of Christian-controlled countries but usually remained as a separate society, they were always suspect. They were a convenient scapegoat whenever needed. Christian maltreatment and persecution of Jews has been one of history's constants.

Traditional anti-Semitism is generally directed against the Jews as a race, although it is difficult to separate Jewish racial or cultural behavior from Jewish religious behavior. Generally speaking, Jews avoid categorizing themselves as either a religion or a race and try to have the best of both and the worst of neither by calling themselves a "religious people." This also permits a logic to adherence to the concept of religious nationalism, whose goal has always been the revival of a separate nation of Jewish people. Central to Jewish belief though it was, however, such a state was almost never realized.

Associations had long been established in Europe, principally in Eastern Europe, to develop a Jewish political identity, but until the horror of the *Übermensch* they failed to gain much of an organized following among Jews. It was generally felt that a return to Zion (Palestine) was where Jews should go "home." The idea of returning to Zion came to be called Zionism, and was espoused with varying degrees of fervor by different Jewish communities, reaching its apogee in 1897 with the formation of an international political council whose ultimate goal was the creation of the nation of Israel. Zionists were always characterized by varying shades of philosophical outlook; many were atheists or at least secular in orientation. While their religious and political views often differed from the mainstream of Judaic thinking, however, numerous common denominators existed: they sought a return to Zion, an idea most Jews did not oppose, even those who did not personally wish to move to Palestine; they felt that a recognized national homeland would provide them with security, or at least the sense of it; they believed that having a national identity would allow them an independence from the *goyim*, the "large nations," non-Jews, with whom they could then relate on a more equal basis. These goals characterized traditional Jewish attitudes, and continue to do so.

[The writings of the Prophets] are the earliest known pamphlet literature
of immediate political actuality.

—Max Weber

I know how men in exile feed on dreams of hope.

—Aeschylus, *Agamemnon*

VI

In Defeat, a Social Contract

The monarchy of the eleventh and tenth centuries B.C.E. was characterized by both peaceful autocracy and an unfortunate corollary: bur-
dening taxes and compulsory labor. Yahweh was apparently not yet
a social reformer.

During this period the nation of Israel was forged in the crucible of
social realities, ultimately leading to a modified understanding of the
covenant as prophets rose to challenge the power of kings. The oppression
of the poor led the prophets to cry out against social wrongs. They did so
tactically however, by couching their protest in terms of a golden past in
which a parallel "social" covenant had allegedly been in force. This naturally led to an embellishment of the historical facts of antiquity and to an
expansion of the concept that religion supervises most human concerns.

The prophets saw social reform as best achieved by invoking higher
principles, elevating social crimes to the level of religious sins. Deuteronomy, the Pentateuch's critical "Book of Laws" (or the materials on which it
is based), is believed to have been written during this time of the Jewish
nation's long decline, from the division of the monarchy through subjugation, Exile and Return, roughly 1100 to 500 B.C.E.

The responsibility of the Jews under the modified covenant was no
longer simply worship of Yahweh alone, although that requirement was
further emphasized. More significantly, the code of personal ethics listed
in the Decalogue was given much higher priority. Transgressions by those
in power attracted particular attention from the prophets, the social con-

science of this age much as journalists are today.

They gave force to this ideological effort by interpreting contemporary events in terms of alleged past transgressions against the now modified covenant. This was amplified by also predicting that misfortunes would befall those who did not adhere to this idealized covenant of religious antiquity. Kings and priests were a common target of these attacks. Prophecies abounded, but this was not new. The listing of events that would bring down divine anger—crimes of man against man, particularly of rulers against ruled—were.

Jeremiah offered the most direct (and colorful) of prophetic social criticism, saying to rich Jews oppressing their poor brethren, "Be circumcised to the Lord, and take away the foreskins of your hearts" (Jeremiah 4:4). Sinfulness was defined as the commission of social oppression and the penalty, Jeremiah warned, would be invasion and subjugation by a more enlightened, neighboring empire. This of course was interpreted by the princes of the day as little less than treason. They responded by arresting Jeremiah repeatedly.

Isaiah more clearly postulated an entirely new Yahweh, one loving rather than bitter, concerned with justice rather than war: "Why do you consume my people and grind the faces of the poor?" he is quoted as asking God in Isaiah 3:15. He predicted on the one hand a kingdom of embers should the Jewish nation maintain its practice of oppression, and on the other hand a virtual utopia of jewels and fruit groves should it turn to the ways of justice. "Unloose the heavy burdens and let the oppressed go free," he commands in Isaiah 58:6. "The Lord hath anointed me: he hath sent me to preach to the meek, to heal the contrite of heart, and to preach a release to the captives and deliverance to them that are shut up."

Isaiah is well known for his prediction that nations "shall turn their swords into ploughshares, and their spears into sickles," but the historical context of such a revolutionary pronouncement is little discussed. A defeated nation of militarists had reaped only a harvest of destruction from centuries of conquest, and now, firmly conquered itself, had to fashion an ideology of peace from the reality of military impotence.

In effect, a system of social ethics was creeping deeper into Jewish community life. The covenant, at first primarily a military pact with God, began a transformation into a standard for class as well as personal behavior. The covenant was becoming a form of social contract, three millennia before Rousseau! This was expressed in religious rather than secular terms, however, giving birth to a history-shaking idea: the Jewish nation was not necessarily a merely terrestrial one. (The incipient notion of an afterlife, as yet completely unformed, would shake the Western world—

but paradoxically with an effect opposite to its origins; in Christian practice it would be used to denigrate the importance of the material conditions of human life.)

The idea was born of a Jewish people which transcended territorial states and was instead a divine instrument for harnessing nature, this by a supernatural process expressed through the course of history. The development of this idea was haphazard—and driven in no little part due to the inability of a subjugated people to construct the engines of war—but essentially gathered force for seven centuries, culminating in the codification of a reinterpreted covenant by Ezra in the fifth century B.C.E. Much had happened in the meantime, including Exile and Return, the rule of successive foreign empires, and an apparent increase in the economic polarization of Jewish society. All contributed to the evolution of Jewish thought. First disaster had to befall the Jewish people, so that prophetic wisdom could be vindicated: God would in fact punish his recreant people. For the prophets, punishment was always impending, and their predictions gained influence as natural calamities regularly came to pass and the rising power of contiguous foreign nations became increasingly obvious to the naked eye. Plague, drought, military defeat and flight were constant visitors to the Jewish people. It would culminate in the fact of a permanent Diaspora. The concept of a Jewish nation which transcended territory, and a covenant expanded to include the widest range of human behavior, social and political, was the result.

When Ezra and Nehemiah returned to Jerusalem after the captivity, they attempted to impose a strict orthodoxy developed in exile. Due to the destruction of the Temple during the Babylonian conquest in 586 B.C.E., where alone sacrifices were offered, Jewish rituals changed; nonsacrificial offerings supplanted the physical rituals. This resulted in the formation of synagogues (from the Greek *sunagoge* meaning "assembly") in which Jews congregated to read the scriptures then in existence. The Sabbath was emphasized as the day for such readings. Most significantly, during this period the Law (the Torah) came into formal being. Along with the rituals, it provided secular as well as theological unity.

The Temple of Solomon was now rebuilt and Hebrew society reorganized. Both efforts required intellectual and physical labor. Reconstruction of the new Temple was financed by the Persian king Darius, who looked with favor upon the Jews. A Jewish woman named Esther, later a queen of the empire, was an influential member of his court. Ezra's eventual colleague in the reorganization of Jewish society, Nehemiah, was the civil governor of the territory.

When the new Temple was completed, the old Jews wept at how insignificant it was compared to the old one, so that the prophet Zechariah felt compelled to prophesy that it was only symbolic of the house of God.

During this period (586 B.C.E. to 70 C.E.) the scribes replaced the prophets and the high priests replaced the kings. No new prophets seemed to be required since the scribes had written down the teachings and ideas of past prophets, theretofore passed down mainly through (unreliable) oral tradition. This combination of high priests and scribes, disavowing the need for kings and prophets, led quite naturally to a halt in the introduction of new ideas and, consequently, the development of a conservative ortho-doxy. The scribes gathered all past ideas, writing them down into an organized collection which came to be called "the Bible" from the Greek *byblos*, meaning "paper" or "book." (One of the many advantages of writing centuries after the fact is that it is easier to describe "prophecies" and make sure they have come true.)

During this time, Ezra tried to ensure the unity of the Jewish popula-tion by insisting that all mixed marriages be banned and that non-Jewish spouses and their children be sent away. He forbade the Jews to "join in marriage with the people of these abominations," it is recorded in Ezra 9, and decreed, "Give not your daughters to their sons, and take not their daughters for your sons, and seek not their peace, nor their prosperity forever." Only by purging the Jewish community of non-Jewish contami-nation could the evils riddling Jewish society be destroyed. Although many spouses and parents believed that there were less chaotic and more sensi-tive ways to assure the safety of Jewish orthodoxy, Ezra proclaimed "a covenant with the Lord our God, to put away all the [foreign] wives, and such as are born of them." He then ordered that "rulers be appointed" to implement the proclamation "until the wrath of our God be turned away from us for this sin."

Fortified by his emerging intellectual influence, Ezra later undertook (with Nehemiah) to organize Jewish laws. By solidifying the Torah as the central guide for Jewish conduct, Ezra would provide the intellectual foundation of all future Jewish beliefs.

The Torah is the body of Jewish literature and oral tradition as a whole containing the laws and teachings passed down through the generations. The Hebrew *torah* means "laws," and was in turn derived from *yarah*, meaning "to teach." The Torah is the basis of Jewish belief and conduct. (The Torah should not be confused with the Talmud, which is a later work of post-biblical Judaism.)

Ezra and Nehemiah established the Torah as a religious and political constitution of sorts, the final stage in assuring a religious foundation for a proposed second Jewish commonwealth. It was a theocracy in the making. In 444 B.C.E. an assembly was held on the first of Tishri, the first month of the civil year in the Hebrew calendar and the beginning of Rosh Hashanah, the Jewish New Year. The Jews gathered in the Temple to listen to Nehemiah pray and Ezra read from a scroll the history of the religious tradition of the Jewish people. At the end of the reading, the people pledged to adopt the scroll (the Torah) as the fundamental law of the newly established commonwealth. The Torah became the legal constitution of Hebrew society.

The Diaspora had a great influence on the Torah. The Jews of Alexandria had become Hellenized, even to the point of forgetting their native tongue. The religious writings so important to their culture needed to be translated into Greek. This resulted in the Septuagint, after the Greek word for "seventy," so called because tradition asserts that seventy Jewish scholars performed the translation. The Pentateuch, the first five books of the Bible, was translated in the middle of the third century B.C.E. *Pente* is the Greek for five, and *tenkhas* is the Greek word for a case to hold papyrus scrolls or for the scrolls themselves. Thus—from the Diaspora—did two of the basic texts of the Jewish religion come to have Greek names.

Following the period of Ezra, Judaism was obscured from history, surviving primarily in a small territory around Jerusalem where, from what we know, the Jews practiced their religion in peace. The empire of Alexander broke into parts after his death, and Palestine fell first to Egypt, then (in 198 B.C.E.) to the Syrians.

Once again the Jews began to forget their tradition and the covenant. To combat this, a group calling themselves the "Hasidim" ("the holy") arose, not to be confused with later Jewish cultural and religious movements of the same name. The Hasidim were agricultural people, by some accounts ancestors of the Pharisees. Many scholars believe that the Essenes were an offshoot of these Hasidim, and that Jesus Christ was the reputed "Teacher of Righteousness" of the Essenes, a group which was to have a significant influence on primitive Christianity.

The First Book of Maccabees recounts the history of the original Hasidim. Beginning in 175 B.C.E. the Syrian King, Antiochus IV, full of hatred for the Jews, made a determined effort to exterminate them and their religion. According to one Bible history, "He devastated Jerusalem (168 B.C.E.), defiled the temple, offered a sow on its altar, erected an altar to Jupiter, prohibited Temple worship, forbade circumcision on pain of death, sold thousands of Jewish families into slavery, destroyed all copies of Scripture that could be found, and slaughtered everyone in possession of such copies, and resorted to every conceivable torture to force Jews to renounce their religion."[1]

The Jews resisted; they were persecuted. Out of this unexpected repression and other events rose internal doubts as to why the virtuous, who believed in Yahweh, were not being rewarded on earth. The traditional Hebrew rationalization would have been that God was displeased by something the Hebrews did—or did not do. However, when persecution fell upon even the most virtuous, it was evident that virtue was not necessarily rewarded on earth. Another explanation began to take form: there must be rewards after life; otherwise, where persecution was not warranted by Jewish misconduct, Yahweh's sense of justice would be held in question.

The Jews had been exposed to the concept of immortality of the soul during the conquests of Alexander the Great.[2] A century and a half later, impotent to defend themselves against Antiochus, they developed the belief that he would suffer eternal damnation for his acts of persecution. One group, the Sadducees, would not accept this notion, and we know that even up to the time of Christ they refused to believe it. Nonetheless, the possibility of immortality eventually gained widespread acceptance among the Jews.

The repression of Antiochus ultimately led to rebellion. Judas Maccabeus, a military leader, led a revolt against the Syrian tyrant and recaptured Jerusalem in 164 B.C.E. Once successful, he turned his skills to persecution, forcibly circumcising and even killing Syrian prisoners.[3] The valiant Jewish determination to defend the right to practice their religion turned into exercises in military excess.

The moment of Jewish political and military resurgence did not last long. Soon the Jews fell under the dominance of neighboring states acting as proxies for the Romans. Except for the existence of the Hasidim, Judaism may have disappeared, partly through persecution and conquest and partly due to Hellenization.[4] If this is true, ironically, it means that the ultra-conservative Hasidim have some responsibility for the existence of Islam and Christianity, both of which borrowed fundamental beliefs and ideas from Judaism.

The theological and secular significance of the Law gradually attained increasing dominance in official Jewish affairs. Maccabees is the last of the Old Testament books. New prophets and their teachings would be allowed no entree to the canon. Nevertheless, the Book of Enoch, not part of the Old Testament but important in Jewish literature, emerged during this period, probably because its authors were Hasidim.

In Enoch Scriptural justification for eternal hell (*sheol*) enters Judeo-Christian psychology. The idea was invented earlier, as we have seen, but embodiment in the form of Scripture allowed it to become accepted with fervor. Enoch consists principally of parables which give cosmic descriptions of heaven and hell. One is of the Last Judgment, which is brought about by the "Son of Man who hath righteousness." Though men may be happy and successful all their lives, the souls of some were said to descend into hell to suffer "darkness and chains and a burning flame." Among the candidates assured of this fate were Hellenized Jews and all non-repentant gentiles, the *goyim*, people from "good families" or "large nations." One of the pains of hell, as described in the last words of Enoch, is that "the sinners shall cry aloud and see them [the "righteous"] resplendent [in heaven]." (Later on Thomas Aquinas, the Christian theologian of the Middle Ages, would add to the drama from the opposite perspective, asserting that one of the joys of heaven is to observe the eternal suffering of those in hell.[5] Believers can certainly be a compassionate bunch.)

A system of angelology and demonology had existed in the period of Exile (722 to 538 B.C.E.), and it formed the basis for the development of a Satan figure. Considered part spirit, part human, angels were seen as a link between God and man. Many of the angels were described as sentenced to the eternal fires of hell for revealing "eternal secrets" of metallurgy to mortals, that is, for assisting men on earth. It was considered impious to impart knowledge to humans. One is reminded of the Greek demigod, Prometheus, who was condemned to have his liver eaten out by an eagle for all eternity because he brought the secret of fire to mortals. (Theology, in whatever form, has always been opposed to science; science lessens man's dependence on the divine, and therefore on theologians.)

By the beginning of the first century B.C.E. Judaism was divided into factions. Two of the most important, each in their way the advocates of Jewish tradition, were the Pharisees and the rival Sadducees. The Pharisees demanded strict observance of orally based holy law, while the Sadducees based their belief on the Torah. Armed struggle between the two groups resulted in direct Roman intervention in 53 B.C.E., a secular restraint of interreligious strife that would become a pattern in history. Chafing under Roman rule, Jews under the leadership of a group called the Zealots revolted in 66 C.E. against the legions of Nero and later Vespasian, whose son Titus destroyed Jerusalem and the Temple in 70 C.E.

It was during this period that a band of Jews numbering less than a thousand fled to the mountaintop of Masada and defended it against the Roman legions. Rather than be captured, they committed suicide. Today a visit to the mountain of Masada is required of elite Israeli soldiers when they have finished their training; they are inspired to believe that they may have to die rather than surrender. The "Masada complex" instilled in Israeli soldiers has broader implications when applied to Israeli leaders, who have the option of precipitating a nuclear war: it becomes a variant we might call the "Armageddon complex," and is apparently so emotionally compelling that Christian leaders of the United States have adopted variations of it in their approach to the threat of Marxism.

After subjugation by the Romans Judaism once again became more introverted and orthodox, just as it had when in exile. At this period Christianity began to develop, and Judaism would never be the same again. As Christianity spread, it stimulated anti-Semitism, initially through Christian religious zeal for converts, but later for theological and political reasons. Ironically, Judaism's intolerance of other gods was an attitude passed on to the Christians who, now having a god of their own, were not tolerant of the Jews. Christians even propagated the belief that the Jews were responsible for the death of Christ. The fact that it was the Romans who crucified Jesus did not temper Christian hostility; the Christians had their own problems with the Romans, who were (until growing Christian influence forced Roman adoption of Christianity as the state religion in 313) too strong to attack.

The period from approximately the first to the fifth century C.E. is also known as the Talmudic era, a time when rabbis came into prominence in Jewish society. The term rabbi (from the Hebrew *rabh*, meaning "master"), referred to sages such as Jesus and Akiba Ben Joseph. The rabbi, or *rav* in Talmudic times, was an expounder or interpreter of the Bible and the oral law; occasionally they were preachers, and by the sixteenth century they were the heads of yeshivas (Talmudic schools). With the Jewish Reform movement of the nineteenth century they became appointed and salaried employees of religious congregations.

The Talmud (from *talmud*, "learning") itself is the most important work of religious law in post-biblical Judaism. The basic text of the Talmud is the Mishnah, a codification of oral law. The second part of the Talmud is called the Gemara, which contains discussions of the Mishnah. The Gemara exists in two forms, the Babylonian and the Palestinian; the Mishnah is the same for both. It is from the Talmudic era that rabbinical humanism begins, influencing the early tradition of a pacifist Christianity; these two sects would eventually go separate ways. The former would expand and shrink in influence, but always remain an important undercurrent of Jewish thought; the latter would virtually disappear with the onset of a secularized papacy, rising again only with the advent of Protestantism.

The rabbis were to exert great influence on the development of Jewish conduct and thought. The covenant had been changed, as we have seen; worship of one god only had been supplemented with mandates of ethical conduct. After the persecutions of Antiochus, the rewards for such obedience were transformed as well. Divinely assured success in conquest was supplanted by divine provision of lasting peace. Rabbinic teachings emphasized the "wholeness of peace," or *shalom*. "Seek peace and preserve it" developed as a central tenet of later Judaism, and the Talmud has many instances of this mandate: "Great is peace, for it equals everything"

(Numbers Rabbah 11:7). "Great is peace, for God's name is Peace" (Leviticus Rabbah 9:18).

The mass emigration of Jews following the second destruction of the Temple was to be steadily maintained in the succeeding centuries. Jewish religious, cultural and economic life remained centered in Palestine for a while, some say until the breakup of the Roman Empire in the fifth century C.E., but eventually few Jews were left there and Jewish life became "centered" in the Diaspora.

It was decidedly stateless. A second major revolt against the Romans in 131 was crushed, leading to complete dissolution of any semblance of a Jewish state. The Jews were forbidden to live in Jerusalem, the center of Jewish religious life. With persistent emigration, there was eventually no state entity identifiably Jewish even in population.

In defeat, the Jews fashioned *shalom* from Torah's "man of war." There was, however, no lesson learned from that. The concept of theological imperialism had taken root and was now part of Mediterranean culture, soon to be introduced into the political science of the West. Religious militarism had become an accepted part of human life. When the Jews dropped the torch of imperialist theology, it was seized, in the third century, by the Christians. In the seventh century the theoreticians of Islam lit their own fires of religious hatred. These two creeds created cultures whose *raison d'etre* was religious conquest. They were to last in this form until supplanted by the rise of purely secular states in the nineteenth and twentieth centuries. Indian religion claims a world of cycles, however, and perhaps it is so. In 1948 some Jews reclaimed the tradition of religious militarism forsaken by their ancestors.

One man with beliefs is equal to a thousand with only interests.
—John Stuart Mill

Lashana Haba Baiyurusaleim ("Next year in Jerusalem")
—Hebrew prayer

VII

Israel: The Caesarian Birth of a Nation

J ust as an age had passed between Abraham and Moses, and another between Moses and Ezra, so in the twentieth century, after eighteen hundred years of quiet, the covenant was reinvoked as a means to unify the descendants of the Hebrews in a common national objective. Once again the theology of imperialism became ascendent, this time supported by Jewish atheists and, more importantly, fundamentalist Christians. Although territorial ambition remained limited to the lands of old, the repercussions in a nuclear age would be fraught with more risk for the world than in the time of Moses.

By 1948 the confluence of East-West politics, burgeoning Zionism among Jews, and the need to resolve the post-war "Jewish problem" combined to create the state of Israel.

The theology of conquest, endemic to Judaism's hopes since the era of Moses, was reinvigorated by the ideology of materialism that characterized the nineteenth century. Ancient theology inspired a Jewish nation, but it was one that needed, in the words of Isaiah, to "make a covenant with death." To survive the new state had to forsake *shalom*. The story of Israel is an essay on the nature and power of theology, even among economically advanced people of the modern day. Put into power, theology today acts much as it did one, two, and three millennia ago. In the case of Israel, popular analyses obscure this fact with pro-Western biases and the minute dissection of geopolitical forces. The attempt here is to provide sufficient detail to conclusively counter this misunderstanding of modern history.

The Arab nations vowed to crush the new country, to "drive the Jews into the sea." From that day to the present, the Jewish nation has been engulfed in violence. Its will to survive is a tribute to the character of the Jewish people. Its ability to do so has more pedestrian origins: international assistance born of the East-West power struggle, Jewish political influence in the United States, and worldwide Jewish financial aid. Nonetheless, the implications of Israel's survival remain at issue in Washington, Moscow and in the Arab world. The cost in worldwide blood and treasure so far is inestimable. Given Israel's internal Arab demographics, even its permanence as a Jewish state is unlikely.

Fortified as in biblical times by the belief that God is their commanding general, the Israelis reassert the centuries-old claim that God ordained them to inherit certain geographical areas as described in the legends of Abraham and Moses. They are undismayed by the knowledge that most nations, constrained by the material realities of power, have lost territories they once possessed. Like the ancient people of Canaan, most Moslem nations of course do not share this view of divine ordination. Biblical Christians, however, mindful of their Judeo-Christian tradition, support modern Jewish claims to ownership of Palestine.

The modern concept of Israel was born in the nineteenth century, an era of flowering nationalism throughout Europe. Like all peoples, Jews gave expression to national aspirations; Zionism (literally: a return to Palestine) was born. It was a political movement with the purpose of creating a Jewish state in the Holy Land.

Nationalism among Jews was spurred by persecutions in this period in Russia and Austria, and the centuries-old dream of the Return began to be realized as some Jewish farmers and artisans emigrated to Palestine. Intellectual debate among Jews on the issue was intense. Successful Jews were generally "assimilationists," with little inclination to abandon what had taken generations to build. Less well-off Jews, deriving little benefit from life in host countries, especially those in Eastern Europe, and ever mindful of outbreaks of persecution, were more interested in Zionist ideology.

The movement gained greatly in influence with the holding of the first World Zionist Congress in 1897, organized by Theodore Herzl (1860–1904) in Basel, Switzerland; in the same year he published a book entitled *The Jewish State*. Zionist groups soon formed all over the world.

Modern Israel began to take form during World War One, with a British invitation to Jews in 1917: make a homeland in Palestine. Britain had purchased Egypt's interest in the Suez Canal in 1875 (putting it in partnership with private French shareholders), and desired a strategic buffer to protect its investment against resurgent Arab nationalism. The British hoped to avoid the political fallout of direct intervention, however.

The solution was in the creation of a neighboring client state. In 1917 Britain created a homeland for Jews who would presumably return the favor by acknowledging British hegemony over them. (It was a plan with successful contemporary precedent: in 1903 the United States assisted the secession from Columbia of the people living in what is now the country of Panama. In return for military protection and diplomatic recognition, the United States would be allowed to build the Panama Canal—and control it as a virtual country within a country.)

The *Manchester Guardian* opened the campaign for a Middle East buffer state in an editorial of late 1915:

> There can be no satisfactory defense of Egypt or the Suez Canal so long as Palestine is in the occupation of a hostile or probably hostile Power. . . . If Palestine were now a buffer state . . . the problem of Egypt in this war would be a very light one. It is to this condition that we ought to work. . . . On the realization of this condition depends the whole future of the British Empire as a sea Empire.[1]

The British foreign minister, Arthur J. Balfour, made it official on November 2, 1917, with announcement of British support in principle of a proposed home for the Jewish people in Palestine. What came to be called the Balfour Declaration had not been issued without a struggle. One of the major impediments to the plan was the body of anti-Zionist English Jews, many in important positions in the government, who saw Zionism as a threat to hard-fought Jewish citizenship in Western countries. Others were afraid (correctly, as it turned out) that the move would be interpreted as British sponsorship of a new state, something Britain was probably not prepared for.[2]

Several elements worked in favor of the Declaration, however. It would help enlist worldwide Jewish support for the Allies. It would repay a debt of gratitude owed Chaim Weizmann (later to become the first president of Israel), a Russian emigre chemist who in a matter of weeks had successfully developed a synthetic acetone, critical in the manufacture of gunpowder, just as a shortage of wood-derived supplies of the essential substance threatened to cripple the war effort. And it could help secure the Middle East militarily, also important for the war effort. The price to the British seemed small—merely "a small notch" of Arab land, as Balfour fondly called Palestine—only ten thousand square miles. It would secure British interests.[3]

Other factors may have contributed to the decision. British prime minister David Lloyd George noted that Jews were in the forefront of the Bolshevik revolution, which, if successful, could take Russia out of the war, strengthening Germany's Western front. Jews were prominent on the Central Committee of the Bolshevik party, and included such luminaries as Leon Trotsky, Gregorii Zinoviev and Lev Kamenev. With the Balfour Declaration, perhaps they would temper agitation to take Russia out of the war—perhaps even their energies could be diverted to the Zionist cause.

The creation of a Jewish homeland in Palestine could also enlist the aid of Jews in America—to help bring the United States into the war. Historian Barbara Tuchman writes that Lloyd George "says specifically in his *Memoirs* that it was hoped to secure for the Allies both the sympathy of the Jews of Russia, who 'wielded considerable influence in Bolshevik circles,' and 'the aid of Jewish financial interests in the United States.' "[4]

Winston Churchill hoped the Balfour Declaration could even help abort the Bolshevik revolution itself. "Zionism has already become a factor in the political convulsion of Russia," he said, making it possible that "schemes of a worldwide communistic State . . . are directly thwarted and hindered by this new ideal, which directs the energies and hopes of Jews in every land towards a simpler, a truer, and a far more attainable goal." Churchill concluded that the "struggle which is now beginning between the Zionist and Bolshevik Jews is little less than a struggle for the soul of the Jewish people."[5] The Balfour Declaration was issued four days before the Bolsheviks seized power.

Tuchman nearly dismisses the manifold suppositions of British geopolitical strategy, however.

> Lloyd George's afterthoughts on the motivation of the War Cabinet in issuing the Balfour Declaration have bewitched and bewildered all subsequent accounts of this episode. Unquestionably he doctored the picture. Why he did so is a matter of opinion. My own feeling is that he knew that his own motivation, as well as Balfour's, was in large part a sentimental (that is, a Biblical) one, but he could not admit it. He was writing his *Memoirs* in the 1930's, when the Palestine trouble was acute, and he could hardly confess to nostalgia for the Old Testament or to a Christian guilty conscience toward the Jews as reasons for an action that had committed Britain to the painful, expensive, and seemingly insoluble problem of the Mandate. So he made himself believe that the Declaration had been really a reward for Weizmann's acetone process or, alternatively, a propagandist gesture to influence American and Bolshevik Jews—an essentially conflicting explanation, neither so simple nor so reasonable as the truth.[6]

Jewish immigration between the wars was strong, and tensions with indigenous Arabs began to rise. British authorities were faced with the need to protect the interests of Palestine's original inhabitants. The Balfour Declaration had promised that it would be "clearly understood that nothing should be done which may prejudice the civil and religious rights of existing non-Jewish communities in Palestine." The new settlers apparently did not have a copy of the document; disputes arose, and Britain was forced to take steps to protect Arab rights. However, the biblical mandate under which the Jews operated had not protected the ancient people of Canaan, and would not now protect the Arabs of Palestine. The Zionists sought a Jewish nation. "Thus, when Palestine came within reach Britain was trapped . . . It put her, to her dismay, in the role of accoucheur to a new state."[7]

The Balfour Declaration alone could not bring Jews to Palestine, however. The rich Jews of Europe in particular had since Herzl's time shown little interest in emigration to a poverty-stricken, hostile land, homeland or not. Herzl had therefore resolved to create a "movement of the poor" to populate his future Israel. However, such people do not a prosperous country make. It would take something more than a dream to bring the skilled and financially well-off to Palestine.

After World War I, many poor Jewish immigrants flowed into Palestine. By 1932 the influx had reached almost ten thousand a year, reaching thirty thousand in 1933, forty thousand in 1934, and sixty thousand in 1935.[8] By 1936 Arabs were complaining that the proportion of Jews in the population had risen from 10 percent to 30 percent in less than fifteen years.[9]

Much financial support of the nascent Jewish economy in Palestine came from Europe's Rothschild family, particularly from Edmond Rothschild. An assimilationist Jew *par excellence,* Edmond had no personal inclination to emigrate to the barren sands of Palestine, but he was consumed by a passion to help those who wished to do so. To Edmond is attributed the saying that a Zionist is an American Jew who gives an English Jew money to get a Polish Jew to Palestine.[10]

Although not ideologically committed (he too was afraid that Zionism could intensify the perception of Jews in the West as "other"), Edmond's sympathy impelled him to generosity. "His money helped start new soil cultures in the Holy Land: almond trees, mulberry bushes, jasmine, mint tobacco. He not only pressed for the introduction of viticulture, but guaranteed its financial survival by purchasing the entire grape crop of all Jewish settlements year after year—at a higher price than the quotations on the world market."[11] Decades later the Edmond James Rothschild Memorial Group "contributed one million dollars to the Weizmann Scientific Institute in Tel Aviv, gave three million dollars toward the construction of the Knesset, and foots the bill for many of Israel's archaeological expeditions."[12]

In addition to European and American Jewish money, financial support of Jewish emigration to Palestine between the wars came from another source: Germany. Over a fifth of the Jews who went to Palestine through 1937 were from Germany, for obvious reasons.[13] More surprising, however, was the direct support given Zionism by the Nazis. Hitler simultaneously wished to stabilize the German economy, ingratiate himself with Great Britain, and further his campaign to purge Germany of the Jews. It all added up to a program in support of both Jewish emigration and the viability of the economy of Palestine.

Hitler saw Germany and Britain as natural allies without major areas of conflicting interests, a subject he discussed in both *Mein Kampf* and *Secret Books*.[14] Hitler also recognized that he could not afford British hostility to his ambitions for *Lebensraum*, increased "living space" for the German people. It was necessary for Britain to at least acquiesce to Germany's expansionist moves. With sixty-eight million inhabitants on 460,000 square kilometers, and no secure source for many raw materials, Germany sought expansion to the east. This strategy was propounded by one of Hitler's principal advisors, Alfred Rosenberg, who promulgated the *Blut und Boden* ("blood and soil") ideology which "rejected overseas colonies and called for a vast continental empire in central and Eastern Europe at Russia's expense in alliance with Great Britain."[15] "The *Blut und Boden* ideological current of the 1920's postulated that Germany's only enemy was Jewish-Bolshevik Russia."[16]

Geopolitically, Hitler saw the British Empire as a known quantity and feared that a collapse of that empire would only benefit Japan, the United States and others—but certainly not Germany.[17] Hitler went so far as to suggest an alliance to Lloyd George "based on spheres of interest, with Britain supporting German hegemony over Europe and Germany guaranteeing the British Empire."[18] To assure Britain of the integrity of his intentions, Hitler was even prepared to provide Britain his own troops to sustain its empire, and to allow Britain to "fix the relative strength of both navies, ensuring Britain about a three-to-one advantage."[19]

Hitler's offers should not be construed as merely a *quid pro quo*, however. The proposed collaboration was also a manifestation of Hitler's racial *Weltanschauung*. The Anglo-Saxons were viewed as a central part of the Germanic concept of the master race, and the British Empire was seen as the living vindication of the white supremacy notions of the Nazi racial doctrine. Hitler observed with unbridled enthusiasm the fact that a small country like Great Britain could achieve total domination over hundreds of million of non-whites in India and the Arab world. He celebrated this state of affairs in *Mein Kampf*.[20]

Hitler also observed that Britain, in its white imperial wisdom, was promoting a policy of sending white European Jews to seize "a small notch of land" from the dark-skinned Arabs in the Middle East. He could also not help but notice that Britain's strongest colony, South Africa, had its own pronounced policies of white supremacy and was one of the most ardent supporters of Zionism.

Hitler's general notions of white racial superiority with respect to both the Jews, a highly accomplished people, and their Zionist enterprise, were in obvious conflict with his anti-Semitism. The resolution of this contradiction was predetermined, however: his dream of *Lebensraum* required a conciliatory policy of *Englandpolitik*. Emerging Arab nationalists were openly supportive of the new Germany and lined up in the Middle East to become members of the German National Socialist party, formed for the benefit of Germans living in the Middle East. In the interests of larger policy, cooperation with Arab Nazi sympathizers (who were, above all, anti-British), was officially discouraged.[21] Despite his pronounced anti-Semitism, "for reasons of power politics and racial ideology, Hitler was not prepared to support the Arab cause in Palestine."[22]

Hitler's anti-Semitism, whatever its sources, was intensified by his advisor Alfred Rosenberg. Together they perceived an international Jewish conspiracy, orchestrated by the strange admixture of Bolshevik Jews in Communist Russia and the capitalist Jews of Europe epitomized by the Rothschild banking family—"the Führer's favorite abomination."[23]

Further intensifying Hitler's anti-Semitism was the spotty international Jewish boycott of German export products, at a time when Germany was in desperate need of hard currency to pay the costs of the Versailles Treaty. In February 1933 the leading German industry and trade body had pressured Hitler's government to promote exports as the best possible method of reviving the economy and reducing unemployment. Hitler's rise to the German chancellorship the month before, however, had moved Jews around the world to direct action: boycott of the German economy. Hitler's belief in the worldwide Jewish conspiracy intensified.

Before resorting to the atrocities of the concentration camps, Hitler sought to make Germany *Jüdenrein* ("free of Jews") by sending them abroad. However, with justifiable fear of Jewish intelligence and political ingenuity, he opposed their emigration to neighboring countries, lest they become a political force against him in Europe. To send them to Palestine would sidestep this hazard, and would also put Germany in cooperation with Great Britain. Hitler accordingly initiated a process to promote the departure of German Jews to Palestine. The Third Reich allowed Palestinian Jews to conduct promotion campaigns and economic training programs in Germany, and subsidized Zionist schools—even allowing Zionist flags to be flown over them.[24] The German foreign office provided German Zionist leaders with multiple exit and reentry visas to expedite their organizing efforts, noting in one memorandum that, "There exists no reason to paralyze Zionist tendencies in Germany because Zionism does not contradict the National Socialist goal of gradually eliminating the Jews from Germany."[25] At least one Palestinian Zionist worked for the Deutsches Nachrichtenburo, the German news service, and Germany even supplied weapons to the Haganah, one of the most important of the Zionist recruiting organizations based in Palestine.[26] The Zionist newspaper *Jüdische*

Rundschau was unaffected by the mass suppression of publications after the Nazi assumption of power, and it enjoyed comparative press freedom. "*Jüdische Rundschau* was free to preach Zionism as a wholly separate political philosophy—indeed, the only separate political philosophy sanctioned by the Third Reich."[27]

For their part, the Zionists pressed for more official cooperation in the hope that it would persuade reluctant assimilationist Jews—the most valuable of potential immigrants, since they were usually the most economically well-off—to support the Zionist effort.[28] The German consul-general in Palestine reported that Zionists there had recognized "the opportunities for Zionism and the development of Palestine that have emerged from the misfortunes of the Jews in Germany."[29]

In his saddening book, *The Transfer Agreement*, Edwin Black reveals that the foundation of the Israel economy during the 1930s and 1940s was laid by secret agreements between Zionists and the Third Reich, agreements which decapitated an anti-Nazi worldwide Jewish boycott that might very well have toppled the Hitler dictatorship. It is a story understandably painful for Jews to hear, but it is unimpeachable: Black, a son of Holocaust survivors, labored five years over tens of thousands of pages of original documents to find the truth.

With the rise of Hitler to the German chancellorship in January 1933, Jews around the world spontaneously resolved to boycott the German economy. Many in the Jewish leadership resisted such action, at first because they believed that open hostilities would endanger the lives of German Jews. Another reason soon arose.

The Zionists saw an "opportunity" (the word was actually used by some Zionists at the time) to transform the feeble economy of Jewish Palestine, enabling it to become a nation—Israel. The means was the possibility of entering into a secret contract with the Third Reich: in exchange for the transfer of German Jews and their assets to Palestine, the Zionists would help break the general economic boycott organized by other worldwide Jewish agencies. According to Black, "Zionist leaders understood that the success of the future Jewish Palestine economy would be inextricably bound up with the survival of the Nazi economy. So the Zionist leadership was compelled to go further. The German economy would have to be safeguarded, stabilized, and if necessary reinforced. Hence the Nazi party and the Zionist organization shared a common stake in the recovery of Germany. If the Hitler economy fell, both sides would be ruined."[30] More explicitly: "The price of this new nation would be the abandonment of the war against Nazi Germany. Whole branches of Judaism would wither, but the trunk would survive—Herzl's words."[31]

The Zionists envisioned the Jews in Palestine as export representatives of the Nazis, through a company set up by the Zionists. Called the Near and Middle East Commercial Corporation (NEMICO), it "operated a regional sales network in Iraq, Egypt, Syria, Cyprus and elsewhere in the region . . . Mideast markets were open for a vast array of key German exports, from Volkswagens to municipal bridgeworks."[32] This provided the Nazis with export markets and with hard currency. Meanwhile, the Jews in Palestine wanted to sell the Third Reich Jaffa oranges and other citrus crops. "If Germany could not sell her exports, there would be no money to purchase 15 percent or more of the 1933-34 citrus crop."[33] By June 1936, Germany was second only to Great Britain among countries exporting to Palestine; by June 1937 it was first. Palestinian Jews aided Hitler in order to expand their own industries—with questionable regard for the fate of Jews in Germany.

The Zionists also wanted German Jewish capital. "The wealth had to be saved."[34] The Zionists wanted a minimum of two thousand British pounds per Jew (about eight thousand dollars at the time, much more in today's currency) who immigrated into Palestine from Germany. Half would be "controlled by official Zionist entities on behalf of the immigrant."[35]

The small Anglo-Palestine Bank was designated to handle these arrangements. As a consequence, it would become "one of the top one hundred banks in the world. And it would change its name to Bank Leumi—the most important bank in Israel."[36]

During the period of late 1933 to 1941 approximately a hundred million dollars flowed into Palestine or was transferred "via corollary German commercial agreements and special international banking transactions, this during a period when the average Palestine Jew earned a dollar a day. Some of Israel's major industrial enterprises were founded with these monies, including Mekoroth, the national waterworks and Rassco, a major land developer. And vast quantities of material were stockpiled, including coal, irrigation pipes, iron and metal products for companies and enterprises not yet in existence."[37]

Thus, during the Hitler era, the Zionists "sought a means of turning the miseries of German Jewry into a new impetus for a Jewish homeland in Palestine."[38] In sum, Black asks, "Was the continuing economic relationship with Germany an indispensible factor in the creation of the State of Israel?"

Black's studied conclusion: "The answer to that is yes."[39]

In late 1935, the Nineteenth Zionist Congress met in Lucerne, Switzerland, to discuss the transfer of Jewish assets from Germany to Palestine and the related business relationships between Palestine and the Third Reich. The Nazis had an official representative at the congress, which approved the transfer agreement. A few days later the Nuremberg laws were published, officially banning Jews in Germany and opening the door for Jews to move to Palestine, where they would activate the agreement and assist the Nazis in developing German exports to the Middle East. The name of the Nazi representative at the meeting was Adolf Eichmann.[40]

Of Jews who opposed him Herzl had said, "Perhaps we shall have to fight first of all against many an evil-disposed, narrow hearted, short-sighted member of our own race."[41] That attitude was rife among the Zionist organizations who played a role in the fate of Europe's Jews during World War II.[42]

After the Allies had crushed the Nazis in 1945, the Zionists developed their own agenda. Jews and capital still needed to be attracted to Palestine. The fresh memory of the Holocaust, aided by a strong Zionist recruitment drive, stimulated a massive immigration. Some Zionist factions, it should be noted, were selective in this effort, preferring young people who could build a nation to old people who would be a burden on the state. Propagating the recent lessons of history was not the only means used to implement this emigration program. Zionist terrorist organizations such as the Irgun (eventually led by Menachem Begin) and the Haganah (one of whose officers was Moshe Dayan) were willing to use force. Author Steven Green, a specialist on disaster and humanitarian relief efforts, writes in *Taking Sides*, a book on America's secret relations with Israel, that, "Irgun recruiters beat some of those who refused to 'volunteer' to fight the Arabs in Palestine, and others were threatened with death if they did not go. While prospective recruits were being persuaded, the main gates to the [Duppel Center Displaced Persons Camp] were closed to prevent escape. . . . An elite, paramilitary group within the Haganah called Sochnut began to appear in [U.S. military] report after report of threats, beatings, and intimidation."[43] One intelligence report cited reports that of three hundred people leaving the Tikwah displaced persons camp, 65 percent had been "forced to go through the application of various degrees of pressure."[44] In short, Green concludes, "Jewish victims of Nazi terror again were forced to flee friends and family to escape Zionist terror."[45]

The drive was successful. With large numbers of Jews flowing into Palestine, the demographic reality of Israel soon came to seem assured. For their part, even in the 1930s the Arabs had perceived, quite accurately, that if the Zionists were supported by both Great Britain and Germany, the number of immigrants would eventually force the Jews to adopt a *Lebensraum* policy of their own. The required land would, of course, have to come from the dark-skinned Arabs.

But first there would have to be Jewish nationhood. With rising Arab resentment at the unprecedented post-war influx of foreigners, military matters became of prime importance to the Zionist movement. The formation of an army and the acquisition of the arms to equip it became priorities. Soldiers could be recruited from immigrant citizenry. But arms required money, and a source. The Zionists got the money from America's Jewish community, still reeling from news of the Holocaust. And they found a source for needed weapons—and training too—behind the Iron Curtain.

The Soviet Union was most anxious to eliminate the British presence in Palestine, and even more anxious to prevent the Americans from re-placing them. As Abba Eban says, "The support of Israel by the Soviet Union lasted for nearly three years, which was long enough to see the British position in Palestine eliminated and the Negev in Israeli hands. The Soviet Union had feared that a British base would remain in the Negev even after Israel's establishment. Once the immediate tactical aim was achieved, the USSR turned its back on Israel and began to seek friendships in the Arab countries."[46]

So for the time being the Eastern bloc proffered its assistance. It came in the form of money, equipment, military training and even military intelligence. Manpower was provided too, in the form of Jews allowed to emigrate from the Soviet Union and Eastern Europe. The Zionists were already obtaining weapons from dozens of sources, but the Eastern bloc became the main Zionist supply depot. In March 1948 U.S. intelligence officials "learned of the new source of arms supply (and, to a certain extent, training) for the Zionist underground: Czechoslovakia. In the last week of March, the [U.S.] Military Attache in Prague had reported that the Stern gang was recruiting in the Czech army with, he thought, the approval of the Soviet government."[47] Czechoslovakian Airlines often provided the planes to ship the weapons to Palestine; the loading of the planes was even protected by Czech security police. American Zionists were involved as well. The CIA reported that "U.S.-owned aircraft and U.S. crews are directly participating in their activities."[48] The U.S. government objected, but did not prosecute the Americans involved, despite their violation of provisions of the Neutrality Act.

In response to formal American objections, Soviet and Czech diplo-mats said that Americans involved would be sent home; they were not. North of Bratislava the Zionists set up a new air operation far from the prying eyes of the U.S. intelligence agencies. "The new base was not just an air transport depot. Russian and Czech Air Force officers trained Israeli Defense Force pilots. Fighters and bombers purchased by Israel were reconditioned there and used for training."[49]

The Zionist army was receiving Soviet and Czech largesse too. "The U.S. Air Attache in Prague reported that between 4000 and 5000 Israeli military personnel were being trained in Czechoslovakia."[50] The Zionists also routinely recruited American Jews (including retired U.S. military officers) to fly their planes and to obtain U.S. military intelligence for the emerging Jewish state.[51]

Not only did Stalin personally "encourage . . . [the Eastern bloc] to supply the weapons with which the Zionists fought their war of independence,"[52] but Soviet support was eventually extended to the diplomatic realm as well. Joseph Stalin and Andrei Gromyko became two of the leading world spokesmen for Zionism. In fact, "In 1948 [Stalin] acted as godparent to the new state of Israel. His representative in the United Nations pleaded for recognition of that state when many governments still disputed its legality . . . When Israel's first diplomatic envoy, Mrs. Golda Meir, made her first appearance in Moscow, she became the object of tumultuous ovations."[53] The Soviet Union was the first nation in the world to grant diplomatic recognition to Israel. Why? Arkady Shevchenko, a major Soviet intelligence official who defected to the West, explained it simply as "ambition for a foothold in the Middle East."[54] In aid and comfort to the Zionist cause, the Third Reich had been deftly replaced with the Soviet bloc.

At this point, President Harry Truman began to act. He was inclined against the creation of the Israeli state, but at the same time interested in maintaining the U.S. geopolitical presence in the Middle East and particularly concerned lest the United States were to come into open conflict with a Soviet-Zionist alliance in Palestine. In such a scenario the American Jewish community would be active—but how and in what way? Truman was generally sympathetic to the Jewish cause in these post-Holocaust times; more importantly, his political instincts told him that "the Jewish vote might well be crucial to the presidential election of 1948."[55] Truman jumped on the Zionist bandwagon, and Francis Spellman, the Roman Catholic cardinal of New York, used his influence to help deliver the "Catholic vote" in the diplomatic realm, i.e., official recognition of the new nation by the Latin American countries. Thus, on the Procrustean bed of *Realpolitik*, assisted by the midwife of violence, the Caesarian birth of Israel was performed.

By the time of the Israeli war of independence, American money and Eastern-bloc arms had made Israel the most powerful military machine in the Middle East. Contrary to popular Zionist mythology, Israel was not the underdog when war broke out. In 1948 the U.S. Joint Chiefs of Staff assessed the military strength of Jews in Palestine at 185,000 soldiers under arms. Arab forces added up to only 140,000 men.[56] In addition, while the Israelis were armed with tanks, airplanes and artillery, the Arabs were wondering how to secure ammunition for their arsenal of predominantly WWI-vintage rifles. The outcome of the Israeli war of independence was a foregone conclusion.

The preparation for the creation of Israel, under United Nations supervision after British withdrawal in May 1947, had included much Zionist terrorism. It was hardly limited to the well-known attacks on Arab families and community organizations. Zionists were strongly implicated in the shocking September 1948 assassination of the head of the U.N. mission to Palestine, Folke Bernadotte. According to James McDonald, the first American ambassador to Israel and strongly pro-Zionist, the Israelis considered Bernadotte "an obstacle to their military conquest of Jerusalem and perhaps the remainder of Palestine."[57] According to Green, "On September 16, the Israeli Foreign Minister, Moshe Shertok, publicly accused U.N. Mediator Bernadotte of bias against the State of Israel and in favor of the Arab states. . . . The next day, Bernadotte was dead."[58] By mid-October, "the U.S. government believed that the Israeli government, or some part of it, had directly participated in Bernadotte's assassination." American intelligence suggested that a specially trained team had been flown in from Prague to do the job.[59]

Throughout the early post-war period the Zionists sought military assistance from the Americans, but refused to allow the United States to monitor Israeli military activities. It was a one-way street. Israeli terrorist and military organizations even harassed American officials, kidnapping one and threatening others with death if they did not accept Israeli ground rules.[60] American intelligence and diplomatic officials reported the cause: Israel did not want U.S. interference in the machinations of its territorial and military ambitions. It wanted American money and military supplies with no strings attached.

Once the Zionists had founded the state of Israel, the classic pattern of empire, "defensive" expansion, was inevitable. Although Israeli liberals and moderates sought accommodation with their Arab neighbors, their views did not prevail. Apart from Israel's foreign minister, Moshe Sharett, Israeli leaders were generally in continuous search of more territory and more weapons. Border clashes were provoked to provide an excuse to occupy more land, and persistent attempts at peace by moderate factions were deliberately thwarted, even sabotaged.

In 1954, Sharett was close to securing a treaty of cooperation with Egypt, which, because of its internal problems, had no reason or desire to enter into serious hostilities with Israel. In fact, Gamel Abdel Nasser, Egypt's prime minister, had in October become one of the few heads of state to decline an offer of military assistance from the United States. All he wanted was economic aid.[61] Nasser had already decided that he should rely for military aid on a less pro-Israel source, namely the Soviet Union.

However, Ben Gurion, Moshe Dayan, and other Israeli leaders sought territory not peace. Green reports that, "Dayan convoked a meeting of the Mapai [one of Israel's two leading political parties at the time] ministers to propose a series of military moves into Egypt to precipitate a war with that country. The next month [February], both [Defense Minister Pinchas] Lavon, and Ben Gurion (the latter from his retirement retreat) proposed what Sharett referred to as a 'blitz-plan' to invade and occupy territory in Syria, at a time of political turmoil in that country."[62] Sharett vetoed the plan because he was near to achieving *detente* with the Middle East's most powerful Arab nation.

Nonetheless, the Israeli militarists won the day. The Israeli defense ministry, headed by Lavon, covertly bombed American and European diplomatic installations in Egypt and tried to blame it on Arab radicals.[63] The Israeli agents were caught and prosecuted and the negotiations with Egypt collapsed. The potential Camp David of the 1950s was scuttled. The tit-for-tat of small-scale terrorism between Egypt and Israel was allowed to continue, and the stage was set for thirty years of serious military conflict.

The Americans expressed brief anger but dropped the matter. Nasser, surprised that the United States tolerated Israeli bomb attacks even against its own facilities, turned increasingly to the Soviet Union for military assistance. The other Arab countries took note of the U.S. attitude and Egypt's reaction. Meanwhile, within the Soviet Union, a Soviet military intelligence report of 1954, called the "Locomotive Report," asserted that "to wreck the 'Locomotive of Capitalism' it was not necessary to smash the engine, only to deprive it of a critical ingredient [oil]. Immediately after this the Soviet penetration of the Arab nations began."[64] Israel thus provided the USSR with the opportunity to infiltrate and appear to befriend Arab nations, and to threaten U.S. geopolitical interests in the oil world.

The Egyptian military buildup strengthened the hand of Israeli hawks urging a preemptive strike against Egypt. "Sometime in June [1956], David Ben Gurion (and Moshe Dayan's) plans for the preventive attack against Egypt were finalized. All that remained was for the right occasion to arise that would provide the justification for a full-scale attack without incurring the extreme wrath of the United States, Britain and France—the Tripartite Agreement signatories."[65] In 1950 the three nations had signed this agreement, supposed to be the cornerstone of their collective foreign policy in the Middle East. The most important provision of the agreement was that all three powers desired to "promote the establishment and maintenance of peace and stability in the area" and stated their "unalterable opposition to the use of force between any of the states in that area."[66] Israeli officials had been strongly opposed to the agreement in private, but nevertheless feared open defiance of the nation's benefactors. If Israel were to attack Egypt, it needed a strong pretext.

Yahweh couldn't have given Israel a better one: in late July 1956 Nasser nationalized the Suez Canal (declaring his intention to pay the full current stockholding price for it, however), apparently because the United States backed out of plans to finance the Aswan High Dam. Told by U.S. officials that he should pay for it himself, Nasser looked to Suez revenues.

Both Britain and France were livid. In his autobiography, Moshe Dayan admits that he saw an opportunity to launch an attack on Egypt, and recommended to Ben Gurion that the occasion should not be missed.[67] According to Ritchie Ovendale in *The Origins of the Arab-Israeli Wars*, "Israeli policy had been decided in 1955; what was needed was the opportunity to implement it."[68] Israel could disguise its aggression by "merely participating" with England and France, who were willing to take the responsibility. Israel enlisted in their immediately formed plans to take back the canal by force.

The United States, meanwhile, was preoccupied with a presidential election and the Soviet occupation of Hungary. In order to camouflage its intentions, Israel explained to the United States that its troop movements were "security measures" for the defense of Israel. Like the Japanese ambassadors in the United States during the attack on Pearl Harbor, when the invasion of the Suez occurred Foreign Minister Abba Eban was in Washington lying (to the then Secretary of State John Foster Dulles) about Israel's peaceful intentions. Eban noted in his autobiography that he was asked to leave the secretary of state's office with the sarcastic suggestion that he "find out exactly what is happening in your country."[69]

Israel invaded the Sinai on October 29, in accordance with the plan. On the following day Britain and France issued an ultimatum demanding that both Israel and Egypt withdraw their forces ten miles from the coast, failing which Anglo-French forces "would intervene with whatever strength may be necessary to ensure compliance." Since Israeli forces were not even near the canal, Israel readily compiled. For Egypt to submit to the ultimatum would have meant abandoning territory not yet lost; Nasser refused. The Anglo-France forces attacked.

Three thousand Egyptians were killed in the ensuing air, sea and land invasion, until the United States intervened. President Eisenhower used the diplomatic and military might of the United States to stand behind Egyptian sovereignty. Much wood had been added to the fires of Arab hostility, however. There was now certainly no turning back to "cooperation."

In 1967 Israel's militarists once again prevailed over its peacemakers. "Defensive" expansion was again on the march, but this time the circumstances were much more complex, and fault perhaps not quite so easily discerned. Despite victory, Israel had received a bit of a shock with the events of the Suez War. Its benefactors, particularly the United States, had not proven entirely stalwart in their support of the nation's military ventures. They had preferred compromise and cease-fire to conquest, even when it was suitably dressed up. Israel was no longer even confident it could rely on its Western allies for timely aid in the case of Arab invasion.

Israel's response was to develop a strategy of preparedness that relied primarily on the pre-emptive strike. According to Ovendale, "It was evident that Israel would be exposed if it relied on a defensive strategy; Israel had to be ready to take the initiative and to be ready to make a pre-emptive counterattack to destroy the opponent's forces. Any future war would have to be short, and fought on the opponent's territory. . . . In the years following the Suez-Sinai War, special emphasis was therefore placed on developing the offensive and striking power of the Israeli army."[70]

It was a cautious and reasonable policy on its face, but embedded in that prudence was the inevitability of the Greek tragedy. First-strike power in the hands of religious militants presupposes its use. Israel's preparedness was not to be used simply to decapitate a planned attack. The political and intelligence process for discerning such an attack is often out of the control of participants, and is also easily manipulated by provocateurs of rank. No one really planned to attack in the first moments of World War I, but mobilization led to mobilization, accidental clashes to full-scale war. Likewise "rogue" elements, as in the Lavon affair, can precipitate crisis by carrying out actions with contrived sponsorship and target. Israel's first-strike capability, required though it might have been, was an accident waiting to happen.

The Six Day War was not precipitated by an imminent Arab invasion, unless "imminent" includes speculation on long-term developments. Israel provoked the Six Day War by spreading the rumor of its own imminent attack on Syria. "Through leakages to the Russians, and by absenting armored formations from the Independence Day parade in Jerusalem on 15 May, Israel gave Nasser the impression that an attack on Syria was imminent. That day Nasser declared a state of alert in Egypt, and sent Egyptian troops into the Sinai . . . On 22 May, Cairo closed the Gulf of Aquaba [Israel's only outlet to the south] to Israeli ships and others sailing to Eilat with strategic cargoes."[71] Trade in general was not hindered. In addition, Egypt instructed the United Nations to remove its border patrols from Egyptian territory, arguing that there were no such forces on the Israeli side.

Israel had successfully laid the groundwork for war. "The next day, [Prime Minister] Eshkol told the Knesset that interference with shipping in the Gulf of Aquaba and the Straits of Tiran constituted a violation of international law, and an act of aggression against Israel."[72] The United Nations offered to mediate and Egypt agreed; then it sought Israel's permission to station U.N. troops on the Israeli side of the border, in order to maintain a calming presence while negotiations were under way. Israel declined.

On June 5, Israel launched an air strike on Egypt, claiming an Egyptian invasion was imminent. Having destroyed the Egyptian Air Force on the ground Israel turned to Jordan. The West Bank was mouth-watering fruit hanging low in a neighbor's orchard. After redeploying its forces, Israel renewed the attack. "Next year in Jerusalem" came the next day. Since the Jordanian forces were negligible, it became obvious that the purpose of the war was to justify Israel's seizure of the West Bank.

It was at this time that an American surveillance vessel, the USS *Liberty*, was in international waters in the Mediterranean Sea monitoring war communications. At Israel's request, the National Security Agency ordered the ship to leave the area, but the command was apparently never received. In the meantime the *Liberty* overheard a conversation it would wish it hadn't. Israel apparently intended to seize Jordan's West Bank despite the cease-fire, but it had laid plans to make the invasion seem justified.[72] Israel wished the world to believe that its forthcoming attack on Jordan was defensive, and feared U.S. knowledge of the ruse because Arabists in the State Department might leak word to the world press.

Exposure of the scheme would abort the invasion. For Israel territory was more important than ethics. There was only one course of action to take. Israeli aircraft initiated an assault on the *Liberty*, strafing and bombing the decks with wave after wave of fighter planes. Thirty-four Americans were killed and 171 wounded, but the ship miraculously escaped being sunk.[74] According to one CIA document, an Israeli general opposed to the attack protested to Moshe Dayan, "This is pure murder."[75] Dayan, who ordered the attack, was unconcerned. Instead, Israeli helicopters bearing boarding parties were sent aloft, presumably to kill any Americans left alive; "They didn't want *anyone* to live," said one survivor.[76] Israel had to eliminate any chance that its secret would be revealed. The helicopters were hovering over the *Liberty* when U.S. Navy aircraft came to its rescue.

The USS *Liberty* was neutralized. The Israelis invaded Jordan and seized the West Bank. Whatever the American government may have wanted to do to prevent the invasion was of no matter once it had been effected. Israel was an ally and of course would be protected. The American government conspired with Israel to treat the *Liberty* "incident" as an accident. Former Congressman Paul Findley (R-Illinois) gives the reason why. "President Johnson was worried about the reaction of Jewish voters."[77] Had the public known what had happened at the time, Johnson would have been forced to action he would regret at the polls.

A co-founder and former head of Washington's most powerful pro-Israel lobbying group, the American Israel Public Affairs Committee, I. L. Kenen, conveniently neglects to mention the *Liberty* incident in his account of Israeli-American relations, *Israel's Defense Line*. As for Israel's provoking a Jordanian invasion to provide a pretext for occupation of the West

Bank, Kenen dares to say, "An inexplicable mystery of the 1967 war was [King] Hussein's costly intervention. There had been no need for him to enter, and he paid for his folly."[78] Coming from a man with access to nearly the highest level of inside information, this is little short of an outright lie. It is typical of Israeli lobbying propaganda, however, and is publicly swallowed by American governments unwilling to challenge the political muscle of the Israel lobby.

Boiling the matter down to its essentials, the United States is willing to countenance Israeli aggression even against itself—this is the extent of the grip of the Israel lobby on the American government. Winking at the attack on the *Liberty* was no passing lenience. To this day America tolerates extensive Israeli espionage within its borders. Simply put, Israel can do whatever it wants to its indispensable benefactor and suffer no consequences. At the same time, domestic critics of Israel are fearful of being labeled anti-Semitic. Left-wing "anti-imperialists" who label Israel a U.S. client state have it nearly backwards.

The territorial dreams of the early Zionists were being realized. Gradually Israel had come to occupy the Golan Heights, the West Bank, the Gaza Strip and the Sinai Desert, territories acquired from Syria, Jordan and Egypt. Unlike the early people of Canaan, decimated by their Hebrew conquerors, the Arabs have not succumbed so easily to their Israeli invaders. As facts were fabricated to justify the naked aggression of the Hebrew imperialists of biblical times (the "covenant"), so has history been conveniently written to justify the Israeli expansionism of modern times. The facts of Israeli provocation of its Arab neighbors, Israeli initiation of repeated Middle East wars, and complete Israeli disdain for even courteous treatment of its sole source of survival, the United States, have all been written out of the popular consciousness. Instead Israel is widely believed to be the innocent lamb among a pack of Middle Eastern wolves, the tiny victim of barbarous, hate-filled Arab aggression, America's only friend in a region that reviles it. Despite its vaunted objectivity, the Western press writes a modern Deuteronomy at nearly every opportunity.

Israel and its militarism are now intertwined for reasons perhaps even less mutable than millennia-old theology: military industry is the basis of Israel's economy. Not having the economic resources to develop many industries at the same time, Israel has elected to make weapons production its principal export industry. More than a *quarter* of the Israeli workforce is employed in the military-industrial complex.[79] Israel supplies sophisticated weapons to a score of countries, including such paragons of international moral virtue as Chile, South Africa, the People's Republic of China, and even Iran, to whom it sells tens of millions of dollars of weapons every year. It was the desire to sell armaments to Iran that caused Israel to

persuade the White House to do the same in 1986. Israel sought to eliminate U.S. pressure to reduce Israel arms sales to Iran, the simplest way to
do so was to get the United States to participate in such sales. On a
per-capita basis Israel is the largest supplier of weapons in the world (the
United States is the largest gross exporter of arms).[80] Furthermore, because
of its desire to avoid inspection of its nuclear military capability, Israel
refuses to sign the nuclear Non-Proliferation Treaty.

International opportunism is a hallmark of Israeli foreign policy. After
the United States, Israel's closest foreign ties are probably to South Africa,
with whom it cooperates economically, technologically, politically, and
militarily—most frighteningly in the area of nuclear weapons research.
The common ground is that both are treated as pariah states internationally, subject to various military and economic sanctions. It is ironic that
Israel would have such a close relationship with South Africa, whose
government is run by the political descendants of Nazi sympathizers, men
jailed during World War II for agitating against the Allied war effort.

It is tragic that a country set up to provide Jews a place to live in
peace can only sustain itself by becoming the largest per-capita supplier of
weapons in the world. The conclusion is inescapable: when religion seeks
political power, any means are justified and morally sanctioned.

It is safe to say that Israel's "defensive" imperialism has spawned a
wave of terrorism longer-lasting and more widely dispersed than any
other. Much of the Western world has been unavoidably drawn into the
maelstrom of the Hebrew covenant. It is a cold and windy land not easily
departed: as terrorism continues unchecked and uncheckable, Israel's
militarists inexorably gain influence; they predictably launch further "defensive" efforts and their victims inevitably vow battle to an even bitterer
end. For every step to Camp David, there are two steps to Lebanon.
It is a self-accelerating downward spiral. Given likely Israeli nuclear
capability and ever-increasing Arab fanaticism, the end result could even
be Armageddon.

The hundreds of thousands of Palestinian refugees from Israeli militarism live a life with no future, only the frustrations which fuel ever more
frantic terrorism. This creates, in turn, ever-widening Israeli "defensive"
measures.

The latest and most extreme venture of this kind came with the effort
to decapitate the Palestinian Liberation Organization in 1982. Israel
launched a military invasion of Lebanon despite the likelihood of severe
international condemnation and the impossibility of any but the shortest-
term success. Religiously inspired militarism, a world view detached from
reality, was in full flower. Using cluster bombs supplied by the United
States (and proscribed for any but defensive use), Israeli aircraft killed thou-

ands of Lebanese, mostly civilians and including many women and children. Not satisfied with cluster bombs, the Israeli air force also dropped white phosphorous firebombs on population centers to teach the Lebanese citizenry the danger of harboring the PLO. In mustering American support for these actions, the Israeli lobby in Washington referred to the military invasion of Lebanon as a "crisis" for Israel—euphemism at its worst.

"The Israelis wished to remain in Beirut until they could achieve two political objectives: the expulsion of the PLO . . . and the replacement of Syrian hegemony over the Lebanese state . . . by the hegemony of Israel."[81] To do this Israel sought to influence the Lebanese election by its military presence in order to have its own allies put into power. The two governments would then sign a peace treaty on Israeli terms, terms which would assure Israeli military suzerainty. Implicit in these matters was the reality that Israel had already diverted the waters of the Litani and Jordan rivers. For years the Israelis had carried out huge dam and pipeline construction projects in order to channel water away from the Arabs and Palestinians and into Israel.

In securing southern Lebanon, the Israeli Defense Forces tacitly condoned the massacre of Sabra and Shatila's helpless Palestinian refugees by Israel's military allies, the Lebanese Christians. Over eight hundred people, disproportionately women and children, were murdered. Jewish humanism was finally aroused. Some American rabbis were heard to cry out, "This is not Jewish, what they are doing," while hundreds of thousands of Israelis took to the streets to protest their government's conduct. For the first time, the sacrosanct IDF was regarded by thousands of Israelis as less than a benevolent protector; even the morale of Israeli soldiers began to decline. The spirit of rabbinical humanism finally arose from its slumbers, but it was still only a minority voice. In the few years since the invasion of Lebanon, it has fallen back into its pre-invasion torpor. With the rise of Hebrew fundamentalism, particularly in the growing Sephardic population, Israeli militarism appears to face an unimpeded future.

From all appearances Israel is less the realization of millennia-old dreams of a homeland for living in peace and more a compensation of Jews for their centuries of persecution. Israel is largely a Jewish affirmative action program, substantially paid for by the non-Jews of America. The United States justifies its financing of Israel's continual deficits by rationalizing that it is America's most stable ally in the region. The cost, however, is enormous. Israel has one of the largest per-capita debts in the world, and remains solvent only because of more than four *billion* dollars in American aid per year. According to the *Washington Post*, "What life-support systems are to medicine, American foreign aid has become to Israeli life. Without the continuing flow of that aid—roughly 19 percent of the government's budget in 1985—Israel would not be able to defend itself and to maintain a society that boasts five universities, sees one-seventh of its citizens travel abroad annually . . . and has 29 percent of its civilian workforce on the government—which is to say the public—payroll."[82] There is no evidence that this dependent relationship will change anytime soon; on the contrary, Israel requests, and is given, more U.S. aid every year.

America's military rationale for its massive support of Israel—primarily Israel's Middle East intelligence gathering network—is clearly not sufficient. When all the costs are added up, it would be cheaper by half to build a U.S. military base in Palestine than to support Israel through subsidies. Recurrent and insoluble tension rather than stability for America's interests in the region has been the only result. All the friendly governments of the Middle East walk a tightrope of inclination toward the United States but fear of fundamentalist revolt if they are open about it.

The relationship with Israel costs the United States more than the sum of its subsidies to the Jewish state. Oil cost three to four dollars a barrel in the early 1970s. Then the emerging Arab oil cartel was suddenly galvanized by the realization that oil could be used as a weapon against Israel. Embargos cause pain to vendor as well as consumer, however; it was soon clear that cartel-enforced price hikes could accomplish the same end. This in turn allowed the effortless financing of anti-Israel terrorist organizations. The price of oil was raised, eventually to thirty-two dollars per barrel and more. Even after dramatic price declines in the mid-1980s, caused by Saudi determination to discipline its fellow cartel members, the West is in the unsatisfying position of paying four times as much for oil as it did in the early 1970s, with the knowledge that part of the proceeds will be used against Israeli interests and even to blow up Americans in far-flung military outposts. The West is in the schizophrenic posture of making huge outlays in support of Israel, being severely penalized economically for such support, and indirectly underwriting anti-Israel organizations all at the same time. Furthermore, many of Israel's enemies purchase their weapons from the Soviet Union—with American dollars garnered from the cartel-derived increases in oil revenues. This puts the United States in the bizarre position of indirectly financing Soviet arms sales.

Israeli foreign policy reflects the practical theological principle that it is easier to obtain forgiveness for sins than permission to commit them. Israel accordingly conducts military forays at will and expects the world to forgive and forget. Only forty years old, Israel has initiated military attacks on Egypt, Jordan, Syria, Iraq, Tunisia and Lebanon— and even the United States in the attack on the *Liberty*.

How can Israel get away with all this? It has clout in Washington. The political influence of the American Israel Public Affairs Committee and other groups, the pro-Israel lobby in Washington, has assured Israel that it will suffer no serious consequences for any of its actions. AIPAC successfully puts out the fires sparked by Israeli pursuit of the aggressive foreign policy of its choosing. Claiming fifty thousand members and a six-million-dollar budget of its own, AIPAC gives cues to between seventy and a hundred pro-Israel political action committees (PACs) throughout the United States.[83] They, in turn, vigorously help elect politicians who support Israel and, even more vigorously, aid the election-time opposition of those who do not.

AIPAC also lobbies against arms sales to Arab countries, even when they are American allies, thereby causing billions of dollars of weapons contracts to go to European manufacturers and in the process creating the loss of thousands of American jobs. AIPAC influence forces the U.S. government to give licenses to produce U.S.-designed military goods to Israeli companies. These companies then compete with American companies internationally, generating another set of exported American jobs. In 1983 Congress approved aid for Israel's development of its Lavi fighter aircraft, direct competition to the Northrop F-20 and the General Dynamics F-16. The bill, crafted by AIPAC, "authorized privileged treatment Uncle Sam had never before extended to a foreign competitor. It was extraordinary for another reason: it set aside a U.S. law that requires that all foreign aid procurement funds be spent in the United States." As Congressman Nick J. Rahall of West Virginia concluded, "Americans are being stripped of their tax dollars to build up foreign industry. They should not have to sacrifice their jobs as well."[84] The cost of the plane, which has tripled since it was originally proposed in 1981, has already run to two billion dollars. Israel plans to produce three hundred of them, estimated by the Pentagon as costing $6.6 billion. Most of the money to pay for the Lavi, of course, will be American.[85] Ironically, one of the principal critics of this boondoggle is a deputy secretary of defense, Don Zakheim, a rabbi. The United States subsidizes Israel's military efforts in every possible form, even when serious military threats to Israel are far from imminent and in any case unlikely to succeed. Since the 1973 war, Israel has achieved unrivalled military dominance in the region.

Despite the enormous gains for Israel's security, the issue of support for Israel has come in recent years to dominate the political agenda of the vocal elements of America's Jewish community. Civil rights, abortion rights, and strict separation of church and state, areas of traditional Jewish political interest, have been increasingly subordinated to this single issue. In one reporting year, 1983–84, Democrats received 80 percent of the political contributions made by America's pro-Israel PACs. In the first six months of 1985, however, they received only 45 percent.[86] AIPAC—and more significantly, the PACs it influences—has proved increasingly willing to support conservatives who oppose the traditional Jewish political agenda—if they will go to the mat for Israel on command.

Admiral Thomas Moorer, former chairman of the U.S. Joint Chiefs of Staff, summarized the influence of the pro-Israel lobby in two lines: "If the American people understood what a grip those people have got on our government, they would rise up in arms. Our citizens don't have any idea what goes on."[87]

Efforts on behalf of Israel by its American lobby go beyond electoral participation. AIPAC and the pro-Israel political network in the Congress, Pentagon and State Department have often been accused of using influence in Washington to acquire U.S. military and trade secrets for Israel. In his book *The Armageddon Network,* Michael Saba documents many of these events and the measures taken to cover them up.

Saba himself overheard a luncheon discussion he suspected concerned espionage on behalf of Israel, and his follow-up was revealing. He reported the matter to the FBI and was interviewed by both FBI agents and representatives of the National Security Council—all of whom repeatedly asked if certain officers of AIPAC had been present. Saba told them no—but was surprised that the question had been asked, and asked repeatedly; he had never mentioned any AIPAC members. American security officials are clearly familiar with charges of close ties between Israeli intelligence and America's pro-Israel lobby. The investigation was eventually dropped because the FBI was unable to independently confirm many of the details Saba had provided.[88]

If that connection has not yet been subject to any conclusive government action, the activities of Israeli diplomats certainly have been. The 1986 capture and confession of Jonathan Pollard, an analyst for the U.S. Navy with a "top secret" security clearance, gave the issue wide American publicity for the first time ever. Pollard provided U.S. military secrets to Israel in collaboration with the Israeli embassy in Washington. Once Pollard was apprehended by the FBI, the Israeli government denied any knowledge of the events, and an official investigation eventually yielded a story of "renegade" Israeli field agents acting without authorization. Their activities were sternly punished by the Israeli government: several of the men involved were promoted.[89]

A particularly egregious instance of Israeli espionage was carried out in 1969, according to the *New York Times*'s Seymour Hersh. In *The Price of Power,* a study of Henry Kissinger's years in the Nixon administration, Hersh writes that federal authorities uncovered evidence that the Israeli intelligence service, Mossad, "had been responsible sometime in the mid-1960s for diverting highly enriched uranium from a private company, the Nuclear Materials and Equipment Corp. in Apollo, Pennsylvania." Its owner, Dr. Zalman Shapiro, was known to have close ties to the Israeli consulate in New York. "Some officials believed that the processing plant, which did classified work for the U.S. Navy and authorized foreign countries, primarily NATO allies, had been set up with Israeli-supplied funds—and might have been created solely to divert enriched uranium for Israeli nuclear weapon production," Hersh says. One aide to Henry Kissinger, commenting on the halt to the investigation, said, "You don't mess with the Israelis."[90]

The purpose of Israeli nuclear espionage is simple—its military strategies call for the possible use of nuclear weapons. Israel has had nuclear reactors for decades; the principal one is at Dimona in the Negev Desert. Israel cooperated with French nuclear scientists for twenty years, then added to its atomic program with American nuclear secrets, obtained both openly and through spying. The Weizmann Institute in Tel Aviv established a Department of Isotope Research in 1949. Long-rumored Israeli possession of nuclear weapons was finally confirmed in October 1986, when the *Sunday Times* of London reported that Mordechai Vanunu, an Israeli nuclear technician said to be disgruntled because he had been laid off, revealed that Israel had secretly stockpiled between one hundred and two hundred nuclear warheads.[91] The *Washington Post* reported speculation that the information had been intentionally leaked by Israel as a veiled threat to the Arab world.[92]

Military and trade secrets are both important to Israeli intelligence. Saba cites a top secret CIA report made public in 1979:

> Israel's program for accelerating its technological, scientific and military development as rapidly as possible has been enhanced by exploiting scientific exchange programs. Mossad plays a key role in this endeavor. In addition to large-scale acquisition of published scientific papers and technical journals from all over the world through overt channels, the Israelis devote a considerable portion of their covert operations to obtaining scientific and technical intelligence. This has included attempts to penetrate classified defense projects in the United States and other Western nations.[93]

The CIA seldom "goes public" with its reports, leading some to call its release an effort by CIA Arabists to stir up public opinion against this decidedly unfriendly Israeli practice. One could also conclude that higher officials were (and, apparently, continue to be) unwilling to take substantive action through less public channels. Thus, forms of indirect pressure by the CIA. Four billion dollars in annual American aid to Israel should give the United States at least some leverage, but government officials seem unwilling to use it.

The pattern is long-lived and clear: the Lavon affair of the 1950s, the attack on the *Liberty* and the Pennsylvania nuclear processing activities of the 1960s, and ongoing espionage ever since, culminating in the Pollard affair of the 1980s. Together they demonstrate that in effect Israel has ever viewed its strongest ally much like a hostile power. One is reminded of Johnson's postscript to the definition of gratitude: "Now obsolete."

American authorities continue to investigate Israel's espionage activities in the United States, if only for the sake of form. According to John Davitt, a long-time head of the Justice Department's internal security section, Israeli intelligence services during his time in office were second only to the KGB in scope, and were "targeted on the United States about half the time and on Arab countries about half the time." Over the years, Davitt said, several Israeli diplomats suspected of espionage have been quietly told to leave the country.[94] The magnitude of Israeli espionage in the United States, the avowed militarism of Israel's foreign policy, and the shift in AIPAC's political priorities, all of these realities are at issue among American Jews, many of whom rightly fear that militarists have captured their agenda and transformed it from traditional Jewish concern for human rights into a condonation of any and all acts of Israeli militarism. Although AIPAC often labels its critics as mere anti-Semites, the reverse may be the case: AIPAC and Israeli militarism give many people an unjustified impression of the American Jewish community. Even the Israeli government has disagreed with AIPAC efforts. One notable case was AIPAC's pressure to move the U.S. embassy from Tel Aviv to Jerusalem, and act which would have created turmoil in Israel.

The Middle East, as former Israeli minister of defense Moshe Arens has said, is an odyssey in brutality and intolerance with little value attached to human life. It is an area of short fuses and long memories, of aroused religious beliefs and consequent militarism, of only occasional tranquility amidst perennial spasms of violence. It should not escape our notice that this area of the world, the cradle of the world's principal religions—Judaism, Islam, and Christianity—has been the center of more wars than any other place on the planet during recorded history. That should tell us something about the general relationship between religion and war!

In no small part this is due to the diversity in nearly every fundamental respect of the people who live in the region. The Israeli population of approximately four million people (several hundred thousand of whom reside abroad) is composed of the Ashkenazim (Jews descended from those who settled in middle and northern Europe), the Sephardim (descended from the Jews of Spain, Portugal, Africa and Asia, and those who remained in the Middle East), some Christians and Druze, and Palestinian Arabs generally of the Sunni Moslem faith; non-Jews make up about 16 percent of Israeli citizens. In addition to this general population, not including the hundreds of thousands of Palestinian refugees and their children who live in neighboring countries, there are nearly one million Palestinians on the West Bank and half a million living in the Gaza Strip (one of the most densely populated areas in the world), both areas militarily occupied by Israel since 1967.

The Ashkenazim are generally more educated, wealthy, and liberal, the Sephardim less educated, working class, and religious. The Sephardic (55 percent of Israel's Jewish citizens) and Palestinian populations are growing faster than the Askenazic, due to both higher birth rates and less emigration.

This reality is a demographic time bomb, since by and large the Sephardim are less tolerant of Arabs, both those who are citizens of Israel and those who live in the occupied territories. Exemplifying the growth of anti-Arab racism in Israel is the rise in popularity of Rabbi Meir Kahane. The leader of Israel's small Kach party, Kahane openly advocates violence against Arabs in Israel, participates in violent demonstrations against Arab rights, and has even led gangs of thugs into Arab neighborhoods. Despite widespread condemnation in Israel, Kahane's party continues to grow, and has even gained a foothold in the Knesset.

The future of Israel can accordingly evolve in only two directions: incorporation of Arabs in the occupied lands into the Israel body politic, resulting in an Israeli population more than a third Arab and Israeli politics accordingly transformed, or exclusion of these Arabs from citizenship and the creation, already in process, of an apartheid Israel.

Since Israel is defined by law and biblical tradition as the "Jewish State," discrimination against non-Jews, particularly Arabs, is both legal and theologically mandated. Israel and its occupied territories already have much of the social structure of apartheid. And since the demographic future of Jewish Israel is Sephardic, two things are fairly sure: Israel will not give up control of its occupied territories (it has already annexed the militarily significant Golan Heights), and, because current law confers citizenship on residents of annexed territory unless they choose otherwise, the indefinite perpetuation of military occupation in the populous West Bank and Gaza Strip. A de facto apartheid Israel seems certain.

The recognition that Israel may ultimately be compelled to incorporate Arabs as citizens in its body politic inspires the government to give great attention to the level of immigration. More Jews are needed in Israel to offset the potential increase in Arab citizenship—especially since Israel suffers a regular loss of its Jewish citizenry, particularly talented professionals, through emigration. Those who emigrate are called *yored*, "those who have fallen." Over half a million Jews have departed Israel's shores since the 1973 war; Israel has even gone to the lengths of adopting currency and other economic restrictions to inhibit the tide of departure. Conversely, the government's department of immigration expends substantial resources to attract new Jewish residents, but its efforts have met only limited success. Most new arrivals lack financial resources and professional training, placing added strain on the Israeli economy. Even to attract these less desirable immigrants has proven to require sophisticated persuasion. For example, Soviet Jews hoping to emigrate to the United States often go first to Israel, a destination that makes it easier to gain permission to leave the Soviet Union. It is Israeli government policy to grant such immigrants instant citizenship for its own purposes. On arrival the immigrants are immediately presented citizenship papers, and, often unwittingly, they sign away the right to travel on to the United States. "U.S. law recognizes Soviet Jews as political refugees and exempts them from the strict quotas that limit the flow of other immigrants into the United States. But a Soviet Jew who comes to Israel is immediately granted citizenship . . . losing refugee status and the right to move to the United States." In February 1987 the Israeli government asked the United States to end its policy of automatic refugee status for emigrating Soviet Jews. The claimed rationale was that the practice played a role in the Soviet government's reluctance to grant exit visas to Soviet Jews. Defending his government's immigration practices, Hillel Butman, a lawyer with the state ombudsman's office, declared, "I'm not in favor of free emigration for Russian Jews to go anyplace they want. We need these people here."[95] One is reminded of the strong-arm tactics of the Haganah before and after World War II. The natural rights and human aspirations of persecuted Jews are being subordinated to Zionist policy.

For the time being, the potential citizens who live in the occupied territories pose mostly a problem of administration. Jewish settlers in these areas are protected by Israeli civil law, but resident Arabs are governed by Israeli military law, which permits the government to arrest and imprison them (called "administrative detention") indefinitely without charge. As a result of these powers, Israeli treatment of the Arabs on the West Bank is characterized by systematic economic and police oppression. A basic reference work on this topic is the 1986 report of the West Bank Data Base Project, supervised by the American Enterprise Institute and published by the *Jerusalem Post*.

The Arabs on the West Bank are economically exploited and politically subjugated. They are used as "a dumping ground for low quality products, forbidden for sale in Israel, especially pharmaceutical and metallurgical products," in order to stimulate foreign sales for Israel, according to the Data Project; the West Bank is also exploited as "an auxiliary and subservient sector of the Israeli economy, a source of cheap, unskilled labor and agricultural surpluses." The West Bank seems in fact much like imperial colonies of old, since Israeli policy is one of "preventing any competition with Israeli economic enterprises . . . aimed at discouraging the growth of a viable Palestinian economic sector."[96] Strong stuff from the *laissez faire* American Enterprise Institute.

Palestinian farmers are forced to pay "almost four times more for water than Israeli farmers," although the water itself comes from the West Bank territories. The water supplies of the West Bank are exploited to the limit by Israel: 4.5 percent is allocated to the West Bank, and 95.5 percent goes to Israel;[97] the Israeli authorities do not permit the residents of the West Bank to expand their use of the water resources, making it impossible for Palestinian farmers to prosper. Arab residents are also charged more than Jews for electricity—but only twice as much.[98] Electricity is apparently less dear to the Israelis than water.

Roads and other infrastructure on the West Bank are built in ways that assure that Arabs remain impoverished, and to allow Israeli settlers the opportunity to excel at Arab expense. "Road networks are designed to bypass Arab population centers, but also to fragment and dissect Arab settlement regions."[99] Road construction is generally used to increase Israeli military preparedness in the occupied territories, and to improve government-expropriated land (now nearly half of the West Bank and 40 percent of the Gaza strip) for the purpose of expanding Jewish settlements.[100]

Palestinian workers are denied pay equal to Jews, and have fewer rights than Israelis with regard to insurance, pensions, sick leave, recuperation, clothing and vacation. In addition, "a sum of 20 percent of wages is deducted [from the wages of West Bank non-Jews] . . . and, in effect, constitutes an 'occupation tax.' " Furthermore, "no payments . . . are made for old age, widowhood, dependent children, survivors or for disability or unemployment, though deductions are made from [Palestinian] employees' salaries."[101] The working conditions of the Palestinians are deplorable; "many are forced to spend the night within Israel illegally, in subhuman conditions, sleeping on tables in restaurants where they work, crowded into unsanitary cellars and attics; they are reported as being searched, arrested or harassed in other ways on an average of twice a week." Under these working conditions and for a usually longer day, the West Bank workers in Israel receive "less than one-half the monthly pay of an Israeli worker."[102]

Attempts by Arabs in the occupied territories to bring legal actions against Israelis are often thwarted, since "Israeli citizens may not be brought to trial or sued before a local court," and the "military government is authorized to close any file or halt any judicial procedure on cases already begun."[103] Things are even worse when the government takes legal action against Arabs. The "demolition or sealing of houses [can] precede legal proceedings, and is considered a form of deterrent and collective punishment, since it affects the suspect's extended family residing in the house itself. The residents are not entitled to any compensation."[104]

In the political sphere the Israeli authorities have adopted stringent enforcement procedures to halt any public display of criticism of Israel. Student demonstrations and displays of material labelled seditious have resulted in the detention of the students, the deportation of their leaders, and the closing of several universities for lengthy periods.[105]

Finally, the Palestinians are forced to pay for the oppression they suffer. Because the Palestinians pay substantial taxes "the occupation does not constitute a fiscal burden on the Israeli treasury."[106]

In sum, Israel has developed an apartheid policy and is systematically exploiting the Arab population. Palestinian attempts to assert various human rights are met by arrest and "administrative detention." Israel's historical and systematic approach to governing the 1.3 million Palestinian Arabs under its control can reasonably be pointed to as one of the principal causes of Palestinian terrorism. When peaceful processes are denied, violence is ordained. In the summary opinion of the West Bank Data Base report, "The Israeli view of all political expression as subversive activity, and the Palestinian view of Israel as an illegitimate ruler, makes the clashes inevitable."[107]

Thus Israel is the unlikely architect of an apartheid system. The comparison to South Africa's system of racial separation is not glib; Israel and South Africa are close militarily and diplomatically, since both countries are shunned internationally, and their relationship is historic, due to their common origin in British imperialism. Both colonial enterprises had at their root the "Christian" concept of white supremacy, "the white man's burden." As historian A. P. Thornton explains, "It was supposed that Jews when inserted into Palestine . . . would act as injections of European culture and technology into a decaying Asiatic trunk."[108] Zionism was not an ideology only of Jews; it was also a strategy in the imperialism of white Christians.

The friendship between Israel and South Africa predates the issuance of the Balfour Declaration. It began with the unflaggingly pro-Zionist efforts of General Jan Christiaan Smuts, leading architect of the Union of South Africa after the Boer War, its prime minister from 1919 to 1924 and 1939 to 1948, and critically important as a Zionist due to his membership in the British war cabinet during WWI. Smuts' support for the unofficial new country was unwavering in the cabinet discussions of the Balfour Declaration, during the creation of the League of Nations shortly after World War I, and through to the debate over partition of Palestine into Jewish and Arab sections at the fledgling United Nations in late 1947.

In his *Weizmann & Smuts*, Richard Stevens places Smuts as surprisingly influential in the British war cabinet, despite the fact that his very presence in it was "quite without precedent."[109] According to Smuts' biographer, Dorothy Wilson, Lloyd George relied heavily on Smuts, sending him on sensitive diplomatic missions, requesting reports on the state of the armed forces, even using him to mediate labor disputes. Smuts "was called the 'Orator for the Empire'. . . . invaluable in the cabinet."[110]

Stevens summarizes Smuts' attitude to a Jewish Palestine as essentially imperial in origin: "Smuts naturally saw the political wisdom in embracing the Zionist vision. . . . In what better way could Britain provide continental security, in the most economical manner, than to deliver Palestine, at the very crossroads of Africa and Asia, to the Jews?" It was not idle philosophizing. Smuts considered Zionism so important that he called it "one of the great objects for which we fight this war [WWI] . . . to provide a national home for the Jewish people."[111] This despite the fact that the only Jew in the Lloyd George government, Edwin Montagu, secretary of state for India, strongly opposed British involvement in the Zionist enterprise on the grounds that a "national home" for the Jews would raise again the question of dual loyalty.[112]

Politics was at work too, however. South African Jewry had a "general identification with Smuts' political party,"[113] largely because his Het Volk organization had early on rejected anti-Semitism as contrary to the need for white unity in the face of African nationalism. According to Sarah Millin's *The People of South Africa*, "Fully 99 percent of South African Jews were Zionist affiliated."[114] Unlike the Jewish communities of Europe, there were few "assimilationist" South African Jews arguing against Zionism as a threat to Jewish citizenship in host countries. The rabid racism of the Dutch-descended Afrikaners and their Nationalist party was perhaps too close for that.

When he died in 1950, Smuts was eulogized as a national hero in Israel. Acting Prime Minister Joseph Sprinzak declared that, "General Smuts is written on the map of Israel and in the heart of our nation."[115] In 1952 Israel dedicated to Smuts a forest on the southern slopes of the Judean hills, appropriately overlooking a forest named for Chaim Weizmann.

South Africa's 1948 elections put the Nationalist Party into power, and Daniel F. Malan, a recognized anti-Semite and Nazi sympathizer, was its leader. South Africa's support for Israel survived Smuts' reign, however. Like the Reich he revered, Malan was an anti-Semitic Zionist.

In 1930, it had been Malan who introduced the quota bill restricting Jewish immigration from Eastern Europe. The anti-Jewish policies of Malan's Nationalist Party often bordered on virulent and blatant anti-Semitism. Malan was known as a whole-hearted supporter of Hitler and as a Nazi collaborator. But, notwithstanding this long record of anti-Semitism, the Nationalist Party found reason to modify at least its overt anti-Semitism at approximately the same time as the goal of the political Zionist movement, the creation of a Jewish state in Palestine, was about to become a reality. It was the Nationalist Government under Malan which, immediately after its narrow victory over Smuts on 26 May 1948, extended *de jure* recognition to the Jewish state.[116]

Thus, when Israel achieved statehood in 1948, the basis for a close relationship with South Africa had been securely established. With Israel's increasing international isolation as the decades went by, the ties became ever closer. The two countries are said to cooperate in the matter of evading the international oil embargo that afflicts them both. Israel is a central processing and transshipment center for South African diamonds, second only to gold as a critical export for the apartheid state. Both countries are said to have constructed nuclear weapons using technology and processed uranium stolen from American and European facilities. Both have developed large domestic small-arms industries, and are commonly known to have sold arms to many of the world's renegade governments, irrespective of ideology. Israel supplies South Africa with security systems and training used to enforce apartheid.

It is an unfortunate alliance. A nation of refugees from the European apartheid horror intimately consorts with the political descendants of the architects of that horror. As Conrad observed, you can not long look into the face of such a thing without being consumed by it.

Ironically, Israel's ascendent coalition of conservative political parties, called the Likud, wishes to annex the West Bank, despite the fact that under current law the whole of its mostly Arab population would become Israeli citizens. But even when Likud has been in power there has not been sufficient support in the Knesset for such a radical action. As a result, Likud attempts at least to assure that control of the West Bank is never returned to the Palestinians. This is accomplished by accelerating the creation of Jewish settlements in the overwhelmingly Arab region, settlements which would have to be removed and Jewish citizens relocated if Israel were ever to withdraw. As the struggle to relocate the fewer Jews who had settled in Sinai showed, that would not be politically easy.

Compared to the status quo, Likud's overt expansionism is at least honest. It advocates direct conquest and annexation of the lands required to reestablish Eretz (biblically defined) Israel. Likud's program would even have democratic side effects—annexation in the Israeli constitutional context implies the granting of full citizenship to the members of incorporated populations. Paradoxically, such an annexation would change the character of Israel, making it less a predominantly Jewish state.

Likud's major opposition, the Labor party, opposes annexation of the occupied territories and from time to time has opposed Jewish settlement in them as well. Instead it has fostered the "temporary" approach (now twenty years long and no end in sight) of apartheid until the matter of occupation can be resolved. Labor has been as intransigent as Likud in the matter of negotiations for a withdrawal from the occupied lands, however. Despite appearances, it may in fact advocate the more oppressive of the two approaches to policy in the occupied territories: for Palestinians neither independence nor equal rights.

Neither party has in recent times been able to amass a majority in the parliament of Israel's unicameral political system, so the central and thorny issue of policy toward the occupied territories has essentially been in stalemate for years. Likud's approach, however apparently repugnant, at least offers a hope for progress in the long term. The half a loaf of lessened oppression through citizenship is surely better than Labor's implicit policy of standing pat forever—no loaf at all. Perhaps a dose of democratic rights, available nowhere in the Arab world, and some equal economic opportunity, would calm the ever-stormier waters of Palestinian rage.

Domestic political confusion, aggravated by strife between various Jewish sects in the context of an increasingly secular society, is likely to be Israel's lot for the foreseeable future. Almost all of Israel's political and economic problems, from relations with Arabs to the country's monstrous external debt, are being solved by postponement, and time is not working in the tiny nation's favor. Paralysis is the principal danger threatening Israel's Jews, not the supposed tens of millions of hate-filled Arabs that surround them.

Time for Israel is in fact a bomb with its fuse already burning, length unknown. This bomb is packed with the refugees from the Israeli nation, over a million displaced Palestinians, nearly all dedicated to securing their own land. One would think Jews would empathize with the desire of a displaced people for their own homeland. Yet Israel fiercely resists the creation of a Palestinian state. It argues that to permit the creation of a neighbor composed of people it has dispossessed would jeopardize the nation's security. The Israelis rationalize that national security is somehow served by the presence of embittered refugees resident in bordering camps, frustrated because essentially homeless, economically unstable and hopeless, prey to the fanaticism of self-serving demagogues. Apartheid is somehow preferable to accommodation.

The survival of Israel's state is dependent on American financial assistance, the survival of its economy on the production of weapons of war. The military-industrial complex has come to dominate both the Israeli economy and its foreign policy. Contrary to the belief of many Israeli leaders, and their critics as well, these respectively dependent and evil states of affairs are not unalterable. A partnership between Jews and Palestinians within Eretz Israel could create an economic miracle, an international center of trade, finance and diverse entrepreneurship. The United States could foster such a revolutionary relationship by creating a "Marshall Plan" for the West Bank and Gaza Strip, instead of supplying Israel with billions of dollars for more weapons. Such a marriage might also eliminate much of the motivation for terrorism, and would attract foreign capital—even from Arab nations. A dream? So too was the creation of Israel. Like that post-Holocaust act of will, the realization of the dream of Jewish-Palestinian cooperation will require the bitter determination of the people of Israel. Certainly their leaders, pandering and hypocritical, cannot be relied upon for such vision.

The Hebrew religion was founded for the specific purpose of taking other peoples' lands and possessions by force. After centuries of dominance among Jews, Judaic humanism has, in many ways understandably, been subordinated to that ancient impulse. Judaism in Israel has of late mortgaged its humanistic soul, and the interest is paid by slowly selling off humanitarian principles. The humanism of Israeli liberals and the majority of Western Jews is being trampled by the twin boots of Israeli militarism—theology and the economic grip of military industry. The atrocities of Lebanon shocked world Jewry, but they were long implicit in Zionist practice. Although religious beliefs galvanized the Jewish people into creating their long-needed refuge from the storm of goyische anti-Semitism, doing so required compromises. The benign and compassionate imperatives of rabbinical Judaism have in the process become silent victims.

The Western world seems stable today. It is hard to conceive, ever again, a Nazi fit of anti-Semitic carnage. But it was the Great Depression that spawned the Third Reich, and who is to say that great depressions are behind us? Jewish people needed an Israel in the 1930s, as their ships of the damned were turned away from port after port. Some Jews may very well need again a land with a Law of Return, a haven from the bloody whims of their fellow man.

But does such a place require religious militarism as its central element of cohesion? It is difficult to separate the religious and other facets of the culture of the Jewish people, but the Israelis have refused even to attempt it, and so have made religion a cornerstone of their state. When state power is bound up with religion, the result is predictable: intolerance. In the case of Israel, continued survival as a nation will ultimately depend upon the resiliency of its institutions, not upon its religion. It is the drive to control forever "biblical Judea and Samaria" that will do Israel in. The first step on that path is the sacrifice to the God of War that which is most humane in Judaic belief. Benign values are being subordinated to bellicose ones; the military imperative of *Realpolitik* is the suppression of compassion for one's fellow man.

The Israelites have come to a fork in the road of their long odyssey through Exodus, Exile, Diaspora and Return. To the left lies the evolution of a Jewish-Arab nation, to the right the awful denouement of events rooted in the days of religious barbarism.

The question is which way will be taken: the militaristic road marked out by the Torah's theology of imperialism, or the peaceful road of Judaic humanism, epitomized by the beautiful Hebrew word *shalom*?

Part Two

THE THEOLOGY OF POWER

I am the light of the world; he who follows me will not walk in darkness but will have the light of life.

—Jesus Christ, John 8:12

I call Christianity the one great curse, the one enormous and innermost perversion, the one great instinct of revenge, for which no means are too venomous, too underhand, too underground and too petty—I call it the one immortal blemish of mankind.

—Friedrich Nietzsche, *The Antichrist*

Blessed are the peacemakers, for they shall be called the Sons of God.
—Jesus Christ, Matthew 5:9

The kingdom of God does not consist in talk, but in power.
—St. Paul, I Corinthians 4

I

Humble Beginnings?

C hristianity has the laudable distinction of being the only major religion founded on the idea of love, and the shameful record of having produced more reasons for hate than almost any other religion in history. Only Marxism, which traces much of its psychology to Christianity, outstrips it in this regard. But Marxism was not founded on love; it was founded on a hatred of the aristocratic and bourgeois classes, and in this regard its practice is consistent with its basis. Christianity, however, epitomizes Shakespeare's well-worn couplet,

> For sweetest things turn sourest by their deeds,
> Lilies that fester, smell far worse than weeds.[1]

Judaism, as we have seen, was founded to facilitate conquest; Islam, as we will see, to legitimize plunder; Buddhism was founded to offer escape from the tribulations of life; Marxism to bring secular justice to the poor. Christianity was founded on love, but, beginning in the fourth century, developed instead a systematic philosophy and theology of dread. Judged by its deeds rather than its pronouncements, Christianity has completely subverted its moral basis, its *raison d'etre*.

Christianity is derived from *Christos*, the Greek translation of the Hebrew "Anointed One," "the Messiah," a figure foretold in prophetic literature as presiding over alternately a restoration of the Jewish nation or the coming of a new age in which all would be judged. A man named Jesus came to be regarded by some Jews as "the Anointed One," Christ, after he developed a following. Many believe that Jesus may have been influenced by the Essene community, a group of pious Jews living near the Dead Sea who came together out of a common contempt for society's pervasive corruption and a corollary vision that the coming of a messiah was imminent.

What we know historically of Jesus comes principally from the four Gospels of Matthew, Mark, Luke and John, all of whom were followers of Jesus and whose accounts, therefore, must be viewed critically, and from the epistles of Paul, a contemporary convert to Jesus' teachings who never actually met him. Modern scholars have found differences of purpose and character between some of the Gospels, which are the best source of information on Jesus, and not a few contradictions within them. Our purpose, however, is not to analyze the alleged divinity of Christ, but to observe the nature of the religion he has come to stand for, and what relationship it has had to organized violence.

According to the Gospels, two Jews named Joseph and Mary were planning to marry when Mary became pregnant with Jesus. She was twelve years old. A fundamental article of Christian faith is that Jesus was not created through the sexual process, however, but rather "conceived by the Holy Ghost" and "born of the virgin, Mary." (One can only imagine the look on Joseph's face when Mary tried to explain this pregnancy to him!)

We are told that Jesus was born in the town of Bethlehem during the reign of the Roman governor Pontius Pilate. Joseph was a carpenter and Jesus pursued this trade, it is said in the Gospels, until he was about thirty years old. One day he decided to seek out John the Baptist, one of many Hebrew prophets of the time, who predicted that the end of the world was at hand, an event in which heavenly judgement would be dispensed and the kingdom of Israel would be reestablished. John administered a ritual cleansing in water, baptism, to those "pledging themselves as penitents to the promised king."[2]

Jesus himself was baptized by John, allegedly to a panoply of heavenly sights and sounds, and then "brought by the Spirit up into the wilderness" to be tempted by the devil. He fasted for forty days, the traditional length of time needed in the Middle East for anything important to happen, all the while rejecting the devil's offers of temporal rule and his demands that the Christ prove his powers.

The test of his character over, and hearing news that John had been imprisoned, so the Gospels say, Jesus took up preaching. His message was much like John's, that the kingdom of heaven was at hand. Evidently Jesus was convincing, because he quickly gathered disciples. The first was Peter, a net fisherman talked into becoming a "fisher of men."

Jesus' teaching was hardly without precedent, but it was nonetheless startlingly new in many ways. He preached the traditional "Thou shalt love the Lord thy God with thine whole mind and soul," but also added a revolutionary commandment: "Thou shalt love thy neighbor as thyself." Jesus' "eight beatitudes" were particularly humanitarian. He said one should show charity to one's fellow man, have a "hunger for justice," be humble ("blessed are the meek") and create peace ("blessed are the peacemakers"). He also decried wealth and preached the value of shunning material things. Jesus' influence was great not merely because he had a powerful message, but because "he himself lived by [his] standards and showed their working in his daily life, so that Jesus himself was 'the Way.' "[3] It didn't hurt that Jesus could perform in ways that passed for miraculous, generally to underscore a point he was trying to make in his preachings. One such favorite point, of course, was his contention that he was the "Son of Man," or "Son of God," that he was in fact the Christ, the Anointed One.

As Jesus attracted more followers, he became a social issue in Palestine; and, as always happens when people develop a following, he became more outspoken and critical of existing institutions. Jesus began to criticize the routine activities of religious leaders, the scribal teachers and their Pharisaic lay followers; he interfered with long-accepted abuses in the temples; he criticized scribal traditions, reinterpreted the law, and maintained an independence from official leaders secular and religious. Finally, on a sojourn in Jerusalem, he openly challenged the priestly hierarchy responsible for keeping the temples, traditions and laws. The authorities began to denounce Jesus and, so it is claimed, seek his prosecution by Pilate.[4]

For a few months Jesus adjourned his activities, withdrawing to the northeast, but eventually he returned to Jerusalem awaited by large crowds probably mobilized by his followers. The religious authorities feared this clear show of support from the populace and were threatened financially by Jesus' brazen attempt to cleanse the Temple by removing the money changers and the bazaars from "the house of prayer for all people." In fact, Jesus was continuing in the tradition of Jeremiah and Isaiah, speaking out against the monied establishment and ruling class. Jesus, it might be said, was an ancient socialist.

As a result, according to the Gospel accounts, the Jewish religious hierarchy of Jerusalem pressured Pilate to put Christ to death by crucifixion. That is the official story, but there is good reason to believe that the Gospels, written late in the first century, *after* the epistles of Paul, were in fact designed primarily to appeal to the Roman audience being evangelized at the time. Defenders of the Gospel accounts claim that the Sanhedrin, the supreme Jewish council, had no authority to execute condemned prisoners in this period, such an end requiring appeal to secular (Roman) power. This is not the case. Religious authorities in Palestine retained the right to try people for capital crimes and to execute them by stoning. The stated reason for the appeal to Roman authority is blatantly incorrect, casting into strong doubt the fact of such an appeal.[5] The process used by Pilate to decide Christ's fate, as described in the Gospels, is similarly suspect. It would have been unthinkable for any Roman governor to submit to the decision of a mob in his affairs, least of all Pilate, particularly known for his ruthlessness.[6] The Romans surely did execute Christ (crucifixion was an exclusively Roman form of execution), but they had reasons other than the appeal of Jewish priests and their followers for doing so. There is a plausible explanation for such extreme biblical variance from likely fact: to exonerate the Romans, transfer the blame for Jesus' death to the Jews and thereby make Jesus acceptable to a Roman audience. The efforts of the chief Christians of the day were directed above all to the spread of Christianity in the Roman Empire. As authors Michael Baigent, Richard Leigh and Henry Lincoln report in *The Holy Blood and the Holy Grail,*

> The Gospels were composed during and after the revolt of A.D. 68-74, when Judaism had effectively ceased to exist as an organized social, political and military force. What is more, the Gospels were composed for a Greco-Roman audience—for whom they had, of necessity, to be made acceptable. Rome had just fought a bitter and costly war against the Jews. In consequence it was perfectly natural to cast the Jews in the role of villains. In the wake of the Judean revolt, moreover, Jesus could not possibly be portrayed as a political figure—a figure in any way linked to the agitation in the war. Finally the role of the Romans in Jesus's trial and execution had to be whitewashed and presented as sympathetically as possible. Thus Pilate is depicted in the Gospels as a decent, responsible and tolerant man, who consents only reluctantly to the Crucifixion.[7]

The roots of Christian anti-Semitism may run farther back than is commonly understood, back in fact to within a hundred years of the death of Christ.

What then might have been the true reason for Jesus' crucifixion? Baigent, Leigh and Lincoln suggest that Jesus was bidding for rule of the Jewish people in direct challenge to Roman authority. Jesus was crucified, a form of execution reserved for crimes against the empire. There is substantial support for this theory in text of the Gospels themselves. Jesus was apparently an educated man, perhaps even having undertaken schooling for the rabbinate, and also seems to have "consorted as frequently with wealthy and influential people as with the poor—Joseph of Arimathea, for instance, and Nicodemus. And the wedding at Cana would seem to bear further witness to Jesus's status and social position."[8]

In fact, Jesus may very well have been of royal blood, as explicitly reported in Matthew, and accounting for Herod's alarm at the birth of Christ, registered in the Gospels as causing him to massacre the kingdom's male children. Jesus' repeated designation (in all four Gospels) as the "King of the Jews" is generally presented as spiritual in biblical criticism, but a temporal reading is very plausible. Jesus was a Jew claiming to fulfill the role of a messiah predicted for centuries. In the Jewish context, this messiah was usually connected to a royal line descended from King David and was seen primarily as restoring the Jewish nation to its rightful place of preeminence. For such a job the title of "King of the Jews" is perfectly fitted, and it is also historically likely. The Christian authors of the Gospels would certainly not have invented it, since it runs counter to Christ's supposed disinterest in temporal power as demonstrated in his rebuff of Satan's offer of just such a thing while in the mountains.

In Mark, Pilate asks the assembled crowd, "What then shall I do with him whom ye call the King of the Jews?"—evidence that many Jews did in fact call him that. Pilate calls Jesus by this title over and over again. "There is no reason to suppose that [Pilate] does so ironically or derisively. In the Fourth Gospel, he insists on it quite adamantly and seriously, despite a chorus of protests."[9] Jesus himself admits his claim to the title in three of the Gospels. The account in Mark 15:2 says, "And Pilate asked him, 'Are thou the King of the Jews?' He answered and saith to him, 'Thou sayest it.' " Baigent, Leigh and Lincoln note that in English "this reply may sound ambivalent—perhaps deliberately so," but that in the original Greek the meaning is perfectly clear—"It can only be interpreted as 'Thou hast spoken correctly' "—and that the same Greek phrase is so translated everywhere else in the Bible.[10]

Jesus' historical reality can finally be only speculative. What is clear, however, is that the Gospel accounts of his life are often both contradictory and (even when in agreement) at unbridgeable odds with what is known. The most important scriptural basis of all Christian belief seems clearly corrupted in the service of evangelism, that is to say, finally, in the service of power. Against this conclusion we can pose the fact of Jesus' general message as it appears in the Bible, and the dedication of the early Christians to spreading the revolutionary commandment to love and bring about a world of social justice. The charge of a corrupt desire merely to acquire power, at least in the first and second centuries, cannot be credibly used to blacken the actions of the early Christians. But at the heart of the dedication to spreading their word lay a motivation perhaps as pernicious and no different in type. Like ambition, evangelism is subject to the expedient. In expedience both historical fact and the original emphases of the Word could be altered. In expedience social reality could come to have less importance than rarefied religious constructions. In expedience the option of salvation offered by Jesus could become the imposition of salvation by his followers. In expedience, finally, the dictates of an ideology of love and social justice could be entirely reversed.

Christ died on the cross, but the climax of Jesus' story, as related in the Gospels, is his resurrection from death. It is a fundamental tenet of Christian faith that within three days of death Jesus was both physically and spiritually resurrected. Some modern scholars, however, maintain that the body might have been stolen, or that Christ never died on the cross.[11] The Gospels' contention that Christ was removed from the cross and placed into a private grave is particularly criticized, since such a practice was foreign to the traditions and regulations accompanying crucifixions. Even the language of the Gospels is not unanimous as to whether this was a spiritual resurrection only, or also a physical one. The preponderance of scholarship and, of course, church teaching, is that it was both. Christ's life, death and resurrection, the prophecies of these events, and the humility and love of Christ are together the foundation of Christian belief.

What came to be built on this foundation as the centuries went by was something entirely different. Christian myth begins where Jewish myth does, in God's creation of earth and humanity, and it concurs in the story of Adam and Eve. Both Christian and Jewish interpretation disdain the discoveries of modern philologists, who tell us that in early writings the Hebrew *ahdam* means "mankind," rather than "man," and that *eve* means "living one" or "breath of life." With little intellectual basis, both Jewish and Christian traditional interpretations reject the reasonable conclusion that these words refer to concepts rather than particular persons.

Christian and Jewish interpretation also agree in the mythical account of the early lives of Adam and Eve. They were living in the Garden of Eden, a virtual paradise, but then God cast Satan out of heaven for disobedience and Satan sought revenge by coming to earth in the form of a serpent to woo the first couple away from God. He tempted them with knowledge, falsely portrayed as the distinguishing feature between God and man. Eat of the apple and "your eyes shall be opened, and ye shall be as gods," Satan said to Eve. She succumbed to the temptation, and Woman was the first to sin, naturally, being that the authors of the legend were male. Then Eve tempted Adam, who followed her into sin by also eating of the apple. From this seminal event thousands of years of libel against women have been promulgated.

Christian and Jewish interpretations of human origins agree that eating that apple was a very bad move—but just how bad, this is the basis of some of the fundamental differences in theology between Christianity and its parent Judaism. First God threw Adam and Eve out of the Garden, both religions agree, condemning them to a life of toil scratching out their living from a reluctant earth. More importantly, they were denied the ability to live forever. Aging and death instead would be their lot.

It is here that Christianity and Judaism diverge. The story so far is the whole of the Hebrew myth of Adam and Eve as told in the Old Testament. But as if the consequences of that ancient agricultural transgression as recorded in the text weren't bad enough, the Christians teased out a monstrous web of theological specifics, a psychological torture rack of philosophical idiocy collectively called "original sin." Paul, early Christianity's leading missionary, is credited with this delightful innovation.[12]

For Christians, the original sin was an insult of ingratitude to God that resulted not merely in the physical punishment described by the Hebrews—limited life and having to work hard for a living—but in spiritual punishment as well: human beings would possess an innately flawed spirit, leading to a death that was not death but rather life in an eternal hell. And the blemish on the soul of all those descended from Adam and Eve was nearly ineradicable—until God granted a reprieve in the form of Jesus. By embracing him one's spirit could be saved from its appointed travails.

This is the Christian interpretation of Christ and his meaning. It is not, from what little knowledge of Christ's thought we have, the message of Christ as he delivered it. Christ declared that by accepting his teaching one could be saved from a wrathful judgement soon to be passed on humanity. It was a pronouncement not terribly different in kind from those of many a Hebrew prophet before Jesus, but the Christians transformed it into something far more complex, in fact, into its opposite. With no basis in the Gospels or the Old Testament, Jesus was said to have come to the earth to save mankind not from the consequences of contemporary wickedness, but from its *innate* wickedness, a bizarre proclivity to evil handed down by Adam and Eve. The benefit to be gained from acceptance of Jesus is the same in Christ's words as it is in the Christian interpretation of them. It is the conception of self that is different. Christian ideology suggests that the self is something to loathe.

Jewish prophetic tradition and the Old Testament are equally essential to Christian belief. Christ explicitly declared that he had come to fulfill the prophecies of the Old Testament. Christians however claim that Jews misunderstood the nature of those Old Testament prophecies. Their meaning is quite clear, however. They were metaphorical prophecies of deliverance from the physical bondage of imperial rule, a restoration of the Promised Land. Christians contend that Christ came instead as a deliverer from the bondage of sin; the Promised Land for Christians was not the Land of Canaan, but paradise in an afterlife.

There is little contest in this debate. Whatever other vagaries they contain, the Old Testament prophecies of a messiah hardly predict a Jesus as the Christians represent him. Neither do the words of Christ himself. The concept of original sin, and therefore of Jesus' purpose on earth, is a complete fabrication by Paul, massively elaborated by Christians who followed him, most influentially Augustine. But to hold their theology together Christians were compelled to take the position that for centuries the Jews had missed the point. "The Messiahship of Jesus is asserted, then sidestepped in order to disclose him in a light more congenial to Hellenic rather than Jewish concepts," writes one historian.[13]

Partially a social and political movement, but mainly a reformed Judaism, Christianity was originally preached by Jews to Jews. Its expansion into non-Jewish circles is principally attributable to a Roman centurion who became a convert to Christianity and eventually one of its greatest saints. His name was Saul of Tarsus, who, we are told, persecuted Christians until one day a bolt of lightning struck him from his horse and a voice said to him, "Saul, Saul, why dost thou persecute me?" Saul became a Christian, spread Christianity near and far, and was later canonized as St. Paul.

Probably born not too long after Jesus, Paul was a Jew raised in strict accordance to Jewish tradition. Despite the fact that he never met Jesus, Paul was not simply a missionary, but a theologian—Durant calls him the first Christian theologian—and an organizing theoretician as well. Many historians consider him the founder of Christianity. Paul had specific ideas for spreading his new faith. Above all he wished Christianity to become more accessible. "The expansion of Christianity from a Jewish sect into a World Religion was Paul's consuming passion, in pursuit of which he broke every hindering tie, and strained every faculty of mind and body for upwards of thirty years."[14] Despite his strict Jewish upbringing, and his pride in it, Paul thought the best way to attract gentiles would be to drop many of the cultural requirements inherited from Judaism, specifically circumcision and submission to Mosaic law. His reasons were many, but three practical ones are worthy of mention. First, in this age of dissolving faiths, many a gentile was seeking a religion in which to believe. Circumcision had long been a serious impediment to conversion to Judaism, however, and it certainly would not help the spread of Christianity. Second, Jewish food laws were seen by many as unacceptable ritual, superstition, or mere foolishness. Thirdly, the Judaic claim to being "the Chosen People" understandably offended the pride of other ethnic groups.

Paul began his ministry in Antioch, a city in what is now central Turkey, as a joint effort with his friend Barnabas. He met with enormous success in converting members of the local Jewish community, quickly building the church in Antioch into the largest known to that time. Some of the converts were merchants and a substantial fund to spread the gospel was eventually established. Local pagans, probably with disrespect, called members of the new group *Christianoi*, "followers of the Messiah." After a successful trip to spread the word among Jews in Cyprus, Paul made a fateful decision to begin preaching to Antioch's gentiles, which for some reason incensed the leaders of the local synagogue. They managed to persuade the municipal authorities to have him thrown out of town. Paul took his message to Greece, perhaps the most momentous odyssey in Western history.

After a brief sojourn in Athens, Paul moved to the nearby city of Corinth. The Diaspora was well established in Greece, and Paul found a receptive audience in the local synagogue, soon converting the rabbi. His success alarmed unconverted Jews who, as in Antioch but for opposite reasons, took their case to the authorities. The Roman governor, Gallio, refused to intervene, and matters soon turned into violence. Intimidated, Paul decided to focus his efforts on gentiles, causing him to begin to "interpret Christianity in terms familiar to the Hellenistic mind."[15] By Hellenizing Christianity Paul universalized it, that is, made it comprehensible, even attractive, to the whole of the Roman world. For a start, large numbers of Greeks flocked to his ministry.

Although James and to a certain extent Peter wished to limit proselytizing only to Jews (they preached mostly in temples, which were attended by the disciples even after the death of Christ), Paul proceeded on his own course. Paul's views were shaped at a distance from Jesus' more immediate followers. He was better equipped to apprehend the transcendent message of Jesus and felt less constrained by what amounted to local custom. For Paul, Mosaic law was in many ways beside the point. In Acts and Galatians Paul makes clear his differences with James and Peter over the method for spreading this new form of Judaism. James wished to keep many of the basic elements of the parent faith; Peter avoided uncircumscribed Christians altogether.

The Galatians of central Turkey, some of Paul's earliest converts (Antioch was in Galatia) eventually·fell under the influence of "Judaizers," those who insisted that one could be a Christian only by embracing Judaism. Paul wrote "a wrathful epistle in which he broke completely with the Judaizing Christians, and declared that men were to be saved not by adherence to the Mosaic Law, but by an active faith in Christ as the redeeming Son of God."[16]

The general issue had enormous import, both for history and the Christian missionaries of the day. "To most Jewish Christians it was unthinkable that a Gentile could accept Messiah, but not the Israel for whom Messiah came. Gentile converts must, therefore, be circumcised and keep the Mosaic code."[17] The efforts of the Judaizing missionaries to Galatian Antioch, and Paul's bitter opposition to them, proved to be the ground on which the issue of adherence to ancient Jewish custom would be fought on.

Paul and Barnabas realized that if these emissaries had their way, Christianity would never be accepted by any significant number of Gentiles; it would remain "a Jewish heresy" (as Heine was to call it), and would fade out in a century. They went down to Jerusalem [about 50 C.E.] and fought the matter out with the apostles, nearly all of whom were still faithful worshipers in the Temple. James was reluctant to consent; Peter defended the two missionaries; finally it was agreed that pagan proselytes should be required only to abstain from immorality and from the eating of sacrificial or strangled animals. Apparently Paul eased the way by promising financial support for the impoverished community at Jerusalem from the swelling funds of the Antioch church.[18]

Although the certainty of Jewish practices and beliefs allowed Jews to maintain a cohesive religion despite the chaos of their time and place, the more liberal religion preached by Paul was attractive to both Jews and the innumerable gentiles seeking the firm hand of monotheism. Converts would soon discover, however, that the ritual simplicity of Paul's Christianity was offset by complex theological constructions. Throughout its evolution, Judaism had avoided metaphysical complexities; its only real mystery was the motive of an omnipotent god in selecting a group of desert nomads to be the Chosen People of his earth. In its basics Judaism was a simple religion easily understood by anyone. Not so Christianity.

By the end of Paul's life, and largely owing to him, Christianity was possessed of vastly increased numbers, stretching all the way to Spain, and of a coherent ideology greatly differentiated from Judaism. Most significantly, Paul had successfully defeated the forces in the church who found it difficult to imagine believers in Christ who did not also believe in Israel—that is, were not Jews, were not invested in Christ's role in reestablishing the Jewish nation. It was a fateful turn of focus, this evangelizing of the gentiles. It was a turn from a monotheism dedicated to creating and sustaining a nation to a monotheism dedicated to the saving of souls and accordingly able to justify the taking of nations.

To develop political influence for the saving of souls, however, required from the outset that the new ideology of love promote hate. As the centuries passed, Christianity incorporated a great deal of intolerance in its teachings about ideas, actions, and peoples. Despite their Jewish origins, the earliest Christians directed many of their first polemics against other Jews. Just as Jesus had made himself the traditional community scapegoat for the collective sins of humanity, the early Christians made the Jews the scapegoat for the travails of Christianity, starting with the troubles of Christ himself. In response to his rejection by certain Jewish congregations and in order to separate himself from other Jewish sects, Paul elected to develop an anti-Semitism. This also facilitated his task of proselytizing the pagan citizens of Rome. The early development of general Christian anti-Semitism was not the sole province of Paul, however. The Jewish Revolt of 66 C.E. became the event separating the various leading followers of Jesus from the other Jewish sects. Internecine Jewish violence and Hebrew rebelliousness against Rome sparked Roman retaliation and lit the fires of early Christian anti-Semitism.

According to the first-century Jewish historian Josephus, in his *The Wars of the Jews,*

> All the people of every place betook themselves to rapine; after which they got together in bodies, in order to rob the people of the country, insomuch that for barbarity and iniquity those of the same nation did no way differ from the Romans; nay, it seemed to be a much lighter thing to be ruined by the Romans than by themselves . . . moreover, besides the bringing on of the war, they were the occasion of sedition and famine therein . . . For there were, besides these, other robbers that came out of the country, and came into the city, and joining to them those that were worse than themselves, omitted no kind of barbarity; for they did not measure their courage by their rapines and plundering only, but proceeded as far as murdering men . . . At length, when they were saturated with the unjust actions they had done towards men, they transferred their contumelious behavior to God himself, and came into the sanctuary with polluted feet.[19]

To quell the rebellion the Romans responded with full-scale military measures, destroying Jewish documents and places of worship and killing everyone connected with the house of David in order to deter any other members of the Hebrew royal family from inciting insurrection against the Roman Empire.[20] As a result, the members of the emerging cult of Christianity prudently sought to distance themselves from the idea that they were another rebellious Jewish sect challenging the authority of Rome. Since both people and documents related to Jesus had been destroyed, the authors of the Gospels took the literary license of ascribing to Jesus words and ideas which would find receptive ears in a Roman audience. Many sayings attributed to Jesus in Mark "seem to refer to a slightly later date,"[21] after the Jewish Revolt, in order better to promote the new ideology. Mark 13:20 has Jesus saying,

> For in those days there will be such tribulation as has not been from the beginning of the Creation which God created until now, and never will be. And if the Lord had not shortened the days, no human being would be saved; but for the sake of the elect, whom he chose, he shortened the days.

Mark's opening sentence tries to suggest that Jesus is prophesying, but the next sentence talks of *past* events. Since during Christ's life there existed no catastrophe of the magnitude alluded to here, "this apocalyptic vision seems extremely likely to refer to the destruction of the temple in A.D. 70."[22] New Testament prophecies, like those of the Old Testament, were often written after the fact. They have another common denominator: they were poorly edited, so their inconsistencies are transparent.

Even Jesus' conduct was now rewritten for history. As the eminent historian Michael Grant says in his *The Jews in the Roman World*, "What the Gospels said more than a generation after [Jesus'] time, in the light of the Jewish revolt, is clear enough: they asserted that Jesus, unlike the rebellious Jews, had been loyal to the Romans."[23] Thus Matthew 22:21 ascribes to Jesus the commandment to "Render therefore unto Caesar the things that are Caesar's, and to God the things that are God's." With careful propaganda Jesus, who was crucified by the Roman procurator, was carefully converted into a loyal citizen of Rome.

To promote Christianity in a Roman audience unlikely to embrace a Jewish cult, the Gospels of Matthew, Mark, and John (like the books of Paul) thus intensified Christian anti-Semitism. "Mark's attacks on the Jews . . . are numerous and savage, both in connection with Jesus' career from its outset, and in relation to his arrest and death."[24] Mark, the translator and interpreter of Peter, deemed it necessary to edit and emphasize Jesus' words (or at least what Mark claimed Peter so often said were Jesus' words) in order to appeal for converts to a Roman congregation sensitive to Rome's condemnation of Jewish rebelliousness. Mark makes it clear that the Jews, not the Romans, wanted Jesus dead, as when he says, "And [the Jews] all condemned him as deserving death" (Mark 14:64). Likewise when Matthew 26:52 declares that, "All who take the sword shall perish by the sword," it is likely that "the sword proclaimed by Matthew was, above all, destined for the Jews who had killed Jesus."[25] John is even more virulent, portraying Jesus himself "as telling the Jews that they are the sons of evil and darkness."[26] John 8:44–45 has Jesus declaring that,

> Your father is the devil and you choose to carry out your father's desires. He was murdered from the beginning, and is not rooted in the truth; there is no truth in him. When he tells a lie, he is speaking his own language; for he is a liar and the father of lies. But I speak the truth, and therefore you do not believe me.

Acts is similarly hostile to the Jews, repeatedly stressing their responsibility for the crucifixion of Jesus. In Acts 10:39, one of many such passages, we find, "And we are witnesses to all that he did both in the country of the

Jews and in Jerusalem. [The Jews] put him to death by hanging him on a tree." Acts tries to claim that Jesus was a victim of Jewish violence just as other faithful Roman citizens had been. "Like the Gospels, it is very eager to show that the early Christians had never shared Jewish disloyalty towards Rome."[27]

These biblical authors must be viewed as politicians and propagandists promoting a new ideology; but while their anti-Semitism is clear, their personal authenticity is not. The actual authors of these Gospels is questionable. As Grant puts it, "The supposed authors of the Gospels are Matthew and John, 'apostles of Jesus,' Mark, 'disciple and interpreter of Peter,' and Luke, 'beloved physician' imprisoned with Paul. But on chronological, geographic, and cultural grounds alike, none of these attributions is generally accepted."[28] The Gospels were written two decades after the epistles of Paul[29] and were undoubtedly influenced by Paul's anti-Semitism; the authors shared Paul's political impulse to further anti-Semitic hatred in order to proselytize a Roman audience in an empire suspicious of Jews. These early efforts at propaganda dramatically impugn the integrity of the Bible itself as divine revelation. They ensured that anti-Semitism imbued Christian psychology down to the present day.

The acquisition of Greek converts assured the introduction to Christianity of detailed intellectual inquiry. Greeks were often disposed to at least a rudimentary philosophical discourse. This would be a model for the development of Christian ideas. Particularly in the spread of Catholicism, the conversion of foreign peoples to Christianity has been most successfully accomplished by transforming local customs and beliefs into various forms of Christian practice. This absorption of pagan customs resulted in Christian belief as fundamental as the existence of saints (to allow an easy transmutation of long-standing pagan gods into Christian corollaries) and the observance of Christmas Day (originally a European pagan holiday celebrating the winter solstice). The willingness to transform foreign beliefs and practices into a Christian scheme, a quality of Christianity as responsible as any other for its spread, made it necessary to develop workable explanations for each new group of converts, each of differing beliefs, to explain how they could fit into the same Christian fold; this in turn necessitated the alteration of overall theological structure in order to assure a consonant whole.

To explain Christianity to the Greeks required blending Hebrew scriptures and Mosaic law—even Paul would not divorce them from Jesus' thought completely—with Greek philosophy and culture. With the onset of the influence of Origen (185–254 C.E.), this synthesis became systematic.[30] Origen lived in Alexandria, which, owing to its position as a trading center and its possession of a university, was a center of syncretism, the effort to unite different doctrines and practices. More than simply reconciling Greek philosophy and Hebrew scripture, Origen laid the groundwork for the church's later philosophical position that reason as well as faith could sustain belief. For all of these accomplishments Origen was considered one of the fathers of the church. His influence did suffer one setback, however; he was later excommunicated and declared a heretic. The development of modern Catholic theology was highly political.

In *Against Celsus*, Origen adumbrates the argument in favor of apprehension of God through reason, fully established (by Thomas Aquinas) only a thousand years later. Celsus apparently claimed in a text since lost that Christians belonged to illegal organizations, properly condemned by the authorities; Origen agreed, but asserted that civil disobedience is a virtue. Celsus claimed that Christianity came from Jews, who were barbarians; Origen said that application of Greek intellectual sophistication to the Gospels would demonstrate their veracity, but that in any case

> the Gospel has a demonstration of its own, more divine than any established by Grecian dialectics. And this diviner method is called by the Apostle the "manifestation of the Spirit and of power"; of "the Spirit," on account of the prophecies, which are sufficient to produce faith in anyone who reads them, especially in those things which relate to Christ; and of "power," because of the signs and wonders which we must believe to have been performed, both on many other grounds, and on this, that traces of them are still preserved among those who regulate their lives by the precepts of the Gospel.[31]

This argument presages the two-fold argument for belief which characterizes Christian philosophy today: that pure reason, rightly exercised, can establish many of the essentials of the Christian faith, notably the existence of God, immortality, and free will; and that the divine inspiration of the Scriptures is authenticated by the fact that the prophets foretold the coming of the Messiah, by miracles, and by the beneficial effects of belief on the lives of the faithful.

Origen's arguments were augmented, systematized, and made triumphant in the thirteenth century by Aquinas, who attempted to synthesize Greek philosophy with the Gospels in order, among other things, to combat the infidel threat of Islam. Origen also anticipated later Catholic philosophy if not practice in his position on church-state relations. He maintained that Christians should take part only in the affairs of the "divine nations," i.e., the church.[32] This view is later implied by Augustine in his differentiation between the City of God and secular (civil) governments, and, much later, in the Western concern with separation of church and state.

Unfortunately for non-Christians, the church only subscribed to Origen's doctrine when it lacked political power; otherwise it relentlessly pressured governments to implement its political, social and religious agenda.

In the first three centuries after Christ, the church concerned itself with making converts (usually clandestinely, since Christianity was persecuted in the Roman Empire), and with developing and systematizing its beliefs. Church government developed slowly, since Christ did not give detailed instructions regarding organization. The primitive church was far less encrusted with procedure and hierarchy than it soon would be. Priests were not anointed, bishops were elected by popular vote, and there were no distinctions between clergy and laity as we know them today.

When almsgiving developed, the acknowledged leader of the community controlled the purse, thus allowing him (or her) to decide who among the mob of the destitute should receive the money. This function was handled by a "clerk" or "cleric"; thus the power of the clergy began. The original, often multiple, supervisors of the ceremonies were called simply "elders," Greek *episkopoi*, Latin *biscopi* ("bishops"), and could be men or women. This changed slightly as early as 150 C.E., and "bishop" became the name of the single leader elected by the people of a large congregation. By 251 "Cyprian taught that the episcopate is a universal core, in succession to the Apostles, of divinely authorized interpreters of doctrine."[33] Accretions of power to the clergy mounted rapidly with Christianity's assumption of state power in Rome under Constantine. The bishops were given judicial and administrative functions. "The hierarchical structure of the church grew in response to practical needs. In the imperial age provincial, or metropolitan, sees were elevated above others 'since all who have business gather to the metropolis,' as stated in a council of 341."[34]

The bishops of Jerusalem, Constantinople, Antioch, Alexandria and Rome soon obtained authority over surrounding regions. Central government developed among Christians. The bishop of Rome, already considered *primus inter pares* (first among equals), quickly came to regard himself as the church's leader, and therefore as *primus supra pares* (first *above* equals). He was called *Papa*, an abbreviation of *Pater Patrum*, meaning "Father of Fathers," "pope" in English.

It is not yet well understood why the church developed in Rome rather than Jerusalem. The destruction of Jerusalem could have prevented Christianity from mobilizing there, but, on the contrary, could also have created fertile ground for the spread of Christian beliefs. It is assumed that the pagans of the Roman Empire proved more receptive to evangelism, prompting more rapid church development there. It has also been suggested that Christianity's spread in the Middle East fell behind that in

Europe because evangelism there was largely limited to the relatively
small audience of Jews.

This shift in the center of Christian organizing came very early on—
Peter himself went to Rome, where he was executed about 64 C.E. According to church legend, he was crucified upside down because he told his
executioners he was not worthy to be crucified in the same manner as
Christ. Church history has Peter as the leader of the community in Rome,
possibly sharing his responsibilities with Paul, but his role there as a first
pope or even the first bishop, not even asserted until the second or third
century, is unlikely. There was neither so much unity nor so much hierarchy in the church of his time.[35]

Persecuted by the Roman authorities, Christians had to practice and
preach their faith in underground caves and caverns which they dug beneath the city of Rome, the "catacombs." It is probably from this era that
the term *underground* arose to describe illegal activity. Christianity grew
for many reasons. Gibbon assigns five causes:

> 1) the inflexible, and, if we may use the expression, the intolerant zeal
> of the Christians, derived, it is true, from the Jewish religion, but purified
> from the narrow and unsocial spirit which, instead of inviting, had de-
> terred the Gentiles from embracing the law of Moses;
> 2) the doctrine of a future life, improved by every additional circum-
> stance which could give weight and efficacy to that important truth;
> 3) the miraculous powers ascribed to the primitive Church;
> 4) the pure and austere morals of the Christians;
> 5) the union and discipline of the Christian republic, which gradually
> formed an independent and increasing state in the heart of the Roman
> Empire.[36]

Early on the Christians believed that they alone would go to heaven,
that all heathens would go to hell. How they developed these beliefs with
such firmness is difficult to say. The Jews, as we have seen, had lately
developed a general belief in an afterlife, probably obtained from the
Greeks, whose Orphic cults postulated a kind of reincarnation. The general
concept of immortality was given intellectual standing by Plato and was
popular in Greece and later in Rome as well, where it flourished in Mithraism, an Indo-Iranian mystery religion which declared the passage of souls
to their place of origin in heaven. As a result, the notion was not foreign to
the bulk of Christianity's early converts.

The Orphic cults and other mystery religions in Greece and Asia also
possessed a central myth of a god who dies but rises again. For some,
Christ's resurrection was accordingly reasonable. Christianity's possession
of sacred scriptures was a powerful impetus to its spread. Impressive in

their own right, these writings were also an effective element of cohesion. Sacred texts, as definitive evidence of origin and consequent legitimacy, are common to most of the world's long-lasting religions, e.g. the Old Testament of the Jews, the Koran of the Muslims, the collected works of Marx, Engels, and Lenin of the Communists. The New Testament was Christianity's personal book, a wondrous focal point of reference around which the faithful could mobilize.

The early moral discipline of the Christians was exemplary. Even Pliny, whose job it was to persecute them, attests to it. Christians distinguished themselves by their moral purity, gained respect even among their enemies, and gained converts and supporters ever more quickly. Gibbon asserts "the union and discipline of the Christian republic" as one of the reasons for the spread of Christianity. As we know in our century, well-organized pressure groups can effect powerful political persuasion. Christian successes were surely due to zeal and discipline, but they were no doubt helped because so many others, apparently, were disorganized. Pressure was steadily applied by the Christian populace, by the Christian underground, the extent of which was not fully known and consequently feared by Constantine, and by the Christians in the Roman military, numerous because soldiers on the frontiers and elsewhere had little to do in their spare time and were accordingly receptive to conversion. The gradual Christian infiltration of Roman society and its military, and the dedication and cunning instilled by inherited Jewish zeal and Roman persecution, combined to create a formidable force that eventually could not be denied.

Christ was a reformer, a prophet in the tradition of Jeremiah and Isaiah. He was the modern-day equivalent of a socialist, calling for a radical social transformation that would address the problems of the poor. But his ideas met with resistance not only from the Hebrew ruling class, but also from the Roman occupation forces interested in social stability above all, as imperial power always is.

When Christianity took root, principally in southern Europe, it was a creed which continued to challenge the ruling classes, now those of Rome itself, not by violent rebellion but by a peaceful revolution of social conscience. However, the more successful its appeal to the oppressed became, the more followers it attracted, the broader its base of social power grew— the more, apparently, it came to resemble its adversary. Christianity would grow so strong that it compelled adoption as the religion of the Roman state. But with incorporation into the ruling structure, rather than transforming the nature of rule Christianity took on its traditional characteristics. Soon it would go so far as to become the mirror image of that which had oppressed it. Despite an ideology of love both on earth and above, Christianity soon would turn to oppressing those who denied it, even those who merely differed with it.

Like all successful revolutionary vanguards, Christianity's elite ultimately formed a new hierarchy of oppressors, proving eager to tinker with Christian essence—doctrine—in the interest of greater control over land, wealth, and the lives of believers. This course seems to be a deep structure in the pattern of human affairs, but the particular figure who set Christianity on this road was a wily Roman emperor named Constantine.

In this sign you will conquer.

—Divine revelation to Constantine

Alas! Constantine, how much misfortune you caused . . . by the dowry which the first rich father accepted from you.

—Dante, *Inferno*

II

Political Rise, Theological Consolidation

C onstantine is one of the most important figures in Christianity because he gave the young religion the form it would hold for fifteen hundred years. First, he contributed to certain basic Christian doctrines; second, he transformed Christianity from the faith of peace and love into a religion of conquerors; third, he introduced Christianity to wealth and power.

Constantine was born in 280 at Naissus (modern Nis, Yugoslavia), the son of Constantius I and the concubine Helena (later St. Helena). Thus by Christian standards Constantine was an illegitimate child born to a woman living in sin, which, of course, did not prevent her from being canonized. Roman rule of the time was in the form of a tetrarchy, a junior (*caesar*) and senior (*augustus*) emperor for each of the two halves of the empire. The division of the empire and the system for ruling it was inaugurated by Diocletian (293) in the interests of imperial stability. Constantius I became *caesar* of the West under the system, advancing to *augustus* in 305, and with his death a year later Constantine began what would be a seven-year campaign to win rule over the West. His efforts culminated in the invasion of Italy in 312 and a climactic attack on the Roman leader Maxentius at the Milvian Bridge near Rome. During the battle, according to Christian legend, Constantine saw a cross in the sky emblazoned with the words *In Hoc Signo Vinces* ("In this sign you will conquer"). His troops' shields were quickly inscribed with the divine call to arms, Constantine succeeded in taking Rome, and the victory is said to have been hailed as a Christian defeat of paganism. *IHS*—a symbol of Roman military combat—would come to be second only to the cross (ironically, an emblem of Roman oppression) as the most widely used symbol of Christianity down to the present day. *IHS* is stitched on the vestments worn by all Catholic priests when they say mass.

Despite the general acceptance of this tale by today's Catholic faithful, it is likely that Constantine's vision was not Christian at all. He

> appears to have had some sort of vision, or numinous experience, in the precincts of a pagan temple to the Gallic Apollo, either in the Vosges or near Autun. According to a witness accompanying Constantine's army at the time, the vision was of the sun god—the deity worshipped by certain cults under the name of "Sol Invictus," the "Invincible Sun." There is evidence that Constantine, just before his vision, had been initiated into a Sol Invictus cult. . . . The state religion of Rome under Constantine was, in fact, pagan sun worship; and Constantine, all his life, acted as its chief priest. Indeed his reign was called a "sun emperorship," and Sol Invictus figured everywhere—including the imperial banners and the coinage of the realm.[1]

Constantine's role in the elevation of Christianity to state power would be great, but it was expedience and chance which determined it, not faith. Constantine hoped to unite the three principal religions of the empire—Sol Invictus, Mithraism and Christianity—into a single institution that would serve to support the state rather than undermine it.[2] Like Diocletian, Constantine had long-term stability of rule uppermost in his mind. Diocletian had turned his efforts to the construction of a complex system of collective rule bound by adoption and family intermarriage. Constantine focused on religion.

He had promising material to work with. All three religions were essentially monotheistic. Mithraism shared sun worship with Sol Invictus, but it also shared important elements of the Christian faith—immortality of the soul, a future judgement and the resurrection of the dead. Constantine accordingly attempted to establish beliefs and practices that would progressively blur the distinctions between the three religions. Thus, for example, Constantine was interested in consolidating Jesus' position as a god rather than a mortal prophet, and for this and other purposes he convened the Council of Nicaea in 325. Jesus was confirmed as divine on a vote of 218 to 2, no abstentions. "As a god Jesus could be associated conveniently with Sol Invictus. As a mortal prophet he would have been more difficult to accommodate. In short, Christian orthodoxy lent itself to a politically desirable fusion with the official state religion; and in so far as it did so, Constantine conferred his support on Christian orthodoxy."[3]

To further harmonize the relationships between the three religions, and to distance Christianity from its Judaic origins, Constantine undertook to change the traditional birth date of Jesus. It had been, until the fourth century, celebrated on January 6. However, by an official edict Constantine made it December 25, the birthday of Mithra and the festival of Natalis Invictus, the birth (or rebirth) of the sun, when the days began to grow longer.[4] This change served the purpose of combining the holiest celebrations of all three religions into one. In 321 Constantine issued an edict ordering the law courts closed on "the venerable day of the sun," making "Sunday" the sacred day of the week for worship, rather than the traditional Sabbath inherited from Judaism, dusk on Friday to dusk on Saturday.

At the Council of Nicaea Constantine altered the day of the resurrection of Christ, the "Christian passover," from the Sabbath to Sunday, and its name was changed to "Easter," from east, its Latin equivalent meaning "the direction of the sun." To simplify the chore of codifying the new canons, Constantine ordered the destruction of pagan and Christian writings about Christianity that he considered heretical. Then, in 331, he commissioned new copies of the Bible, facilitating the task of the new guardians of orthodoxy—instant scriptural support for recently prescribed tenets of faith. "The importance of Constantine's commission must not be underestimated. Of the five thousand extant early manuscript versions of the New Testament, not one pre-dates the fourth century."[5]

A more defined structure of belief engineered to political specifications naturally required a financial and organizational structure that could uphold and extend it. The authority of bishops was expanded, and the process of concentrating ecclesiastical power accelerated. Constantine arranged for a fixed income to be allocated to the church and installed the bishop of Rome in the Lateran Palace.

Constantine altered the face of Christianity by making it an officially supported religion of the Roman Empire. This caused a fundamental change in Christian psychology; persecuted for centuries, Christians moved overnight into the seat of secular and spiritual power. The cross now emerged as a Christian symbol. While a persecuted religion, the believers had not wanted to unnecessarily remind potential converts that being a Christian could result in a death by crucifixion; the fish, selected because the first letters of the Greek for "Jesus Christ Son of God Saviour" spelled the Greek word for "fish," had become the secret sign that Christians used to identify each other and, eventually, the official symbol of their faith. Constantine now officially abolished crucifixion as the supreme method of execution of the empire,[6] allowing the cross of death to become Christianity's insignia. It was a prophetic symbol.

Constantine had an inestimable effect on doctrine; he is referred to in history as "the thirteenth Apostle." Although he helped formulate some of the basic doctrine of the church, he did so while still a pagan. Perhaps to mitigate the fact of a heathen's tremendous influence on its most important theological principles, church tradition holds that Constantine was converted to Christianity on his deathbed. This fiction was spread throughout Christendom in a romanticized version of the life of Pope Sylvester, *The Acts of St. Sylvester,* and repeated in a document attributed to Constantine that transferred temporal authority over the whole of the Western Empire to the bishop of Rome. The "Donation of Constantine," as it is called, was of course a forgery.[7]

Although Constantine claimed to have received many inspirations directly from God, the most practical one regarded Byzantium, the city on the Bosporus, founded by the Greeks nearly a thousand years earlier. The location was far more magnificent than Rome in most respects. One day Constantine announced that he had received a direct instruction from God to rebuild the city.[8] Its name, he decreed modestly, would be changed to Constantinople. Constantine's desire for the scenic beauty of his new capital would eventually be purchased at the expense of the unity of the Roman Empire, which would not survive the construction of a second capital. The move to Constantinople (330) ultimately engendered the Hellenization, even the Orientalization, of the empire. This would eventually lead to political strife between the bishop of Rome (by now called the "pope") and the patriarch of Constantinople, whose power gradually rose as the locus of ecclesiastical authority shifted to the east along with secular power. Centuries later the final outcome would be a complete schism between the Eastern and Western Christians, which lasts to this day.

Constantine's enormous political power impelled both secular and church leaders to seek his guidance in their affairs. Constantine's role in the Council of Nicaea was typical. He called what has since been recognized as the first of the church's sweeping ecumenical councils, which define essential elements of faith. (There have been less than two dozen in Roman Catholic history; the most recent was the Second Vatican Council, held in 1962.) Constantine's particular concern was the rise of Arianism as a significant Christian movement. Arius, a cultivated priest in Alexandria, maintained that Christ, the Son, was not equal to the Father, but was created by him—that is, Jesus was not divine. This creed came to be called "Arianism," and could be called an early attempt to define the relation between God and Christ according to natural reason. A synod of bishops excommunicated Arius in 321, but his doctrines continued to gain influence, posing problems for Constantine's master plan to unite the religions of the empire. Thus the chief item of business at the Council of Nicaea in 325 was the repudiation of Arianism.

Probably on the advice of his counselor, the Spanish bishop Hosius,

Constantine opposed to Arian doctrine the concept of "consubstantiality," which simply means that Christ "shares the substance" of the Father and is equal to him. He must have been convincing. Arianism was summarily defined as heresy by the Council of Nicaea and the notion of consubstantiality was inserted into what came to be known as the Nicene Creed. With some modification, the Nicene Creed forms the basis for all of Christian belief today, summarizing the basic tenets of the Christian religion. It does not seem to bother Christian believers that Constantine oversaw the writing of this essential doctrine while still a convinced pagan and for decidedly secular purposes.

After a few years of reflection, Constantine apparently had some second thoughts about the doctrine he had just formulated for all of Christianity. After all, what did he, a pagan, know about theology? In 331 Constantine decided to receive Arius to discuss it, eventually ordering Athanasius, champion of orthodoxy at Nicaea, to receive Arius back into the church. Athanasius refused, was deposed by the Synod of Tyre (335) and exiled to Gaul. Constantine then commanded the bishop of Constantinople to restore Arius to communion.[9] Arius died on the day of ceremony, however. The Nicene Creed remained.

The third person of the Blessed Trinity was left in a logical limbo by the Council of Nicaea. No one seems to know much about the Holy Spirit, except that Christ made periodic reference to it. It was postulated, therefore, that there was another component to the divine godhead; so the notion of "three persons in one god" developed. Even though Christian teaching states that Christ was conceived by the Holy Spirit, we are assured that he is not the son of the Holy Spirit. The medieval theologian Thomas Aquinas hastens to point out that the existence of the Holy Spirit cannot be deduced from reason alone. No one would doubt him on that point. In fact, in Acts 19:2 Paul asks some disciples if they have been baptized into the Holy Spirit. They answer, "No, we have never even heard that there is a Holy Spirit." Church leaders apparently needed the Holy Spirit to hold the theology together. To settle the issue the church called the Holy Spirit a "mystery" of the faith and made belief in it mandatory. Thus was born one of the basic doctrines of Christianity. Arcane though it is, the matter would be of great moment. The Eastern and Western church would split in the eleventh century over the relationship between the three persons in the Blessed Trinity.

From the time of Constantine until the eighteenth century the interests of church and state were merged in all Christian countries; even today only a handful of them maintain a true separation of church and state. The result has been the use of state power to enforce theological beliefs. At first this was regarded as a blessing by God, but eventually would be seen as a curse by all except those who wielded the power; the French Revolution would show how bitterly the citizenry could come to resent state-enforced religion. All too quickly, the church would sacrifice its morality, even tamper with the tenets of its faith, in the interest of gaining or maintaining secular power. One might say that even the persecution of Christians did not end with Christian acquisition of state power. They would use its instruments against each other. Once the Roman state became predominantly Christian, new opportunities for wealth and power became available to ecclesiastics and laity; theological quarrels became contests for worldly gain rather than disputes over purer or more coherent theological principle. This would characterize Christian conduct down to the present day.

In line with his plan for merging the three dominant strands of Roman religious belief, Constantine did not wish to convert to Christianity. Instead he bestowed the bulk of ecclesiastical power on Pope Sylvester I, and with it a good measure of secular authority and wealth. This marked the beginning of the church's role as more than mere handmaiden of the ruling class, and, as a necessary corollary, the beginning of the church's growing proclivity to corruption. As Dante wrote, "Alas! Constantine, how much misfortune you caused, not by becoming Christian, but by the dowry which the first rich father accepted from you." When Constantine moved to Constantinople, leaving Sylvester in charge of most ecclesiastical affairs in Rome, the church gained power by virtue of increased independence. Eventually the papacy claimed, based on a fabricated document, that Constantine had granted it Rome and the Western Empire.

The church's ascension to power came in the nick of time. The empire was slipping into decay under the onslaught of barbarian migrations and, some say, spreading moral turpitude. Constantine's attempt to unite Rome's various religions faltered under succeeding emperors and some malcontents insisted that it was the rise of Christianity itself which was destroying the empire—abandoned pagan gods were taking their revenge. Once again Christianity was under attack, prompting a round of theological introspection that, in Augustine (354–430), would have an impact second only to that of Paul. How should Christians live while awaiting the Second Coming of Christ? How should influence with secular power be handled? Augustine provided the theological framework for church orientation toward rule that would last until the nineteenth century.

Augustine converted to Christianity in the midst of a long period of bawdy living described in detail in his *Confessions*. He wound up in 396 as the bishop of Hippo, a town near Carthage. A lustful man in a North African bishopric, Augustine would nonetheless go on to organize, refine and extend the theology of Pauline Christianity, distilling it to a form that would remain fundamentally untouched for a thousand years, until Aquinas.

In 410 Rome fell and was sacked by the Goths. Pagan citizens attributed this calamity to the abandonment of the ancient gods, particularly Jupiter, who, they claimed, ceased to protect Rome once it had a Christian emperor. To answer this attack on Christianity, Augustine wrote *The City of God*, a tome which differentiates at length the metaphorical City of God and the "city" of the world. During this era the Roman Empire was disintegrating due not only to overwhelming economic and political difficulties but also to the absorption by Roman society of various barbarian subcultures. Hedonism and debauchery ate internally at the basic morality of Rome, while externally the military forces of the barbarians were lurking in the long shadow that was uncivilized Europe. Most church leaders concerned themselves mainly with sexual morality, particularly the preservation of virginity, while ignoring broader moral issues. Augustine was different; while remaining obsessed with sexual matters, always the easiest for moralists to discuss, he went beyond them in an attempt to develop a moral framework for society as a whole.

This was particularly essential for Christians in this era because the ongoing collapse of Rome reminded them that the Second Coming was overdue. Christ was supposed to return in a time just such as this. If not now, when? Although Augustine clearly believed that the Second Coming would not take place in the immediate future, he did think that the Christian faithful were in any case completely unprepared for the Last Judgement. He set himself to the task of revising Christian theology so that when Judgement Day came, Christians would be ready. This of course required the revitalization of the morals of the Christian population. But, just as Paul had with the example of his life's work, Augustine also emphasized that there was another critical element in Christianity's preparation for judgement—the taking up of determined efforts to enlighten the whole of the world to the possibility of its salvation.

In *The City of God*, one of the most important books in Christian literature, Augustine attempted to deal with all of these concerns. Writing it over a period of thirteen years, he was able to address the burning issues of the day and in the process formulate a cohesive theology for life in the secular world. While Jerome provided a systematic written frame of reference by organizing and legitimizing the Scriptures, Augustine provided an intellectual structure by making Christian theology coherent, applying it to every crevice of human experience, present and future.

Augustine posited an eternal city in which man would dwell when the secular city of earthly existence decomposed. By expanding the conception of the afterlife to dimensions previously unknown, Augustine expanded as well the sense of security Christianity could offer its followers. In the process he reconciled the division between the secular and sacred of the Old Testament, and taught Christians how to conduct themselves in the secular world while awaiting Christ: they should spread the word of the Gospels and the salvation theology of St. Paul. While awaiting Jesus, they should save the world. It was in fact a Christian duty to bring to the heathen the message of Christ; the dedication to carrying out this duty was a factor in one's personal judgement to come.

Augustine strongly believed in the separation of church and state, but his was a much different concept than what we know today. As Bertrand Russell summarizes it, Augustine believed that the state "could only be part of the City of God by being submissive towards the Church in all religious matters."[10] Despite the form in which it was declared, this amounted to an advocacy of theocracy, and it was eagerly embraced as such by the church thereafter. "All through the Middle Ages, during the gradual rise of the papal power, and throughout the conflict between Pope and Emperor, Saint Augustine supplied the Western Church with the theoretical justification of its policy . . . The weakness of the emperors, and of most Western medieval monarchs, enabled the Church, to a great extent, to realize the ideal of the City of God."[11] Not only should Christians not feel responsible for the decline of Rome, Augustine says, but the vacuum of power caused by the collapse of the pagan system could be filled with the Christian spirit.

Among the themes of *The City of God* is the claim that worse disasters had fallen upon other cities and countries in pre-Christian times; Christianity therefore could not be blamed for the fall of Rome. On the contrary, when Roman legions conquered cities, they had often treated them more brutally than the Goths had Rome. The fact of Rome's relatively mild treatment, Augustine suggests, was due to the influence of Christians there. The Christians who suffered in the invasion, Augustine explains, had no justification for being upset; God would punish the Goths in the hereafter. If all sins were punished on earth, there would be no need for a Judgement Day; revenge belongs to Jesus. Regarding the rape of Rome's women during the invasion, Augustine says that chastity is a virtue of the mind and is not lost by physical rape, but he then goes on to imply that God might permit the rape of women too proud of their virginity. Pride, it must be remembered, is a sin.

The City of God is the society of the elect. One can only acquire knowledge of God through Christ, and for knowledge, Augustine says, Christians must rely on the Scriptures, not on reason. Here Augustine differs from other church fathers and theologians. He argues that it is folly to try and understand time and space before the world was created, since there was no time before Creation, and no place when the world was not.

Augustine was greatly concerned with the doctrine of original sin. This trespass by Adam, Christianity's first human, brought the consequence of eventual physical death to mankind, who, presumably, would have had eternal physical life had Adam not sinned. Adam's sins also brought down eternal damnation on all humans, but God saw fit to give mankind one more chance to redeem itself, dispatching Christ to die for its sins and thereby providing humans the opportunity to obtain salvation through "grace."

Grace is the most important element in Catholic understanding of the process by which man is saved. It is described as an unmerited gift from God, through which he brings people to a perfection which transcends their natural limitations. Augustine maintains that man would only do that which was right if man's will were properly directed and sustained by grace. This was an incipient proclamation of the doctrine of predestination, which led to questions as to whether man's will was free to choose right and wrong or required grace to do so; and, if so, who received grace—only those chosen by God? If so, how could there be free will? And if not, what good was grace? While grace is one of the essentials of Christian belief, eternal salvation being the most important thing in Christian theology, Christians up to the present day cannot agree upon what it is or how it works, or if it contradicts other doctrines such as free will or (in the case of the Calvinists) predestination. With the rise of Protestantism in the sixteenth century, the concept of grace became controversial; disagreements over it were settled militarily.

Grace comes from the Latin word *gratia*, meaning "pleasure, favor, thanks," from which we derive the word *gratitude*. To be in someone's "good grace" is to be in their favor; so also, Augustine tells us, with God. Humans need God's favor on earth in order to acquire eternal salvation. Grace is to Christian theology what ether once was to physics: an all-pervading, massless medium postulated to explain the cohesion of certain elements; in theology it is meant to explain the bond between God and man. In physics "ether" gradually lost its rationale, as physicists learned the details of the workings of electromagnetic waves. In order to prevent grace from losing its plausibility, by contrast, theologians *invented* the details needed to substantiate its workings.

One of the hallmarks of theological methodology is that if something cannot be explained it must be even further obfuscated, under the guise of pretending to give it more detailed exposition. Such an exposition will preferably have practical applications, say, increasing revenues. So grace was divided by church theologians into two categories: "sanctifying" grace, an undeserved gift from God, and "actual" grace, which moves people to perform good works and thereby assists them in acquiring salvation. Feeling compelled to leave unknowable God's methods of distributing sanctifying grace, the clergy pretended to possess a detailed knowledge of how actual grace was acquired. If good works were performed, believers could safely assume that they had been the recipient of actual grace. (No similar assumptions were made about sanctifying grace, a mystery which remained a source of employment for the graduates of the church's many divinity schools.) Good works became the only visible evidence that actual grace was operative. The logical next step was to say that good works gained the believer credit with God against the roster of his sins. This credit was gradually labeled an "indulgence" from God, to be applied against the punishment due for sins. This eventually resulted in directing the congregation to earn indulgences (God's "indulgence"), the suspension of accrued punishments for sin. If believers had not acquired actual grace in time to fortify their character against sin, their punishment could be lessened through indulgences earned and quantified by performing works or prayers, or making donations to the church. Soon the clergy claimed to know how much of a given currency could avert how many years of punishment in the afterlife. Church officials were the bookkeepers adding and subtracting columns of figures recorded in God's Great Ledger. With indulgences available for purchase, the practical need for actual grace diminished, at least among the well-off; who needed actual grace to gain salvation if one could buy a pleasant afterlife?

It was never explained if a French franc, for instance, had the same divine purchasing power from one century to the next. Consumer price index schedules were never officially appended to these contracts with God. Inflation, currency devaluations, and the like are important considerations in determining how much time in punishment could be bought back from God. Different prices for the French and German congregations, for example, could create enormous disparities in the administration of divine commutations.

Corrupt in its very conception, the sale of indulgences by church clergy became so corrupt in practice as well that it began to generate protest. If any theological minutia can be credited with sparking the Protestant Reformation (some historians attribute it to the rise of capitalism), this blatant merging of material interest with spiritual guidance was it. Protestantism's Martin Luther was the most virulent critic of the practice, and his attack on the sale of indulgences soon led to a theological construction rejecting the doctrine of the role of good works in salvation, from which the concept of indulgences derived. Luther maintained that grace alone, without good works, was adequate to attain eternal salvation.

The rancor eventually generated by Luther's attack on indulgences, mortally threatening to church finances, is almost beyond description. Four centuries of bloodshed between Catholics and the Lutherans and their descendants resulted, and the matter was only settled in 1983, when it was determined that the two faiths really did not disagree after all, but that if they did the Lutheran interpretation was now acceptable to Catholics. Since this reconciliation is ambiguous and confusing, the congregations of both churches appear to be most pleased with it. Intellectual confusion is the cornerstone of theology.

Sex and lust were among Augustine's greatest interests. After all, he had become a personal authority on the subject. Once he grew older, found Christianity, and tired of his own sexual promiscuity, in that order, Augustine defined the parameters of sexual morality for all succeeding Christians. In his ambivalent period, Augustine is reported to have said, "Lord, give me chastity and continence, but not just now." When he finally chose chastity over the good times, however, Augustine implanted a rigorous sexual purity as a tenet of Christian faith. The resultant doctrines were ludicrously restrictive and permeated with hellfire.

His theory is essentially that sex contains the elements of lust and pleasure because of the sin of Adam. According to Augustine, sex before Adam was a pleasureless pursuit, useful only for producing offspring. (Physiology was not one of Augustine's strong suits, despite the fact that his practical experience in the field was prodigious.) When Adam sinned, human will lost control of sexual activity, and sex became part of the emotions instead of a physical routine like defecation. Since lust contests the will, it is evil; and since sex produces pleasure, which undermines the will, sex too is evil. Augustine even counsels married people to avoid lust when having sexual intercourse to produce children. Augustine was most specific in these matters; his first translator, perhaps led into temptation by some of the detail of Augustine's prescriptions, decided to leave some of the text in the obscurity of the original Latin. Augustine does not explain why God chose lust as a form of punishment for Adam's sins, but his self-proclaimed affliction by lust in especially large measure perhaps explains the excessive repression he advocated. With such a bizarre and repressive theology of sexual morality, it is not surprising that Augustine's attitude toward women was also repressive, but this was traditional. The subjugation of women in the church had been given its first organized impetus by Paul, who said that women should serve their men as the Church served Christ. "Man was not made from woman, but woman from man. Neither was man created for woman, but woman for man," Paul declares in I Corinthians 11.

The City of God describes a world that has been divided into two cities, one which will ultimately stand shining on the left hand of God, and one which shall be condemned to eternal torment with Satan. Abel, the virtuous son of Adam and Eve, belongs to the City of God, and his brother Cain, who killed Abel, belongs to the city of the devil. Augustine summarizes both sacred and secular history in order to demonstrate his thesis. In the process he delineates a double standard in which acts considered virtuous for Christians could at the same time be vices for pagans. This, he suggests, is because Christians can act in the name of God or for God, and pagans cannot. The implication is that human activity is not inherently good or evil (most scientists and liberal criminal lawyers might agree, but theologians generally, and Catholic theologians most of all, stand united against this relativism), but are *rendered* good or evil by the belief system of the actor. A pagan giving a cup of water to a thirsty man is not virtuous, in the theological sense, earning no points for the accounting on Judgement Day; but Christians giving that same cup of water, even if keeping two-thirds for themselves, will contribute to the saving of their souls.

In conformity with this logic, Augustine conceived the Christian concept of a just war. Its central tenet is that "war is not contrary to the divine law and evil in itself."[12] This is church teaching still, and reasonable when practiced by, if we may use so vague a term, reasonable people. It could and would also be used to justify untold carnage wreaked under purely opportunistic banners of piety.

Augustine contends that all should believe in Scripture as the word of God, and all, accordingly, should base their conduct on it. However, he never resolved the inextricably linked issue of the accuracy of this source of reference. There were equally prestigious translations of the Scriptures available in Greek and Latin. In the Old Testament they differed greatly. The Greek version was made up of the Septuagint, a translation of the Old Testament written at the request of an Egyptian king in the third century B.C.E., and the copied and recopied books of the New Testament originally written in Greek. The Septuagint in particular was alleged to have been translated by seventy separate translators, and all of their translations said to have been in total agreement—it was divinely inspired, although the scribes who had copied it since could have made errors.

The Vulgate on other hand was translated into Latin directly from the oldest and most authoritative manuscripts available at the time (Jerome worked on this project from 382 to 404). Jerome used Hebrew manuscripts in his translation of the Old Testament, though they were probably later than those available to the translators of the Septuagint. Jerome was apparently able to eliminate both clear errors in the original translation and many of the additions and mistakes present in the commonly available versions of the Septuagint. Many Christians, however, thought the Hebrew text had been falsified in the areas where it predicted the Messiah; this was anti-Semitic suspicion.

Jerome translated the New Testament as well, producing much of what is still today the official Catholic version of the Bible. Jerome accepted assistance from Jews in preparing the translations, and his finished product met redoubled anti-Semitic hostility as a result, but he successfully enlisted the support of Augustine and by 800 the Vulgate was overwhelmingly the most widely used (in Latin, *vulgatus,* "popular") version of the Bible.

Jerome completed the Gospels first; he reproduced the rest of the New Testament (it is believed), virtually untouched, from one version of the Old Latin. But Jerome's patron, Pope Damasus, died in 384, and Jerome fell out of favor with the Roman clergy. Able to secure financial support from his friends, he moved to Bethlehem determined to finish his project with or without official sanction. There he took up the translation of the Old Testament in 390, finishing it in about fifteen years. Thanks to Jerome, the Catholic Bible is far truer to the purported original word of God than it would have been, but this is not saying a great deal.

The texts which Jerome worked from were questionable from the outset. First, the Gospels were not written until after 75 C.E., from memory decades after Jesus lived, and the original manuscripts of these documents, called in hermeneutics "Q," "M," "L," and "proto-Luke," are not extant.[13] More importantly, Jesus' sayings and the events of his life were clearly interpreted by the authors of the Gospels in the context of their evangelical mission. "We cannot ignore that in the interest of theological doctrine, contemporary circumstances, and effective story-telling, nothing wrong was seen in creating views for Jesus to express, altering the sense of traditional sayings of his, supplying and coloring episodes with the help of non-Christian literature."[14] Second, the Gospels of both Matthew and Luke are now understood to have drawn from Mark, but the accuracy of Mark's Gospel is doubtful, since he never met Jesus and relied upon Peter's sermons (Mark was Peter's interpreter) for his account of Jesus' ideas and sayings.[15] Third, it is universally acknowledged that Paul's intent in his recitation of sayings attributed to Jesus was to embellish Jesus' words in order to comport with his own salvation theology. It is thought by some that Mark's Gospel was an attempt to reconcile Peter's Palestine-based approach to Christian history with Paul's Hellenistic one. Fourth, the revolt of the Jews against the Romans in 66 had caused two serious repercussions which afflicted the Scriptures: the Romans had destroyed most of the literature which had been prepared by those in Palestine, and had killed many of the people who had known Jesus. Thus, most collateral support for the truth of the Gospels was removed from review. With the Gospels themselves of questionable veracity, any translation by Jerome was doubly so.

Jerome's Vulgate has problems of its own—Jerome included in the Vulgate several books (Tobit, Judith, and the Greek additions to the books of Daniel and Esther) reluctantly, under pressure from friends. More significant a difficulty in the Vulgate was introduced by the labors of Cassiodorus, who in the sixth century compiled the still-separate books translated by Jerome into the Vulgate that forms the basis of the Catholic Bible today. Cassiodorus added to Jerome's collection five books that Jerome thought uncanonical, called by Roman Catholics Deuterocanonica, substituted a version of Jerome's translation of Psalms that Jerome had specifically rejected, and used in the New Testament "Acts, Epistles, and Revelation, according to the Old Latin, but whether revised, and by whom, is uncertain."[16]

As close a translation of original manuscripts as was possible for the time, the integrity of Jerome's translation would be seriously eroded by the passage of the centuries. Copying of the Vulgate was by hand; without rigorous, centralized authority to approve these copies, errors were necessarily introduced. These copies would in turn be copied by hand, introducing further errors, and at various points self-appointed scholars would even make insertions intended to reconcile contradictory aspects of the text, particularly in the Gospels, and these in turn would be copied by hand with compounding errors.

This would be of less import in modern times if there were a willingness by Christian authorities to issue retranslated versions of the Bible based on the most authoritative available material. Unfortunately, this has not necessarily been the case, particularly in Roman Catholicism. In the early sixteenth century, with the revival of European interest in Greek and Hebrew learning, several attempts were made to undo the centuries of deterioration in the Bible's integrity. Numerous new Latin translations of the Bible and emendations of the Vulgate based on comparison with original Hebrew manuscripts were made. The result was more confusing than ever, and prompted the holding of the Council of Trent, 1545–63, to take up the question of an authoritative version of Christianity's version of the word of God. Far from commanding what was required—the commissioning of a comprehensive scholarly effort to find the earliest possible sources and translate an entirely new Bible—those assembled at Trent merely decreed that the Vulgate had superior status to all the new Latin translations. The council took no position on the standing of the Vulgate relative to the Hebrew and Greek original manuscripts, and resolved only to determine the most authoritative Vulgate. Even this was finally never accomplished.

After several abortive projects an expert commission appointed in 1586 by Pope Sixtus V (r. 1585–90) prepared in two years an excellent text, based on the best surviving Vulgate manuscript, the *Codex Amiatinus*, which represents the text tradition stemming from Cassiodorus. Unfortunately, Sixtus, disturbed at the quantity of matter thus omitted from the text then familiar in the church, insisted on editing the work himself and largely nullified the commission's labors by restoring many of the old interpolations and corrupt readings.[17]

The result was so dissatisfying that ten days after Sixtus died the cardinals withdrew the new version from circulation. Another, called the Sixto-Clementine, was soon issued, but it was only a partial return to the original produced by the expert commission. Nonetheless, this Vulgate is the version that remains the official Catholic Bible to the present day.

Augustine's backing of Jerome's translation made possible a Bible that was several degrees less false than it would have been without his help, but his impact on Christian theology is far greater than that. Theology in Christianity has only the most distant relation to Scripture. Augustine's influence was enormous, altering Christian psychology in at least two major ways. First, to forget the collapse of Rome and the problems of living, Augustine focused Christian attention on an afterlife. Second, although the early Christians were led to expect the Second Coming of Christ as imminent, it now became clear that it was not so near as they had been taught to believe. The faithful were accordingly admonished to imitate the divine by creating the City of God on earth.

Augustine's bifurcation of reality gave strength and solace to Christians experiencing political, financial and spiritual difficulties, for it gave them cause to hope in another life, "not of this world," as Rome was crumbling. It also crystallized the notion that the eternal battle between good and evil was being played out on earth, and that Christians would eventually play a military role in that battle.

It was an ideology admirably suited to the unalloyed Christian rule soon to come. The social problems apparent during such rule could be dismissed as relatively unimportant, given the glory of the afterlife for the right-thinking; the victims of a Christian ruling class could be more easily dominated in a theological schema where they would receive their reward in heaven.

At the same time Augustine's ideology prepared the masses for military service of lord and state on behalf of God. It would be difficult to conjure up a more prestigious and inspiring commanding general. Yahweh's military visage had reappeared, although as yet just in outline, but this time it was not merely for the purpose of seizing a very specific, few thousand square miles of land. God was now outfitted for the salvation of the entire world. His first vehicle would be constructed by the church out of the ruins of Rome. A Christian theology useful in the justification of imperial aims was taking shape. The military legions of the Roman Empire would have a moral rationalization for acting on political ambition; they would become soldiers of Christ. Apparently without embarrassment, this divine partnership would come to call itself the "Holy Roman Empire."

Despite the sacking of Rome, the fall of the empire was no immediate thing and not completed in the Eastern Empire. Roman civilization was so old and had been so powerful that it could bargain even when defenseless before an invader. There remained for much of a century a Western central authority which could direct Roman armies here and there. The fifth century as a whole marked the end of the Roman Empire, but also the beginning of nationhood for England, with the invasion of the Teutonic Saxons; the makings of France, carved out of Roman Gaul by invading Germans called Franks; the conversion of Ireland to Christianity by Britain's Patrick; the emergence of little kingdoms in Germany to replace the empire there; and the advance of Attila the Hun, a visitor from Asia, into Europe with his Mongol hordes. Precious little philosophy was developed during this period, but several theological controversies did arise, contributing to fifth-century life several dollops more of destruction and cruelty.

Attila the Hun pushed southwest the Goths of central Europe, relieving the pressure on the Eastern Roman Empire; the Goths accordingly attacked the Western Roman Empire by invading Italy. In previous periods the unskilled soldiers of these barbarian forces would have been no match for Roman soldiers, but since the reign of Diocletian (284–305) many of the Goths were trained as Roman mercenaries. They had learned well. The Goths sacked Rome in 410 under the leadership of Alaric, who died the same year. In 476, the Ostrogoths of southern Russia under King Odovaker completed the destruction of the Western Roman Empire, ruling until 526.

The final dissolution of Rome had not come without a fight. Frustrated in an invasion of Gaul by an unlikely alliance of Romans and Goths, in 451 Attila turned his attention to Italy. It is doubtful that the legions of Rome could have stopped him. Although lacking in much military strength of his own, Pope Leo was able to save the day. Recognizing that Catholic theology would not deter Attila, effective though it might be against other Christians, he invoked pagan superstition and hastened to remind Attila that Alaric had died shortly after sacking Rome. The same fate would befall Attila, Leo told him, if he transgressed the inviolability of the Seat of the Church. Attila apparently paused for a year to reflect upon this possibility, and while pausing, died. The Huns dispersed. Had Leo's bluff not met with success, Attila would have sacked Rome, and, in his fashion, probably have destroyed the libraries and seats of learning, preventing Christianity and the pope from filling the political vacuum that had become the empire. Attila's retreat enabled Christianity to seize political control of Europe and to shape European life and destiny for more than a thousand years. From that day on, separation of church and state in Europe (and its colonies) would be an abstraction never put into political practice, at least not voluntarily.

During the period between the fifth and ninth centuries, the powers of Europe would fight sixteen major groups of wars. This averages out to one every twenty-five years. The various smaller wars and battles are too many to mention, including the internecine conflicts that were fought between popes, emperors and various nobles. While these military adventures were confusing the political boundaries of Europe, the Christian theologians undertook to confuse the boundaries of sanity by entering into a theological controversy on the subject of the Incarnation.

Nestorius, patriarch of Constantinople, maintained that there were two persons in Christ, one human and one divine, and that the Blessed Virgin was only the mother of the human person. She could not justifiably be called "the Mother of God," as some people were starting to do. Cyril, patriarch of Alexandria from 412 to 444, held the opposite view, asserting that there was only one person in Christ, and the Blessed Virgin was the "Mother of God." The controversy generated great passion and anger, threatening to jeopardize the stability of the Eastern and Western halves of the Christian world.

Cyril was traditionally on the side of unity at any cost, in theology as well as in politics. Compromise, however, was not his method of achieving it, as evidenced by his initiation of pogroms against the Jews of Alexandria, and by his purging of the city's thinkers whose views were contrary to the church as he saw it. One notorious example cited by Gibbon was the cruel torture of Hypatia, a well-known Alexandrian woman who studied mathematics and taught the philosophy of Aristotle and Plato. Cyril viewed her teachings and popularity with distaste and concern. According to Gibbon she was "torn from her chariot, stripped naked, dragged to the Church, and inhumanly butchered by the hands of Peter the Reader and a troop of savage and merciless fanatics: her flesh was scraped from her bones with sharp oyster-shells, and her quivering limbs were delivered to the flames."[18] As Russell wryly observes, "After this Alexandria was no longer troubled by philosophers."[19] Nonetheless, Cyril's life eventually recommended itself to the church fathers, and the kindly fellow was duly canonized. To this day Christians seek Cyril's guidance in prayer.

To decide the controversy over the personage(s) of Christ and the corollary concern of Mary's biological role in Christian theology, Emperor

Theodosius called a council in 431 at Ephesus, in western Asia Minor, a city with a history of venerating female deities. The people of Ephesus had come to adopt the Virgin as their own local object of veneration, substituting her for the Greek goddess Artemis, the daughter of Zeus, who was also a virgin; Ephesus had been an important center of her cult. Having rejoiced in the idea that their new virgin was the Mother of God, the citizens of Ephesus did not want her to lose status by demotion to motherhood of only his human person.

It was the development of just such cults that some church figures wished to hinder, while at the same time, it seems, finding a way to channel into the Christian fold the pagan followers of other cults of female deities. Since most of the Eastern bishops favored Nestorius, Cyril and the Western bishops arrived early and locked the doors to those who did not arrive on time. Cyril presided over the group assembled and of course the issue was decided in his favor. Nestorius was condemned as a heretic but the excluded Eastern bishops held their own council and excommunicated Cyril. Nonetheless, by 433 support for Nestorius had eroded and he was deposed. In the words of Gibbon, "This episcopal tumult, at the distance of thirteen centuries, assumes the venerable aspect of the Third Ecumenical Council."[20]

Cyril's code of conduct was evidently compatible with Christian philosophy, since it resulted in one of the dogmas of the Catholic church, that there is only one person in Christ. Nestorius and his followers maintained their beliefs, however, which spread throughout Syria and to Christian communities in India and China. Later attempts by the Catholic church to eradicate Syrian Nestorians weakened both parties, inadvertently assisting Islam in its conquest of Syria two centuries later.

However, the issue at Ephesus may have had more to do with Mary than with Christ. The Council of Ephesus both defined Christ's nature and elevated Mary's role in his birth. Mary was rapidly being referred to as *Theotokos*, "Mother of God," rather than *Anthropotokos*, "Mother of the man," or *Christokos*, "Mother of Christ." Nestorius objected to the term *Theotokos* on the grounds that it was illogical to suggest that Mary, a creation of God, could be the mother of the Creator. This position is eminently reasonable, but reason was not the determining power of the discussion. At the Council of Ephesus the church decided in favor of Mary's divinity as "a response to the fact that Mary was a figure who appealed to a large segment of the Church's new constituency."[21]

In pre-Christian times, the motif of a virgin made pregnant by a god was not unusual. Indeed, Romulus himself, the mythical founder of the city of Rome, and his twin brother, Remus, were supposedly born to a mortal virgin impregnated by Mars. In the second century, Justin Martyr discussed the divine birth of Perseus from the virgin Danae.[22] A virgin cult would find a receptive audience in the Roman Empire. Indeed, in the fourth century an aberrant but growing dedication to chastity was spreading along with the cult of Cybele, the most important mother goddess in the Roman pantheon and often called the "mother of the gods."[23] Perhaps to compete for her converts, the church began to reconstruct Mary's virginity. It was not an easy period for theologians.

Beginning in the third century, Cybele's attributes became more and more anti-sexual, until at some point she was deemed a virgin by many of her believers. The various female deities, Ceres (originally Eleusinian), Minerva (Athenian), Venus (Cyprian) and Diana (Cretan), all had much in common. One could merely add the Virgin Mary to the list: "All these goddesses are in some sense the same goddess," says Michael P. Carroll in *The Cult of the Virgin Mary.*[24]

Cybele, however, was the principal mother deity of the Roman Empire, and her qualities were fashioned by and for Rome's poorest citizen class, the *proletarius*, whose members were the recipients of the pacifying "bread and circuses" and whose only social functions were to procreate and, by the third century, to be used as imperial cannon fodder. As a result of its social condition, according to Carroll, this class was characterized by a "father-ineffective family" seeking a female deity with virginal qualities.[25]

The priests of this cult were called *galli*, and they developed an increasingly anti-sexual sentiment, possibly in psychological reaction to the perceived role of their class as useful only for procreation. Their fervor in this respect led the *galli* to go beyond venerating Cybele as virginal; to please her, they abstained from sex and quickly developed the practice of an ultimate tribute to her—self-castration, which was ritually carried out each March 24, called *dies sanguinis*, "the day of blood." On this day new *galli* were initiated and already-castrated devotees would flagellate their limbs, perhaps because they were penis-like, by means of a scourge studded with knuckle bones.[26]

In this ambience of the fourth century the cult of Mary began to develop. The church had already learned from Constantine that efforts to achieve religious unity could usefully adapt pagan rituals to facilitate conversion. The degree to which this may have influenced the development of the cult of the Virgin Mary is not reliably known; however, "many churches dedicated to Mary were erected on the ruins of temples devoted to Cybele, and . . . there is an obvious similarity between the title 'great mother of the gods' and the title 'mother of God.' "[27] It is also impossible to know the influence of the cult's self-castration practices on the Christian church. The serious practice of celibacy by Christian clergy is known to have come into official being during this period, however.[28] Occasional attempts at institutionalizing celibacy had been made by individual bishops, but "what is certain is that there were no formal regulations whatsoever requiring clerical celibacy in any region of the Western Church" until 300. In parallel with the rise of the cult of Cybele and its self-castrating priests, "the movement to impose celibacy upon the clergy began in earnest only toward the end of the fourth century." This was the time of the influx of the Roman *proletarius* into Christianity.[29]

It was not simply the cult of Mary which grew during this period, but also the preoccupation with her virginity. The male equivalent for her priests, celibacy, grew likewise, as it had in the cult of Cybele. Thus began Christianity's obsession with sex, which has permeated and influenced the creation of Christian dogma ever since, creating an educational system based on guilt-ridden sexual masochism and a social policy in resolute opposition to contraception—responsible every year for the needless birth of millions of children into starvation and physical abuse. Today's Christian *galli* are the moral arbiters of the sexual behavior of a fourth of the world's people.

Because the Council of Ephesus decided that Christ had one person, Mary was confirmed in her capacity as the "Mother of God." The Ephesians who venerated her had staved off a reduction in Mary's importance, and soon they dared the attempt to further entrench her status. Fortified by the victory over Nestorius, a synod of Ephesus tried to enhance Christ's theological unity by maintaining that he had only one "nature" as well, causing the followers of this view to be called "monophysites." In 451 Emperor Marcian called for yet another meeting, the Council of Chalcedon, to decide this further ambiguity: Christ was one person, but did he have two natures, one human and one divine? It was merely a restating of the previous dispute but Cyril was dead now and this time the Eastern bishops arrived on time. The Council of Chalcedon decided that Christ exists "in two natures," one human and one divine, while at the same time ratifying the previous decision that Christ was only one "person"—divine. With this reasoning, the possibilities for expense-paid trips all over the world were now endless; councils could perhaps be convened to determine the human or divine "will," "psyche," and "intellect" of Christ.

Central to the decisions of Chalcedon was the influence of Pope Leo the Great, whose *Tome of Leo,* a collection of essays, laid out the orthodox position regarding the two natures of Christ. Leo's book was approved in its entirety, making his discussions of Mary the official position of the church. Leo supported not only Mary's *in partu* virginity, that is, her purity at the time of Christ's birth, but also her perpetual virginity. Unfortunately, the latter conflicts with the Bible. In Matthew 1:25 it is recorded that, "[Joseph] knew her not until she had borne a son; and he called his name

Jesus." This is a definitive statement that Mary had sexual relations with Joseph after the birth of Jesus. The Bible also refers to Christ's resultant siblings; Paul claims in Galatians to have met a brother of Jesus named James, and in Luke 8 Jesus' "mother and his brothers" are recorded as having come to see him near Galilee, but having been blocked by crowds. "Roman Catholics, because of the doctrine of the perpetual virginity of Mary, are obliged to hold that the brothers and sisters of Jesus were the children of Joseph by a former wife. The Gospels give no warrant for the teaching."[30]

As if the theological minutiae of Marian virginity were not complicated enough, the church also had to reconcile Mary's nature with Paul's concept of original sin. A tainted woman certainly couldn't have given birth to God. Already overworked, theologians had to go back to the boudoir to search for more hidden doctrines. It must have come to one of them in the middle of the night: an Immaculate Conception! Mary was in a state of grace when God conceived Jesus in her, of course. But surely for this to be possible Mary must also have been *born* in the state of grace. Yes, yes, that was it! God had plans for Mary. It was a good thing that the idea of grace itself had been conceived by this time (by Augustine, barely a half century before). No support for the concept of the Immaculate Conception can be found in the whole of the Scriptures, however, even in the New Testament written by the early Christians. "There is virtually no warrant for it in the Bible, and the passages sometimes cited in support (Genesis 3:15, Luke 1:28, 30-31) have to be stretched to carry the meaning," declares Rev. Charles Sheedy, a prominent Catholic theologian.[31] "Stretching the meaning" of biblical text is a mild description of this fraud. Genesis 3:15, recording a speech by God to Satan, states, "I will put enmities between thee and the woman, and thy seed and her seed: she shall crush thy head and thou shalt lie in wait for her heel." It took a long time to massage the passage into an enunciation of the Immaculate Conception. This tortured derivative of the doctrine of original sin did not become official Catholic dogma—it is rejected by most Protestant faiths—until 1854. Despite the centuries of theological exertions, in the end the whole of this prodigious study of Mary's nature was perhaps superfluous. Since the lives of Adam and Eve, according even to many Catholic theologians, are now largely regarded as metaphorical, Mary was not the only person conceived without original sin. She numbers as merely one among all of humanity.

With the rise of the Reformation in the sixteenth century, the Protestants would take the easy way out and simply repudiate most of the beliefs and doctrines surrounding Mary. The Catholics of course would embellish Marian legend to its present cult status, endorsing even in our own century the legitimacy of paranormal events such as the claimed weeping of statues of Mary everywhere, and the appearance of apparitions at one such statue in Fatima, Portugal. It has become impossible for any reasonable person to accept the doctrines about Mary as other than badly contrived, but, having based so much of its creed on Mary, Rome cannot afford to abandon her. By now, most Catholic theologians are celibate and unable to divorce the supposed virgin whom their celibacy honors.

Over the centuries the benefits to the church of the cult of the Virgin Mary have been manifold. Many of the devotees of Cybele did became converts to Christianity. The cult's successful promotion of sexual repression has enabled Christianity to imprison the minds and emotions of its adherents by focusing their attention on sexual conduct to such a degree that Christian morality is generally regarded as primarily sexual morality. This allowed Christian theologians and the ecclesiastical superiors for whom they labored to carve the excesses of the powerful out of the domain of Christian morality. The imbalance has been addressed in recent years, but the anti-sexual legacy of this unfortunate expedience haunts the Catholic world.

The cult of the Virgin Mary has also long provided the Roman church untold revenue through donations made on her behalf to the myriad of churches named after her, and through the sale of Blessed Virgin literature, prayer books, holy cards and souvenirs. The rank commercialization of Elvis doesn't even compare in profitability. The largest of Mary's shrines is in Lourdes, France, and it is the most popular holy place in the world. Incredibly enough, the shrine at Lourdes attracts more people annually than the entire cities of Mecca, Jerusalem, even Rome! By 1986, over five million people a year were visiting Lourdes, mostly the poor, the sick, and the maimed, and their families. These people spend their savings on a superstition, fully endorsed by the Catholic church. The massive inflow of money from the ever-hopeful in search of a miracle supports four hundred hotels, several hundred restaurants, and over seven hundred souvenir shops. The church stages a religious ceremony in an enormous sanctuary each evening, and more than forty thousand people participate in a candle-light procession through the streets, all the while proffering donations.[32] These vigils are only held from April to October, however; the ski season must get underway. Besides, the mother of Christ does not perform miracles in the cold. She is, after all, Palestinian. It is of no matter to the businesses of Lourdes; skiers may be fewer in number, but their pockets are deeper than those of the sufferers from religious hope.

Christianity's ecclesiastical authorities are able to command such devotion to figures such as Mary because they have long instilled a primitive fear of God in the minds and hearts of their congregations. Despite the "good news" of the Gospels and the hopes thereby engendered, sermons on eternal hellfire have long been constant reminders that fear should be the predominant attitude towards God. The regular torture and murder of heretics helped give credence to the notion that one did not have only eternity to fear; God's representatives in this world were perfectly able to impose hell on earth.

In the face of a tempting world and a potentially awful hereafter, to whom could one take one's problems? The place of the individual believer in the Christian scheme was small but very heavily weighted, and only a little unburdened by the nature of Christianity's major figures, the Father, the Son, the Holy Ghost, and Mary. Though conceived in the context of love, Christianity's revered tetrarchy was nonetheless not really that approachable. God the Father retained the image of severity that had come down from the Judaic vision of Yahweh. The Holy Ghost was abstract, difficult for uneducated people to relate to and impossible to identify with or seriously emulate. Jesus and Mary were both figures of kindness, but in the first case, as Durant says, "He too was God, and one hardly ventured to speak to Him face to face after so thoroughly ignoring His Beatitudes,"[33] and the second was so untouchable a figure of virtue, had had so much of her humanity drained from her persona, that personal entreaties to her were often felt best left to utterances of a ritual nature.

Born of Christianity's twin urges to honor its pioneers and absorb rival pagan deities, the pantheon of Christian saints came to serve as the average person's intermediary with the divine. A saint sat in heaven, but he or she had usually been a very real person, sometimes within at least family memory, and was a figure one could treat as a guardian. For divine creatures, saints could also be reassuringly mundane, concerned primarily with common aspects of daily life that were nonetheless important to existence or the pursuit of happiness. "All the poetic and popular polytheism of antiquity rose from the never dead past, and filled Christian worship with a heartening communion of spirits," so much so that "every nation, city, abbey, church, craft, soul and crisis of life had its patron saint as in pagan Rome it had had a god."[34] St. Bartholomew, who had been flayed alive, logically became the saint of tanners; St. Blaise, who had allegedly helped a choking boy, was the patron saint of sore throats; St. Gall looked after chickens; St. Anthony was the guardian of pigs and the finder of lost objects. For every crisis or ailment there was a friend in the sky. By the tenth century, more than twenty-five thousand saints had been canonized.[35]

The competition was thus intense to obtain the surest sign of a saint's importance—a designated day on the calendar. To add veracity to the existence and influence of one's patron saint, competing clergy and laity often discovered relics—bones, hair, clothing, and anything which the saints might have touched while inhabitants of the planet earth. Exeter Cathedral boasted possession of parts of the burning bush from which God was said to have spoken to Moses. The Cathedral of Amiens enshrined the head of St. John the Baptist in a silver cup, though several other churches also claimed to possess it; perhaps St. John had had the powers of Hydra. It was claimed that interred in the Basilica of St. Peter were the bodies of both Peter and Paul. Each of three churches in France professed to have the complete corpse of Mary Magdalene. The abbey of St. Denis claimed to house Christ's crown of thorns. So many churches claimed to have pieces of the True Cross that, together, the alleged relics made up a lumber-yard. Churches in Constantinople claimed to have the lance that pierced Christ on the cross, the rod that scourged him, and pieces of his corpse, including hairs from his beard. Not to be outdone in the contest of reposi-tory prestige, five churches in France vowed that they had the apex of holy collectibles: pieces of the tip of Christ's penis from his circumcision![36]

Possession of such relics enhanced the sanctity of the churches con-cerned and could generate visits by the thousands and donations practically without limit. In 1220, when the bones of Thomas a Becket were trans-ferred to the cathedral at Canterbury, the worshippers in attendance con-tributed sums of money which today would come to more than $300,000.[37] Relics came to provide such substantial commercial revenues and religious prestige that abuse was only natural, culminating in the wide practice of "dismemberment of dead saints so that several places might enjoy their patronage and power."[38] During the centuries of the Inquisition, this prac-tice was followed in reverse for heretics. Their graves were opened and the bodies removed, mutilated, and set afire, so that the corpses would burn like the damned souls they allegedly had harbored.

The number of saints declined with illiteracy and by the nineteenth century the process of canonization was strictly defined. A number of beloved saints were lost along the way, some because they had never actually lived (Christopher, the saint of travellers, was merely a meta-phorical figure for those said to have helped Christ carry the cross to Calvary), others because their devotees lost interest in them.

But Christianity's reverence for saints remains strong, as the millions of prayers made to them daily amply demonstrate. The phenomenon is a subtle acknowledgment by many Christians that they do not really trust in the justice, compassion, or mercy of their god.

Constantine had put Christianity on the right hand of the emperor and accelerated the centralization of its hierarchy, positioning the church to use its state status to best advantage when the emperor was gone. Paul had given Christianity its theological thrust and Augustine fleshed it out and confirmed it for history. And while Paul had fitted Christianity to the

Procrustean bed of its evangelizing mission, Constantine had given the church an acceptance of fashioning custom eclectically that would allow it to succeed in that mission all over Europe and eventually the world.

With such strengths, the Christian church was able to weather the dissolution of the mightiest empire known to its time.

These two halves of god, the pope and the emperor.

—Victor Hugo

How do you dare, Bishop who holds the place of the Apostle, school your people in War.

—Erasmus

III

Papacy—Depravity

P ope Gregory I, Gregory the Great, one of only three popes in history to acquire the title "Great," was sixty-fourth in the line dating back to the Apostle Peter. He is perhaps the most important pope in history. In fourteen years as pope (626–40) Gregory came to grips with a startling fact: the church was the only unifying authority in Europe. The Eastern Roman Empire had become thoroughly Greek in character (Constantinople was renamed Byzantium, after its former Greek name, in 629), and though desirous of reconquering the Western empire (it held most of Italy, but was losing its toehold on Spain), Byzantium was unable to accomplish such a difficult task.

At thirty Gregory was governor of Rome, at thirty-four he became a monk, at thirty-nine a papal envoy to the emperor of Constantinople, and at fifty he assumed the papacy. Rushing to fill the cultural and moral vacuum created by the breakup of the Roman Empire, Gregory determined the attitudes, theology, piety, music, moral practices and philosophical disposition of the West lasting down to the present day. When Gregory died, the Western world would be completely overrun by armed hordes of "barbarians," Vandals, Goths, Lombards and Franks in the millions plundering Europe and its treasures and finally bringing down what had been in the offing for two centuries, the Dark Ages. But a structure had been set up by Gregory to weather the times of chaos to come. Nine or ten centuries later Europe would finally absorb its occupiers and burst into the light of the Renaissance. The church was able to preserve the heritage of Roman and Greek culture that would be the basis for the revival of Western civilization. It was Gregory who gave the church the power to do so.

Two factors influenced the development of the church's political power and the accompanying spread of Christianity to the whole of Europe: the emergence of monasteries, and the growth of the papacy as one of the most powerful forces in Western history.

Sometime around 320 an Egyptian named Pachomius founded the first monastery. People had long been hermits, the most notable another Egyptian, Anthony, best known for enduring years of lustful visions in the desert without committing sin. A monastery was a gathering of such hermits. Women accounted for enough hermits to eventually organize into convents of nuns. There seems to be no description of what lustful temptations, if any, these women experienced, but history was generally written by men. The monks in Pachomius's monastery lived without private property and shared common meals, shelter, prayers and religious observances. They engaged in agriculture and other work with the hands, deemed a way to avoid obsessive preoccupation with the temptations of the flesh.

The monasteries were first well organized by Basil in the mid–fourth century and developed as spontaneous movements outside of the organization or control of the church. But Athanasius, who introduced the monastic concept to the West around 339, also took steps to ecclesiasticize monasticism by promoting the idea (eventually the rule) that monks should be priests. Jerome promoted this way of life and personally practiced an asceticism common to early monasticism—contemplation of sin, particularly the sins of the flesh, long periods spent praying and fasting, and the reading of only Christian materials. In a moment of temptation Jerome had brought his diverse library with him into the desert, but eventually decided it was sinful to read pagan books. The discipline and regimentation of monasticism was apparently quite appealing, perhaps simply because it offered a strict ordering of life and thought. In the dark times to come, the monasteries would be repositories of classical literature and centers of learning, particularly of history. With time they would establish a tradition of social service, which included hospitality, care of the poor, and the establishment of monastic schools.

Probably the most important person in Western monasticism is Benedict. Born of a noble family, he went to a cave at the age of twenty, leaving behind him the pleasures of Rome. After three years in the solitude of the cave, around 520, he founded a monastery at Monte Cassius. Benedict imposed limits on ascetic practices in order to improve the monks' poor physical and mental health, caused by competitions in ascetic fervor. Disease and hallucination were rife in the monasteries. Some monks believed that cleanliness was sinful, that lice were "the pearls of God." Candidates for sainthood boasted that except for crossing rivers, water would never even touch their feet, let alone higher parts of the anatomy. It would be many centuries before the aphorism "cleanliness is next to godliness" held sway; during this period, "dirt was divine."

Socialist in many senses, monasteries were nonetheless quite dictatorial. An abbot was in full authority over the lives of the monks, having even the power to prevent them from leaving the monastery. All monks vowed poverty, chastity, and obedience and the all-powerful abbot enforced these vows. This did not necessarily mean the abbot was party to them. Gibbon comments that, "I have somewhere heard or read the frank confession of a Benedictine abbot: 'My vow of poverty has given me a hundred thousand crowns a year; my vow of obedience has raised me to the rank of a sovereign price.' I forget the consequence of his vow of chastity."[1]

Benedict lived in the monastery he founded until his death in 543. Later the monastery was sacked by the Lombards, and the monks fled for a while to Rome but were able to return. Most of what history knows of Benedict was written by one of his monks. We are told that Benedict was twice nearly poisoned by monks jealous of his piety or annoyed by his rules; that Benedict worked various minor miracles, such as repairing a broken sieve, mending a broken tool, and breaking (with his Benedictal blessing) a glass containing poisoned wine given him by another priest; and that Benedict was frequently tempted by women and plagued by the thought of them, and on one occasion threw himself into a briar patch naked so that the pain and damage to his body would overcome his lustful thoughts. Benedict's biographer was the young man who become Pope Gregory the Great.

Gregory was born in 540 to a wealthy senatorial family in Rome. Highly educated, well traveled and generous, he rose by the age of thirty to the highest civil office in Rome, *praefectus urbis,* director of the city, and gave his riches for the establishment of monasteries and to charity, finally leaving public life to become a Benedictine monk himself. Initially he was inclined to subscribe to a fiercely ascetic life, which would in later years prove to have damaged his health irreparably. After eight years Gregory accepted a commission from Pope Pelagius II as one of seven deacons of Rome and in 579 was sent as Rome's envoy to the Byzantine court which tenuously ruled Italy.

Up to Gregory's time, the pope was *primus inter pares* ("first among equals") as bishop of Rome; yet despite nominal recognition that it was the seat of the church, Rome was not able to dictate to other centers of Christian power. This would change with Gregory's ascension to the papal throne, though he apparently did maintain a belief that the papacy was not superior to the patriarchate.[2] Through charm, manipulation, cleverness, erudition and his *Book of Pastoral Rule* Gregory was able to draw to himself authority over fellow bishops and secular rulers alike. "He became the founder of the worldly power of the papacy in Italy, and thereby gradually the secular ruler of the city of Rome."[3] By blessing and admonishing, cajoling and threatening, Gregory gradually arrested the practice of promoting priests and church officials through bribes and in general slowed the corruption of ecclesiastical affairs. He also sought to limit secular education, believing that pagan learning was harmful to morality since "the praises of Christ cannot find room in one mouth with the praises of Jupiter."

Despite a devotion to piety in his youth, Gregory's sense of morality did not extend to affairs of state. When a Roman centurion and Christian named Phocas deposed Byzantium's Emperor Maurice, killing the poor man only after slaughtering his five sons before his eyes, Gregory wrote to Phocas, "May Almighty God in every thought and deed keep the heart of your Piety [i.e., you] in the hand of His grace; and whatever things should be done justly, whatsoever things with clemency, may the Holy Spirit who dwells in your breast direct."[4] Gregory dealt with more abstract questions of piety as well, however, including a troublesome matter originally brought up by Augustine: should spouses who have had intercourse the previous night be allowed to come to church? Gregory decreed that they should, if they have washed themselves. He did not go into details.

Gregory's legacy of amassing the first concentration of secular papal power is due in large measure to his skillful use of the vast amounts of real estate owned by the church. He organized these scattered parcels of land into a vast business empire, "replacing a corrupt civil administration with devoted clergy, and keeping strict control over the entire business operation." Soon "the entire population of central Italy looked increasingly toward him to supply their needs, and their plea strengthened his hand."[5] It was *de facto* secular power. "Though never challenging openly the [Byzantine] imperial rights, he finally bypassed . . . the imperial representative in the West . . . negotiating separate agreements with the Lombards, who stood twice at the gates of Rome during those years."[6] The road was taken. Church history would become one of business and secular rule.

The Dark Ages is a term used by Western historians to refer to the period between 600 and 1000, during which time there was a dearth of intellectual, artistic, and cultural development. It should be remembered that the term refers only to Europe, since other cultures such as those of China and Japan were not suffering stagnation. Furthermore, the territories under the control of Islam were flourishing with astonishing centers of art and learning that for a while were the most lively and advanced on earth.

The Dark Ages of Europe were highlighted by at least three central church developments: the growth of the power of the papacy in ecclesiastical and political affairs, achieved by further accumulation of real estate through fraud, deception, extortion and murder; the nearly complete moral decay of the church, despite the labors of Gregory; and the split between the eastern and western halves of the church, which lasts to the present day.

During this period the church devoted a great deal of attention to its relationship to the state. The Eastern church was largely subservient to the Byzantine emperor, who deemed himself authorized by God to decide matters of faith as well as to appoint and depose priests, bishops and patriarchs alike. The Eastern patriarchs tolerated this, although in any case they had little choice, in large part because they preferred it to domination by papal authority. In the West relationships were less clear. Power swung between pope and emperor in direct ratio to the relative need each had for the other at any given time, likewise between pope and more local secular power. Italian monarchs were often desirous of papal legitimization in their struggles with rivals. For this the popes often received land and stakes in commercial ventures. With the accrual of material wealth far and wide, the popes in turn frequently had need of secular power to defend these assets. "During the four centuries from Gregory the Great to Sylvester II, the papacy underwent astonishing vicissitudes. It was subject, at times, to the Greek emperor, at other times to the Western emperor, and at yet other times to the local Roman aristocracy; nevertheless, vigorous popes in the eighth and ninth centuries built up the tradition of papal power."[7]

In the seventh century the military power of the Byzantine emperor protected the popes from the incursions of the Lombards, threatening from just north of Italy; from 685 to 752 most of the popes were Greek or Syrian. In 751 the Lombards seized Ravenna, in north Italy, the seat of Byzantine power in the West. It was not all bad news for the papacy since "this event, while it exposed the popes to great danger from the Lombards, freed them from all dependence on the Greek emperors."[8]

New alliances could be fashioned. For two decades the popes had turned to the Franks for aid against the Lombards, and the Frankish leader, Charles "the Hammer" Martel, had defeated the Moors at the Battle of Tours, thereby saving France for Christianity. By 754 circumstances permitted the firmest alliance of papacy and Frank to date. A man named Pepin had come to power among the Franks, but his monarchy was illegitimate. He wished papal sanction to cement his rule and in return promised to secure Italy for the church and officially grant the conquered lands to the papacy. "The Lombards did not submit tamely to Pepin and the Pope, but in repeated wars with the Franks they were worsted."[9] The bargain was fully consummated in 774, when Pepin's son, Charlemagne, marched into Italy, routed the Lombards completely, had himself recognized as their king and confirmed the church's agreement with Pepin. The territory concerned covered approximately sixteen thousand square miles and supported a population of nearly three million people.

Acceptance by the church of temporal rule over this land was fateful. Although many a devotee had made substantial donations to the church and its leaders, the grant of Pepin, eventually called the Papal States and not ineradicably separated from the church until the late nineteenth century, immersed the church body and soul into the secular world. Political concerns henceforth would always matter more than spiritual ones. The significance of the bequest included more than its riches and the security it offered Rome. Much of the land had only a few years before been under the control of Byzantium, and since "it could not be expected that Constantinople would recognize such a gift, this involved a political severance from the Eastern Empire."[10] A religious separation would not be terribly long in coming.

It was sometime in this period that the "Donation of Constantine" (not claimed by a pope until 1054) was forged. Perhaps in an effort to confer an air of legality on its new-found control of Italy, someone created a document which purported to be Constantine's personal grant, after his move to Constantinople, of the "old Rome" and all its territories to the bishop of Rome. "Constantine" declares his reason to be gratitude for Pope Sylvester I's curing of his leprosy, and further notes that he was baptized in the process. The forgery was accepted as genuine, even by the enemies of the papacy, until 1439, when a Latin linguist named Lorenzo Valla revealed that it was undeniably a fraud.

The church's relationship with Byzantium was a dead letter even in practical terms by the end of the eighth century, and the time was ripe for the establishment of a new empire of the Christian faith. The assumption of secular power over the city of Rome in the centuries since the collapse of the Western Empire had set the standard by which future popes would act. The military successes of Charlemagne offered the opportunity for the church to paint on a much larger canvas. "The Popes of his time, Hadrian and Leo III, found it to their advantage to further his schemes in every way." Already king of the Franks and having declared himself king of Italy, Charlemagne "conquered most of Germany, converted the Saxons by vigorous persecution, and finally, in his own person, revived the Western Empire."[11] Charlemagne was crowned emperor by the pope in Rome on Christmas Day, 800, and the Holy Roman Empire was proclaimed.

It was a partnership in expansion. During this period Germany was converted, largely through the efforts of Boniface, an English missionary loyal to the pope but also a friend of Pepin and Charlemagne. Boniface founded a great number of monasteries in Germany before he was killed by heathens. Legend tells us that it was Boniface who transformed the pagan fertility celebration of fir trees into the Christmas tree ceremony we observe today. Monasteries proliferated in England as well, and were, in contrast to the church of Ireland, loyal almost exclusively to Rome.

When Charlemagne died, Pope Nicholas I (ruled 858–67) seized the opportunity to expand papal power to unprecedented heights. He used the church's authority of solemnizing and nullifying marriages to keep the kings in tow and to balance rival royal factions. He was able to prevail in the matter of making bishops formally concede that they owed their office to the pope. The authoritarian transformation of a church whose priestly officials once were elected by popular acclaim of the faithful was complete.

During the tenth century the Roman aristocracy controlled the papacy, and that aristocracy was controlled by women: Agiltruda of Spoleto, Theodora of Theophylact and Theodora's daughter Marozia, often called "the Nymph" and "the woman pope," although she never actually assumed the title.

Morality in the church reached new lows in this time, but that was perhaps the price paid for ever-greater entanglement in affairs of finance and state. By the end of the tenth century it would be inappropriate to associate the term "holiness" with the Roman church. An obsession for political and military power and the acceptance of murder and sexual depravity pervaded the clergy, particularly the upper hierarchy of bishops and popes.

Agiltruda, a Lombard, became enraged when Pope Formosus passed over her son Guido and crowned Arnulf of Germany Holy Roman emperor in February 896. She led an army against Rome and captured the city, but the newly appointed Emperor Arnulf came with his own armies, forcing her retreat. Agiltruda's anger only increased. Logs were thrown on the fire when Pope Formosus decided to march an army to her beloved city of Spoleto; he died of a stroke (some accounts have it that he was poisoned by Agiltruda) before commencing the attack.

The citizens of Rome, using both wisdom and weapons to guide their choice, then installed Boniface VI as the new pope; among his credentials for the papacy were twice having been defrocked for lewd behavior. Within two weeks Agiltruda assassinated him and managed to install her own candidate, who became Pope Stephen VII. His *vita* included a generally acknowledged insanity and a tendency to uncontrollable and violent rage.[12] Stephen VII, generally speaking, was well qualified for the job.

Pope Formosus' untimely death had not quieted Agiltruda's anger against him. On the contrary, her ire had been increased by the lost opportunity for revenge. Corporeal realities did not deter Agiltruda, however. She ordered Stephen to dig up Formosus' corpse and bring it to the Lateran Palace fully clothed in pontifical vestments. As the rotting remains sat propped up on the papal throne, Stephen and his cardinals conducted a ritual. They were trying the corpse for capital crimes. The accused is not recorded as having said much in its own defense, of course, but was noted to have given off an enormous stench, perhaps in silent comment on the proceedings. In Catholic history this sacred gathering is called *Synodus Cadaveris*, "the Corpse Synod."

The verdict was never in doubt. The pious prelates found the corpse guilty, tore off its vestments, ripped off the three fingers of the right hand with which the papal blessing is given, and dragged the corpse out of the building and through the streets of Rome. The shouts of the crowd and the throwing of mud and stones added to the sanctified air of this unusual mourning rite. Finally the corpse was thrown into the Tiber River. The theologians had triumphed over sinfulness.

In 897, Stephen himself was imprisoned and strangled, and Agiltruda installed another lackey as Pope Romanus—for four months—then removed him and put a third puppet into office as Pope Theodore II. This foolish man decided to act on his own; within twenty days he was deposed. While Agiltruda was shopping around for a successor, her only remaining heir, Lambert, died of gangrene contracted after a horse-riding accident. With no reason to go on, Agiltruda retired, perhaps believing she owed it to herself after the trials of an active Christian life.

Another woman, Theodora, rushed in to fill the spiritual vacuum. She belonged to the wealthy house of Theophylact and had long had plans; hadn't she taken her daughter, Marozia, to the Corpse Synod at age six? Now was the opening for an investment that would pay dividends for almost a century. First Theodora made one Pope Benedict IV, but he died in 903, only three years later. Next was Leo V, but he reigned only the month of July 903 and was imprisoned by one Cardinal Christopher, who thought he was better qualified to carry out God's work. A certain Cardinal Sergius also felt the divine calling, however. With the assistance of Theodora he imprisoned Christopher, assassinated both Christopher and Leo in prison, arranged the assassination of all the cardinals who opposed him, strangled his enemies at court and proclaimed himself Pope Sergius III.

Two years later, in 906, Sergius took as his mistress Theodora's daughter, Marozia, now grown to fifteen years of age. Sergius died after seven years as pope, in 911, a peaceful death as befits the innocent and holy. Theodora had to scout around for another pope, finally settling on a man who took the name Anastasius III. She felt compelled to arrange his death two years later, however, and installed a fellow named Lando, but his was only an interim papacy; Theodora needed time to think. Six months was all that was required. Lando was killed and by force of arms Theodora conferred the venerable and pious mantle of the papacy on her lover of many years, Bishop John of Ravenna. He took the name of John X, no doubt in pious memory of John IX, known for his corruption.

We now approach the era of Theodora's daughter, Marozia, the best known of the women pope-makers. In the ninety years of papal rule by the house of Theophylact, Marozia was its most accomplished agent. She was

> the mother of one pope, whom she conceived by another pope, and was the aunt of a third pope, the grandmother of a fourth pope, and with the help of her own mother, the creator of nine popes in eight years, of whom two had been strangled, one suffocated with a cushion and four deposed and disposed of in circumstances that have never come to public light.[13]

During the reign of John X, a Lombard prince named Alberic began to assert himself in Rome, threatening to upset the family plan for continued domination of the papacy. Now in her early twenties, Marozia was assigned by Theodora and John to keep Alberic happy. They married and had a son.

While satisfying Alberic sexually, Marozia was drawn into his political ambitions. Alberic attempted to seize Rome by force, failed, and John forced Marozia to view her husband's defiled corpse. To what extent Marozia was involved in her husband's machinations is not known, but despite John's effort to teach her not to diddle the legions of the Lord, Marozia seemed only to learn how better to play the papal game.

Marozia acted at the first opportunity. After Theodora died she married a man named Guido, who joined forces with the enemies of John, imprisoning and then suffocating the good pontiff. Marozia and her allies arranged for their own candidate to become Pope Leo VI. Like her mother, always firing the help, within seven months Marozia arranged for the disappearance of Leo and installed a man who took the name Pope Stephen VIII. He lasted until March 931, then mysteriously disappeared. After all, Marozia had a son by her first liaison, Pope Sergius III. The boy was more than qualified for the job: he had reached age sixteen; Marozia had been a year younger when she commenced her relations with Sergius. Yes, it was time to anoint a child as Pope John XI, the latest in a long line of distinguished Holy Fathers. It was a beautiful ceremony.

When Guido died, Marozia married King Hugo of Tuscany. The marriage ceremony was of course performed by her son, the pope. Marozia had plans for the entire family. "Her dream: she as queen-empress, Hugo as emperor of all the Romans, and her son, Alberic [by her first husband, Alberic], as the emperor to succeed Hugo."[14] Unfortunately, Marozia was dilatory in communicating her grand scheme to the young Alberic, who had felt left out in the cold. Alberic had his mother's ambitious blood, but her sense of family loyalty was somehow missing from his character. In 931 Alberic seized the city of Rome, ran King Hugo out of town and threw into prison both Marozia and Pope John XI, his half brother. Marozia would remain there the rest of her life.

Theodora was dead and Marozia was in prison, but the family dynasty that the papacy had become would go on. Alberic appointed as pope successively Leo VII, Stephen IX (imprisoned and mutilated after participating in a conspiracy against Alberic), Marinus II and finally Agapetus II. Nearing his death in 954, Alberic called a meeting in St. Peter's Basilica of all the Roman nobles and clergy. He wanted them to swear an oath on the head of Peter the Apostle that his illegitimate son Octavian (Marozia's grandson) would be appointed pope when Agapetus died—and that the papacy would thenceforth be a heredity dynasty!

The assembled church hierarchy agreed—surely it was a stroke of doctrinal genius! Agapetus died within a year and Octavian, aged fifteen, was consecrated pope in December 955. He chose the name of John XII, since his uncle, Marozia's son by Pope Sergius II, had been Pope John XI. "Octavian as Pope John XII was the absolute nadir . . . Surrounded by boys and girls of his own age and rank, he spent his days and nights eating sumptuously, playing at the tables, hunting, and in love affairs. The pope's palace was frequented by courtesans and prostitutes."[15] Presumably this did not interfere with the church's ongoing development of Christian moral teachings.

Temporal realities cut short this gay life. In 963 John concluded an agreement with King Otto of Germany acknowledging papal subordination to the Holy Roman monarchy. In return John received Otto's pledge to defend the church and its possessions, reaffirmation of the territorial agreements agreed to by Pepin and Charlemagne, and "significant additions which extended the papal state to about two-thirds of Italy."[16] The terms were good, but when Otto left Rome John began to intrigue against him. Otto returned to Rome enraged, prompting John to flee to Tivoli with the papal treasure. Otto convened a synod which deposed John and appointed one Pope Leo VIII.

Now the fun began. Otto left Rome to rejoin his army and his absence allowed John to return and triumphantly reestablish his authority. According to a contemporary document of church accusations against Marozia, John "evicted Leo VIII, cut off the nose and tongue and two fingers of the

Cardinal-Deacon, flayed the skin off Bishop Otger, cut off the hands of Notary Azzo, and beheaded sixty-three of Rome's clergy and nobility."[17] Given the ancient church principle that no earthly power can judge the Holy See, these were moderate measures for restoring the inviolable sanctity of the papal office.

Licentiousness reasserted its rightful residence in the Lateran Palace, but the celebration couldn't go on forever. Otto promptly marched on Rome and John fled once again, this time to Campagna. There the evils of John's life came to a head. According to the document of charges, "During the night of May 14, 964, while having illicit and filthy relations with a Roman matron, he was surprised in the act of sin by the matron's angry husband, who, in just wrath, smashed his skull with a hammer and thus liberated his evil soul into the grasp of Satan."[18]

In May 986, Marozia, still alive in prison after fifty-four years, was allowed to confess her sins. On the order of Holy Roman Emperor Otto III, she was then suffocated "for the well-being of the Holy Mother Church and the peace of the Roman people."[19] The papal house of Theophylact had come to an end.

This century of piety in Western Christendom did not go unnoticed in Byzantium. Never the primary impetus behind the forces of dispute between the Western and Eastern church and itself hardly a paragon of moral virtue, the Byzantine church was nonetheless seriously beginning to question the sanctity of its counterpart in Rome. At one time the Eastern clergy had felt the opposite—since it was not controlled in the long term by secular power, Rome perhaps had more theological legitimacy. It was impossible on its face to believe this in the tenth century.

Between 800 and 1000 the Eastern church grew increasingly distant from its Roman kin. To adopt the materialist analysis, the separation was probably caused by the rivalry between the empires to which each was attached. "While Rome flourished militarily and economically, Byzantium shrank territorially, barely survived militarily, and staggered economically."[20] The papacy's ties to the emperor had become stronger than to its Eastern mate, the patriarchate; the papacy was concerned with religious unity more for imperial advantage than for spiritual advance. The church of Rome, abetted by secular power, gradually extended its Roman rites into areas formerly under Eastern domination. Spiritual disputes became more antagonistic. As a partner rather than a servant of empire, it turned out, the Roman church was considerably more worldly than its Eastern counterpart. The nearly total disappearance of morality among the members of the Roman church hierarchy showed this clearly.

The relationship between the Eastern church, centered in Constantinople, and the Western church, centered in Rome, was always contentious. When Constantine built his new capital and centered Roman political power there, he brought much church power with him. Constantinople became the "New Rome." Western church leaders, particularly the pope (the bishop of Rome) sought to assure that the "old" Rome would not become moribund or second in importance.

With competing loci of secular power, it was perhaps inevitable that theological differences would begin to surface. Much church doctrine arose out of compromise struck between the differing theological views and political considerations of Constantinople and Rome; these disputes were settled by councils convened to define dogma, sometimes, it is true, under the influence of the polished instruments of treachery and force of arms, but the settlements were usually accepted nonetheless.

Some emperors, including Constantine, thought they were God's chosen leaders on earth in spiritual as well as political affairs. Accordingly they sought to maintain definitive influence over the appointment of pope or patriarch; very often they were successful. For their part, the popes and patriarchs believed they were God's appointed spiritual leaders on earth, and as such it was their obligation and right to choose the emperor, and at times they were able to do so, though this proved possible only in the West. Legally, no one in the West could be emperor unless crowned by the pope in Rome; nonetheless, for centuries every strong emperor claimed the right to appoint or depose popes and often did so. Add to this ever-boiling kettle of Western imperial and clerical rivalry the claims of the Roman populace and lower clergy, of Roman, Italian and French nobility, and of church officials outside the papal states: each group believed that it was entitled to choose the pope and each was sometimes able to do so.

Control of the Eastern church was not nearly so chaotic, primarily because it was never able to establish much independence from secular power. In general the patriarchs of the East remained under the complete domination of the Byzantine emperors. Although it had less influence in wordly affairs, the Eastern church at the same time was less subject to the corruption that accompanied such influence. It can be fairly said to have been more interested in religious affairs for their own sake and somewhat less concerned with the ramifications of doctrinal matters in the balance of power. Despite its pretensions to tradition, universality and consistency, the Roman Catholic Church has far less claim to purity of doctrine than the Eastern church.

It is thus no surprise that the weight of scholarly opinion places on Rome the primary blame for the Eastern Schism to come between East and West in the eleventh century. The split was officially over interpretation of doctrine, aspects of the Nicene creed, but the underlying tensions were purely secular, and more Rome- than Byzantium-driven. Rome was intent on extending its power as far as possible, and while expansion could not be said to have been of no interest to the Eastern church, it had less interest in gaining influence at the expense of its Siamese sibling. It preferred the pagan north for such enterprises.

The theological cover for Rome's religious imperialism was a dispute over a single word, the Latin term *filioque* in the Nicene Creed. Rome believed that the Holy Spirit proceeded from the Father and from the Son. In Latin, "and from the Son" is expressed in the word *filioque*. The Eastern church maintained that the Holy Spirit proceeded only from the Father, coming close to the Roman interpretation only by conceding that it came into being *through* the Son: in Greek *dia tou viou*. In general it was Rome that forced this issue. The original Nicene creed had no *filioque* clause; it was added for Spanish Christians at a synod (regional council) held in Toledo in 653, probably to combat heresy there, but insisted on by the Romans only much later, at the beginning of the eleventh century. The *filioque* clause was never approved by a church-wide council before the schism. Theology finally had little to do with the break. This was competition.

> The religious dispute between Rome and Constantinople was real enough, but its effective props were territorial and economic. Both churches were sending out waves of missionaries. By the end of the ninth century, Constantinople had converted the majority of Bulgars, Serbs, Moravians (inhabitants of modern Czechoslovakia), Albanians, many Poles and Romanians to Eastern Orthodoxy. Within another hundred years [by the end of the tenth century], there was a national Orthodox Church in these places tied politically and culturally and religiously to Constantinople. And, by then, too, Vladimir of Russia had converted and Greek missionaries started on the conversion of Russia's Slavs. The "New Rome," "the Second Rome," was expanding to the north and west even as it withered in its original heartland.[21]

In May 1003 Pope Sylvester II was murdered. His successor, John XVII, was poisoned within seven months and replaced by John XVIII. He died and was succeeded by Sergius IV (ruled 1009–12), who immediately sent "statutes of faith" to the patriarch of Constantinople for his unconditional acceptance. It was implicitly a demand for Eastern submission to papal authority. Sergius included the *filioque* clause despised by the Greeks. This was a slap in the face and the patriarch refused even to respond, sealing the counter-insult by also refusing to inscribe Sergius's name in the Diptychs, the official records of the Eastern church. "In the complicated protocol of the time, this was tantamount to declaring Sergius an imposter."[22] In 1014, Pope Benedict VIII used the *filioque* clause in the coronation ceremony of the German Henry II, reportedly at Henry's insistence. The Greeks walked out of the ceremony. When Benedict died, his brother had himself ordained priest, consecrated bishop and crowned Pope John XIX, all during a single twenty-four-hour period on June 24 and 25, 1024.

In 1003, John XIX died under questionable circumstances and his relatives proclaimed John's son, a lad probably in his twenties, Pope Benedict IX. It was quite a spectacle, a lay novice barely of age "issuing excommunications, giving his papal blessing, formulating decrees, consecrating bishops, deciding theological matters," but the fellow was further recommended for papal office by his affection for bisexuality, sex with animals and dabblings in witchcraft and Satanism.[23] (In the mid–nineteenth century the Catholic church would face the complex task of reconciling Benedict's colorful life—and that of dozens of popes like Benedict—with the pope's newly understood power to enunciate Catholic doctrine infallibly!)

Roman moral corruption spanned the range of the Ten Commandments. King, pope and cardinal sold bishoprics; bishops in turn sold whatever ecclesiastical preferments they could. Sylvester II (ruled 999–1003) represented one of them as saying,

> I gave gold and I received the episcopate; but yet I do not fear to receive it back if I behave as I should. I ordain a priest and I receive gold; I make a deacon and I receive a heap of silver. Behold the gold which I gave I have once more.[24]

The proceedings for the consecrations of bishops provides some insight into the depths to which official church morality had sunk. According to Byzantine documents of the time, regarded as authoritative by Malachi Martin, a former Jesuit professor and aide to Pope John XXIII, several questions were asked of a prospective bishop during his ritual consecration. These questions included: "Have you fornicated with a nun?"; "Have you sodomized a boy?"; and "Have you sodomized any four-legged animal?"[25]

What goes around comes around. Judging from the questions and the height of the office of bishop, one can only imagine the depth and variety of the moral depravity of the clergy. Doubtless lay morals were better, not worse, than those of the laity's moral shepherds. St. Peter Damian in his *Book of Gomorrah* confirms in detail the venality, bestiality, perversion, violence, greed and homicidal tendencies of his fellow clergymen.

Although young, Benedict IX proved resourceful, holding on to power for more than ten years. Discontent with his degeneracy led to an attempt on Benedict's life in 1044, forcing him to flee, and the citizens of Rome shortly elected John of Sabina as Pope Silvester III. Silvester was quickly run out of town by Benedict's relatives and Benedict was returned to the throne of St. Peter. Perhaps the job had proven too trying, because in two months time Benedict arranged the sale of his office to a rich priest, Giovanni Graziano, who took the name Gregory VI. Benedict's religious mission had yet a while to run, however. He was permitted to maintain a residence in the Lateran Palace, where he took to ministering to wayward women. Benedict's residence was reputed to be the best brothel in Rome.

There were now three consecrated popes living in Rome—Benedict IX and Sylvester III, permitted to return after his overthrow and take up residence at St. Mary Major's Church, and Gregory VI, the reigning pontiff. Holy Roman Emperor Henry III liked none of them and came to Rome in September 1046 to simplify things; with his army he expelled all three and installed one of his German bishops as Pope Clement II. Now there were four living popes! (Fortunately for theologians, the doctrine of papal infallibility had not been invented; if the four had ever been seated in a room writing disquisitions on morals, who would be enunciating church teaching properly if two arose to defecate but two maintained concentration on their work?)

Benedict IX liked the idea of simplicity but disdained Henry's approach; he had Clement II poisoned in October 1047 and climbed back onto the throne himself. Henry stormed back into Rome eight months later, chased Benedict from his high chair and put another German bishop on the papal throne as Pope Damasus II. Benedict IX found him no more pleasing, and managed to have him poisoned twenty-three days later. But, apparently of the opinion that he had more German bishops than Benedict had poison, Henry put another German bishop on the throne as Pope Leo IX. Henry was right and Leo managed to die in office of natural causes, but not before he initiated the events from which the schism with the Eastern church is officially dated.

> Angered by [Leo's] interference in south Italy in areas claimed by Byzantium, not least by his holding of a synod at Siponto, and his naming Humbert archbishop of Sicily, the fanatically anti-Latin patriarch Michael Cerularius (ruled 1043–58) shut down the Latin churches in Constantinople in 1053 and launched a violent attack on western religious practices, such as the use of unleavened bread in the Eucharist.[26]

Leo responded by sending a delegation of three cardinals to Constantinople to discuss the differences between the two churches, but things had already gone too far. Leo died while the effort was in progress, both Cerularius and the Roman delegation proved intransigent, and the trio one day in 1054 took it upon themselves to stride into the Basilica of Hagia

Sofia while the patriarch himself was saying mass and lay upon the altar a document of excommunication. By this act, Rome declared the patriarch, all Eastern bishops, priests, nuns, laity and even the Eastern emperor to be excommunicated and damned for all eternity to the fires of hell. Cerularius responded in kind.

The Eastern Schism was not really caused by dispute over doctrine, of course. Economics and ecclesiastical power were the invisible hand of the affair. The popes and their families had invested heavily in the shipping industry of Genoa and Venice, and these ships, commercial and military, were taking over Greek markets in the Mediterranean. Theological rationales were used as covers for political hostility. There were sporadic efforts at reconciliation over the succeeding four centuries, but all proved fruitless or impermanent; the two halves of the church were firmly attached to different empires. The day would come, and soon, when Christian holy warriors would even sack Constantinople.

Do not think that I have come to bring peace on earth; I have not come to bring peace, but a sword.

—Jesus Christ, Matthew 5:9

IV

The Theology of Carnage

While internal bloodletting preoccupied the church in the tenth and eleventh centuries, the twelfth and thirteenth centuries were characterized by a return to more basic Christian doctrine: killing non-Christians.

Europe was a feudal-clerical society, with the various barons, bishops and feudal lords continually at war with one another. Meanwhile the Seljuk Turks, a nomadic people of central Asia, converted to the Islamic faith and were transformed into a people on the march. "Unlike Christianity, which preached a peace never achieved, Islam unashamedly came with a sword."[1] The newest upstart monotheists overran Western Asia, defeated the Byzantines at Manzikert in Armenia in 1071, and assaulted Asia Minor, threatening Constantinople. Other Turkish bands entered Syria and in 1076 captured Jerusalem from the Egyptians. Meanwhile, Jewish merchants were prospering as traders around the Mediterranean, a fact repugnant to Christian anti-Semitism. Spurred intellectually by the possibility of reducing strife in Europe itself, the combination of these developments inspired Christian action—the Crusades.

The Crusades were wars against the Muslims, officially organized by the popes but often led by princes. They were also brutal wars against the Jews, who were active in trading Eastern goods throughout Europe, a limitation on Italian shipping merchants who were often related to members of the church hierarchy. In 1095 Pope Urban II organized the Council of Clermont to address, among other things, the problem of incessant armed conflict between Christian nobles and clergy. More than three hundred of Western Christendom's most prominent figures were in attendance, including King Philip of France, soon to be excommunicated by the council for bigamy and adultery (popes, bishops and abbots alone were exempt from church fulminations against sexual misbehavior), and the bishop of Cambrai, excommunicated by the council for simony.

The council initiated decrees against clerical marriages and lay investiture. The latter eliminated the practice of lay (usually royal) appointment of bishops, one more step in the direction of centralizing the power of the church in the clergy. The two most significant matters before the council however were advocacy of a proposed "Truce of God" between warring Christian principalities, and the inauguration of "holy wars" against spreading Islam.

Theologically one would think these were contradictory efforts, but there was a logic to the pairing. The Truce of God was advocated to contain fighting between Christians; the "holy wars," the Crusades, were an attempt to channel against the heathen the resulting bottled-up enthusiasm. Urban's initiatives were in fact beautifully complementary. The Truce of God was a compromise between theology and violence; the Crusades were a union of the two. The endearing faults of the human psyche did not need to be disturbed; instead they could be harnessed for the greater glory of Jesus.

The Truce of God was first suggested by Pope John XV in 950. Almost eighty years later, in 1027, a council meeting at Elne, France, decreed that military operations cease between 9 P.M. Saturday and 3 A.M. Monday.[2] In 1038, the archbishop of Bourges organized "Leagues of Peace," ordering every man over the age of fifteen to take up arms against anyone who did violence to other Christians. This approach backfired, as castles of recalcitrant nobles were destroyed by troops of armed peasants led by the clergy. One such band burned down the entire village of Benecy but the Count of Deols routed them on the banks of the river Cher. Seven hundred clerics perished in the battle.[3] Violence between Christians continued, but now had the sanction of the church.

To minimize the carnage only exacerbated the leagues, later versions of the Truce of God prohibited fighting variously on the Sabbath, on major Christian feast days, on Saturdays and Sundays, and during the periods between Advent and Epiphany and between Ash Wednesday and Easter week. In Burgundy the church had attempted to allow fighting only between Monday mornings and Wednesday evenings but met with little success.

Even the church's strongest supporters would violate a command to truce if it gained them strategic advantage. William the Conqueror was an enthusiastic advocate of the church's truce arrangements, but strategy prevailed over theology in his pursuit of the English crown. He fought the decisive engagement of his career, the Battle of Hastings in 1066, on a Saturday.[4]

Urban would have better success in his call for holy war. Saint Augustine had held that wars could be waged at the command of God, and the developing code of Christian knightly chivalry both gave prestige to the military hero and put a mark of disrepute on pacifism from which it has yet to recover. Pope Leo IV had declared in the mid–ninth century that those dying in battle for the church would win a heavenly reward; Nicholas I (ruled 858–68) thought that men under church sentence for their sins might "bear arms against the infidel" (Nicholas was eventually sanctified); and John VIII (ruled 872–82) called soldiers dying in a holy war martyrs whose sins would be forgiven.[5] The theology of war was endemic to Christian teaching.

Thus the Crusades could be an effective escape valve for frustrated Christian aggressiveness. On November 27, 1095, a little more than a week after the opening of the Council of Clermont, the pope announced that the Christians of Byzantium needed help against the Muslim terror. Jerusalem needed to be recaptured for Christendom. The pope was not enthusiastic about helping the Greek church, since in 1054 the Greek and Roman churches had excommunicated each other, but it was imperative that Christians cease slaughtering each other in Europe. The love of God and of fellow Christians had proved an ineffective deterrent to aggression. Directing elsewhere the urge to violence might succeed where merely moral prescriptions had not. The Muslims (and the Jews) were elected to be the victims. Steven Runciman, perhaps the world's foremost historian of the Crusades, vividly paraphrases Pope Urban's impassioned plea to the council assembled as, "Leave off slaying each other and fight instead a righteous war, doing the work of God."[6] The First Crusade was thus initiated, consecrated, and readied for delivery in wrapping paper of holy white topped with a bow of glistening red.

The word *crusade* comes from the old French *crosier*, "to bear the cross," because the Christians were carrying the cross of Christ into battle against the non-Christians. The Crusaders stitched red crosses on their cloaks to indicate that they were soldiers of Christ, pilgrims under arms,[7] fulfilling the age old Christian battle cry, *In Hoc Signo Vinces*.

From the first crusade of Urban II at the eleventh-century *fin de siecle*, to the last in the late thirteenth century, Christianity's holy wars were a nearly continuous struggle against the Muslims and the Jews. "The papacy grasped the moral leadership of Christendom and turned the warlike energies of an illiterate and brutalized feudal baronage into a religious channel that would carry them far away from Europe."[8] As Robert the Monk reported Urban to have observed to the nobles gathered at Clermont, "In this land you can scarcely feed the inhabitants. That is why you use up its goods and excite endless wars among yourselves." In the interest of all concerned, in other words, go kill people where it will do us some good. The oppressed economic condition of the peasants was exploited by con-

trasting it to the riches of plunder available in Palestine. The church mag-
nanimously volunteered to safeguard the possessions of those who went to
holy war; the disposition of the goods belonging to those unable to return
was not clearly detailed, however. Countless tens of thousands would be
slaughtered, raped, maimed and reduced to poverty when all was said and
done, but, as in our own age the industrialized nations export their poverty,
so in the Middle Ages Christendom exported its urge to carnage.

A shower of meteorites in 1095 presaged a large movement of peoples,
and to fuel the fire of passion the pulpit was used to preach that the
Second Coming would not happen until the Holy Land was restored to
Christian hands. The church taught that sin could be expiated by pilgrimage,[9] a bloody variant of the practice of selling indulgences. Credit for the
perfidy of this enterprise was claimed by the papacy. "Urban wished to
make it clear that the expedition was under the control of the church. Its
head must be an ecclesiastic, his legate. With the unanimous consent of the
Council he nominated the Bishop of Le Puy."[10] Urban was unsuccessful in
his effort to maintain church control of Christian aggression, however, as
we will see.

Dozens of minor crusades were sent throughout Europe and the Mediterranean, to wherever the infidel or the heretic could be found, but there
were nine major crusades sent to the Holy Land. They were not pretty affairs; the wars were graced by "every barbarity," which were justified only
by their "high spiritual aim."[11] The First Crusade was preceded in the
spring of 1096 by an undisciplined group of poor peasants who rushed
south and east without any training or preparation. They were led by spiritual provocateurs such as Walter the Penniless and Peter the Hermit; reaching Constantinople in the summer, they were quickly transported to Asia
Minor by the Byzantine emperor, Alexius I, and immediately defeated.

By early 1097 a group of about thirty-five thousand under the leadership of various princes had assembled in Constantinople. Alexius was fearful of so many foreign troops camped within his borders and demanded
from them oaths of fealty. Eastern leadership of the Roman crusade was
certainly not Urban's original intent, since the Great Schism was only forty
years old and still fresh in Catholic memory, but England's William Rufus
was busy ruthlessly consolidating Christian power in England, and Henry
IV of Germany and Philip I of France had been excommunicated. It was
hard to ask favors of people no longer officially spoken to. Christian
monarchs sufficiently pious to introduce Palestine to holiness were in short
supply that year.

In July 1097 the crusaders routed a Turkish army at Dorylacum and
battled across the central plateau into Syria. In June 1098, after a long
siege, Antioch fell. In 1099 the crusaders stormed Jerusalem and met with

no solid resistance. Nonetheless, the Christians "used to their full extent the rights of victory . . . Everywhere one could see nothing but heads flying, legs hacked off, arms cut down, bodies in slices . . . they killed the very children in their mother's arms to exterminate, if possible, that accursed race, as God formerly wished should be done to the Amalekites."[12] In sum, "The Muslim and Jewish inhabitants, to the number of at least 10,000, were pitilessly butchered."[13] The Muslims had been fighting internecine battles of their own and had been weakened by them. It was this weakness which allowed the Christians to conquer them. Jerusalem was restored as the urban shrine of Christian piety.

Having achieved a victory for Christ by decimating the local population, most crusaders saw no reason to hang around. So, carrying whatever plunder they could manage, most returned to Europe leaving a relatively small force to guard the Holy Land. Eventually the inevitable occurred: the Muslims counterattacked and in 1144 attained their first victory, capturing Edessa, at the eastern edge of Asia Minor. Christendom was shocked by the Muslim victory; such impiety of course required retaliation. Supported by the powerful and popular abbot Bernard of Clairvaux, Pope Eugenius III called for a second crusade. This time both Conrad III of Germany and Louis VII of France were available to lead the effort. Unfortunately, both dearly wanted to be in charge. There was only one solution to the dilemma: they traveled separately and did not coordinate their efforts. The price of this rivalry was paid for with the blood of their soldiers.

Rather than attacking the defined objectives, both kings first plundered Byzantine territory, then senselessly attacked Damascus, which could have been a useful buffer between the crusaders and the hostile principality of Mosul. The attack was repelled and the crusade collapsed in 1148. The two kings returned home discredited while the corpses of their men lay unacclaimed on the sands of Syria.

It was not a period of total loss for Christianity, however. A party of English and Flemish crusaders travelling to join the Second Crusade reached the mouth of the Douro River on the Iberian Peninsula. They decided to settle rather than fight. There they found not only infidels but lands as rich as any in Palestine. They would have this land, and were wise enough to recognize that the desire to have it was a form of divine intervention rather than simple human greed. The pious soldiers of Christ massacred the Muslim inhabitants and installed themselves on their lands, founding Portugal. The consequences of this migration were significant for world history, but otherwise the Second Crusade served no purpose.

Unlike the Jews, who react to defeat by entering into a new phase in the cycle of guilt, Christians respond to defeat by searching for a new object to hate. The Kurd Saladin recaptured Jerusalem in 1187, providing the impetus to mobilize Christian hostility. The fall of sacred Jerusalem was so horrifying to Christian sensibilities that the three principal sovereigns of Europe undertook to lead the Third Crusade to recover it—Holy Roman Emperor Frederick I, Philip II Augustus of France, and Richard the Lion-Hearted of England. Before the crusade even reached Syria, however, Frederick fell into a stream and drowned, perhaps because his armor was so heavy he could not rise. He had barely reached Asia Minor, but at least was able to sack Adrianople. Philip and Richard managed to attack Acre in 1191 and they defeated forces led by Saladin, but the pair quarreled afterwards and Philip went home in a pout. Richard was left with insufficient strength to recover Jerusalem but was able to conclude a five-year treaty by which Christians were accorded free access to the holy city. In his passage to the Holy Land Richard recovered some of his out-of-pocket expenses by seizing Cyprus from Byzantium, but otherwise the Third Crusade was another failure. The thousands of dead bodies strewn across Asia Minor had not resulted in many notable accomplishments, and the crusade was regarded as a bitter disappointment for Christian theology. It is possible the crusaders could have done as well by taking up peaceful negotiations from the start.

There had been at least some non-theological benefits from the futile effort, however. First, the Christians had now spent two centuries directing some of their aggression against non-Christians instead of one another. Second, the devastation and disruption caused by each of the crusades had both blunted long-term Islamic expansion and destroyed Jewish commercial strength in the Mediterranean. Capturing Jerusalem again by military force did not seem to be possible anytime soon, but since an agreement providing Christian access to Jerusalem had been reached, one would think peace could be in order. Such utopianism was soon rejected.

The Fourth Crusade was preached in 1202 by Pope Innocent III, called by Russell the first *great* pope in whom there was no element of sanctity.[14] Innocent was a towering figure of power. He referred to himself as "King of Kings, Lord of Lords,"[15] not exactly an appellation inspired by Christian humility. Innocent's accomplishments included forcing King John of England to yield his kingdoms to the church, with Innocent returning them as a "papal fief." Innocent also secured guardianship over the infant Frederick, son of Holy Roman Emperor Henry IV and Constance of Sicily. These were very creditable extensions of papal power.

For all of his shrewdness and influence, Innocent still had difficulty organizing the Fourth Crusade. The soldiers of Christ were to have embarked to the Holy Land from Venice, because only the Venetians had enough ships to carry them. But the Venetians believed that schismatic Byzantium was at least as wicked as the infidels. Besides, Constantinople was far richer for plunder than the small town of Jerusalem, and anyway it was closer. The Venetian senators found it easy to persuade the crusaders to make a small diversion in their route and attack Constantinople first. "The appropriate passions of orthodoxy and cupidity were inflamed; amid scenes which put the massacres of Antioch and Jerusalem in the shade, the crusaders, having entered [Constantinople] as allies, seized and sacked the greatest city of Europe."[16] Innocent was powerless to halt the seige, so he decided it could be put to good use; force of arms might even be able to unite the church. In the long run that was not to be, and in the short term resources intended for the crusade were squandered in the assault. Venice profited from the developments, however, and Jerusalem stood in relative peace; apparently both had Christ on their side against the successor of St. Peter.

To keep other holy swords sharp, Innocent in 1208 launched a crusade within Europe. The victims were the Albigenses, a strange group of heretics in southern France who believed that the God of the Old Testament was evil and that wicked souls transmigrated to animals after death. For this reason they were largely vegetarian, a practice complemented by an urge to pacifism. This combination of hateful characteristics was too compelling for good Christians not to act. A savage, five-year war destroyed the people and country of southern France along with the heretics.[17]

This affair was quickly followed by more debacles of military pilgrimage to the Holy Land. Most pathetic was the Children's Crusade of 1212. "Led by a visionary French peasant boy, Stephen of Cloyes, children embarked at Marseilles, hoping to succeed in the cause that their elders had betrayed. According to later sources, they were sold into slavery by unscrupulous skippers." Another group of German children died from hunger and disease in Italy.[18] The Fifth Crusade (1217–21), directed against the strongest Muslim power, Egypt, and led by Austrian and Hungarian nobility together with the titular king of Jerusalem, John of Brienne, ended in defeat after some initial success.

While the soldiers of Christ were consolidating territory for Jesus overseas, on the theological front Innocent began to codify canon law in a manner that increased the power of the Roman Curia. The new code was called by Walther von der Vogelweide "the blackest book that hell ever gave"[19] because it was a blatant Machiavellian ploy to centralize papal power under the pretense of standardizing church law. Meanwhile, to expand his influence in secular affairs, Innocent arranged to settle the dispute between Philip of Swabia and Otto IV of Brunswick over rightful rule of the Holy Roman Empire. He put his charge, Frederick, already crowned king of Sicily at the age of four, on the throne. The scheme was successful and the ensuing wars were eventually settled in Frederick's favor, although the principal factions, called the Guelfs and the Ghibellines, would remain at odds for more than two centuries.

Frederick was progressive for his day, but he was also a man who understood power. His court at Sicily was one of learning—Frederick is supposed to have launched Italian poetry,[20] and he founded the University of Naples to educate his officials—but at the same time he centralized the government by assuming the administrative functions of the feudal nobility, designed an efficient bureaucracy to run this government, and established a comprehensive legal code. In short, Frederick built the first modern state in Western Europe.

Frederick also assumed full leadership of the church in Sicily, to the consternation of Innocent and his successors. Italian by upbringing and interest, Frederick handed over the Holy Roman emperorship to his son, Henry, and prepared to extend his own rule to include Lombardy, which encompassed much of northern Italy. Feeling the threat of encirclement, in 1227 Pope Gregory IX excommunicated Frederick on the pretext that he had not fulfilled a pledge to lead a crusade. This had the result of strengthening the opposition against Frederick in Lombardy.

Frederick accordingly made the Sixth Crusade in 1228. This submission only increased Innocent's ire; it was most inappropriate for an excommunicate to lead a holy war for Christ. As husband of the heiress to the Jerusalem monarchy, Frederick already called himself king of Jerusalem. The idea of leading an attack against his relatives was a bit troublesome; Frederick's preference was to obtain Jerusalem peacefully. Upon his arrival in Palestine Frederick explained to the sultan, Kamil, that Jerusalem was not of strategic importance to Christians but was of religious significance to Christianity. Negotiations were successful and in 1229 Frederick secured the peaceful return of an unfortified Jerusalem to the Christians. "This made the Pope still more furious—one should fight the infidel, not negotiate with him," explains Russell.[21]

From the hallowed halls of the Vatican the pope exacted his revenge. He invaded Frederick's Italian territories with papal armies while Frederick was in the Holy Land. The move backfired. "The attack by the Pope himself on the lands of an absent crusader shocked Christian opinion. Even St. Louis, King of France, was horrified."[22] So in 1230 Gregory made peace with Frederick, enabling them to participate together in the afterglow of success surrounding the return of Jerusalem to Christianity. Frederick was again made a son of the church, and everyone celebrated the wisdom of Christ and the Holy Ghost.

The peace lasted only briefly. In 1237 trouble erupted again when Frederick defeated the Lombard cities and sought to extend his sway over the island of Sardinia, regarded by the papacy as its fief. The pope went on the offensive, but when he "preached a Holy War against the emperor it seemed that the whole idea of the Holy War had become ridiculous." Nonetheless, "the Pope was implacable. The struggle lasted on bitterly throughout his pontificat[e] and was maintained by his successors."[23] Although the crusades channeled some Christian hostility towards the infidel, it seems that there were adequate reserves left for domestic struggle. When Gregory died in 1241 his successor, Innocent IV, declared Frederick deposed and undertook a campaign to sponsor "anti-kings" in Germany.

Frederick died in 1250, leaving a legacy of erudition, governmental improvement, and the notable distinction of having been the only crusader who tried to avoid bloodshed. Gregory, the pope who had excommunicated Frederick for dodging the call to holy war, became recognized as one of the most influential popes in history. For one thing, he had established a complete code of canon law, published in five volumes under the title *Decretals*. The result was unprecedented centralization of authority in the clergy, which has been maintained until the present day. Gregory is also responsible for developing inquisition as a method of extirpating heresy. "His appointment of several [Dominican] friars to investigate the remnants of the Albigensian heresy in southern France is usually taken as marking the beginning of the papal Inquisition."[24] Restrained by secular powers from killing foreigners to his fullest satisfaction, Gregory channeled his religious enthusiasm into setting up the machinery that would torture the people of Europe for six centuries; although frustrated by Frederick in the matter of butchering Muslims and Jews during the Sixth Crusade, Gregory did not have to worry—his place in the history of Christian compassion could be assured.

Three more crusades would be launched, two abortive sorties to North Africa and a landing at Acre by England's Prince Edward that ended in truce, but Islam steadily occupied Christian strongholds throughout and the last, Acre, fell in 1291. A final episode suitably caps the moral debacle of the Crusades, however. The fifteenth-century church of Pope Innocent VIII faced innumerable problems, caused in large part by the debts incurred by Innocent's predecessor, Sixtus IV. To pay for his own carnal pleasures, Innocent called for a crusade in 1486, decreeing in its support "a tithe on all churches, benefices, and ecclesiastical persons of all ranks."[25] Although money was received, no crusade came to pass. Instead Innocent entered into one of Catholicism's stranger manuevers. The Ottoman Empire had by this time supplanted Byzantium as the dominant power in the Middle East and it was considered a threat to Christian Europe. Like any court, the Ottoman royal house was subject to intrigue. Its latest problem was the ambition of the sultan's brother, Djem. The affair had seemed to end with his flight to Europe, but the sultan considered the threat sufficiently serious that he was willing to pay Djem's hosts, the Knights of St. John, ensconced on an island in the Mediterranean named Rhodes, the sum of 45,000 ducats to keep him out of circulation. As an ever-looming threat to the Ottoman sultanate, Djem was more than a financial asset, and for this reason Innocent was interested in securing custody of the meandering Muslim. "After a temporary sojourn in France, Djem was won by the Pope together with his subsidy at the price of two cardinalships, one for the Grand Master of Rhodes and one for a candidate of the French King."[26]

Next, the stroke of brilliance. Innocent had a plan to eliminate the Turkish sultan and replace him with Djem, who on ascending the throne would return the Christian favor by withdrawing Turkish forces from Europe. This was an idiocy matched since only by the American sale of arms to the Iran of Khomeini. "Even if [the plan] had been believable, it is not clear how replacing one Moslem with another constituted Holy War."[27] Until the fruition of his machinations, Innocent VIII used the monies gathered for the crusade to properly bribe Djem. Amidst pomp, parties, and praises, Djem, by now called the "Grand Turk" for his sumptuous habits, lived in Rome at a royal suite in the Vatican apartments. Innocent died in 1492, Djem died in French custody a few years later, and the entire affair was a fittingly ludicrous end to the idea of the Crusades: commenced as a way of channeling Christian hatred against the infidel, Christianity's holy wars were concluded by papal merrymaking with him.

As a military enterprise the Crusades were a failure. They were even less successful as a first experiment in modern European colonialism; killing the natives and plundering their cities right off was not conducive to organizing colonies. Nonetheless, the Crusades engendered sweeping change in the West. Violence in the name of God gained prestige; the Inquisition was in embryo. The Crusades also demonstrated a seminal political truth: overseas wars do wonders for domestic politics. The problem of population growth in Europe, one impetus of the Crusades, found part of its solution in the experience gained during crusading travel. On the way to the Holy Land or returning from it many crusaders would simply stop and settle, setting up new farms, towns and cities. The Crusades lessened the parochialism and accompanying intellectual and entrepreneurial lethargy that had condemned Europe to the stagnation of the Dark and Middle Ages. In his *The Rise of Christian Europe*, Hugh Trevor-Roper suggests that the Crusades were responsible for the Western obsession with world exploration soon to come. Colonialism with a Christian face was born. The Christian holy wars stimulated Western trade by heightening an appetite for Eastern goods and services and increasing Christian control of Mediterranean trade routes formerly dominated by Jews. Venice was the font of this development. According to Trevor-

Roper, it had been only reluctantly drawn into the crusading effort,

> but as the Crusades went on, requiring constant sea-transport and finan-
> cial refreshment, the coastal towns of Italy saw their opportunity. They
> provided the transport, they invested the funds, they secured payment in
> concessions of every kind—their own quarters in captured seaports, privi-
> leges and monopolies of trade, farms of taxes—until, in the end, they
> became the living, thriving link whereby Europe was once again in regu-
> lar contact with the East . . . Moreover, thanks to the trade of the Medi-
> terranean, and an industry financed by it, the Italian towns drew back
> into Europe the essential motor of such commerce: gold.[28]

For this reason, some credit the Crusades with hastening the end of feudalism by strengthening the power of the kings and the middle class and
creating the need for an efficient system of taxation to pay for war.

In 1270 the Treaty of Tunis was signed. It was an agreement for peace
between the Christians and Muslims but also a pact of mutual trade between the Muslim ruler of Tunis and Philip III of France, Charles of Sicily
and Thibaud of Navarre. Theology became subordinated to trade and the
Muslims became more useful as business partners than repositories of
excess Christian militarism. The pursuit of profit produced a peace which
had eluded religion.

The greatest achievement of the Crusades might be that it created the
"idea of Europe." This was one of Pope Urban's original objectives, lo,
two centuries before. The overseas solution to domestic problems was a
new awakening for Europe, which would soon embark on an era of
colonialism. Given its origins in adventuring, it is no wonder that so young
a kingdom as Portugal would quickly advance to colonial preeminence.
European conquistadors would seek to spread the word of God in South
America, led by such paragons of piety as James the Moor-Killer, but "he
would do to kill Red Indians too." Bernal Diaz del Castillo, the companion
of Cortez, would write that they came *para servir a Dios y hacernos
ricos*—"to serve God and become rich."[29] To do that European explorers
would bring Christ to Africa, the Americas and the Far East. In these
places the communion did not need to be celebrated with only symbolic
flesh and blood.

Sad to say, however, the Christians hardly refrained from killing each
other during the period of the Crusades. The contests to control Sicily,
Italy, and Germany were perhaps even heightened by the Crusades, and
the idea of them was used to reinvigorate bloody campaigns against individuals and even whole towns suspected of harboring heresy. These resulted in the death of thousands by torture and the destruction of many of
Europe's most beautiful towns and villages. When the Crusades to the

Holy Land died out, the popes could spend more time laying waste to Europe over various of the panoply of theological issues. There would be the Inquisition, torture made into an art form, then the rise of Protestantism, when nationalism garbed as heresy would serve as the motor of religious war. In the Crusades, Christianity had only begun to realize its murderous potential.

The Inquisition

Heresy is the lifeblood of religions. It is faith that begets heretics. There are no heresies in a dead religion.

—Andre Suares, *Peguy*

The crusades to restore Christianity to the Middle East had immediate repercussions in Europe. Long-standing disgust at the "wealth and wickedness" of the Christian clergy was compounded by doubts generated by the failure of the Crusades. In this fertile soil the ideas of superior Muslim culture, carried back to Europe by the returning crusaders, became the seeds of heresy. Inevitably this led the church to attempt to reassert its theological supremacy, an effort which took many forms. One was the development of a comprehensive Christian theology by Thomas Aquinas, explicitly a response to the ideas of the Muslim infidel. Another was an attempt by the papacy to control the thinking of the faithful. This it did by creating the Inquisition.

The early Christians had used non-violent methods to locate heresy and eradicate it, but when Christianity became the official religion of the Roman Empire in the fourth century the faith of love turned to the techniques of torment to check aberrant beliefs. In the days of Roman rule, heresy was more often a badge of rebellion against imperial authority than a dedication to a different form of worshipping God. Imperial response to heresy was more an assertion of authority than an interest in purity of thought.

Faced with the heresy of the Donatists in the fourth century, Augustine had advocated state punishment of heretics by exile, confiscation of property, or prison. With joint church and state responsibility for belief, heresy was sometimes as broadly interpreted as "national security" is in our age. It was the vehicle used by ecclesiastical and secular authorities to interrogate and repress anyone who was a threat to the unity of the society, that is, to those in power. First the papacy but ultimately the bishops and secular nobility as well assumed the responsibility of rooting out ideas which did not conform to church teaching. It was no matter that the church was not clear on its teaching, that theological ideas were hotly disputed even among theologians, and that with no widely available written Bible belief was based on word of mouth; if anything this increased the usefulness of heresy as a political tool.

Contemporary heresy (the term derives from the Greek *hairetikos*, "those who are able to choose") was at first an isolated phenomenon. In 1017 King Robert II of France burned thirteen heretics at Orleans. In 1051 Holy Roman Emperor Henry III hanged a group of heretics at Goslar. But with time heretical sects proved to be a continent-wide plague of dissent. The first general papal legislation in these matters did not come until 1163, when Pope Alexander III instructed the clergy at the Council of Tours to be diligent in locating and punishing heretics, and requested any possible assistance from the lay princes, including help with carrying out imprisonment and confiscation of property. The latter punishment was perhaps an inducement for lay participation in the papal campaign, but it also assured that the princes could never be objective judges of heretical belief. The official procedure laid down for an inquest into heresy began with the interview of witnesses under oath by a judge or ecclesiastical commission. There were then steps to be taken to decide the guilt of the accused. This procedure, *per inquisitionem*, "through inquiry," is the basis for what came to be the institution of the Inquisition.

Heresy continued to spread, so at the Third Lateran Council in 1179 Alexander prohibited the faithful from providing protection to heretics, urged lay princes to commence a crusade against them, and reiterated papal authorization of confiscation of the property of heretics and their reduction to servitude. It must be kept in mind that printing had not yet been invented, nor of course was literacy widespread, and so people believed things by learning of them through word of mouth. There was in fact not yet even an officially agreed upon version of the Bible. Since Christian theology is very complicated and most people were uneducated, many people did not even know what constituted heresy. It is accordingly impossible to say how much repression was based on genuine heresy and how much on simply an urge to plunder.

In 1184, with the assistance of Emperor Frederick Barbarossa, Pope Lucius III developed even harsher papal legislation. All lay princes were instructed to assist the church hierarchy in prosecuting heretics or face excommunication, loss of lands, or interdict (the forbidding of the prince's population from receiving certain sacraments, such as Christian marriage and burial). An interdict could have the effect of creating an insurrection against the lay prince. The punishments of the heretics now ranged to exile, hanging and death by fire at the stake, all depending both on the offense and the disposition of the authorities on any given day. Only torture had yet to be officially sanctioned.

At the turn of the century Pope Innocent III faced the particularly flourishing heresy of the Albigenses, a sect first entrenched in the town of Albi but soon spread throughout southern France. The count of Toulouse agreed with Albigensian doctrines, gave the sect protection, and, after a time of fruitless condemnations, Innocent urged a crusade against the infidels. The count's lands were offered to those who would conquer them and soon Norman warriors commenced a savage war. Thousands were killed, heretic and non-heretic alike were robbed of their lands and possessions, and the invaders acted in general like "savage buccaneers." Peace was finally established in 1229; the land was desolate, but orthodox. The legal justification for this particular fit of barbarism came from the Fourth Lateran Council of 1215. Innocent was very knowledgable of Roman law, and among his writings on the subject are legal opinions that heretics are guilty of spiritual treason. Since civil treason is punishable by death, how much more severely must treason against Jesus Christ be punished?[30]

The formal establishment of the Inquisition as a papal tribunal run according to official laws of the church, *inquisitio haereticae pravitatis*, came soon after, during the reign of Pope Gregory IX. After a century of scattered attempts to contain the spread of the heresies, Gregory formalized inquisitorial practice between 1231 and 1235 and sent the Dominicans and Franciscans to establish the Inquisition in France. The inquisitors themselves were the special legate of the pope, answerable only to him. This nearly absolute power led to innumerable abuses, for although the inquisitor was supposed to abide by certain rules of trial, such as the public interviewing of witnesses and a public hearing of the accused, in fact the inquisitor could do what he liked. The accused were not allowed any legal defense, nor to know who their accusers were. Therefore any of a person's enemies, personal or political, could make accusations of heresy; the testimony of only two accusers was required to condemn a suspected heretic.

Christian envy managed to rear its head even in so sick a setting. The various bishops and cardinals in each locality were becoming resentful, since they did not enjoy authoritarian power equal to that of the inquisitors. This forced the papacy to associate them more closely with the persecutions. The Council of Vienna in 1312 decided that the bishops possessed equal authority and power to the inquisitor in matters of heretical inquiry. This was helpful to local church treasuries.

The Inquisition was an itinerant operation, its agents roving restlessly through the territories of their jurisdiction. The inquisitors were usually forced to conduct their business in fortified locations because their presence often provoked the local population to violence, but their enormous power also attracted the services of spies and the gamut of thugs and ruffians to help apprehend suspects. If the accused had an advocate, rather than being allowed to argue in his client's defense the advocate himself became responsible for convincing the accused to confess his guilt. If an advocate foolishly insisted on offering a defense for the accused, he would be rendered infamous—made ineligible to practice law and perhaps put on trial himself.[31] The procedure was trial by fear and psychological torment. Deceiving the accused into "confessing" was standard procedure, as was, of course, intimidation. Punishment was summary, and severe if there was much delay in confessing.

Intimidation, extortion and the like were not enough to satisfy the church's thirst for cruelty. In 1252 Pope Innocent IV officially authorized the use of torture by the inquisitors. It goes without saying that torture had been employed sporadically before, but it now became official church policy.

> Torture was in several cases used to force witnesses to testify, or to induce a confessing heretic to name other heretics. It took the form of flogging, burning, the rack, or solitary imprisonment in dark and narrow dungeons. The feet of the accused might be slowly roasted over burning coals; or he might be bound upon a triangular frame, and have his arms and legs pulled by cords wound on a windlass. . . . Some men had been so drawn on the rack that they had lost the use of their arms and legs; some had died under torture.[32]

After a suspect's arrest, interrogation, torture and conviction, sentence was generally announced and carried out at the Sunday religious ceremonies. After all, conviction of a heretic was a religious event. For those convicted who abjured their crimes, the standard punishment was life imprisonment. For those convicted who were impenitent, the church practice was to abandon them to the secular authorities for the execution of the death penalty. The way in which this was done reflected a curious guilt on the part of the church itself.

> The Church never pronounced a sentence of death; her old motto was *ecclesia abhorret a sanguine*—"the Church shrinks from blood"; clerics were forbidden to shed blood. So, in turning over to the secular arm those she had condemned, the Church confined herself to asking the state authorities to inflict the "due penalty," with a caution to avoid "all bloodshed and all danger of death." After Gregory IX, it was agreed by both Church and state that the caution should not be taken literally, but that the condemned were to be put to death without shedding of blood—i.e., by burning at the stake.[33]

As a concession to compassion, those who abjured at the stake were sometimes strangled before the fire was lighted. The property of those condemned to death or life imprisonment was confiscated, thereby often condemning their relatives and descendants to poverty. Sometimes the Inquisition would even stretch its powers into the grave, posthumously convicting the dead of heresy, digging up their corpses and burning them, and confiscating the property of their survivors.

As the authority of the Inquisition grew, its range of interest moved from belief to practice; those who committed blasphemy and "crimes of immorality" began to be put on trial—this in the same period that the popes held orgies in the Lateran Palace! Increasingly the Inquisition became a political tool for disposing of one's enemies. Joan of Arc was legally executed in inquisitorial proceedings when she fell into the hands of the English. The French retaliated twenty-five years later by inducing a new pope to schedule a retrial, called the Trial of Rehabilitation. It exonerated Joan by declaring the original trial fraudulent and null and void. As partial recompense Joan was sanctified in 1920, making her a canon figure of the church which had officially condemned and killed her.

The Roman and Universal Inquisition in Italy, also called, apparently without embarrassment, the "Holy Office," was most active in the sixteenth and seventeenth centuries, when religious upheavals in Europe were at their height and modern science was born. The Italian Inquisition's willingness to persecute anyone was most dramatically revealed in its execution by fire of Giordano Bruno (1548–1600), regarded then and now as one of the outstanding thinkers of the Renaissance. Moments before he was burned alive Bruno is reported to have declared, "You perhaps tremble more in pronouncing the sentence than I in receiving it."[34] Another well-known recipient of the Roman Inquisition's divine justice was Galileo, whose sentence to life imprisonment was commuted to life-long house arrest only because he had powerful friends in the church hierarchy.

The Spanish Inquisition is the most infamous example of political repression masquerading as theological morality; it was a church-state consanguinity of blood. The Christians, Jews and Muslims of Castile had lived together peacefully for over a hundred years, when, in the fourteenth century, Spain's urban middle class began to gain wealth and power. Its Jewish members were conspicuous, resulting in pogroms and forced conversions which created what were called the "New Christians" or *conversos*. Eventually Ferdinand of Aragon and Isabella of Castile decreed the expulsion from their lands of all Jews, causing many more to convert in order to remain in what had become their home.

These *conversos* were suspected (usually correctly so) of practicing Christianity in public but retaining Jewish beliefs in private. To ensure a religious homogeneity they thought essential to the unity of Spain, the Catholic monarchs asked the papacy to establish an inquisition in Castile to ferret out the "secret Jews" among the *conversos*. Pope Sixtus IV complied on November 1, 1478, delegating to the secular monarchs the authority to appoint and dismiss all inquisitors.

The result was far beyond the scope of the original request—massive persecution of Jews, Protestants, Muslims, even high-ranking servants of the crown and the church itself. At the height of its activity, the Spanish Inquisition was virtually invulnerable, beyond the control even of the papacy. Like the inquisitions in other parts of Europe, it was largely a political tool of the ecclesiastical and secular members of the ruling class, used to control internal dissension, eliminate enemies and acquire their wealth. The most brutal tortures imaginable were frequently employed, although, as in the rest of Europe, they were usually accompanied by prayers of compassion. Tomas de Torquemada, the most fanatical of the Spanish Inquisition's leaders, ruled as grand inquisitor general for only fifteen years, from 1483 to 1498, but in that short time he held over a hundred thousand trials and carried out over two thousand executions, usually by ritual burning at the stake called *actus fidei generalis*, or *auto-da-fe*, "act of faith." Torquemada paid special attention to the "secret Jews" despite the fact that he had some Jewish blood.

Most people assume that the Inquisition was abolished hundreds of years ago, but it was active into the nineteenth century. It was moribund in its last years, but the Holy Office was not abolished until 1965, when its name was changed to the Congregation for the Doctrine of the Faith and its decisions of religious consequence limited to examining the theological disposition of church officials. It is this body which has examined University of Tübingen theologian Hans Küng, Catholic University theologian Charles Curran and Seattle's Archbishop Raymond Hunthausen, to name the most publicized examples. The first two were forbidden to teach and the third to exercise many of his ecclesiastical powers. The Congregation has also been busy investigating the "liberation theologians" of South America and elsewhere, mostly priests who have insisted on political involvement on the model of the life of Jesus as the best way to alleviate the problems of the poor.

The ideology and methods of the Inquisition have disappeared in most of the West, but they hold sway nearly everywhere else, equally severely in the right-wing dictatorships and the Marxist "democratic republics" scattered around the globe. The most systematic enforcer of doctrinal purity in our age, however, holds court in Christianity's "Third Rome," Moscow. Communism's fanatical suppression of independent thought has far outstripped the excesses of the Inquisition. May the blessing of civilization decree that its lifespan is accordingly shorter.

Suppressing the rise of science

The strongest guard is placed at the gateway to nothing. Maybe because the condition of emptiness is too shameful to be divulged.
—F. Scott Fitzgerald, *Tender Is the Night*

The seventeenth century was the century of science, the time when the foundation for the modern world was laid. In the light of unfolding possibilities of rationality, the use of human ingenuity for peaceful purposes, the sixteenth century's preoccupation with brutality showed it to have been a time of barbarism.

The seventeenth century saw the removal of theology from the center of things by a Pole who had lived a hundred years before. Nicolaus Copernicus's interest in astronomy led him to suggest a humbling possibility: the sun was the center of the universe, not the earth. Earth was of course the center of the universe, else why would Christ have come to it? The Mediterranean Sea was in like manner regarded as the center of the world because Christ was born on its shores; the Latin word *mediterraneus* means "middle of the earth." Jerusalem was at the center of all maps made up to the middle of the seventeenth century because Ezekiel had revealed, "Thus saith the Lord God; this is Jerusalem: I have set it in the midst of the nations and countries that are round about her." The words of the Vulgate were *umbilicus terrae*, "navel of the world." Maps in medieval times were as much theological pictures of the world as tools of geography, locating the Garden of Eden, Jerusalem, and "the land of Magog," the mythical terrestrial abode of Satan.

The theological conception of world geography was a prime impediment to Western exploration of the world. Discoveries that the earth was round put knowledge in direct clash with ecclesiastical authority. Faith and knowledge were in conflict, but the maps to represent that knowledge were written by believers. Explorers of this time accordingly needed theological fortitude as well as physical courage. They had to be willing to risk falling off the edge of the world and going to hell.

Modern science was conceived in this bizarre atmosphere. Scriptural citations eventually proved no match for the gradual march of mathematics and astronomy and the empirical evidence of the telescope. Copernicus (1473–1543) initiated this conflict when he discerned flaws in the Ptolemaic conception of the universe he had learned in school. He set about reviewing the literature on the subject in order to fix them. In the course of his inquiry, Copernicus came upon a long-neglected minority view, held by Aristarchus and Nicetas among others, that the sun was the center of the universe. It was this "heliocentric" conception that he resolved to investigate.

Copernicus did so without the aid of a telescope; he turned on its head humanity's understanding of its place in the universe merely on the basis of deduction from phenomena visible to the naked eye. Fully aware of planets and their distinction from stars, earth for Copernicus became simply one among many heavenly bodies. With this understanding the concept of heaven disappeared and was replaced by the idea of space; up and down became relative. Given Christianity's central heaven-up/hell-down dichotomization, the theological ramifications were enormous. Copernicus knew his assertions were an assault on theology, but certainly did not intend them as such. A faithful ecclesiastic, Copernicus dedicated his *De revolutionibus orbium coelestium* ("Concerning the Revolutions of the Heavenly Bodies") to the pope.

Having failed to prevent intellectual conception in the womb of fertile minds, the church found itself in the unpleasant position of searching for a way to terminate a pregnancy. The attempt was not only Catholic. There were also the tirades of Martin Luther against Copernican ideas, citing Joshua's command that the sun, not the earth, stand still, and Calvin's denunciations based on the Scripture's declaration that, "Yea, the world is established; it shall never be moved" (Psalms 93:1). Despite all invocations of Scripture disputing him, Copernicus was right and Scripture was revealed to be myth.

Naturally the church wound up addressing the issue by putting scientists into prison, burning their books, and condemning people to hell if they taught or even read science's "theories of Satan." This approach definitely lacked a certain civility, of course, not to mention intellectual integrity, but in the long term it did little to delay the dawn of truth. It did however prolong for yet a few more score of years the rule of fear in humanity's engagement with the world, giving the theologians a century to determine how scientific truth comported with the Scriptures.

It gradually became obvious that Scripture and science were not always reconcilable. One solution for theologians was to reinterpret scriptural texts in the context of "cultural history"—a euphemism which allows a literal scriptural passage blatantly contradictory to scientific fact to be viewed as having been true only during the time and in the culture of the author, but no longer, or as being all along metaphorical. Despite the polysyllabic vocabulary used to defend these complex interpretations, the result is that Scripture must be prepared to yield whenever scientific discoveries contradict it. The theologians were dragged kicking and screaming to the alter of empirical truth.

Copernicus escaped persecution since his principal work was published the year he died. The church in any case did not discern its meaning for more than twenty years and only then, ironically, because of the fulminations of its theological archenemy, Luther; Copernicus's books were eventually ordered burned by the ecclesiastical authorities. The church has long loved the light of fire, on earth or below it. *De revolutionibus* remained on the church's Index of Forbidden Books until 1835.

The suppression of Copernicus's work was *de rigueur,* but with the assertions of Galileo (1564–1642), the principal founder of modern science, full-scale war between religion and science was finally taken up in the Western world. Galileo is important in the history of science for his theoretical formulations, but they were born of his observations of the universe. Galileo linked physics and astronomy with mathematics, revolutionary for the time. Before Galileo, physics was treated as a branch of Aristotelian philosophy and not as an experimental science. He founded dynamics, the study of the laws of motion, and enunciated the law of falling bodies, the uniform change in the velocity of projectiles, and the method of calculating the collective effect of separate forces (for example, where does a human walking downstream on a ship traveling upstream in a crosswind "stand" at any given moment?). Galileo's march into astronomical history began with his construction in 1609 of a telescope that substantially improved upon the prototype invented by Hans Lippershey the year before, but his problems with the church arose only when he accepted the theory that the sun is the center of the universe. It was the Roman and Universal Inquisition that had the general task of halting the advance of science. This it carried out by means of exile, imprisonment and execution. Christ's admonition that "the truth shall make you free" was supplanted by the church practice of the warning that "the truth shall make you flee"; not to do so was to face persecution.

Not originally interested in astronomy, Galileo was excited by Lippershey's invention of the telescope. The next year he built his own to study the planets. In 1611 Galileo took his telescope and some of his discoveries to Rome to show church dignitaries and while there was elected to the Accademia dei Lincei, founded in 1603 and the Western world's first scientific society. In 1612 Galileo published a book supporting Archimedes and refuting Aristotle on the subject of the laws of floating bodies. The book was assailed by four professors at the universities of Pisa and Florence and an opposition group began to form against him. In 1613 Galileo published *History and Demonstrations Concerning Sunspots and Their Phenomena,* in which he openly endorsed the views of Copernicus that the sun, not the earth, is the center of the universe. Many priests and professors attacked him on religious grounds, inducing him to write a letter to his friend and pupil, Benedetto Cartelli, a Benedictine monk, arguing that biblical authority should not be invoked against scientific theories.

In 1614, a copy of this letter was sent by a Dominican preacher to

Rome for action by the Inquisition. The church fathers saw a frightening light at the end of Galileo's telescope, because it was on darkness that their world, and their privilege too, was based. Believing that he had to defend freedom of scientific inquiry as well as his own life, Galileo expanded his previous letter into a famous defense of free science known as the "Letter to the Grand Duchess Christina." It was widely circulated in 1615 and late that year Galileo went to Rome and argued publicly for acceptance of the ideas of Copernicus. This aroused the anger of Pope Paul V, who appointed a commission to examine this theory of the earth's motion. The commission declared the theory contrary to the Bible and possibly heretical. In February 1616 the pope ordered Robert Cardinal Bellarmine to advise Galileo to abandon the Copernican system or face imprisonment. Galileo decided to maintain silence on astronomy.

In 1623 one of Galileo's old friends, Maffeo Barberini, was elected pope, taking the name Urban VIII, and the next year Galileo petitioned the new pope to allow him to teach Copernican views and to halt the vilification he was receiving at the hands of professors and priests. To support his request, Galileo dedicated to Urban a new book, *Il Saggiatore* ("The Assayer"), in which he set forth principles by which scientific research should be guided. Urban gave Galileo permission to write a book comparing the old and new understandings of astronomy, provided that both were treated hypothetically and impartially, and Galileo published his *Dialogue on the Two Great World Systems* in 1632.

In the *Dialogue* Galileo recorded many of his findings and observations concerning the rotation of the earth and the nature of the sun. To minimize the reaction to so sweeping and controversial a project, Galileo chose to write the book in the form of a discussion between three characters, one an Aristotelian simpleton. Galileo's enemies managed to convince the pope that he was the figure of ridicule. With Urban's support, the Inquisition moved against the greatest scientist who had ever lived. At sixty-nine years old Galileo stood trial for failing to treat the subjects hypothetically, and by clearly espousing the Copernican view being "vehemently suspect of heresy."[35] Under threat of torture he recanted.[36]

Galileo was condemned to life imprisonment, the sentence was ordered read in all university cities, Galileo's books were forbidden to be printed or reprinted, and the *Dialogue* was burned. If his enemies, a number of Jesuit astronomers among them, had had their way, Galileo would have met more severe punishment. Instead, because Galileo had friends in the Vatican, the sentence was commuted to house arrest in care of an old friend, the archbishop of Sienna, then to house arrest at his own villa at Arcetri near Florence. Galileo began to go blind as early as 1633, and lost his sight entirely by 1638, but the pope refused him permission to visit Florence to see doctors.[37]

One episode provides an insight into Galileo's character. A friend, Nicholas Fabri de Peiresc, offered to try to obtain a pardon for him. Galileo replied that he had done nothing requiring a pardon, and besides, those who are unjustly condemned could only expect their accusers to intensify their injustice in order to justify their position; but, Galileo said, he was grateful to learn through his troubles of the friendship and goodwill of people he would otherwise never have known. Later Galileo would write in the margin of his own copy of the *Dialogue,*

> And who can doubt that it will lead to the worst disorders when minds created free by God are compelled to submit slavishly to an outside will? When we are told to deny our senses and subject them to the whim of others? When people of whatsoever competence are made judges over experts and are granted authority to treat them as they please? These are the novelties which are apt to bring about the ruin of commonwealths and the subversion of the state.[38]

On January 8, 1642, Galileo died at Arcetri. "Urban was still full of rancor, and positively refused to let his old friend have any memorial erected over his grave. Not until almost a century later was permission given for his remains to be interred under a large monument in the entrance to the Church of Santa Croce in Florence."[39]

Today Galileo is universally regarded as one of the founders of modern science, on whose shoulders we all stand—or fly! Many of our methods of scientific inquiry are descendants of Galileo's scientific method of experiment. Our satellites and flights to the moon are the direct result of Galileo's investigations and discoveries. As for the Catholic church, more than 350 years after the fact it appointed in 1980 a commission to investigate the conduct of Galileo's trial. Was it possible that the church had committed an error? In March 1984 the Vatican acknowledged that Galileo had been right. The four-year investigation had revealed that the earth was not, in fact, the center of the universe.

Some attribute to the Crusades the rise in Europe of both heresy and science. Though stagnant, Arab culture in the time of the Crusades was far in advance of Europe's. Returning crusaders brought with them ideas and outlook which caught the imagination of the West, church or no, and the passage to and fro of Europe's holy warriors brought dramatic economic change.

All the while the church maintained its old corrupt ways. A reckoning was surely unavoidable.

No man is more disgusted than I am with the ambition, the avarice, and the profligacy of the priests [and I would like] to see this form of scoundrels put back into their proper places, so that they may be forced to live either without vices or without power.

—Guicciardini

V

From Depravity to Protestantism

T he Western church always showed its worst face while choosing its *Papa*. At these times people were bribed or killed or armies marched in favor of a candidate, and the choice of a particularly corrupt man showed more clearly than anything else that the church's moral decay was collective. A more orderly way of electing the successor to St. Peter was needed, but, typically, it was not the church that recognized this need for reform or moved to implement it. More typically, nothing changed.

The new way of choosing the pope, still practiced today, was developed in the thirteenth century. Papal elections had always been contentious affairs, since the clergy, the bishops, the wealthy families and the populace all could bring political pressure to bear, and all frequently contested or killed popes they did not approve of. There had developed a tradition in earlier centuries that electors choose a new pope in the city where his predecessor had died; this removed some of the interest groups from the contest and gave more influence to the electors alone. After the church reached the apparent nadir of papal politics during the reign of the female pope-makers in the tenth century, the Third Lateran Council in 1179 bestowed on the Sacred College of Cardinals, formerly a purely administrative body, the sole power to elect the pope on a two-thirds vote. The office of cardinal had until this time been largely honorific; a papal elector had been nearly anyone with enough backing to be appointed one. The aim of this new approach was to simplify the election process and centralize the authority of pope-making.

The Third Lateran Council established a fine, formal mechanism for papal elections, but it hardly assured order. Pope Innocent III died in the northern Italian town of Perugia in 1216, during a time of relative political chaos. Since the personal loyalties and political interests of the cardinals militated against any rapid election of the next pope, to encourage haste as well as divinity among the assembled cardinals "the Perugian civil authorities and the citizenry locked the doors of the house where the cardinals were meeting."[1] As a result Pope Honorius III was elected in one day. It was a first. From this seminal event the term *conclave* eventually came into use, from *cumlavis*, "locked with a key."

Remembering this incident, the cardinals quickly elected Gregory IX on the death of Honorius in 1227. Gregory soon made a mortal enemy out of Frederick II, the powerful German emperor. Frederick eventually invaded Italy and laid seige to Rome. Gregory also antagonized England, France, and Spain, and exacerbated tensions among the bishops, kings, and noble families whose power and wealth were tied to the papacy. When Gregory died in 1241 Rome was a divided city. Frederick and his armies were camped a short distance from Rome, where the city's nobles, bishops and cardinals were in a feeding frenzy over the spoils up for grabs with the election of the next pope. They all agreed, however, that it was imperative to prevent the Germans from seizing Rome and electing a pope favorable to their ambitions. The cardinals nevertheless seemed to dally even as events proposed to overtake them. The coercion of conclave was adopted again, and it would have the effect of institutionalizing the process for the future election of all popes.

The First Conclave, as it came to be called, did not have the venerable aspect of conclaves to follow, however. Pressed by events, the governor of Rome, Senator Matteo Rosso Orsini, bound the cardinals hand and foot and had them kicked and beaten in front of witnesses, shaming them for procrastinating in this dark hour. As a further antidote to their lethargy, Orsini had the cardinals untied and thrown into one large room in the building known as the Septizodium. The windows were covered and the doors locked. Orsini ordered his men to kill anyone who attempted to enter or leave. The first official conclave was under way.

Crude latrines were put into the room with the understanding that they would not be emptied until a pope was elected. There were not enough chairs or cots, and no medical attention or special food was allowed any of the old cardinals. It was summer and no windows were allowed to be opened. Interior gutters were used as garbage dumps and latrines; when the summer thunderstorms poured rain into them, they overflowed and spilled urine, feces, and rotting food onto the sleeping places of the cardinals. Nothing seemed to work. At one point Orsini even threatened to dig up Gregory's corpse and put it in the room with the honorable assemblage. Finally, after fifty-five days in that room, the cardinals elected Godfrey, the cardinal bishop at Santa Sabina, who chose the name Celestine IV. Such was the historical origin of the holy meetings used to elect Catholic popes today.

Godfrey died only two weeks later, however, before he was consecrated pope. To avoid a repetition of the last two months' ordeal, the cardinals tried to elect a new pope by communicating with each other by messenger rather than meeting. A year passed and no pope was elected. "By now it was Emperor Frederick of Germany who was intent on having a new pope. From his armed camp at Tivoli, he sent a message to the cardinals at Anagni: 'We are sending you the two cardinals we imprisoned at Capua (Otto Colonna, Jacopo of Praeneste), and the other cardinals who are in their palaces and fortresses. Get together! The church needs a pope.' "[2] Since the Holy Spirit was still dilatory in providing divine inspiration to this august group, Frederick's armies began to destroy property belonging to the cardinals; Frederick then marched on Rome. Without property and revenue, the cardinals recognized the wisdom of electing a pope quickly. They held secret meetings with Frederick and on June 25, 1243, selected Sinibald Fieschi as Pope Innocent IV.

Eleven years later, in 1254, Innocent died in Naples. As soon as the cardinals heard the news they tried to leave the city secretly. The laity was too quick for them. The governor of Naples learned of the cardinals' attempted flight and locked the city gates. He then apprehended the men, locked them in the house where Innocent had died and instructed them to fulfill their divine responsibilities. In a trice there was a new pope, Alexander IV. This was the Second Conclave; tradition had taken root.

The conclave developed out of Europe's need for political stability. "The political life and therefore the economic well-being of all European peoples revolved around that single bishop of Rome, his policies, his preferences, his family interests, and the dynasties he personally supported."[3] Since the cardinals were politically or financially in debt to various nobles, kings, emperors, or other cardinals, they were subject to intense lobbying pressure from several sources. Power was the name of the game, not spirituality. Spirituality *per se* was less important than the spiritual weapons in the hands of the pope, such as excommunication or consecration of kings and emperors. The papacy was a locus of political power for all Europe and the health of Europe's ruling class depended upon its stability.

Alexander IV died in 1261 and the good cardinals immediately elected a Frenchman, Jacques Pantelon, as Urban IV. Strong memories of the past do wonders to inspire the rapid discharge of spiritual responsibilities. Urban IV died at Perugia in 1264, leaving Europe in a state of potential chaos. At this time the Germans, French, Spanish and Italians all had differing views on the subject of who should control Sicily. The next pope would be a central force in the matter, and the rival national interests were reflected in sharp dispute among the cardinals. "Six months passed before the German emperor rattled his sword and whispered the dread word 'conclave.' "⁴ The two most antagonistic factions, pro-French and pro-German, appointed official compromisers to select two candidates on whom the cardinals would vote. The ultimate consequence of this compromise was the election of the cardinal of Santa Sabina, Guido the Fat of Fulcodi, who took the name of Clement IV, in February 1265.

Unfortunately for the German emperor, Guido's principal objective was to prevent the Hohenstraufen dynasty from appropriating real estate belonging to the papacy, euphemistically referred to as "the patrimony of St. Peter." Guido's loving response to the outrageous Hohenstraufen desire to "de-materialize" the papacy was to attempt the assassination of every member of the German emperor's family.⁵ It is not known if the Holy Spirit suggested this approach. During the three years of his reign, Guido's hatred of the Hohenstraufens was expressed in traditional papal bloodletting and other of the church's orthodox methods; he was largely successful in retaining the papacy's material wealth.

In 1268 Guido died in Viterbo and the cardinals met in the archbishop's palace there to elect another pope. It would take a long time. For two years there was no agreement, and in March 1271, concerned over the interminable delay, Europe's nobles began to arrive in Viterbo, some with their armies and retinues of body guards. In so sacred a matter as electing a pope, bloodshed was of course on the agenda. One faction or the other left mutilated bodies on the street from the previous night's lobbying efforts. One noble even stabbed a prince to death—at mass as he was about to receive Holy Eucharist, in full view of the assembled congregation of cardinals, bishops and nobles. The perpetrator, Guido of Montfort, would later be made commander-in-chief of all papal armies.⁶ In this atmosphere the sacred mission of electing the descendant of St. Peter was being carried out—on stretchers.

With such daunting power assembled in his town, the local governor (one Albert de Montebuono) was moved to follow tradition. He locked up the cardinals and their servants in one room of the archbishop's palace and the Third Conclave was underway. To impress upon the cardinals the need for celerity Albert allowed only bread and wine to be sent into the room; later this was reduced to water. Then the roof was removed (in order, a joke of the time went, to allow the Holy Spirit to enter and inspire the cardinals) and the sun and rain beat down on the venerable electors. The cardinals reacted by threatening to excommunicate their jailers and interdict the town. It was all to no avail. Finally, on September 1, 1271, after an animated sermon by a Father Bonaventure (later St. Bonaventure), the cardinals elected Toebaldo Visconti as pope. Visconti was in Palestine on a crusade at the time, so it was not until March 1272 that he was consecrated in Rome as Gregory X, nearly three-and-a-half years after the death of his predecessor.

Like Cardinal Wolsey of England, and Joseph Stalin of the Soviet Union, Gregory X recognized that great power can flow from control of administrative procedure. He called a general council of the church at Lyons, France, to set up more precise rules for all future elections of popes. Gregory made it church policy to hold a conclave to elect a pope, at which conclave: all doors would be locked; all windows barred; no one could enter or leave; no communication with the outside world would be allowed; all food was to be passed through a guarded window and examined for messages, knives or poison; no cardinal could touch the food or physical person of another cardinal; after three days food would be limited to one meal per day, and after eight days, only water, wine and bread would be provided; if a deadlock in voting occurred, the roof would be removed to expose the cardinals to the weather day and night, whether hot summer sun or heavy rainfalls.[7]

Having established all of these rules to reduce the chaos and politics of papal elections, Gregory gave the perpetual right of custodianship of the conclaves to his friends, the Savelli family. In 1712, with the death of the last Savelli, this right was passed onto the Chigi family, where it remains to this day.[8]

During most of the fourteenth century the pope was a political tool of the king of France. It was a time of growth for Europe's commercial classes, accompanied by a general increase of knowledge among the laity. The worldly papacy spent much of its time raising money and collecting taxes from the population and the nobility, leading many earnest men of the century to come into conflict with the popes.

The last pope before French domination was Boniface VIII, noted chiefly for instituting in 1300 the Year of Jubilee. "Plenary indulgences," remissions of punishment in the hereafter due to sin, were granted to all Catholics who visited Rome and performed certain ceremonies while there. This generated enormous income for both the Curia and the citizens of Rome. The residents of that great city, by virtue of living there, apparently could not receive as many indulgences as could visitors; the benefits of tourism were perhaps partial compensation. The Year of Jubilee had been ordained to be repeated every hundred years, but it produced so much money that it was rescheduled every fifty years, then every twenty-five years, as it is today.

Boniface died and in 1305 the cardinals elected as pope the archbishop of Bordeaux, who took the name Clement V and promptly settled in Avignon, France, partly to escape domination by the Roman nobility. He never ventured to Italy, establishing a tradition that would last seventy years and nearly lead to a permanent schism. Always in need of money, Clement entered into a conspiracy with King Philip, similarly pressed by the demands of war against the English and Flemish, to exploit a group called the Knights of Templar, a French Christian military order founded during the Crusades. In 1307 all of France's leading Templars were arrested, tortured, and made to confess to various religious crimes, including having worshipped Satan. Shortly the pope could rightfully suppress the order (he did so in 1313) and, with the help of the king, confiscate its property. All charges against the Templars were without foundation, according to Henry C. Lea's *History of the Inquisition,* but the purses of king and pope were well fattened.[9]

The domination of the papacy by the French king was to the disadvantage of the Germans, the Italians and the Romans, and it eventually led to a period known as the Great Schism. An initial skirmish was fought when Clement's successor, John XXII, attempted to assert greater control over the Franciscan order, which soon turned to the Holy Roman emperor for help. He in turn marched on Rome and installed a Franciscan as pope. This led to little more than a diminution of the status of the papacy, but events had been set in motion. Four Avignon popes came and went and finally Gregory XI took power. He moved back to Rome. The Italian clergy had by this time built up an enormous hostility to the French and Gregory attempted to appease them by opposing the French cardinals in a number of matters. It was to no avail. On Gregory's death in 1378 "the French and Roman parties in the College of Cardinals proved irreconcilable."[10] The Great Schism was launched. The two factions ended up electing rival popes, one ensconced at Avignon and recognized by France and another in residence in Rome and recognized by the enemies of France. To resolve this theological impasse, a council was summoned in 1409 which met in Pisa and declared both popes deposed for heresy and schism. The council then elected its own pope, who promptly died and was succeeded by an ex-pirate named Baldassare Cossa, who took the name of John XXIII. (In the twentieth century another pope would take the name of John XXIII, with the idea of trying to erase this blot on Catholicism. Hearing of the event, Nikita Khrushchev sent him a book on fifteenth-century history.) The result of all of this maneuvering was only that three popes now claimed the papacy.

With the help of lucky political circumstance, the Great Schism healed nearly as quickly as it had cracked open. In 1414 a new council was convened at Constance. It deposed John XXIII, persuaded the Roman pope to resign and in 1417 elected Pope Martin V. The pope of Avignon, by now one Benedict XIII, refused to cooperate in the divine negotiations, but his successor lost the support of France for political reasons and by 1430 Martin was generally recognized as legitimate. The Council of Constance also attended to some business less fraught with antagonism between the good cardinals, a matter that all compassionate clerics could agree upon: final condemnation of the heretical priest John Wycliffe, who had dared to preach a "priesthood of all believers" and translated the Bible into English for the sake of the unwashed. The council ordered Wycliffe's grave dug up and his bones burned. Thus, despite political rancor and clerical corruption, theological purity continued to advance.

While in church affairs the fifteenth century generated antipopes, increased the powers of the Inquisition, and uncovered the fraud of the Donation of Constantine, in the secular world Vasco da Gama and Columbus explored the terrestrial and Copernicus the celestial realms, the Renaissance was about to be born and humanity develop an idea of its own importance, and human affairs in the West would undergo two major technical revolutions at once with the arrival of gunpowder and printing, both long known in China. The Chinese used gunpowder to entertain themselves with firecrackers, but Europe's Christians quickly realized that God did not create such things merely for entertainment—in gunpowder God was revealing His plan. So it was. Musket and cannon would help a number of Europeans on their way to heaven and the reach of Western imperialism was greatly extended.

Printing, however, transformed the whole of Western society. The power of publishing to spread ideas and the power of the people when motivated by them would demonstrate themselves soon enough. Gutenberg developed a press with changeable type and an ink that could legibly adhere to paper. Use of the process spread rapidly throughout Europe. Predictably, the church responded by 1559 with its *Index Librorum Prohibitorum,* the Index of Forbidden Books. It was merely one of what would become many tools of Catholic censors. To read books on the list was a mortal sin punishable by hellfire and Inquisition. Incredibly, the Index was in force as late as the mid-1960s.

In all fairness it must be noted that Gutenberg and the West were not the first to conceive of this revolutionary device. Even in Europe it is possible that others, Procope Waldfogel of Prague or Coster of Haarlem in Holland, came up with the idea first, but the use of movable type dates at least to eleventh-century China, evolving to perfected metal type in either China or Korea by the fifteenth century and widely used in both countries. In the words of Fernand Braudel, the great modern historian of pre-capitalist Europe, "It does not matter who invented movable type in the West . . . The problem is rather to know whether the discovery was a revival, an imitation, or a rediscovery." Portuguese travellers brought printed books back from the Far East and it is possible that they were circulated in northern Europe and inspired printing there, but this is uncertain.[11]

The ability to mass produce books and pamphlets had of course its greatest effect in education, which now could hope to be granted universally. Nothing short of foreign occupation or plague could transform a society so much. The printed word was quickly understood as a challenge to the power of the church. Average understanding in the West could now increase fantastically. After five thousand years wandering in a field of eye-level theological brambles, Western society happened onto the tiniest sliver of a trail. Disappearing entirely here, suddenly widening there, it was a path to the City of Man, a place nearly free of theological terror at least.

The end of the fifteenth and the beginning of the sixteenth centuries, if it was possible, saw a new low in papal greed and depravity. In 1497 Cardinal Rodrigo Borgia, age sixty-two, was elected to the throne of St. Peter and took the name of Alexander VI. His credentials for Christian piety included a life of simony, seven children by two mistresses said to be mother and daughter, a devotion to poison as a tool of assassination and an uncommon love of debauchery. On Alexander's election to the papacy, Giovanni de' Medici counseled, "Flee, we are in the hands of a wolf."[12]

Borgia obtained the papacy by purchase, eliminating his two principal rivals by paying them bribes. One of them, Cardinal Ascanio Sforza, was paid four mule-loads of bullion "dispatched from Borgia's palace to Sforza's during the conclave."[13] Having no sexual compunctions as a cardinal, Alexander saw no reason to gain them on becoming pope. He boasted openly of his simony, the selling of spiritual favors. To keep his adversaries and critics in line, "Alexander poisoned, imprisoned or otherwise immobilized inconvenient opponents" throughout his reign. When a man named Savonarola called Alexander's papacy "a prostitute who sits upon the throne of Solomon and signals to passers-by," Alexander excommunicated him, arranged for papal examiners to torture him for a confession of heresy, and finally turned him over to the civil executioners to be hanged and burned.[14]

Alexander's daughter Lucretia was betrothed twice to Spanish noblemen and married three times to Italian princes for reasons of political expediency—all by the time she was twenty-two. Lucretia's first marriage was annulled by Alexander to expedite the alignment of the papacy with Spain and Naples against France and Milan. Lucretia's second marriage, to the illegitimate son of King Alfonso II of Naples, was terminated by the assassination of the boy at the behest of Lucretia's brother, Cesare Borgia. A new family relationship was needed with Louis XII of France. The sheets of Lucretia's bed were the sails of the Borgia ship of state.

After Alexander died, however, Lucretia began to lead a moral and exemplary life. She married Alfonso d'Este, and, when he became the duke of Ferrara, successfully transformed his court into a center of art and learning; Titian and Dosso Dossi were among the painters she patronized. The woman who had come to epitomize the moral corruption of the time became a model of moral virtue once freed from the influence of her papal father, a sad commentary on the state of the papacy in this period.

In 1499 Louis wanted to marry Anne of Brittany in order to add her duchy to the French crown. First his marriage to an invalid woman had to be annulled. Alexander accommodated the good king—in return for thirty thousand ducats and Louis's political support for his son Caesare's ambition to marry the daughter of Alfonso of Naples so that . . . The story goes on a long while. Caesare's political career suffered constant setbacks, however, and to raise the boy's spirits Alexander threw a Vatican party known in the history of pornography as "the Ballet of the Chestnuts." The main entertainment was provided by naked courtesans crawling on their hands and knees among the candelabra picking up chestnuts with various parts of their anatomy. Prizes were given in various contests, including a competition among those who could "perform the [sexual] act most often with the courtesans."[15] It is not known if, or how often, Alexander himself was able to rise to the occasion.

The pope's lavish expenses steadily emptied Vatican coffers, so in 1503 Alexander replenished them by creating eighty new offices in the Curia, sold for 780 ducats each, and auctioning off nine cardinalships, apparently worth 120,000 ducats the lot.[16] It was enough for any number of ecclesiastical orgies, with a little to spare for saving souls.

Alexander died that same year, and the public reacted as though a demon had met its end. One rumor had Alexander's corpse foaming at the mouth and dragged to the grave by a rope because it was too terrible to touch.[17] Thus lived and died the 214th inheritor of St. Peter's mantle. In Alexander papal piety had attained full flower.

After the twenty-six day reign of Alexander's successor, Pius III, Giuliano della Rovere was elected pope in only a day and chose the name Julius II. Rovere, it is said, had distributed his bribes before Pius's corpse could stiffen. Julius set the tone of his papacy in 1506 by personally leading an army to reassert papal authority over Bologna and Perugia. Julius's relationship with France ran hot and cold. During a conflict in which French support seemed useful, Julius gave three cardinalships to Louis XII. But then the political winds shifted against France and Julius saw the opportunity to remove French authority and influence from the papal states. The good pope engaged the services of Mathaus Schinner, the bellicose bishop of Sion who had long hated his French neighbors. Placed on a five-year subsidy, Schinner became commander of the papal forces and went to battle wearing the cardinal's hat he had won in the bargain. To inspire the soldiers of Christ, Schinner told his troops that he wished to bathe in French blood.[18]

These military campaigns did not pretend to concern sophisticated theological issues; they were wars to accumulate territory and power. But military outlays were depleting the papal treasury, and Julius needed money to undertake other projects. Art was one of his favorites. Julius was well acquainted with Michelangelo, but their relationship sailed in waters clear or stormy depending on whether the pope paid his debts to the Western world's leading artist. The most serious break came with Julius's refusal to pay for a huge mass of stone Michelangelo had hauled and cut for Julius's own tomb, planned to be thirty-six feet high and graced with forty larger-than-life statues. Michelangelo returned to Florence in a rage, vowing never to deal with the dishonorable pontiff again. Julius, meanwhile, was so inspired by Michelangelo's design of his tomb that he resolved to build a "new St. Peter's as suitable housing for it."[19] In the glory of pope rather than God was the crowning artistic achievement of Catholicism conceived. After endless entreaties conducted through numerous intermediaries, the pope finally was able to regain Michelangelo's services. The project: a statue of Julius himself, three times life-size, in celebration of his conquest of Bologna. "When it was viewed by the subject while still in clay, Michelangelo asked whether he should place a book in the left hand. 'Put a sword there,' answered the warrior pope, 'I know nothing of letters.' "[20]

Short on money due to extravagance and war, Julius had to devise a means of generating income to pay for his many projects, which included both the new St. Peter's and a new Vatican, the one that stands today. Setting up manufacturing companies would be too complicated; selling Vatican real estate was out of the question, since the papacy had made the constant acquisition of property into an eleventh commandment. Orchestrating stock swindles and foreign currency schemes were alternatives not available until the nineteenth and twentieth centuries. The pope was compelled to do what ecclesiastical authorities had done for centuries: sell spiritual favors.

As Tuchman puts it, the sale of indulgences was "a device of fateful consequence"[21]—the abuse of most offense to those who would spark the Reformation. Indulgences were a commodity produced without competition and by the stroke of the papal pen which, for this purpose, never ran out of ink or inclination. Julius initiated the public sale of indulgences to construct the Basilica of St. Peter. It was not finished in his lifetime, and Julius's successor, Leo X, needed still more money to complete the job. The sale of indulgences was extended throughout Europe, and broadened to the maximum extent: for enough money, one could buy "complete absolution and remission of all sins." For the credit-worthy, the bill could be paid over an eight-year term.

In Germany, the financial details were sometimes directly managed by the Fugger banking family. In one case, a young noble, Albrecht of Brandenburg, had purchased three church offices (a bishopric and two archbishoprics) for somewhere between twenty-four and thirty thousand ducats. "Unable to raise the money, Albrecht had borrowed from the Fuggers, whom he was now to reimburse through the proceeds from the indulgences." Agents of the Fuggers then sat in churches throughout the lands, papal banners waving behind them, and collected money from parishioners in return for printed certificates evidencing the pardon of spiritual punishment.[22]

Leo came up with other, equally innovative ways to raise money. One of these concerned Cardinal Alfonso Petrucci of Siena, who allegedly led a conspiracy of cardinals to poison the Holy Father. Arrests and tortures produced various confessions, and Petrucci eventually pleaded guilty and was executed. Leo then pardoned the other cardinals in return for enormous fines. Although some archival evidence suggests that the conspiracy may have been real, "so far-fetched was the plot that the inference could not be avoided that the Pope, seizing upon some informer's tattle, had promoted the whole affair for the sake of the fines."[23]

It was into this atmosphere that a number of men with moral principles rose to challenge the cupidity and depravity of the church. These men—they would one day be called Protestants—turned their revulsion into theological and political revolution. It was long overdue.

The Protestants: Moral Reform or Political Opportunism?

The Bible is for the Government of the people, by the people and for the people.

—John Wycliffe

The corruption of the sixteenth-century church engendered revulsion among the laity, especially as geographical distance from Rome increased and the benefits of Rome's economy correspondingly decreased. Dramatic changes in the character of Europe's economy were at work, coming to a head in this time of trans-Atlantic colonization.

This pair of factors provided an opening for secular rulers, never enthralled with sharing power, to support an outright break with the church. The result was the emergence throughout Europe of several new churches and religious traditions—Lutheran, Calvinist (Reformed), Anglican, Anabaptist, Antitrinitarian—all anti-Catholic in orientation. These are collectively referred to as "Protestant" churches, a term stemming from their "protest" at the 1529 Diet of Speyer against the church's condemnation of the writings of Martin Luther and declaration that he was a political outlaw. The movement that gave birth to these churches was called by its adherents the "Reformation," to express their view that they were reforming the church. It comes from the Latin *reformare*, "to renew"; the reformers believed they were renewing Christianity by returning it to its original biblical sources.

In the long view, commercial factors were perhaps more important than any other in both driving and allowing the revolutionary changes of the Reformation. As Durant describes it,

> The replacement of the Mediterranean-Egyptian route to India by the all-water route, and the development of European commerce with America, enriched the Atlantic countries while helping to impoverish Italy; German trade moved more and more down the Rhine to North Sea outlets, less and less over the mountains to Italy; Germany became commercially independent of Italy; a northern drift and pull of power wrenched Germany from the Italian web of trade and religion, and gave Germany the will and strength to stand alone.
>
> The discovery of America had even more lasting effects upon Italy than the new route to India. Gradually the Mediterranean nations declined, left on a siding in the movement of men and goods; the Atlantic nations came to the fore, enriched with American trade and gold.[24]

This era of the division of Western Christianity was triggered by a Catholic priest named Martin Luther, a professor of theology at the University of Wittenberg. Luther had doubts regarding the theology of indulgences and was scornful of distributing them for material reasons, particularly for cash. In an effort to combat indulgences and other church evils, Luther employed the academic form of submitting theses, or sentences for discussion, to initiate scholarly debate. In 1517 he submitted ninety-five of these theses. They quickly came to public light, and, according to some scholars, were posted on the doors of the Wittenberg cathedral. These theses contained in the main two essential themes. First, Luther condemned papal corruption and depravity, a criticism to which the Christian population of Germany enthusiastically subscribed, having openly denounced the abuses for more than a century. Second, Luther challenged papal jurisdiction over purgatory, claiming that even if the pope exercised such authority over those fiery regions of theological imagination, he should liberate the souls imprisoned there free of charge. The corollary concept of indulgences was denigrated as a papal fiction, since the treasury of the church is the Gospel, not a coffer of accumulated spiritual pardons dispensed in purchase.

Among other, more esoteric criticisms was disagreement with the church's conception of the bread and wine of the Eucharist as literally the body and blood of Christ. Although there is some support for the church position in the Gospels, the idea had not taken root until the eleventh century. Intentionally or not, it served the old purpose of bringing pagans into the fold. Europe was riddled with pagans and former pagans, and most observed ceremonies in which they ate things representing a god (or, in one case, representing the accumulated sin of somebody recently deceased). The concept of the Eucharist, from the Greek *eukharistia*, "gratitude" to the gods, far pre-dated Christianity. Most primitive cultures believed that eating the flesh and drinking the blood of animals sacrificed to the gods allowed human participation in their power; some regarded the animals or crops of a sacrifice as the god incarnate, and accordingly believed they were actually eating the body of the god. This ritual, which created a communion between believer and deity, was practiced throughout Europe, the Mediterranean, Latin America and Africa. It was also well established in Greece and Rome, in the festivals of Dionysus and Bacchus. As James G. Frazer, the renowned anthropologist, explains the practice,

> It is easy to understand why a savage should desire to partake of the flesh of an animal or man whom he regards as divine. By eating the body of the god, he shares in the god's attributes and powers. And when the god is a corn-god, the corn is his proper body; when he is a vine-god, the juice of the grape is his blood; by eating the bread and drinking the wine the worshipper partook of the real body and blood of his god. Thus the drinking of wine in the rites of a vine-god like Dionysus is not an act of revelry, it is a solemn sacrament.[25]

The Protestants challenged various aspects of this rite, some tampering with incidental features and others denying that Christ was physically present at all—the whole ritual was merely symbolic and Christ's words at the Last Supper were only metaphorical. Against this challenge the church of Rome acted, proclaiming doctrinally at the 1551 session of the Council of Trent that the bread and wine contained the physical body and blood of Christ. The council also made it mandatory for all Christians to receive the Eucharist at least once a year; failure to do so was a mortal sin, punishable by hellfire for all eternity.

Luther was the first influential critic to bring all these criticisms to bear coherently and powerfully. The church reacted swiftly, calling Luther to Rome in less than a year to face charges of heresy, but the old game had played itself out. Germany's political and religious climate was strongly supportive of Luther. The site of the inquiry was moved to Augsburg, and eventual papal bulls denouncing Luther went unenforced. Ultimately Luther set up a separate religion, Lutheranism, and his example caused others to set up their own religions, prompted by theological sub-disagreements with Luther and fired by the underlying premise of the reform rebellion: an individual's relationship to God was more direct, less mediated by the church, and, as a logical derivative, local congregations had authority to determine doctrine.

From this time Western Christianity divided. Christians holding allegiance to the pope began to be called Roman Catholics, to distinguish them from their schismatic offspring. The new Protestant churches were in every way a reform of the degenerate institution from which they sprang, but they would be unable to avoid developing the excesses of their forebear. The fragmentation of Christianity provided each of the Christian creeds a rationale to initiate open hostilities against one another, as they vied to demonstrate the righteousness of their respective modifications of belief; theological contests quickly escalated into armed conflict. Christianity could change its form, but not its nature.

The first serious split in the Reformation movement was generated by the founder of Protestantism in Switzerland, Ulrich Zwingli. Long a critic of papal practices, Zwingli was animated by the doctrines and success of Luther and found the secular authorities of the Swiss Federation even more eager than he to foment a break with Rome. Zwingli soon moved from general criticisms of Roman practice to specific criticisms of Roman theology. Strange as it may seem, the most serious of these criticisms was Zwingli's contention that there was no real presence of Christ even in the bread and wine of the Last Supper, but a spiritual one only. Luther could not agree wholly with so radical a departure from Christian tradition, and the dispute between the two most influential Protestants of the time was fiery.

This theoretical division would lead to numerous formal ones in the decades to follow, but Protestant individualism would formally manifest itself more instantly. A pacifist group called the Anabaptists (from a term coined by Zwingli, to "rebaptise" when of age) quickly parted ways with Zwingli and developed a theology of religious independence from any temporal authority. Anabaptist congregations quickly sprang up throughout Europe and were widely persecuted by Catholic and Protestant alike for their anti-state ideology.

In 1522 Luther's colleague at Wittenberg, a man named Carlstadt, publicly criticized the limits of Luther's scope of reform, and two years later Thomas Muentzer accused Luther of capitulating to political authorities in order to obtain secular backing for his growing influence. In the spring of 1525 Muentzer joined German peasants rebelling in central Germany over social and economic grievances. He issued vitriolic pamphlets arguing that the Church could be realized only by suffering and resolute opposition to exploitative rule.

Luther was virulently opposed to the peasant rebellion. "Wherefore, my lords, free, save, help, and pity the poor people," he wrote in a pamphlet entitled "Against the Thievish, Murderous Hordes of Peasants." But to accomplish this noble end Luther recommended that the authorities "stab, smite, and slay, all ye that can. If you die in battle you could never have a more blessed end, for you die obedient to God's Word in Romans 13, and in the service of love to free your neighbor from the hands of hell and the devil. . . . Let none think this too hard who considers how intolerable is rebellion."[26]

In what today is a caricature of German devotion to the state, Luther saw temporal authority as subject only to God and not at all to man. He declared its actions invalid only when in explicit conflict with the Scriptures, but severely mediated even this restriction with the assertion that, even in such cases, resistance should be only passive. It was up to God to punish offending rulers. Luther was the theological precursor of Hegel, Nietzsche, and, ultimately, Hitler.

Another variant of Luther's reformation was Calvinism, founded by John Calvin, an urbane French lawyer and humanist who originally sought to reform the church in France. He attempted to engage in peaceful debate over church policies and practices, particularly at the Sorbonne in Paris, but the ecclesiastical authorities were not inclined to change in Paris any more than elsewhere. His efforts meeting with failure and persecution, Calvin fled Paris in 1533 for the tranquility of the countryside. His life in France continued to be one of travail, however, so he went to Basel, Switzerland, the city of scholars and printers. There, at the age of twenty-six, Calvin wrote *The Institutes of the Christian Religion*, which appeared in 1535. This disquisition emphasizes the awe-inspiring majesty and sovereignty of God and concludes that salvation is determined by a dreadful decree, called *decretum horrible*, in which God appoints to each soul, in advance, eternal happiness or damnation. It was a bizarre and fanatical doctrine in which man is nothing in the scheme of God's universe, but it came to be one of the principal tenets of Calvinism.

Calvin spent much time teaching, wherever the opportunity arose, and traveled extensively to do so. In July 1536 he journeyed to Geneva. Because of his growing reputation, he was approached by Guillaume Farel, who sought Calvin's assistance in reforming the city's church. The following January Geneva's principal governing body, the Little Council, adopted a set of articles for religious reform which had been prepared by Calvin and Farel. These included the imposition of discipline in secular as well as religious affairs, to be carried out by "certain persons of good life and repute." Resistance to this newly contrived authority by much of the population, coupled with the efforts of the church of Bern to impose its own rites on the citizenry of Geneva, compelled Calvin and Farel to flee for their lives. The population of Geneva was not quite ready for sanctity.

But in 1539 Jacopo Cardinal Sadoleto sought to bring back the recalcitrant believers of Geneva to the obedience of Roman authority. Faced with this dreadful prospect, the Genevese determined that Calvin was preferable to the pope. Accordingly they requested him to return to assist them in the developing confrontation with Rome. "There is no place under heaven that I am more afraid of," Calvin wrote;[27] but, submitting to the persistence of the citizens of Geneva, he accepted the divine calling and returned to the city that had cast him out on September 13, 1541. He would stay there the remainder of his life.

Calvin undertook to reform, by force, not merely the church but the whole of the canton society. The city's moral regulations were now elaborated and stringently enforced; gambling, drunkenness, dancing and even the singing of distasteful songs warranted severe punishment. Calvin's opponents quickly became victims and retribution was stern: banishment for lesser theological crimes, death for blasphemy (by beheading) and heresy (usually by strangulation or the pyre). Calvin did not hesitate to encourage the burning of witches. On one occasion, in an apparent spasm of pity, Calvin recommended that his heretical adversary, Michael Servetus, be put to death by the sword. But the fires of passion had already been aroused in the population. For his anti-trinitarian views Servetus was burned alive.

Much of the population of Geneva regretted Calvin's return, notably those who liked to drink and dance, and his life was generally in jeopardy. Calvin's temper, which he called the "wild beast" within his soul, did not ingratiate him with friend or adversary. However, he gained the support of the merchant class by condoning usury, even though it is condemned in the Bible, and his tenure in power was assured. This was only the first step in a sweeping subordination of Scripture to commercialism. Calvin's doctrine of predestination lacked any sure indicators of who God had chosen as his "elect," but it was only reasonable that people so select would meet with success in their brief sojourn on earth. It would make no sense if those ordained by God for eternal bliss should suffer terrestrial privation. This gradually led to the assumption that financial success was a sign of divine favor. In this way Calvinism and its offshoots eventually formed the theological justification for an emerging creed: capitalism. Whatever its contribution in this respect, Calvinism was finally a sweeping denigration of human earthly existence, one of the most repressive theologies ever conceived. As Durant says, "We shall always find it hard to love the man who darkened the human soul with the most absurd and blasphemous conception of God in all the long and honored history of nonsense."[28]

With the death of Luther in 1546, Calvin and his followers were the locus of dynamism in the Reformation. Their descendants became the Reformed and Presbyterial churches of Switzerland, France, Scotland, the Netherlands, Germany and throughout Europe; their Congregational and Baptist offshoots would come to have strong influence in the British colonies, including the United States.

Calvin's role in Europe, like Napoleon's and Lenin's, was that of internationalist revolutionary. Once he had secured nearly complete control of the Geneva city-state (about 1555), Calvin looked abroad. France was his native country; its Catholic millions beckoned.

> Calvin then launched a campaign for the evangelization of France and devoted to this end most of his formidable energies until his death in 1564. Calvin trained hundreds of other exiles in the principles of his theology, at first informally and then, after 1559, within the curriculum of the new Academy of Geneva. His work was supported by dozens of refugee printers, who made Geneva an important printing center and from it distributed thousands of French Bibles, psalters, and works of Protestant theology and polemics. . . . The French exiles trained by the theologians of Geneva were sent back to their homeland as missionary pastors. There they established local churches, and bound them together into an ecclesiastical structure that soon covered much of the nation.[29]

Such success was possible because of the weakness of the French state. In northern Europe Protestantism was quickly triumphant. In southern Europe Catholicism remained secure. In France, however, there was no resolution of the contest between the Roman church and its rebels. Obsessed by the hope of extending French domination over Italy and enfeebled by decades of fruitless conflict with the Hapsburg empire in pursuit of that hope, the French royal house had "squandered the monarchy's wealth and prestige, neglected to check the growth of Protestantism, and failed to build a military-bureaucratic apparatus capable of keeping order."[30] As a result, France would suffer the devastation of the Wars of Religion.

The sizable and militant minority of French Protestants, called Huguenots, numbered many nobles among its ranks. Eventually these came to include princes in the line of succession to the throne. "The Calvinist religious movement and the Bourbon-led political movement began to fuse in 1560, when a number of aristocrats were converted to Calvinism. While many of them were sincere in their conversion, they also found in Calvinism an ideology useful for influencing public opinion and an ecclesiastical structure useful for raising money and mustering troops."[31] Most of the sixteenth century was for France a time of unrelenting skirmishes between Catholic monarchy and Huguenot upstarts.

Between 1559 and 1574 France was nominally ruled by the "sickly youths," Francis II, fifteen years old when he gained the throne and dead in just over a year, and Charles IX, ten years old at his brother's death and dominated by his mother, Catherine de Medicis. Tensions with the Huguenots were increased immeasurably and irreversibly in 1572, when, with thousands of prominent Huguenots in Paris for the wedding of Henry of Navarre, the titular Huguenot leader, to Catherine's daughter Marguerite de Valois, Catherine persuaded her son to order what became known as the St. Bartholomew's Day Massacre. Twenty thousand Huguenots died in the ensuing carnage.

Henry III attempted outright repression of the Huguenot movement immediately on his accession to the throne in 1574, but the effort failed militarily and the king became little more than a mediator between three groups: Huguenots, "Politiques" (Roman Catholics loyal to the king and urging religious toleration), and Catholic extremists unwilling to allow heretical worship anywhere in the realm. The death in 1584 of Henry III's brother left Henry of Navarre, the apex of the Protestant danger, next in the line of succession. Events picked up the momentum of a locomotive. The possibility of Henry Navarre's ascension to the throne prompted the revival of the fanatically anti-Protestant Holy League; the start of war between Huguenot and League, which had enlisted an unwilling Henry III in its efforts; Henry III's flight from Paris, forced by the League on his attempt to end hostilities; his successful plot to assassinate the head of the Holy League; his own assassination at the hand of a fanatical monk; and Henry of Navarre's elevation to the throne (as Henry IV) even as the League remained in control of Paris.

Things were in stalemate for four years, until Henry, now king rather than Huguenot, conceived a brilliant tactic. He converted to Roman Catholicism. "Paris is well worth a mass," he is reported to have explained. The resolve of the League was mortally wounded and in 1594 Henry was able to occupy Paris.

With a clear-headedness exceptional for the time, Henry sought to reduce rather than excite religious hostility in order to unify his land. In 1598 Henry issued the Edict of Nantes, which confirmed Roman Catholicism as the official religion of France but granted the Huguenots freedom of worship. For a dozen years France lived in religious peace, but on May 14, 1610, a fanatic Roman Catholic named Francois Ravaillec stabbed Henry to death in Paris. Henry's successors resumed the persecution of the Huguenots and Europe's experiment with theological coexistence came to an end.

The division of opinion generated by the challenge of Protestantism was perhaps no less severe in England during this time, but the strength of the English monarchy assured a more orderly end to the conflict it caused. The English church was in a state of unrest in the 1520s. Anticlericalism was rampant, Erasmus was preaching humanism and events on the continent were generating great interest. King Henry VIII, the Catholic son of Henry VII, had ascended the throne of England in 1509. He assisted the pope in containing both the ideological and physical assaults on the church, and as a reward Pope Leo X granted him the title *Defensor Fidei*, "Defender of the Faith"; the title would tarnish quickly.

Henry was naturally flamboyant. He was for a while athletic, until he grew older and corpulent, at which time his size was described as "five-foot-six by five-foot-five." Henry styled himself a bit of an intellectual, and he sought popularity. While young, Henry indulged in private pursuits, leaving Thomas Wolsey, the archbishop of York and a cardinal from 1515, to administer both England's church affairs and most of its affairs of state. Wolsey can be compared to Joseph Stalin, since both worked and wormed their way to the top by performing administrative chores disdained by others—until one day they were on top of the political pile. Wolsey wanted to be pope and England was his stepping stone to that end. Wolsey accordingly spent much of his time in foreign affairs, often at the expense of England, much of whose wealth he put in the hands of the church and its monasteries. Resentment towards clerical rule and the accretion of church wealth grew unchecked among the population, and with Wolsey as *de facto* head of both church and state, ill will generated by such things as inflation inevitably attached itself to the church as well.

Henry meanwhile spent his nights trying to produce a son with his wife, Catherine of Aragon, and his days trying to nullify his marriage with her because she seemed unable to bear a child. Henry was also infatuated with a girl named Anne Boleyn, whose presumed biological ability to have children was coupled with her willingness, of course, to do so with the king of England. Henry's ministers attempted to persuade Pope Clement VII to annul the king's marriage with Catherine on the theory that it offended divine law—Catherine was the widow of Henry's brother. Since he was now the "Defender of the Faith" Henry expected a favorable decision. Clement, however, under pressure from the Holy Roman emperor and said to be naturally indecisive, finally refused the annulment.

Henry's marriage frustrations coincided with the rise of anticlericalism in England, and in an orgasmic display of political power he removed Cardinal Wolsey, blaming him both for failing to secure his annulment and proving unable to establish England as the pivotal power on the continent. In 1533 Henry openly defied Rome and married Anne Boleyn. Parliament passed the Act of Restraint of Appeals to Rome, cutting all legal ties between England and the papacy. In 1534 Parliament declared Henry the head of the English church. In the blink of an eye, the Church of England was born. Later Henry would dissolve his relationship with Anne Boleyn and marry again, many times. Many rulers govern with their "head" or rule with their "heart"; Henry VIII was one of those men who rule with their penis. The Church of England was born because of Henry's sexual desires and the pope's unwillingness to indulge them at the expense of canon law. It must be concluded, therefore, that the Church of England was conceived in lust and born out of wedlock.

Whatever his personal motivations, Henry's demolition of papal rule in England had consequences far beyond his intent. "Luther believed that he was establishing, or at least reforming, a universal Church. Henry's church laid no claim to universal dominion. It merely claimed to have absolute, independent jurisdiction over the souls of Englishmen. In doing so, it laid down the principles of nationalism both in politics and in religion."[32] It could be argued that Henry's actions were of farther-reaching historical importance in North America rather than in Europe. Since England had broken with the papacy, it could (and did) contest the pope's granting of the Americas to Spain and Portugal. Had England remained Catholic and therefore obedient to that grant, the United States would have been part of Spanish America, its immigrants of entirely different ethnic extraction.

Having gratified his sexual urges and temporarily resolved his theological problems, Henry undertook during the period from 1536 to 1539 to dissolve England's monasteries, effectively eliminating centers of Catholic propaganda and increasing the king's property while in the process unfortunately also destroying innumerable treasures of art and learning. It is estimated that 20 percent of England's landed wealth at this time was owned by the monasteries. Most of this property was transferred by the king to the nobility and gentry. At the same time, the monks were given a strong impetus to abandon Catholicism and declare allegiance to the new state church.

The archbishop of Canterbury, Thomas Cranmer, had dissolved Henry's marriage to Catherine of Aragon even as the Act of Appeals was being debated. Cranmer would provide regular marital services to Henry, later invalidating his marriage to Anne Boleyn, marrying him to Jane Seymour (who died while giving birth to a male heir), arranging his divorce from her successor, Anne of Cleves, marrying him to Catherine Howard and presiding over the dissolution of that marriage as well, and finally (1543) marrying him to Catherine Parr. She was Henry's last wife. As befits the founder of a church later renowned for its puritanism, Henry died, in 1547, of syphilis.

When the religious dust temporarily settled, the Reformation had created a new group of rulers, both secular and theological. In the secular realm the break with the papacy by England, France and Germany left a void in the minds of the rulers and in the hearts of the population. This vacuum was filled by the enunciation of another doctrine, one loitering in the shadows of the palaces for centuries but now able to come into the open. Since monarchs had the awesome responsibility of ensuring the well-being of their subjects, it seemed only logical that God should deal with them directly rather than through papal mediation. Thus the monarchs came to claim that there was a "divine right of kings" to provide for the welfare of the people on behalf of God. In the words of William McGovern in his *From Luther to Hitler,*

> The Protestant who denied all connection between God and the papacy felt forlorn in the absence of contacts with some divinely appointed institution, until he was told that he could find this contact in the monarch who ruled over him. If his state and the ruler of his state owed their existence and their power to Divine Providence, he could be content even though all ties with other countries were cut. The Catholic who wished to remain Catholic, but who desired to share in the thrill of nationalist emotion which was arising all over Europe, felt that he could do so if he accepted the doctrine that though the pope was ordained by God to rule over purely spiritual matters, his own ruler was no less directly ordained by God to rule over temporal affairs.[33]

Instead of Christian Europe there now stood a Europe of states whose power over their feudal subdivisions was certain. Instead of papal religious authority, there now stood the authority of a host of Protestant theologians, less venal but more severe than their Vatican forebears and often entirely in the service of their kings and the new age of unfettered commercial enterprise.

Avoid, as you would the plague, a clergyman who is also a man of business.

—St. Jerome

For if a man know not how to rule his own house, how shall he take care of the Church of God?

—Timothy 3:5

VI

The Theology of Finance

T he Catholic church had ever been the enemy of the nationalist impulse. The rise of nation states in the sixteenth century had drastically limited the secular power at the disposal of the pope, forcing him to rely almost entirely on the ever-shrinking Holy Roman (Austrian) Empire for its troops. The rise of nationalism as a popular ideology in the nineteenth century, and the ideological hostility of the forces of the coming age, most fearsome at first in the form of Napoleon, threatened soon to end forever the secular power of the church. The thorough-going hatred of the church expressed by the French people during the Revolution, its massive execution of priests and confiscation of church property, told a terrible story of the fate of the church under republicanism.

That part of Italy ruled by the popes was accordingly a bastion of the worst of the old ways. Between 1823 and 1846

almost two hundred thousand citizens of the papal states were severely punished (death, life imprisonment, exile, galleys) for political offenses; another 1.5 million were subject to constant police surveillance and harassment.

There was a gallows permanently in the square of every town and city and village. Railways, meetings of more than three people, and all newspapers were forbidden. All books were censored. A special tribunal sat permanently in each place to try, condemn, and execute the accused. All trials were conducted in Latin. Ninety-nine percent of the accused did not understand the accusations against them. Every pope tore up the stream of petitions that came constantly asking for justice, for the franchise, for reform of the police and prison system. When revolts occurred in Bologna, in the Romangna, and elsewhere, they were put down with wholesale executions, sentences to lifelong hard labor in the state penitentiary, to exile, to torture. Austrian troops were always being called in to suppress the revolts.[1]

After putting down a revolutionary uprising in Rome itself in 1846, the papal victors strangely held a plebiscite. Did the people of the Papal State want to join the Italian republic? The result was hardly what the papacy expected. An astonishing 99 percent of the voters said yes.[2]

The handwriting was on the wall. Victor Emmanual II of the Kingdom of Piedmont-Sardinia to the north annexed three papal provinces in 1860. The London *Times* in 1869 hoped for the dissolution of the papacy itself, sardonically predicting "the final passing of this venerable institution."[3] By 1870 the papacy was left with but an arc of land around Rome, under the protection of troops on loan from the reestablished monarchy in France.

The pope had only spiritual weapons with which to struggle. In 1864, in his *Syllabus of Errors* and the accompanying encyclical *Quanta Cura*, Pius IX warned all Catholics against everything that went under the name of liberalism, progress and civilization. "The papacy denounced unrestricted freedom of speech and of the press. The concept of equal status for all religions was totally rejected . . . [Pius] also made it clear that he disliked intensely the concept of democratic government and that his preference was for absolute monarchies. He further denounced 'the proponents of freedom of conscience and freedom of religion' as well as 'all of those who assert that the Church may not use force.' "[4]

In 1869 the papacy acted on this body of tripe; Pius called what became known as the First Vatican Council. He wanted sweeping new powers to combat the flagrant encroachments of secular power on church authority. The council obediently decreed two fantastic new doctrines: the pope could not err in his pronouncements on "faith and morals" when these were delivered *ex cathedra*, ("from the chair"), that is, in a prescribed, highly official manner; and the pope was the only legitimate spiritual authority over the whole of Christendom, Catholic and non-Catholic alike—there was no valid Christian church outside the Roman Catholic.

These concepts are called respectively papal infallibility and papal primacy, and both served to harden into permanence what was perhaps the worst quality of the Catholic church: its character as a dictatorship. The motive for the creation of this doctrine is transparent. In response to secular attack the papacy retreated into a mentality of seige; ever more piercing lances of spiritual omnipotence could perhaps slay the dragon of secular domination.

The new doctrines were patently false even in terms of Catholic theology, and have been repudiated by honest Catholic theologians who have dared. Among these courageous souls has been Hans Küng, one of Catholicism's principal theologians, predictably banned from teaching for his views. In *Infallible? An Inquiry,* Küng argues that the doctrine of papal infallibility is logically incoherent. The most obvious reason is the historical fact of the church's recognized errors of both doctrine and deed.

> What might be called classical errors of the ecclesiastical teaching office, now largely admitted, may be listed as follows: the excommunication of Photius, the ecumenical patriarch of Constantinople and of the Greek church, which made formal the schism with the Eastern church, a schism which is now almost a thousand years old; the prohibition of interest at the beginning of modern times, on which the ecclesiastical teaching office after a variety of compromises changed its mind, much too late; the condemnation of Galileo and the measures adopted as a consequence of this action, which are essentially responsible for the estrangement between the church and the natural sciences (not yet overcome today); the condemnation of new forms of worship in the Rites controversy, which is one of the main reasons for the large-scale breakdown of the Catholic missions of modern times in India, China, and Japan; the maintenance up to the First Vatican Council of the medieval secular power of the Pope, with the aid of all secular and spiritual means of excommunication, which in large measure rendered the papacy incredible as a spiritual ministry; finally, at the beginning of our century, the numerous condemnations of the approach of modern critical-historical exegesis to the authorship of the books of the Bible, to source-criticism in the Old and New Testaments, to historicity and literary forms, to the Comma Johanneum, to the Vulgate; and also the condemnations in the dogmatic field, particularly in connection with "modernism" (theory of evolution, conception of development of dogma) and most recently of all in connection with Pius XII's encyclical *Humani Generis,* and the consequent ecclesiastical disciplinary measures, etc. The errors of the ecclesiastical teaching office in every century have been numerous and indisputable.[5]

The labors of the First Vatican Council were for nought in immediate terms. Finally unified under Victor Emmanual, Italy successfully annexed Rome in September 1870, when the troops of Napoleon III protecting the pope were withdrawn to fight more important battles against the Prussians. The seizure of Rome was instant and unceremonious.

Bereft of military power, the church naturally became less bellicose, which partially explains its new consistency in preaching a morality of peace. Pastoral letters such as that of the U.S. bishops opposing nuclear weapons (1982) would have been inconceivable anytime before our own century—the church could hardly oppose in principle the tools it needed to retain power. It is no coincidence that the *canon* and *cannon* came from the same etymological root.

The five popes who reigned during the years between 1870 and 1929 assumed a position of involuntary imprisonment within the Vatican, treating Italy's domination as illegitimate. Finally the church had its day in court. It was the 1920s and the "Vatican question" was of great concern to Italy's Fascist leader, Benito Mussolini. He wanted to prevent the dispute from ever becoming a basis for objection to his rule.

In 1929 Mussolini reached agreement on the matter with Pope Pius XI and signed the Lateran Treaty, by which the Holy See was assured state sovereignty over the Vatican, the papal villa at Castel Gandolfo, and about fifty other territorial possessions outside of Vatican City. The Vatican was also paid the 1984 equivalent of $500 million in cash and bonds,[6] part inducement to sign off on the deal and part compensation for losses incurred by the papacy during the nationalist takeover of 1870. Thus the pope now lived in his own country, Vatican City, with its ten thousand halls, suites, rooms, and passages, its thirty squares and streets, a railway station, and four post offices. Vatican City was in every way a state, with a court of law and two jails, its own coinage and postage stamps, and a security force of eighty Swiss guards, a loyal mercenary unit organized in 1506 by Pope Julius II and dressed in uniforms said to have been designed by Michelangelo. The pope had had *de facto* control over much of the facilities of Vatican City in the interregnum of humiliation; it was the huge endowment by the Italian state that was of the most significance for the future of the papacy. "Vatican Incorporated was in business. It has never looked back."[7]

The Vatican moved quickly in its newest secular domain. On June 7, 1929, the Vatican set up a unit known as the Special Administration to handle its finances, and hired one Bernardino Nogara to direct its activities. From the beginning the aim was profit without regard to morality, religious or any other.

Nogara was reluctant to accept the job and did so only when Pope Pius XI agreed to certain conditions. Nogara did not wish to be trammelled by any traditional views the Church might still hold about making money. The ground rules Nogara insisted on included the following: "1. His decisions on what investments to make would be totally and completely free of any religious or doctrinal considerations. 2. He would be free to invest Vatican funds anywhere in the world." The pope agreed and opened the doors to currency speculation and to playing the markets and stock exchanges, including the buying of shares in companies whose products were inconsistent with Roman Catholic teaching. Items such as bombs, tanks, guns, and contraceptives might be condemned in the pulpit, but the shares Nogara bought for the Vatican in companies that manufactured these items helped to fill the coffers in St. Peter's.[8]

These investments were made early on—"When Mussolini needed armaments for his invasion of Ethiopia in 1935, a substantial proportion was supplied by a munitions plant Nogara had acquired on behalf of the Vatican"[9]—but the real gains lay outside of Italy. Immediately on Hitler's assumption of power in 1933, the church concluded a concordant with Hitler that confirmed the *Kirchensteuer* (church tax), a state deduction from the paychecks of German workers representing between 8 and 10 percent of the total income tax collected by the German government. The money collected from workers who were Catholic was directly transferred to the Catholic church. There was a price, however, as in Italy: no political involvement. When Germany invaded Poland in 1939, Pius refused to condemn it, saying, "We cannot forget that there are forty million Catholics in the Reich. What would they be exposed to after such an act by the Holy See?"[10] There was no need to even consider condemning the slaughter of six million Jews.

Church collaboration with the Nazis was not always merely passive, and the benefits could run to facilities as well as money. After the Nazis subdued Yugoslavia in 1941, they set up puppet states to administer the territory. One of these was the "Independent State of Croatia," headed by a right-wing Croatian nationalist named Ante Pavelich, leader of the Ustashi terrorist gang. The aim of his government was "the massacre of Eastern Orthodox Serbs by Roman Catholic Croats, in an effort to make the province of Croatia solidly Roman Catholic."[11] An important collaborator in this horror—six hundred thousand people would be murdered—was the area's Catholic leader, Archbishop Stepinac.

> Stepinac was appointed supreme military apostolic vicar of the Ustashi army led by Pavelich. He was, therefore, in a position to know of the atrocities that were constantly taking place. In May, 1941, after innumerable massacres had been committed, Pavelich went to Rome and was received by pope Pius XII, and on the same occasion signed a treaty with Mussolini. In June of that year more than 100,000 Serbian men, women, and children were killed by the Ustashi. In all some 250 Orthodox churches were destroyed or turned over to Roman Catholic parishes and convents. Documents requesting and authorizing such transfers are now in the state prosecutor's office at Zagreb and Sarajevo, bearing the signature of archbishop Stepinac.[12]

After the war Stepinac was convicted of collaborating with the Nazis and sentenced to sixteen years, but this did not seem to affect his church's attitude toward him; for his labors on behalf of piety he received Catholic honors as far away as New York City, where a high school was named after him. While Stepinac was still serving his sentence Pius made him a cardinal.[13] Such church approval of fascist war criminals was hardly unusual. In office from 1939 to 1958, Pius XII in all that time never excommunicated, or even severely censured, either Mussolini or Hitler, both Catholic. Today, the *Kirchensteuer* provides the church approximately $1.9 billion in revenues each year.[14]

Under the leadership of Bernardino Nogara, the Vatican acquired controlling interests in companies in the banking, insurance, steel, cement, food and real estate industries. In real estate alone, by acquiring a 15 percent interest in the giant Societa Generale Immobiliare, Italy's oldest construction company, the Vatican has had a share of an almost incalculable wealth of properties, including the Rome Hilton hotel, a block of offices and shops on the Avenue des Champs Elysees, the Stock Exchange Tower in Canada, residential dwellings in Oyster Bay, New York, that cover 277 acres, and the Watergate complex in Washington, D.C., the most prestigious address in the most powerful city in the world. The Vatican also acquired shares of stock in General Motors, Shell, Gulf Oil, General Electric, Bethlehem Steel, IBM, TWA and others.[15] When Pope Paul VI issued the papal encyclical *Humanae Vitae*, which set forth the church's position against artificial birth control, he neglected to note that the Vatican at that very moment owned the Instituto Farmacologico Sereno. "One of Sereno's best-selling products was an oral contraceptive called Luteolas."[16] The list of Vatican assets grew so large that Cardinal Spellman, the church's New York district manager, once said that, "Next to Jesus Christ the greatest thing that has happened to the Catholic Church is Bernardino Nogara."[17]

Vatican financial affairs were to become considerably more tainted after Nogara's passing. His successors developed a close relationship with one Michele Sindona, currently holding court in a federal prison in New York. Sindona was the chief financial consultant to the Vatican, in particular to Nogara's *de facto* successor, Bishop Paul Casimir Marcinkus, currently a volunteer prisoner of the Vatican because he is wanted for bank fraud in Italy. Through Sindona, Marcinkus apparently saw fit to involve in the Vatican portfolio members of the Palermo-New York axis of the Mafia, controlled by the Gambino family, and members of P2, an Italian Masonic organization that conducts business in partnership with the Italian Mafia.

Sindona's downfall was precipitated by the collapse in 1974 of the Franklin National Bank of New York; he had defrauded it in the course of his Vatican business dealings. American police managed to apprehend Sindona and U.S. courts made arrangements for him to practice his religion

in a federal penitentiary. The bizarre church-mob network he had facilitated was not revealed until years later, however, with a scandal set off in
1982 by the discovery of the body of Roberto Calvi. He was hanging from
a London bridge with rocks in his pockets. Calvi was head of the Banco
Ambrosiano Group, 16 percent owned by the Vatican Bank (called in
Italian Instituto per le Opere di Religione [IOR]; assets in 1984: $10 bil-
lion[18]). Sixteen percent ownership gave the Vatican controlling interest in
Ambrosiano.[19]

> Within hours of [Calvi's] body being identified in London, the alarm had
> been sounded throughout Italy. On the first day the banks were open
> after [Calvi] had been found . . . the Banco Ambrosiano began to experi-
> ence a heavy run of withdrawals. What is not public knowledge until now
> is that the Vatican Bank suffered the same fate. Many millions of dollars
> were withdrawn by those members of the Italian establishment, who,
> privy to the facts, were aware that a $1.3 billion hole in the Ambrosiano
> Group would soon be public knowledge and that the hole was not un-
> connected with Calvi's long-standing business and personal relationship
> with [Bishop] Paul Marcinkus and the IOR.[20]

In a fast-moving chain of events, Banco Ambrosiano was revealed as
having, in effect, capitalized a series of Latin American companies secretly
controlled by the Vatican—some involved in the international arms market
—to the tune of $1 billion. The transactions were illegal because owners of
substantial shares in a bank are forbidden to loan money to themselves.
The companies, using Vatican prestige and Vatican "letters of comfort"
designed for the purpose, had in turn borrowed hundreds of millions more
from Latin American banks and investors. Unfortunately, the Vatican's
companies were for various reasons unable to pay anyone back—even the
Ambrosiano Group. The scheme had gone too far, threatening even the
Vatican's agent in the affair, the Ambrosiano Group, which now had a
huge hole in its assets. Calvi was said by family members to have nearly
arranged a deal to solve the problem, by obtaining over a billion dollars of
financing from Opus Dei ("the work of God"), one of the church's missionary organizations, which apparently had extra funds available not immediately needed for saving souls.[21] Calvi was assassinated before the
maneuver could be concluded.

There followed an international banking scandal that led to the collapse of a number of European and American banks, and after extensive
investigation the Vatican role in the affair was exposed—the church had
profited immensely from the operation of its companies, but by setting
them up independently the Vatican had evaded legal responsibility for its
debts. Italian investigating and law-enforcement agencies were hampered

by the subterfuges available with the Vatican's status as a sovereign foreign state, but eventually the Vatican Bank agreed to pay a mere $250 million to one of the creditor banks, claiming with traditional Vatican piety that the payment was being made on the basis of "non-culpability" but "in recognition of a moral involvement."[22] Token morality is important for a bank whose official name translates as "the Institute for Administration of Religious Affairs." The other creditors defrauded in the Ambrosiano affair would have to make due with the knowledge that they had contributed to the well-being of God's agents on earth.

The Ambrosiano affair, and a dozen like it, was as nothing compared to the crime committed in the Vatican three years before. The time was September, 1979, and John Paul I, "the smiling pope," had just been elected; he was quickly exposed to the essentials of the Vatican's way of doing business. Possibly not since Francis of Assisi had the church had such a spiritual presence as Albino Luciani, the man who took the name of John Paul I; for that reason Luciani had been called "God's candidate" during the papal elections which brought him into office. But "the smiling pope" was shocked at the extent of Vatican venality he saw in his first few days, and he began almost immediately to take steps to clean house. This, of course, made him a mortal threat to certain members of the Vatican and their Mafia and Masonic partners.

Even while he had been the patriarch of Venice, Luciani had been troubled by his limited business dealings with the Vatican. The spiritual and temporal needs of his own diocese were clearly subordinated to the financial machinations of the Holy See. When he became pope, however, John Paul was shocked to learn the magnitude of the church's financial holdings and the use to which their hundreds of millions in profits were being put: reinvestment. The church's portfolio in the Italian stock exchange was so enormous that when the Italian government in 1964 tried to collect a recently enacted tax on stock dividends, the Vatican quite credibly threatened to ruin the market by selling off everything it owned. The matter was dropped until 1968, when there rose to power a coalition government possessed of more resolve.[23] Worse, John Paul was quickly discovering that P2 and the Gambino Mafia family had an intimate, indeed incestuous relationship with the Holy See itself. Sindona, partner and mentor of the Vatican's chief financial officer, Bishop Marcinkus, was a Gambino boy.

The kindly John Paul, afflicted by what some have called "transparent honesty," could not disguise his disgust at what he was learning. As "a poor man, accustomed to small things and silence," John Paul also failed to discern that his virtue would threaten as nothing else could the financial empires of the Italian Mafia, the Masons of the P2, and numerous officials and bureaucrats in the Vatican itself. That all were inextricably linked was perhaps too stunning a notion to grasp quickly. John Paul failed to understand the character of the Vatican principals with whom he was dealing; this would prove tragic.

The "smiling pope" had other concerns far more dear to his heart. Predominate among them was the church's position on birth control. Luciani had long before concluded that the theory of the *Humanae Vitae* encyclical was born of male chauvinism. "Eminence," he had once said to Cardinal Villot, the Vatican's secretary of state, "what can we old celibates really know of the sexual desires of the married?"[24] But John Paul's concerns went far deeper than emotional difficulties caused among the faithful by church birth control policies. Of far more import to John Paul was the pain and suffering that unplanned births caused the children of the world. This too he had explained to Cardinal Villot. "Eminence," he said, according to a number of those present,

> we have been discussing birth control for about forty-five minutes. If the information I have been given, the various statistics, if that information is accurate, then during the period of time we have been talking, over one thousand children under the age of five have died of malnutrition. During the next forty-five minutes while you and I look forward with anticipation to our next meal a further thousand children will die of malnutrition. By this time tomorrow thirty thousand children who at this moment are alive, will be dead—of malnutrition. God does not always provide.[25]

But Cardinal Villot was to the Vatican's spiritual establishment what Bishop Marcinkus was to the financial hierarchy of the church. He viewed the new pope's ideas with sanctimonious disdain. They were a challenge to the established order—and to his own authority. Villot was, after all, one of the Vatican's staunchest supporters of the anti-birth control policies, and had even attempted to slip into one of the new pope's speeches an official endorsement of these policies. Luciani had removed the text concerned from the draft.[26] If these policies were altered, Villot, as secretary of state, would have to have a strong role in implementing them. But Villot had other reasons to fear this new pope. He happened to be a Mason; membership in Masonic organizations was forbidden by the church and virulently so. Most importantly, Villot was head of the Administration of the Patrimony of the Holy See, more important than the Vatican Bank itself. Villot was a central figure in the Vatican financial empire likely to be closely investigated and completely reorganized by John Paul.

With die-hard, potent adversaries in both the financial and spiritual sectors of the Holy See, John Paul's work would not be easy. But John Paul would not live to face the difficulty. After only thirty-three days as pope, John Paul I, a man in perfect health for his age, was dead. As David A. Yallop explains in his sad book *In God's Name*, "On September 28, 1978, [John Paul] was martyred for his beliefs. Confronted with a man such as Albino Luciani, with the problems his continuing presence would pose, the Italian Solution was applied. The decision was made that the pope must die, and thus 'God's candidate' was murdered." Pope John Paul I, according to Yallop, was poisoned.[27]

It is fantastic to assert an inside plot to murder a pope in this day, but Yallop's reasons to believe it are manifold and completely convincing. John Paul's body was said by the Vatican to have been discovered at 5:30 A.M. by Father John Magee. This was not at all the case. In fact, John Paul's personal secretary of eighteen years, Sister Vincenza, had gone to the pope at 4:30 A.M., just before his usual waking time. She knocked lightly, got no answer and left, returning at 4:45, the latest that the pope ever slept. Still no answer. Sister Vincenza entered the pope's room and found him dead, sitting up in bed with his reading glasses on and papers clutched in his hand.

Soon Villot had been informed.

By 5:00 A.M. Villot was in the pope's bedroom and had seen for himself that Albino Luciani was dead.

If Luciani died naturally, Villot's actions and instructions are completely inexplicable. His behavior becomes understandable only when related to one specific conclusion: Either Cardinal John Villot was part of a conspiracy to murder the pope, or he saw clear evidence in the papal bedroom indicating the pope had been murdered, and he promptly determined that to protect the Church that evidence must be destroyed.

On the small bedside table was the medicine that Luciani had been taking for low blood pressure. Villot pocketed the medicine. From the dead pope's hands he took the notes on papal transfers and appointments. These he pocketed as well. The pope's last will, which had been in the desk in his study, was removed. His glasses and slippers disappeared from the bedroom. None of these items has ever been seen again.

Villot then created for the shocked members of the pope's household a totally fictitious account of the circumstances leading to the finding of Luciani's body. He imposed a vow of silence concerning Sister Vincenza's discovery and instructed the household that news of the death was to be suppressed until he indicated otherwise.[28]

A full forty-five minutes ahead of any official need for their services, embalmers were called. They were picked up by a Vatican car and taken to the papal residence at 5:00 A.M.—thirty minutes before John Paul was said to have been found lifeless in his bed.[29] Instead of a routine embalming check of the body which would have taken only a few minutes, one and one-half hours was spent examining the corpse, an examination from which the pope's personal physician was excluded.[30] Commenting on this procedure, Professor Mario Fontana, head of the Vatican medical service, stated, "If I had to certify, under the same circumstances, the death of an ordinary unimportant citizen, I would quite simply have refused to allow him to be buried."[31]

No autopsy was performed. This is strange because the pope had been thought to be in exceptionally good health—nearly perfect health in the judgement of his doctor, Giuseppe da Ros, who had checked Albino Luciani weekly for more than two decades. The deputy head of the Vatican medical services was told to examine John Paul's body within a couple hours of the body's discovery. "Dr. Buzzonetti made a brief examination of the body. He informed Villot that the cause of death was acute myocardial infarction, a heart attack. The doctor set the time of death at about 11:00 P.M. To establish that the time of death was 11:00 P.M. and the cause myocardial infarction in such a brief external examination is a medical impossibility."[32]

At 7:30 A.M. Villot released a statement. Along with the purely speculative conclusions drawn by Buzzonetti, Villot provided the public with the idea that Father Magee had found the body. Soon Vatican radio gave more of the details surrounding John Paul's death, still provided by Villot. One particularly ill-advised fabrication was that John Paul had been found with a book in his hands, *The Imitation of Christ*, a fifteenth-century work usually attributed to Thomas Kempis. It was well known that the book was one of John Paul's favorites. Unfortunately, there was no copy of the book in the papal apartments. John Paul's personal copy was still in Venice.[33]

Over the next few days the Vatican began to explain John Paul's death as merely the latest in a long history of John Paul brushes with near-fatal illness. He had long been a sick pope, you see.

> With regard to an explanation for the sudden death, the Roman Curia disinformation service had achieved a remarkable coup. Writer after writer talked about a long record of illness. That someone as experienced as Patrick O'Donovan of the *Observer* could be deceived into writing the following indicates just how successful the lies were: "It is only now generally known that Cardinal Luciani had a long record of all but mortal illness."
>
> Exactly what these illnesses were was not stated. It is clear that O'Donovan and the other reporters, fighting to meet deadlines, had no time for personal research but relied on Vatican contacts. Some talked of Luciani's heavy smoking, of the fact that he only one lung, of his several bouts of tuberculosis. Since his death others have been told by Vatican sources about his four heart attacks, about the fact that he suffered from phlebitis, a painful circulatory disease, and about his struggle with em-

physema, a chronic illness of the lungs. There is not a word of truth in any of it.[34]

The deception surrounding the death of John Paul would be enforced by his successor, Karol Wojtyla, who, inappropriately in this context, took the name John Paul II. To halt the barrage of questions, the Vatican called for reverence and prayers, hoping that a surge of universal piety would calm the turbulent waves whipped up by the deception. But even members of the church hierarchy were outraged, their attitude best summarized by Archbishop Marcel Lefebvre, who issued a statement through Abbot Ducaud-Bourget: "It's difficult to believe that the death was natural considering all the creatures of the devil who inhabit the Vatican."[35] Lefebvre can hardly be considered partisan in this view; he leads a group of arch-conservatives who would have been fiercely opposed to nearly any doctrinal reforms initiated by John Paul.

Piety aside, it was vital to continue the theology of finance without interruption in these chaotic times. Stability is crucial in financial affairs, and the Vatican quickly took steps to assure that economic gains would not be jeopardized by the mere death of a pope. As far as the Vatican banks and financial departments were concerned, John Paul I was just a footnote in papal history. The economic chapters were still being written. Bishop Marcinkus himself "had discovered in the person of Karol Wojtyla the most powerful protector a Vatican employee could have."[36] John Paul II promoted Marcinkus, head of the Vatican Bank and a major participant in the nefarious scandal, to pro-president of the Pontifical Commission for the State of Vatican City. Despite the fact that arrest warrants were outstanding for the good bishop by the Italian authorities, he was elevated to what amounted to the mayoralty of Vatican City.[37] "[Bishop Marcinkus] still retained his position as head of the Vatican Bank, and the new post meant that he was automatically elevated to archbishop."[38] In February 1987 Italian magistrates issued another warrant for the arrest of Marcinkus, this time because he was believed to be "an accessory to fraudulent bankruptcy" in the Ambrosiano affair.

The death of a world leader is often followed by the enunciation of conspiracy theories. Usually one of the two fundamental elements of any such argument, motive and opportunity, are lacking in persuasiveness. That is not the case in the claim of a conspiracy to murder John Paul I. Albino Luciani had not sought the papacy and had been elected with stunning suddenness during the conclave which elevated him to it. Those threatened by his election had had no time to organize against it. The man elected so unusually was legendary for his humanity and dedication, but also for his resolve. Those threatened by John Paul had no reason to believe that he would prove a feeble administrator, and no hope at all that he could be bribed or intimidated. With details of the threatened principal figures and their interests filled in, the motive for conspiracy is clear. As for opportunity, those threatened by John Paul, one or another, were well-schooled in the "Italian Solution." Those threatened included important men inside and outside the Vatican, men, one or another, intimately knowledgeable of papal routine and papal security, and able to exploit that knowledge. And these men, many of these men, acted unusually and in some cases inexplicably during and after the death of John Paul. With the details filled in, the opportunity to carry out a conspiracy is clear.

As far as can be known without formal investigation or the appearance of the smoking gun, it is clear that John Paul I was murdered because he threatened to change a Vatican that was and is, to use Nietzsche's sharp words about Christianity, "the one great curse, the one enormous and innermost perversion, the one great instinct of revenge, for which no means are too venomous, too underhand, too underground and too petty." This sentiment is extreme when applied to the whole of Christianity. But of the Vatican, as the murder of John Paul shows with very little doubt, such words are merely accurately and thoroughly descriptive.

In America the television and "crusading" evangelists are at least as sinister as the Catholic church. The "televangelists" raise untold millions of dollars each year from emotionally vulnerable Americans seeking spiritual consolation. Chief among them are Pat Robertson, Ernest Angley, W. V. Grant, Oral Roberts, Jerry Falwell, Jimmy Swaggert and Jim Bakker. Each of these takes in millions of dollars a year from the public. Without embarrassment, these men construct massive building complexes and amass extensive real estate properties on the foundation of "ministries" comprising churches, schools, television production companies, radio stations, and record and publishing companies. These enterprises are supported by some of the most sophisticated direct-mail operations in the world.

All is of course paid for by the penny donations of the most lonely and destitute people in America. The televangelists know their audience and tailor their pitches to the emotions. In January 1987, for example, Oral Roberts let the world know that if he did not receive an additional $4.5 million by the end of March, God had said he might die. "Help me extend my life," Roberts said on television, obviously with grave demeanor, "We're at the point where God could call Oral Roberts home."[39] After his pronouncements on the joys of the afterlife for the righteous, one wonders why Roberts hoped to avert this tragedy. The world waited breathlessly, of course; presumably so did some of Roberts's creditors in his $100 million building project in Tulsa, Oklahoma. Probably fearing sanctions from the

Federal Communications Commission, the radio station over which Roberts issued his plea for listener mercy, WFAA in Dallas, Texas, refused to allow future appeals of such a nature. A spokesperson said that the broadcasts were "inappropriate."[40]

Most televangelical appeals for money are less imaginative. Typical are those made by Jim Bakker. For years Bakker has been soliciting funds to build his religious complex, the cost of which has run into the millions of dollars. By the end of 1986 Bakker was asking people for money because the buildings needed to be graced with paintings and furniture. Monuments to cupidity must at least be decorated in good taste.

Many of the evangelists claim to be faith healers. People with long-standing medical problems ranging from blindness to cancer come on the shows and are miraculously cured before the very eyes of a national television audience. Oddly enough, some dedicated groups actually bother to investigate faith-healing claims. Without exception the recipients of the "cures" who have been investigated either cannot be shown ever to have had the disease claimed or can show no improvement in their conditions. One particularly notorious faith healer is Peter Popoff. He performs his miracles live in tents and halls across the country. Before the show his wife works the crowd, gathering personal information from those in attendance. Popoff goes on stage with a small radio receiver in his ear. His wife, positioned in a suitably obscured vantage point, directs him to marks she has learned something about. Miraculously knowledgeable about their condition, Popoff can dispense appropriate nostrums. To complement the act, confederates in wheelchairs are sometimes wheeled to the front; God's mercy works through Popoff and these perfectly healthy people get up and walk about.

These evangelists are not just harmless con men. In many instances they tell people not to rely upon the medicine which their doctors have prescribed, and instead, to rely on the "medicine of God." It is not reliably known how many people have medically deteriorated, suffered more, or died due to these charlatans. What is known is that the fraudulent cures are published in brochures and magazines for the purpose of fund raising. Staging phony cures on national television and receiving the resultant income has inured these evangelists to any pangs of conscience or sense of shame. "Those who write and design these mailers betray a numbing confidence that they can tell their flocks virtually anything, however manifestly self-aggrandizing, and tell them it came from God—and get results."[41]

Indeed, the U.S. tradition of separation of church and state is used to avoid criminal indictments. Occasionally, however, these people do get into trouble. Jerry Falwell developed difficulties with the Federal Communications Commission for false promises on national television. He was also sued by a listener and lost. Falwell's organization, (formerly the Moral Majority but due to unrelenting bad press now the Liberty Federation) claims over a million members and is a major political and social influence. According to one of Falwell's former employees, in 1984 the Moral Majority was planning to undertake a campaign to stop AIDS, by raising money to launch a nation-wide effort to deny homosexuals the right to be employed at hospitals and restaurants. The estimated cost of the campaign would be $1.5 million; the estimated revenue to be received from solicitations was expected to be nearly $7 million—a $5.5 million projected profit from this exemplary effort on behalf of the public good. There were hardly plans to spend $5.5 million on the AIDS effort.[42] By and large, the American public maintains an intellectual lethargy toward financial abuses by religion, perhaps out of a subconscious sense of reverence for anything religious.

America's religious businesses are not limited to the Catholic church and the evangelists. The Mormon church, a number of other Protestant churches, the Salvation Army, Eastern religions such as that of Guru Maharaji, unconventional religions such as Scientology and countless other religious organizations earn untold millions of dollars each year from investments in stocks, real estate, manufacturing companies, and every nature and kind of commercial activity. All of these investments are subsidized by non-believers due to religion's manipulation of U.S. tax laws. Religion is perhaps America's largest business, but it is not difficult to understand why. The product is salvation, and by the time it proves defective its buyers are no longer around to complain.

Christianity in the twentieth century has become a creed of finance. Through economic strength it seeks to influence politics and the social order, but with limited success. The "born again" Christians, particularly in the United States, are generally on the right wing of the political spectrum, much the same as the religious Jews in Israel, the fundamentalist Muslims in the Arab world, and the orthodox Marxists in the Communist countries. In each instance, the adherents to these creeds are the "hawks," intolerant warmongers who often portray non-believers as the devil incarnate. But the ever-onward advance of technology and wealth gradually relegates the orthodox to the realm of the ridiculous. Free-thinking rationalists, particularly those with a democratic proclivity, are on the rise in countries of free speech. The days of the imprimatur are limited in the Western world.

As the military power of Christianity has declined, its policy toward war has become divided. Christianity's liberals are for peace while its conservatives pressure world governments to fight for Christian beliefs in the form of anti-communism. In the case of Catholicism, the church's radical right supports its favored dictatorships while its radical left supports the "liberation theology" of priests who carry machine guns in support of Marxist revolution. The radical left of the church, however, is a tiny minority; most left-leaning church activists favor non-violent change in the tradition of Jesus Christ. The same cannot be said of the church's right-leaning activists. At the moment the papacy seems to be on their side; in the events just before the ouster of Ferdinand Marcos from the Philippines, the Vatican fruitlessly directed the Philippine church hierarchy to refrain from support of the Aquino insurrection.

What Christian groups of the right and some on the left have in common is a philosophy of violence, but they no longer have the tools to implement it on their own. *IHS* is still an emblem of the Catholic church. The cross, the symbol of Roman repression, remains the symbol of all Christianity. When both are replaced by the dove of peace, we will know that Christianity has begun to return to the tranquil teachings of Christ, "Peace I leave with you, my peace I give unto you . . . Let not your heart be troubled, neither let it be afraid" (John 14:27).

Christianity is largely responsible for an even greater anguish than that caused by war, however. The Catholic church in particular refuses to take certain crucial measures to help relieve the suffering of the impoverished people of the towns and villages around the world struggling desperately to break the bonds of mass misery. Christian missionaries in the Third World teach people to accept hardships for Christ far more than they instruct them in ways to plant crops or build irrigation systems. The ten-year clean-water program of the United Nations International Children's Emergency Fund, intended to bring disease-free drinking water to the world's poor, particularly children, is estimated to cost $100 million. A mere *one cent* per year from each Christian in the world would pay for this effort. Millions of children die each year from diseases caused by impure water. Instead of providing these desperately needed funds for the poor of the world, the churches collect money *from* them, some for charity it is true, but most for Bible classes, silver chalices and additions to the residence of the local church higher-up.

An estimated forty thousand children die each day of starvation or malnutrition-related diseases. Yet, for example, the Catholic church still would have ignorant people believe that they will go to hell for all eternity for practicing birth control, and presumably suffer an even worse fate for terminating a pregnancy. As a result countless thousands of women abort themselves with knives or sticks when they become pregnant, and many thousands more bear children they have no hope of providing for.

Christianity's capacity for cruelty has known no limits, as this brief history demonstrates. The millions who have perished by the swords of the Christian righteous were killed mercifully compared to the millions, particularly children, who die annually of starvation or disease as a result of Christian social and sexual doctrines. If the legendary Christ of the Gospel were alive, surely he would attempt to lift the burden of despair from the tired shoulders of those who are deprived, rather than condemn them to further misery. Those who suffer are those who have no voice, no money, no education. It is time that Christianity returned to the values of Christ "the peacemaker" and to the attitude, "Blessed are those who hunger and thirst for justice, for they shall be satisfied." It is time to free humanity from the weights of superstition and poverty. It is time, in the words of Isaiah the Prophet, to "unloose the heavy burdens, and let the oppressed go free."

But Christ is not alive, and it was not the Jews or Romans of his time who killed him. Constantine killed Christ. If there were a real Resurrection, it would be one in which the compassionate values of Christ were revived. Instead, as St. Paul says in I Corinthians 13:1, "Though I speak with the tongues of men and of angels, and have not charity, I become as sounding brass, or a tinkling cymbal." Rather than raising a moral standard to which the people can repair, Christianity has traditionally instilled in society hatred and cynicism. Although Christian intent may have been to battle evil, hatred of any kind is a poor judge of evil. The subordination of humane behavior to the ephemeral notions of divine justice has tended to supplant spontaneous compassion with doctrinaire notions of morality. Add to this ethical and psychological stew the various differing notions of divine justice even among theologians of the same faith and the result is moral confusion.

Since Augustine Christianity has persuaded humanity not to act in its earthly interest but to subordinate needs and desires and striving to a higher calling—a calling always vague and variously defined except in respect of requiring donations to church coffers. To participate in a cohesive society, human contact is motivated by both a sense of compassion and a sense of self-interest. Christianity has debased compassion by giving it a profit motive. Rather than promoting simple altruism, Christianity teaches that kindness gains an eternal reward.

It is often argued that religion provides society with its morality, and that social and political anarchy can only be avoided by promulgating a litany of useful religious lies. It is hard to see how dread of punishment in an afterlife is a useful lie. The Buddhist theology of successive planes of existence in the next life, an excellent metaphor for the struggles and possibilities in this one, seems far more useful. Yet even as its theology has been far from useful, Christian practice has been worse—two millennia of banality and hypocrisy written in the blood of the helpless and uneducated who forever live in hope. It is a shame of epic proportions that the incomparable message of Jesus has come to such an end.

Part Three

THE THEOLOGY OF PLUNDER

Make war on [the unbelievers] until idolatry is no more and Allah's religion reigns supreme.

—The Koran, 8:40

Unlike Christianity, which preached a peace never achieved, Islam unashamedly came with a sword.

—Steven Runciman

I

The Self-Appointed Prophet

I slam, "submission to the will of God," is the religion of those who follow the teachings of Muhammad, born 570 C.E. in Mecca, in what today is Saudi Arabia. The word "Islam" derives from *aslama*, "he submits," and *salama*, "he was safe." Believers are called Muslims, those who submit. Nearly a billion people adhere in some degree to Islam. These believers are in the traditional Arab lands as well as Africa, Turkey, Eastern Europe, parts of the Soviet Union, Iran, Afghanistan, Pakistan, India, Indonesia, parts of China and Southeast Asia. There are only very small groups in the Americas.

Muhammad was born into an Arabic culture which was polytheistic, polygamous and warring. He is believed to be the son of Abdullah bin Abdul-Muttalib, who died before Muhammad was born, and of the Quraish tribe, dominant in Mecca. Muhammad's mother, Amira, apparently died before he was six years old, so Muhammad lived with his grandfather. We know from the Koran, the sacred book of the Muslims, that he was an orphan: "Did He not find thee an orphan and give you shelter?"[1] Most details of Muhammad's life are unknown, since his "earliest Arabic biographer did not write until a century or so after he died and even his account survives only indirectly."[2] The historical name, "Muhammad," means "highly praised," an honorific title apparently given the Prophet by his followers. In one way Muhammad is like Abraham, Moses and Christ— all seem to have been of dubious parentage.

The Arabic peninsula which gave birth to Islam is largely desert, arid steppe and barren mountains. Then as today the area was inhabited by nomadic tribesmen who grazed their flocks in the desert during the short months of spring and returned to the highland for the remainder of the year. The nomads were disparate groups with no acknowledged ruler and no particular need or desire to become organized into a national entity. They often engaged in trade with the other cultures of the Middle East and frequently took up the sword against one another. Each tribe possessed its flock in common and the members of the tribe adhered to a code of mutual assistance and protection that required any injury to a tribesman or to the honor of the tribe to be avenged in blood, not only against the transgressor but against his tribe. Violations of this code were severely punished. Tribes took enormous pride in their reputation, their honor, the size of their flocks, the quality of their heroes, the beauty and chastity of their women, their superiority over other tribes, the eloquence of their poets, the number of their male offspring and their overall image to the outside world.

This pastoral existence was altered dramatically in the sixth century, with the sudden emergence of Arabia as a crossroads of intercontinental trade. The main trade routes between Europe and Asia, across present-day Turkey and Iran, were disrupted by the wars between the Persian and Byzantine empires. As a consequence, the produce of Asia was taken to the ports of Arabia, where it was transported by camel caravan up the peninsula to the Mediterranean. The towns and cities along this route prospered, but the new riches created a commercial upper class, causing the disintegration of traditional tribal values which even in the urban centers had long served to protect the poor. The number of these poor increased even as the strength of social values protecting them began to wane. Migrants from the countryside, moving in the hope of participating in this new prosperity, merely added to the increasing numbers of the emerging lower class. The irrigation and water-supply systems of many of the towns of southern Arabia began to collapse, for reasons not completely known, and this intensified the population movement to those towns with oases. Through trade and commerce came communication with other cultures and the introduction of new ideas into the Bedouin population, while the growing differences between rich and poor created a breeding ground of social unrest and its traditional sycophant, political opportunism. By the seventh century the Arabian peninsula was ripe for social upheaval. A revolutionary personality could easily galvanize the gradually growing forces of discontent.

Into this setting Muhammad was born. His Quraish brethren had become wealthy as merchants and middlemen because important trade routes leading to Yemen, Palestine, Egypt, Syria and Iraq converged in Mecca. The town had already developed banking and credit facilities, record-keeping and a means of exchange of foreign currencies. The city organized two annual caravans, an equivalent of joint-stock companies in which every citizen, wealthy or poor, could invest. Some of these caravans consisted of as many as twenty-five hundred camels loaded with precious goods, and an accompanying contingent of guards, guides, look-outs and messengers. One of Mecca's principal activities was to provide the capital for these ventures, from which it received a high rate of interest. Mecca was already a center of worship for a number of religions of the time, which conveniently scheduled major ceremonies to coincide with the times of year when food production and merchandise were most available to be traded and sold.

Mecca's commerce led to intercourse with the outside world, probably how Muhammad came into contact with the ideas of Judaism and Christianity, great influences on Islam. Muhammad accompanied his uncle on caravan travels to Syria and is thought certain to have encountered Christian ideas there. Mind expanding travel notwithstanding, there were also negative aspects to the amassing of trading wealth. The Arab love of alcohol and gambling, with money more and more available, contributed to the disintegration of the tribal social structure. Perhaps as bad, the social framework of an Arabian society had assumed that age and noble blood were the logical concomitants of wealth, but this was now changing.

Although Arab nomads had various religious beliefs and practices, religion was not a significant part of their lives. In the main they tended to be animists, venerating spirits that they believed dwelt in various creatures, trees, stones and natural phenomena such as rivers. Some paid occasional worship to broader nature deities. Pilgrimages to sacred shrines was customary. The most important shrine was that of the Kaaba in Mecca, which housed the Black Stone, probably a meteorite, allegedly given to mankind by God. One group, the Hanifs, grew away from these pagan customs and gradually moved toward monotheism. Muhammad associated himself with these people and even considered himself one of them.

At the age of twenty-five Muhammad married his employer, a wealthy and energetic widow named Khadija, fifteen years his senior. While she was alive he apparently remained faithful to her. "Until her death twenty-six years later, Mohammed lived with Khadija in a monogamous condition, highly unusual for a Moslem of means," but perhaps natural for one dependent on his mate for such means.[3] When Khadija died Muhammad practiced polygamy, by example ultimately sanctioning it for Islamic men. Khadija bore the only child of Muhammad to survive him, their daughter Fatima. She was to marry his cousin Ali, becoming the mother of all those who descended from the Prophet, as Muhammad would one day be called. It was his financial relationship with Khadija which gave Muhammad the leisure to reflect upon the Judeo-Christian ideas of God and man which were revolutionary to the animists and polytheists of his land. Muhammad was evidently impressed that the Jews and Christians had complex social organization and a sacred book, whereas his people were backward and had no sacred book.

According to tradition (in religious history a euphemism for myth), Muhammad was meditating in a cave outside of Mecca when a voice spoke to him saying, "Recite thou in the name of your Lord who created, created man from clots of blood."[4] The voice, Muhammad later claimed, was that of the archangel Gabriel, messenger of Allah, the chief god of the Quraish. Their religion had other gods, notably Allah's three daughters, al-Lat, al-Uzzah and al-Manat, but the Quraish reverence for Allah above all others paved the way for Muhammad's development of a monotheistic theology. It was much like Abraham's choice of Yahweh, one among the many gods of the time, as the figure in whom he invested predominant powers.

After what is recorded as a lengthy period of doubt, Muhammad interpreted his first revelation as a divine call to prophethood in the tradition of the prophets of old. The date of the event was later fixed as being at the end of the month of fasting, called Ramadan ("the hot month," the ninth month in the Muslim calendar) in the year 610. Interestingly enough, some translations of Islamic scripture call this moment the "night of power."[5] The voice was later said to be that of Archangel Gabriel.

In his new role as prophet, Muhammad's early utterances took the highly organized form used by oracles, soothsayers and pagan priests. Since he was an umni (an "unschooled man," ignorant and illiterate), to Muhammad's followers the avowed beauty of his recorded sayings in the Koran are clear miracle and proof of his prophethood. Muhammad neither performed nor claimed any other miracles, but the social revolution he wrought was a political miracle in itself, for he transferred traditional tribal loyalties of blood and title to a higher being; a brotherhood of believers became the basis of community and a new kinship group.

At first Muhammad thought he was just another *kahin*, soothsayer, common as a camel in the Arab world. But the visions came fast and furious after Gabriel's first visit. "Often, when they came, he fell to the ground in a convulsion or swoon; perspiration covered his brow; even the camel on which he was sitting felt the excitement, and moved fitfully."[6] The angelic transmission of God's word apparently took no notice of Muhammad's whereabouts. It is possible that these convulsions were not the self-delusions of the holy rollers that we know today. The descriptions of the episodes, particularly Muhammad's assertion that they were accompanied by the ringing of a bell, mesh well with the characteristics of epileptic fits.[7] Julius Caesar, an epileptic, had received political insights in a similar way.

Gradually Muhammad began to believe that he was exceptional, and in 613 he began to preach, in short passages of rhythmic prose taken down in his lifetime on whatever material was available, pieces of leather, camel-bone, palm leaves or wood. Later these writings were grouped in *suras*, chapters, together forming the Koran, Arabic for "recitation," the basis of Muslim belief.

Islam teaches that Muhammad is the last prophet, that when the world falls away from him, that is, from Islam, the end of the world will come. Muslims believe that Adam, Noah, Abraham, Moses and Jesus were also prophets sent by God, but the world remained profane. So Allah chose Muhammad to straighten things out. "The Koran accuses the Jews of corrupting the Scriptures and the Christians of worshipping Jesus as the Son of God, although He had expressly commanded them to worship none but Him. Having thus gone astray, they must be brought back to the right path, to the true religion preached by Abraham."[8]

Since Mecca was a trading city rather than a poor agricultural village, by comparison with other Arab towns it was prosperous and sophisticated. The polytheism of the Arabs was generally on the decline, and the morality of Mecca was accordingly in decay. The civilized world as the Arabs knew it was in tumult over the rivalry between the empires of Persia and Byzantium, giving credence to the idea that an apocalypse was imminent. It was in this setting that Muhammad began to preach his simple message, that the Meccans should abandon all forms of idolatry and surrender themselves to the one true God, who is all powerful and compassionate. This idea of total submission, in Arabic, *islam*, gives Muhammad's followers their name. The only formal rite which the Prophet asked them to heed at this time was to pray, prostrate, in the direction of Jerusalem.

Muhammad's initial teachings concerned the unity of God, an idea still unacceptable to the polytheists of the area, and the existence of an afterlife, certainly derived from his contact with Jewish and Christian ideas. He stressed the eternal reward for the righteous or the eternal punishment of the iniquitous according to his audience. "The doctrine was used as an inducement or deterrent, depending upon the nature of the response."[9]

Deviating from the religious tradition of the region, Muhammad attracted followers mainly from the socially insignificant and economically discontented. He had some prominent supporters, however, including his wife, Khadija, his cousin Ali, who would later marry his daughter, and the merchant Abu Bakr, who on the Prophet's death would become the first caliph (*khalifa*, "successor") of the Muslim community. The Meccans generally disliked Muhammad because his call for submission, even to God, offended their fierce Arab individualism. Initial reactions were condescending ("the Quraish heard him at first with smiling patience, called him a half-wit, and proposed to send him, at their own expense, to a physician who might cure him of his madness"), but some of Muhammad's ideas, particularly those that attacked Kaaba worship as idolatrous, proved threatening to the religious merchants of Mecca. If people began to believe in one God, Allah, the pilgrimage traffic would diminish. As Durant delicately puts it, the merchants "rose to the protection of their income."[10] Muhammad's popularity was not furthered by his notion that Meccan ancestors would roast in the eternal fires of hell for being sinners, an idea highly offensive to people who took great pride in their ancestry.

Muhammad and his followers began to be persecuted and in 615 a small group fled to Abyssinia, now Ethiopia; apparently they felt an affinity with Christians who lived there. Meanwhile the authorities confined Muhammad and those who remained with him in Mecca. The hope was to starve the group into submission to them rather than to God. While in confinement Muhammad claimed to have a revelation in which he was told that Allah was not the sole god, despite the fact that this was the basic tenet of Muhammad's preachings. Three goddesses of Mecca were also genuine, he said he had been told. Satisfied with this concession, the authorities freed Muhammad and his companions and allowed the emigres to return. Muhammad later repudiated this revelation, suggesting that his ordeal had caused hallucinations.

Khadija died in 619, known in Islam today as the "Year of Mourning." Muhammad moved to Taif, a town sixty miles away, but its leaders did not wish to offend Mecca and in any case the population jeered at his ideas. A batch of Muhammad's followers moved to Yathrib on July 16, 622, and Muhammad followed with Abu Bakr in September. This migration came to be called the Hegira (flight), and Yathrib is now called Medina, "the city of the Prophet." It is from the July arrival of Muhammad's followers that the Muslim calendar is calculated, its lunar year of six months of 29 days and six months of 30 days creating a 354-day year. As a result Islam is forty-one years behind the Western World—with respect to the calendar.

In Medina Muhammad managed to add to his standing as religious leader by progressively becoming the arbiter of local disputes. In the most significant instance, nearly the entire community of Medina was seriously disrupted by a blood feud and Muhammad agreed to be the mediator. He was successful in resolving the matter and the people of the oasis acknowledged him as their leader.

Muhammad began to taste political power. He gained political advantage through several marriages entered into for that purpose, while also contracting marriages in order to produce heirs. Some marriages Muhammad arranged for more intimate reasons. On one occasion, apparently, he had an urge to make love to the wife of his adopted son. In such a venture prophethood can come in handy; Allah perhaps could be convinced that His Prophet should be liberated from the distractions of concupiscence, the better to carry out His plan. According to Durant, Muhammad "was not above using the method of revelation for very human and personal ends, as when a special message from Allah sanctioned his desire to marry the pretty wife of Zaid, his adopted son."[11]

One of Muhammad's most important marriages was to Aisha, Abu Bakr's seventeen-year-old daughter. Ambitious and astute, Aisha became a major influence in Muhammad's life and was the transmitter of many of the "Traditions," important sayings later ascribed to the Prophet. Aisha was young and exceptionally attractive, and she garnered special treatment from her important husband. In polygamous marriage this can be problematic, but Allah, the compassionate and merciful, could resolve all things. Muhammad "refused to indulge the extravagances of his wives, but he promised them paradise; and for a time he dutifully spent a night with each of them in rotation. . . . The alluring and vivacious Aisha, however, won so many attentions out of her turn that the other wives rebelled, until the matter was settled by revelation." Allah had sanctioned Muhammad's sexual preferences. Muhammad was also a vain man who "perfumed his body, painted his eyes, dyed his hair, and wore a ring inscribed 'Mohammed the Messenger of Allah.' " It was a vanity that was inspirational. "His followers collected his spittle, or his cut hair, or the water in which he had washed his hands, expecting from these objects magic cures for their infirmities."[12]

With the command of such devotion, Muhammad had little trouble consolidating his authority, making Medina the first Muslim theocracy and the home of the first mosque, its site presently occupied by the Mosque of the Prophet, where Muhammad is buried. As the number of his followers grew, Muhammad faced the responsibility of providing for them. Medina was an agricultural community, but the development of farming techniques proved perhaps too pedestrian for the confidant of an archangel. Muhammad resolved instead to lead his followers in conquest. Some small-scale military ventures brought neighboring tribes under his sway and in 624 Muhammad decided to attack the caravans of Mecca. According to his own theology, fighting was prohibited during Ramadan, Islam's holy month, but this detail did not prevent Muhammad from carrying out his attack in just this month of 624. The battle took place near Badr, twenty miles southwest of Medina. Some thousand Meccan reinforcements came to aid the beleaguered merchants, under the attack of a mere three hundred Muhammadans; nevertheless, the soldiers of Allah won the day. Such a victory could only be explained as divine sanction of the new creed. Scribes took notes and they were later embodied in the Koran's *sura* 3. "This victory at Badr laid the basis of the temporal power of Islam. Ever since then Islam has had a strong military cast."[13] The financial benefits of such piety had understandable appeal to the Prophet and his followers.

Muhammad assumed at first that Jews and Christians would naturally recognize his teachings as God's final and most perfect revelation, but their arrogance was as great as his, and their tradition ancient by comparison. In the religious consolidation of Medina the Jews were in fact the most thoroughly resistant. Their theology was so much more advanced that they saw no reason to adopt Muslim beliefs. To persuade them, Muhammad adopted traditions such as Judaism's holiest day, Yom Kippur, and maintained the practice of directing all prayers toward Jerusalem. The Jews would not be dissuaded from their beliefs, however, so Muhammad instructed his followers to direct their prayers instead to Mecca. He then abandoned Yom Kippur, but retained its practice of fasting for the month of Ramadan. Finally Muhammad required all Muslims to part their hair to distinguish them from Jews, who let their hair hang loose.

The stubbornness of the Jews got Muhammad well and truly angry. He challenged Jewish intellectual honesty, accusing Jews of distorting the teachings of Moses and condemning them for refusing to recognize Jesus as a prophet. Regarding himself as the last of the prophets in a lineage dating back to Adam, Muhammad claimed that Islam accordingly superseded Judaism and Christianity. But, encountering difficulties with the followers of those faiths, he divorced his creed from both religions. In the process Muhammad assured that Islam would retain its Arab character.

In 628 Muhammad entered into a truce with his adversaries in Mecca, thereby guaranteeing his followers the right to perform the pilgrimage. It was a cultural tradition the new faith had proved unable to render moribund. In Muhammad's mind the truce was a temporary necessity in order to gain peaceful access to Mecca, placating followers whose traditional reverence for Mecca remained strong. Muhammad also wished to bring certain Meccans over to his side. In the 629 pilgrimage to Mecca, two men were recruited to the cause of Islam, Khalid Ibn al-Walid and Amr Ibn al-As; they would figure as brilliant leaders in the future military conquests of Islam.

Despite the truce, effectuated principally to restrain his own restive followers, and with his position consolidated and his military forces prepared, Muhammad reciprocated the graciousness of the people of Mecca by successfully cutting off their trade routes and leading an army against them. He was quickly victorious, seized the city, and celebrated his triumph by personally smashing the 360 idols in the Meccan sanctuary, proclaiming, "Truth has come and falsehood has vanished." Unmentioned were the lies of truce that had allowed the "truth" to come. Muhammad's victory over Mecca was marked by uncommon restraint and little persecution, but despite swift military success Muhammad's evangelism of the citizenry encountered protracted resistance. In order to avoid prolonged hostilities, Muhammad negotiated with city leaders, agreeing that if they submitted to Islam he would make pilgrimage to Mecca a requirement of the new religion. This assured a continuation of the present pilgrimage and tourist traffic and even promised a great increase in it. The pagan Kaaba would be transformed into the holiest of Muslim shrines. Muhammad accordingly prescribed that all Muslims should endeavor to make at least one pilgrimage to Mecca during their lifetimes, more if possible. The pilgrimage was called the Hajj. The merchant community quickly realized the material possibilities of this divine arrangement, and submitted to the new theology with an understanding of its economic if not its celestial rewards. Thus did Mecca adopt the Islamic faith. Muhammad had made an offer they couldn't refuse.

The pagan house of worship, the Kaaba, was given a Muslim mantel of theology. Suddenly it was Abraham who had built the shrine, and the sacred Black Stone it housed became a rock taken from paradise and personally delivered to Abraham by Gabriel during the construction. The territory surrounding the Kaaba was declared *haram*, forbidden, or sacred. This proclamation excluded the members of other religions from visiting the shrine, in order that the Islamic faith would remain "pure," a concept we have seen in Judaism and Christianity.

The conquest of Mecca was the turning point in the advance of what would become the largest religion in the world. "With the fall of Mecca, Mohammed was easily the most powerful man in Arabia, and tribes from everywhere in the peninsula came flocking to him. He achieved what no one before him had done—uniting the tribes under a single authority."[14] When Muhammad died in 632 he had accomplished in two decades that which had taken Judaism and Christianity centuries; Islam had emerged from the imagination, taken root in the populace, been extended by the sword and entrenched through compromise with secular power. So little a time, and already Islam was poised to join the ranks of the disciples of destruction.

When you meet the unbelievers in the battlefield strike off their heads and, when you have laid them low, bind your captives firmly.

—The Koran, 47:3

Had we pleased, We had certainly given to every soul its guidance. But true shall be the word that has gone forth from Me—I will surely fill hell with demons and men together.

—The Koran, 32:13

II

Scripture as Political Tool: The Koran

T he Koran is the sacred book of Islam, composed of piecemeal utterances said by Muhammad to have come to him from God in the form of revelations. As Muhammad tells the story, God had delivered his word to a number of messengers, beginning with Adam and running through many of the prophets of the Old Testament and several others mentioned only in the Koran; the latest of these select recipients of the message of God had been Jesus. But each in turn had been repudiated by the people to whom they had been sent, the Jews and Christians, who in time had either ignored or corrupted their teachings.

Muhammad was the last of these messengers, and when the world turned from the divine teachings delivered through him, the end of the world would be at hand. Because of this prophetic tradition and his self-proclaimed role in it, Muhammad respected above all things the great books of Judaism and Christianity. Through a great book, the word could be preserved. All that had been revealed to Muhammad by Allah since that day in the cave would be collected together, recorded in a great book of Islam, the Koran, "the recitation" of God's message to mankind.

The Koran is divided into 114 chapters, or *suras*, each named after a subject, or even a single metaphor, contained therein. The twenty-ninth chapter, "The Spider," for example, compares false gods to the gossamer traps laid by spiders. With one exception the *suras* are introduced by the formula *bismallah*, "In the name of God, the Compassionate, the Merciful."

The text of the Koran as we have it is more authentic than its Judeo-Christian counterpart, the Bible. The Koran was assembled in part under

Muhammad's supervision, and the definitive version dates from 651, less than twenty years after his death. Since Islam did not flourish only in lands outside its place of origin, as Christianity did, nor were Muslims separated from the birthplace of their faith, as Jews were, the Koran is not subject to the errors of translation that afflict the Bible. But Muhammad was illiterate, so that all his sayings were recorded (and, presumably, interpreted) by others. The collection of his words that make up the Koran was organized with no concern for chronological order, and even parts of what are obviously the same stories are in different places in the Koran; many of the revelations known to have been delivered in Medina are for some reason included in chapters written earlier in Mecca. The book appears to have been arranged in order of length, with the longest and most practically oriented chapters first. Much of the Koran is believed to have been taken directly from documents written at the very moment of their utterance, on stones, palm-leaves, even the shoulder blades of camels; but much is also acknowledged to have been taken from the memories of remembrancers who never wrote the revelations down. Inscrutable Arabic letters head certain chapters of the Koran, but scholars have no idea what they mean, or even who wrote them.

Although the text of 651 was assembled very early, it was already a fourth-generation text.

> The Caliph Abu Bekr ordered Mohammed's chief amanuensis, Zaid ibn Thabit, to "search out the Koran and bring it together." He gathered the fragments, says tradition, "from date leaves and tablets of white stone, and the breasts of men." From Zaid's completed manuscript several copies were made; but as these had no vowels, public readers interpreted some words variously, and diverse texts appeared in different cities of the spreading Moslem realm. To stop this confusion, the Caliph Othman commissioned Zaid and three Quraish scholars to revise Zaid's manuscript (651).[1]

Nonetheless, several of the various versions of Zaid's original text are also considered legitimate. "The learned men of the [Muslim] community continue to recognize variant readings, accepting the doctrine that the Koran has come down in seven versions."[2]

Although the Koran is described in nearly all authoritative sources as defined in 651 and unchanged since, some question even this degree of authenticity. Malise Ruthven, a former editor in the Arab affairs department of the British Broadcasting Corporation and author of *Islam in the World*, notes that,

Some Western scholars have, however, radically questioned the Muslim account, using methods adapted from biblical textual analysis. They argue that the Quran as we know it was assembled at a much later date out of fragmentary oral tradition deriving from the Arabian Prophet, but which also included a large quantity of exegetical or explanatory matter developed in the course of polemical disputes with Jews and Christians after the Arab conquest. This revisionist theory of the Quran has radical consequences for the early history of Islam, for it would suggest that the religious institution emerged at least two centuries after Muhammad's time, to consolidate ideologically, as it were, the Arab conquest. It would mean that the Arabs, anxious to avoid becoming absorbed by the more advanced religions and cultures of the peoples they conquered, cast about for a religion that would help them to maintain their identity. In so doing they looked back to the figure of the Arabian Prophet, and attributed to him the reaffirmation of an ancient Mosaic code of law for the Arabs.

The revisionist theory has several attractions. It fits in with the available paleographic evidence, which places the development of the Arabic script much later than the Muslim sources. It provides an explanation of certain archaeological problems, such as the fact that the *qiblas* of certain early mosques in Iraq face Jerusalem rather than Mecca. It would account for the absence of any references in Jewish sources to Medina as a place where the Torah was studied; and it would account for the repetitious and inconsequential character of the Quran which so exasperated Thomas Carlyle as well as countless others who have struggled through translations in various European languages.[3]

The truth of such charges is perhaps irrelevant. For history, and for the world community of today, it is the advocacy of unreasoning militarism that is the Koran's most significant feature, and it can be credibly traced to either Muhammad himself, the Arab Moses, or his disciples, the architects of the *jihad*, the "holy war" of the centuries to follow. The instrument of Islamic conquest in both cases was the Koran, and it served its Muslim masters well, as we will see.

The Koran was to become the "constitution" of the Islamic faith, providing moral guidance, sense of purpose, knowledge of final things, political cohesion—and a theology of conquest. The Koran succeeded because it was a "reflection on the psychological plane of material changes in Mecca itself, where a society of beduin traders was being transformed into one of merchant capitalists. Similar tensions between individualism and group identity had been growing in Medina, where the clan system of formerly nomadic tribes was proving increasingly ill-adapted to the needs of an agricultural community."[4] The Koran contains Muhammad's conception of a judgement day, borrowed from the Jews and Christians, which provided a useful psychological framework for emerging individualism.

Its divine advocacy of imperialism was perhaps the best proof of the specialness of Islam's adherents in the eyes of God.

Like the Catholic Vulgate and Anglican St. James versions of the Bible, the final agreed-upon version of the Koran was a combination of literary consensus and political exigency. The divinity of the revelations was certainly corrupted, not only because Muhammad claimed God's sanction for many of his personal whims, but also by the caliphate, which incorporated in its codes their own dynastic and imperial ambitions. Indeed, it is claimed by some Western scholars that the Koran was primarily organized to justify Islamic expansionism. The Koran is the Islamic Torah, a record of the Arab "covenant" with God, delineating the structure of the twin, inseparable instruments of ruling class power: war and social control. Like the Hebrews, whose concept of social organization after Exodus was understandably the inverse of anything Egyptian (notably a passionate aversion to centralized authority), the Arabs embraced a theology that reversed a millennia-old tradition of social and religious independence. In a single step these individualist nomads pledged spiritual submission to God and political obeisance to his messenger, Muhammad.

The suddenness and extent of this transformation surely has had no equal in history. Complete submission to Allah and the unquestioned authority of his Prophet had to be accepted or rejected in their entirety; there was no room for equivocation. As historian William McNeill says, "Either Muhammad was Allah's latest and only authoritative prophet, and the Sacred Law in every jot and title was the true expression of Allah's will for men, or else these claims were false. No middle ground could be found in logic, and very little was discovered in fact. Islam, in short, shared the doctrinal intolerance of its Judaic and Christian forerunners to the full."[5]

Tradition and the lives of ancestors were highly revered among Arabs in the time of Muhammad, but he nonetheless attacked them as both idolatrous and ignorant. The spread of belief in Islam necessitated a concession to the culture and a transposition of this basic urge to search the past for guidance in the present. The Muslim may want to look to the Koran for guidance in all things, but its scope is limited. For this reason Muslims developed the Sunna, "the way of the Prophet," Muhammadan sayings and tales of Muhammad's life not included in the Koran.

The creation of the Sunna could be said to have begun at the moment Muhammad died. "When, after Muhammad's death, the Muslims faced problems that the Koran alone did not solve, they naturally sought guidance in what people before them had done. The strongest argument a man could advance to prove his views was to show that Muhammad and his companions had acted in a similar way or said something to the same effect . . . The technique for solving all sorts of problems, from politics to the interpretation of the Koran, consisted in searching for precedents."⁶

Such efforts of course ran into the same problem presented by reliance on the Koran alone: informal material concerning Muhammad was limited as well. When this became apparent, "the Muslims quickly began to fabricate traditions to support the causes in which they were interested."⁷ Eventually Muslim leaders developed an approach analogous to the Catholic doctrine of infallibility. "Whenever someone says something true, it is as if I said it," Muhammad was said to have declared. (Humility was not one of his shining attributes.) What could be more perfect? The Muslim leaders could claim Muhammadan authority for nearly anything they wished, suggesting, much as Christian popes claimed to be spokesmen for Christ, that they were the Prophet's certified representatives on earth.

This general enterprise was considered quite legitimate, and at first few accounts were questioned. In terms of orthodoxy, there was extensive theological back-peddling, as the concept of useful Sunna expanded almost out of control. "One party held that Sunna was the custom of the entire early community; another, headed by Malik Ibn Anas, argued for the Sunna of the people of Medina, where the Prophet had lived the most successful part of his life. Still other parties, like that of Iraq, contended for the supremacy of local custom."⁸ In time, the closest equivalent of orthodoxy in Arabic came to be the phrase *ahlu-l-sunna wa-l-jamaah*, which means "people who adhere to the customary way of doing things and to the community." With this ambiguous classification, another codification of Islamic theology began.

Two centuries of this and the danger to the maintenance of any orthodoxy at all became clear. Muslim leaders and the scholars under their direction suddenly turned to advocacy of Sunna only strictly related to the Prophet, and to an obsessive examination of the legitimacy of those texts which fit that category. The jurist al-Shafaa (died 820) is credited with sparking this movement. He declared that the Sunna of the Prophet alone was authoritative, and that it could be legitimately determined only by close study of the line of transmission through various sources of the oral reports, or Hadith, that made up the alleged sayings, actions, approbations and disapprobations attributed to Muhammad but not in the Koran.

In time, the Muslim community created a body of *muhaddithun*, or students of Hadith, to conduct an examination, called *jahr wa tadil* ("wounding authenticity") of the Hadith. The Hadith itself was divided into two parts, the *matn*, or text, and the *isnad*, or chain of transmitters, somewhat like the Talmud's Mishnah, or oral law, and Gemara, discussion of that law. Each of the Hadith was assigned a category, "sound," "good," and "weak," according to the authenticity that could be established for each, and they were then packaged into collections of texts and analyses called the Six Sunnan Books.

Additions to Muhammad's teachings were thus halted, not unlike the manner in which the ancient kings of Israel called a halt to the addition of new scriptures to the holy book of the Jews. In the history of a theology there is always a time when tradition becomes ascendant and innovations are confined to the reinterpretation of existing writings. As we have seen, this only redirects rather than limits theological creativity.

Although the Sunna has come to be considered second only to the Koran in authority, its accuracy is disputed and it is generally acknowledged to be replete with "contradictions, anachronisms, and statements favoring one or another group that came into being after the Prophet's demise."[9] Since the late nineteenth century a number of Muslims have rejected the Hadith and seek guidance only from the Koran.

Koran and war

It was the Koran's doctrinal intolerance that would inform the most successful theology of imperialism known to the time, Islamic *jihad*. More significantly, the kind of holy war conceived by the Muslims was the incipient central ideology of Western imperialism from the twelfth century to the twentieth. It enlarged infinitely on the Judaic covenant, which merely claimed divine sanction of war in the limited setting of the Holy Land, by proposing a divine mandate to save the souls of all who lived. It was conquest on behalf of the conquered. War as charity. Christianity had preceded Islam in the evangelistic urge, but Islam preceded Christianity in the explicit use of war to carry it out. Islam is essentially a political faith, not a theological one.

Muslim faith centers on the one God and the only "mortal" sin of Islam is to deny his unity. *Sura* 112 declares:

> Say: Allah is One, the Eternal God.
> He begot none, nor was He begotten.
> None is equal to Him.

The central feature of the Koran is the *shahada*, the profession of faith, *La ilaha il-Allah, Muhammad-un Rasulu-llah*, "There is no god but Allah, and Muhammad is his Prophet." It is one of what is known as the five pillars of Islam, the rest being the four "acts of devotion"—prayer, the paying of *zakat* (alms), the pilgrimage to Mecca, and fasting during Ramadan.

But there is a critical act of faith that could be called the sixth pillar of Islam, and it has determined the course of Islamic history far more than the others: *jihad*, literally, "striving." The basic meaning is an internal struggle for self-purification, exerting oneself in order to purify one's being. Since humans historically think of resistance to temptation in terms of struggle, usually with an incorporeal force, *jihad* came to mean the "inner battle" against the evil in oneself. Since the most delectable aspect of moral repression is in the sharing of it, this idea eventually came to be concerned with the evil in others—those who did not accept the Islamic faith.

The Islamic caliphate early on found it useful to twist the meaning of *jihad* into a different kind of struggle, a secular one between Muslims and other peoples. The Muslim ruling class turned *jihad* into "holy war" against nonbelievers. To conquer nations was now taught as justified by God's direct approval. "Prophet, make war on the unbelievers and the hypocrites and deal sternly with them. Hell shall be their home, evil their fate," says *sura* 66:9. Such propaganda was enormously effective; the caliphate was able to launch armies equipped with a fervor that became legendary.

According to the Islamic view, the world is divided into two regions, the sphere of Islam, *dar al-islam*, and the sphere of war, *dar al-harb*, so conceived because the sphere of the unbelievers had to be warred upon: the pagans and the "people of the book," Jews and Christians, forced to convert or pay tribute. The waging of war to these ends is considered the sacred *duty* of all Muslims, the very specific will of Allah. Conflict is an acceptable and proper way of life for the Muslim, and, indeed, it is prescribed.

Muhammad had been both a reformer and a military leader. His life's work was the reform of his own society, *dar al-islam*, and the subjugation of all other societies, *dar al-harb*. The Arab society into which Muhammad was born was torn by internecine strife. The message revealed to him was that man should live in community under Allah. This community should be forged immediately. The practical method for establishing such a community was to redirect the traditional belligerence of the Arabs against the heathen and infidel, all those not a part of the newly conceived community of *dar al-islam*.

To accomplish both objectives, Muhammad outlawed intertribal raiding within the *umma*, "community," while promoting conquest of *dar al-harb* in a manner remarkably similar to the later crusades of Christianity. Perhaps Islam was the template of those bizarre escapades—Pope Urban's call to arms, as reconstructed by the historians, suggested a duality quite parallel to Muhammad's: "Lay off killing each other and fight instead a holy war." Islam's *jihad* was not merely sanctioned by Allah, it was a road to his grace. It was a "striving" by the faithful for transcendent goals; the earthly rewards of plunder secured in the process would merely serve to make the wait for grace less tedious.

The *jihad* is a holy war to make the world more fully Muslim, for the benefit of all mankind. "Islam is the least 'other-worldly' of the great religious systems, the one which, above all others, seeks to realize its aims in this world . . . the good society was generally seen as the necessary precondition to salvation."[10] The military crusade to impose beneficence on the world had collateral results as well, however. A dozen new dynastic families were established, and all secured some degree of divine authority.

One of Islam's earlier conquests, sometime between 634 and 644, was of the Hindu-Buddhist kingdom of Sind. There is an Arab account of it in a book called the *Chachnama*, written five hundred years later but based on a manuscript preserved by the family of the Arab leader, Bin Qasim. The account makes it clear that the purpose of the conquest was not the propagation of the faith. "The invasion was a commercial-imperial enterprise; it had to show a profit. Revenge was a subsidiary motive, but what was required from the conquered people was not conversion to Islam, but tribute and taxes, treasure, slaves and women."[11]

Bin Qasim fought under the sanction of the governor of Iraq, Hajjaj.

> When he received the head of the defeated king of Sind, together with sixty thousand slaves and the royal one-fifth of the loot of Sind, Hajjaj "placed his forehead on the ground and offered prayers of thanksgiving, by two genuflections to God, and praised him, saying: 'Now have I got all the treasure, whether open or buried, as well as other wealth and the kingdom of the world.' " He summoned the people of Kufa to the famous mosque of that town, and from the pulpit told them, " 'Good news and good luck to the people of Syria and Arabia, whom I congratulate on the conquest of Sind and on the possession of immense wealth . . . which the great and omnipotent God has kindly bestowed on them.' "[12]

Accounts of Muslim conquests are manifold, and most make little attempt to disguise the fact that Islam's battles were fought for pillage and plunder. As Steven Runciman explains, "Unlike Christianity, which preached a peace never achieved, Islam unashamedly came with a sword."[13]

Islam was merely the excuse to expand tribal warfare into foreign conquests. With success, ignorant tribesmen found themselves in control of cities, wealth and luxury. Although much killing and persecution was carried out in the process of conquest, the desire for riches restrained the Muslims from unbridled repression of those they conquered. This lenience, coupled with the escape valve of conversion to avoid the payment of tribute, allowed Muslim conquerors to amass a startling amount of territory in only a century, and enabled their faith to keep its hold in almost all of these places down to the present day.

None of this is to underestimate the power of the Word in motivating

Islam's foot soldiers. The Koran offers numerous passages supporting the idea of *jihad*, developed very early on in the thought of the Prophet. In Muhammad's first military venture a small Muslim band of just over three hundred met a Meccan force more than three times as large, yet the Muslims emerged victorious. This of course was proof of Allah's sanction. As *sura* 3:13 explains to the faithful, only his intercession could account for triumph over such odds.

> Indeed, there was a sign for you in the two armies which met on the battlefield. One was fighting for the cause of Allah, the other a host of unbelievers. The faithful saw with their very eyes that they were twice their own number. But Allah strengthens with his aid whom He will. Surely in that there was a lesson for the discerning.[14]

In the following year, however, the Meccans returned and defeated the Muslims. Anything can be reconciled in theology, however, and the Koran's explanation is only apparently different from the Torah's explanation of Exile as punishment for sinfulness. Both books maintain God's special relation to his people despite adversity, and put setbacks in the context of faithfulness to him. For the Jews, defeat was evidence of divine displeasure over Hebrew conduct, whereas for the Muslims it was merely a test of faith. Hence, the Muslim response is guilt free:

> If you have suffered a defeat, so did the enemy. We alternate these vicissitudes among mankind so that Allah may know the true believers and choose martyrs from among you . . . and that He may test the faithful and annihilate the infidels.[15]

The cosmology of Islam is elementary at best and does not contain the Christian theme that humanity is a mirrored reflection of a chaotic and conflict-ridden cosmos, that the cosmic battles of good and evil, contests between God and Satan, are fought on earth. But Islam does share with Christianity, and Judaism too, the belief that struggle is ineradicably part and parcel of this world. For Muslims it is struggle by the righteous against the idolatrous that, in theory, is constant.

In Islam man is not by nature socially righteous. "Men are enemies of one another."[16] Because of this, society takes the form of the state, and internal violence is strictly prohibited. The individual has a strict obligation to the state or community of Islam, and this obligation is the *jihad*—a holy battle expanded from the original duty to purify one's soul. Soon there was a mandate to purify one's society and eventually there was the call to a holy war against non-Muslims. Like the conquering Christians who killed their adversaries in order to save the souls of those who remained alive, the

Muslims seek to conquer societies to make converts for Allah. Religious abuses of this sort are always perpetrated in the name of the victims. Like the evangelical Christian's desire to save all the world's souls, the Muslim's motivation is to extend his inner *jihad* to the whole of earth.

There are four types of *jihad*, performed with the heart, tongue, hands, and sword. The first is an inner, personal battle against evil; the second and third are in support of right and correction of wrong; the fourth is the conventional *jihad*, a military endeavor against unbelievers and enemies of the faith (if there is difficulty in conquering minds and souls, then conquer bodies).

Despite Muhammad's attempt to keep peace and unity within the Muslim community, various sects of Islam have developed. They have battled one another throughout history and continue to do so today. Nonetheless, despite the inconceivably bloody confrontation between Iran and Iraq, Middle East Islam in modern times has existed in comparative peace with itself. Perhaps the principal reason is that Muslims have found a common foe towards whom they can direct their bellicose spirit, namely, Israel.

Although for the Muslim war is a fact and obligation of life in the *umma* of Islam, there is some evidence of Islamic pacifism; but this carries little influence in the Muslim world. There are also certain rules of war resembling contemporary principles governing the just war: the caliph or *imam* is responsible for the declaration of war (proper authority); there must be an opportunity to accede to Islam (exhaust alternatives); noncombatant immunity must be granted if possible (though the civilian blood baths which occurred during the Muslim wars of expansion dispute the acceptance of this prescription); and there should be no destruction of the means of livelihood. All of these precepts are of course overshadowed if not openly repudiated in the reality that is war.

Islam derived some of its militarism from the cultural ethos in which it developed. There is nothing unusual about this; Zoroastrianism, Shintoism and Islam all developed in very militaristic societies, and in order to spread they incorporated bellicose characteristics into their world view. This martial mentality would dominate Islamic behavior throughout the centuries, tempered in the our own era only when self-interest was served not by plundering foreign lands with armies but by plundering foreign treasuries through raising oil prices. Also critically important, with the development of oil installations and facilities, Islamic nations became vulnerable to counterattack on their own rich lands. Hence self-interest, through monetary pragmatism, indicated that holy war could also be commercially counterproductive. Thus, although a *jihad* against Israel may be compelled by Islamic theologians and scripture, it is often opposed by Islamic ministers of finance.

The essence of the rise and spread of the Muslim faith was political and economic, not religious. It was political since the Prophet Muhammad saw the folly of constant tribal warfare, and sought to redirect this propensity to violence and use it to plunder his neighbors. It was economic because Arab tribes were poor; prior to their conquests, they lacked the imagination and ideas required to improve conditions of life on their own; plunder was far easier to master. Religion became the political tool most effective for absconding with the hard-earned wealth of others.

When the sacred months are over slay the idolaters wherever you find them. Arrest them, beseige them, and lie in ambush everywhere for them. If they repent and take to prayer and pay the alms-tax, let them go their way. Allah is forgiving and merciful.

—The Koran, 9:5

III

Plundering the Faith

M uhammad died in 632 and the following fifty years were characterized by strife and discord serious enough to be called civil war. The process of selecting a successor, *khalifa* (caliph) developed into internecine struggle. This half century, known as the "patriarchal caliphate," is regarded by the Muslim world as the era of "Rightly Guided" caliphs. However, Allah's guidance met with serious disagreement from his Islamic congregation of the time. "Of the four 'Rightly Guided' successors to Muhammad, only one of them, Abu Bakr, died in his bed. Three were assassinated, two of them by fellow-Muslims."[1] The divine rules of succession were apparently open to interpretation.

Political cohesion required an articulation of the new faith in terms familiar to its adherents. Scriptures would not unite illiterate tribesmen, particularly since the Koran was only in the process of being assembled. Divinely sanctioned conquests, however, had a basic appeal. Ruthven declares that, "The survival of the new community was assured, not, as in Christianity, by the religious devotion of its martyrs, but by the military successes of its rulers."[2] Muhammad had accomplished the difficult task of uniting for the first time a collection of tribes who long had prized independence above nearly all else. In the absence of the Prophet, how could the unity of Arabia be maintained? Largely by force. "Muhammad and Abu Bakr had realized that the only way to prevent the Medinese polity from collapse was to maintain its outward momentum. The fragile tribal alliances upon which it depended would survive so long as the prospect of fresh gains continued to attract beduin support."[3] Thus, immediately after the Prophet's death sporadic Islamic raiding was quickly transformed into determined military conquest. "The successors of Mohammed, the Caliphs, combined, as he had, the powers of Emperor and

Pope."⁴ The era of Muslim conquests began, and continued with fierce speed for the next century. God was again on the march.

The initial military advances under Abu Bakr were probing raids into Mesopotamia to seek ransom and plunder. The Arabian armies were largely inspired by physical need. The Arabian desert was growing less and less capable of supporting the expanding population. Although the Islamic forces did not have an ideology of a "Promised Land," they were already formulating a theology of plunder for similar motives. As the oases became crowded, the hungry fighters of the Arabian desert were spurred on by the need for *Lebensraum*. However, unlike other of history's demographic dislocations, "This time there was a creed to give it direction as well as a simple love of plunder."⁵ Unlike their Hebrew ancestors, the emerging *umma* of Islam would not settle for a small piece of land. Religious ambition had grown since the Exodus.

Abu Bakr lived only to 634, and he chose one Umar to succeed him. "Umar's problem, like that of his predecessor Abu Bakr and Muhammad himself, was to prevent this coalition from collapsing into a welter of competing tribal interests . . . He achieved his task in two ways: by encouraging the expansion of the empire through the continuing *jihad* or holy war; and by systematic indoctrination of his beduin soldiers, aimed at replacing tribal allegiances with loyalty to the new theocracy based on obedience to God and the commandments of His Prophet."⁶ To intensify their enthusiasm, the caliphs told their followers that he who dies fighting for the faith goes to paradise. With the prospect of sharing plunder if he survived, or going to heaven if he died, the Islamic warrior could not lose. The lack of resistance to its raids tempted the caliphate to venture further. In an invasion of Iraq and Syria the astonished Byzantine emperor, Heraclius, tried to protect Damascus, but was soundly defeated at Adzhnadein, in southern Palestine, by the Muslim general Khalid ibn-Walid. Damascus fell in 635, Jerusalem in 638. In 639 the Muslim general Muawiya was appointed governor of Syria. Mesopotamia was conquered in 640. The winter of 639 found the Muslim general Amir ibn al-As attacking al-Arish on Egypt's eastern frontier. The Coptic Christians, harboring hatred for their Byzantine rulers, welcomed the invaders. First the area of Cairo fell, and within another year Alexandria followed suit. By 642 Egypt was defeated.

Umar was murdered by a Persian slave in 644, but military progress was maintained under succeeding caliphs. The Arabs then built a fleet and the taking of North Africa began. Tripoli fell in 645. Cyprus was raided regularly during the 630s and 640s. To the east, Arabic troops had subdued Persia by 657, when the caliph defeated the main Persian army at Kadisiya, and they got as far as Kabul, capital of what today is Afghanistan, by 664. By 711 Muslim forces had pushed two-thirds of the way into what is now Pakistan.

Finally, Europe beckoned. In 712 an Arab army aided by the Berbers of North Africa crossed the Straits of Gibraltar into Europe. By 732, a mere hundred years after the death of the Prophet, the Islamic armies had reached the heart of France—and the end of their expansionist success. Charles "the Hammer" Martel defeated Islamic armies at a battle somewhere between Tours and Poitiers. The warriors of Islam would have to be content with controlling nearly the whole of what is today Spain and Portugal; in any case, it got too cold farther north.

In 669 Constantinople was attacked for the first time, but after two costly and inconclusive contests for that great capital the Muslims decided to let a sleeping dog lie. After a defeat at the hands of the Khazais in Azerbaijan, today part of the Soviet Union bordering Iran, and a victory in 751 over a Chinese army at Talas in the Pamir mountains, the Muslims ran out of theological steam. They had established stable frontiers in Central Asia, the Caucasus, Byzantium and Western Europe. By the middle of the eighth century, having secured an extent of empire exceeded only by Rome, the Arab conquests came to an end.

Various circumstances facilitated the rapid conquests of Islam. The two largest empires of the time, the Byzantine and the Sassanid (Persian) had both been weakened by a long series of wars against each other. Subjects on the edges of both empires seethed with resentment against their respective rulers. The Syrian state had been weakened by the long dispute with Orthodox Christians opposed to Nestorianism, prevalent in Syria. In Egypt the monophysites, tired of persecution by the Orthodox Christians, were ready to welcome invading Muslim armies, who were willing to tolerate all Christian sects so long as tribute was paid. The disarray of what had been the Roman Empire made all the lands on its eastern and southern borders vulnerable to Muslim conquest, and in these various domains the invading forces of Islam often found little serious resistance. Lacking training, the Muslims substituted zeal; lacking equipment to storm fortresses, they used lengthy sieges to starve those inside. Muslim victories were often achieved against superior fighting forces, and this served to further enhance the belief by Muslim soldiers and leaders alike that Allah supported their adventures. Although Allah did not receive a percentage of plunder, *zakat*, alms-giving, may have been viewed as his share.

After Umar's assassination in 644, Uthman, a member of the powerful Umayyad clan of Mecca, became caliph. Uthman's legacy was two-fold. He organized the assembly of the definitive version of the Koran (although some scholars contend that it was not assembled for another hundred years), and he laid the groundwork for a dynastic tradition in the rule of the Islamic world. Uthman's appointments reflected extensive nepotism;

he elevated men who "scorned the puritanism and simplicity of pious Moslems" and made lucrative use of their positions of power. The faith was being corrupted, and in the process, divided. "Islam, relaxing in victory, divided into ferocious factions: 'Refugees' from Mecca vs. 'Helpers' from Medina; the ruling cities of Mecca and Medina vs. the fast-growing Moslem cities of Damascus, Kufa, and Basra; the Quraish aristocracy vs. the Bedouin democracy; the Prophet's Hashimite clan led by Ali vs. the Umayyad clan led by Muawiya—son of Mohammed's chief enemy Abu Sufyan, but now governor of Syria."[7]

The world of Islam was a kettle of simmering rivalry for twelve years, when Uthman was murdered in June 656 by a discontented mob of Egyptian pilgrims, followers of a converted Jew who preached a belief that Muhammad would come back to life, that Ali was his only legitimate successor, and that Uthman "was a usurper and his appointees a set of godless tyrants."[8] Uthman was reading the Koran when the mob broke into his room and killed him. The first serious struggle for the rule of Islam and its empire was on.

Ali became caliph, but it was against the wishes of the Prophet's widow, Aisha, allied with the Umayyads. Ali quickly defeated Aisha's military forces, however, in the "battle of the camels" at Basra, located at the head of the Persian Gulf, and then moved the capital from Medina to the Iraqi city of Kufa, making Arabia of secondary importance in the still rapidly expanding empire.

Meanwhile Muawiya had encamped in Damascus and before a year had passed his forces mounted a revolt against Ali. In the middle of a decisive battle slowly going against the rebels, one of Muawiya's generals devised the ploy of affixing copies of the Koran to the heads of his soldiers' spears, pretending to allow Allah to decide who should be victorious. The defending forces, in their piety, forced Ali to agree to a six-month period of arbitration.

In the meantime, a group of Ali's men turned against him, forming a sect called the *Khariji* or "Seceders." In the embryonic tradition of Islamic social critique they developed a democratic ideology that argued that the caliph be elected and even removable by the people. "Some of them were religious anarchists who rejected all government except that of God; all of them rejected the worldliness and luxury of the new ruling classes in Islam."[9] Ali eventually suppressed these emerging liberals, but the Khariji would come back to haunt him.

Returning to broader concerns, Ali then yielded to the decision of the arbitrators in his contest for power with Muawiya: both should renounce their claims to the caliphate. Ali resigned in 661 but Muawiya reneged on the agreement and had himself proclaimed caliph. The Umayyad clan had finally taken the throne. In the ensuing theological chaos, a Kharijite approached Ali near Kufa and pierced his brain with a poisoned sword. Thus did the adopted son of the Prophet become the latest victim of Islam. Allah had failed to inform Muhammad's successors of the physical risks attendant upon theological inheritance.

Although the Umayyad seizure of the caliphate was never seriously threatened, a standard-issue battle of ideology, not mentioned in the Koran, now erupted among the descendants of the Prophet. A group calling themselves *Shi'a* (from *Shi'at Ali*, "the party of Ali") claimed that only the heirs of Ali had the authority to interpret the Koran, and, as such, should be the hereditary caliphs. Ali had been divinely designated as *imam* and was free of sin and error. Allah's intention, the *Shi'a* assured the faithful, was to have the infallibility of Muhammad transmitted through the descendants of his family. This theological claim apparently did not include Aisha, since she was allied with the archenemies of the *Shi'a*, the Umayyad clan. Muawiya and the Umayyad caliphs who succeeded him had their own supporters, however, the *Sunn*, "people of the way of the Prophet." It was a lie, of course; the Umayyads had as little genuine interest in theology as most rulers, except when it could serve their purposes. Muawiya himself was "a man of the world, who privately put little stock in Mohammed's revelation; religion seemed to him an economic substitute for policemen, but no aristocrat would let it interfere with his enjoyment of the world."[10]

The Shiite schism would last to the present day, but the breakaway Muslims would ever be a small minority. Only 10 percent of the world's Muslims today are Shiite; of the more than two dozen countries with a mostly Muslim population, only in Iran, Kuwait, and Iraq do the Shiites number in the majority. By contrast, the Sunni Islam's toleration and relatively strict orthodoxy "have preserved the Sunni from serious defections and variations." The Shiites however, "have fathered countless sects; among them are the 'Assassins,' the Druse, the Fatimids, the Ismailis, and the Karmathians."[11] This is no doubt due in large part to the marked degree which the Shiite faith has diverged from that of the original teachings.

It is one of the remarkable characteristics of Islam that the Shiite schism is the most serious of only a few such splits, amounting to little in terms of population. In so far as the Muslim world has been divided theologically, it has almost always been due to dispute over the relationship of faith and state. "That the Muslim world should have divided itself over the political question of the caliphate illustrates a characteristic of Islam, that every Muslim thinks of himself as living in theocracy."[12] So it remains. The most serious division among Muslims in the Middle East today derives from the developments in Iran, where the example of direct rule by the mullahs poses the most serious challenge in decades to many of the area's relatively secular Muslim governments.

The Muslim successes resulted in the creation of an empire ruled by Arabs. Given their relatively small numbers, the Arab ability to maintain control over such large territories was made possible only by allowing others to rule on their behalf.

> As they had acquired their empire without severe fighting, there had been little destruction, and the civil administration was kept on almost unchanged. Both in Persia and in the Byzantine Empire, the civil government had been highly organized. The Arab tribesmen, at first, understood nothing of its complications, and perforce accepted the services of the trained men whom they found in charge. These men, for the most part, showed no reluctance to serve their new masters . . . It was only in virtue of their lack of fanaticism that a handful of warriors were able to govern, without much difficulty, vast populations of higher civilization and alien religion.[13]

The invaders exacted tribute only from conquered subjects who were not Muslim. But here a difficulty soon arose. People would convert to Islam to escape the burdensome tax of conquest; a plethora of mostly Christians, and some Jews, began to see the value of acknowledging Allah and His Messenger, no matter how strange it seemed to pray five times a day. This caused an unanticipated problem for an empire with a bureaucracy to support and a ruling class gaining ever more expensive tastes; these things require large and dependable revenues. To their credit however, despite developing budget problems, Islam's ruling dynasties only sporadically limited the right to convert.

There were other problems along this line. Muslim armies frequently impressed those conquered into their employ, replenishing the ranks of their soldiers for the next campaign. This was not as oppressive at it seems at first blush: such soldiers eventually received a share of the plunder, even if it was not as large as that of their conquering comrades-in-arms. Here too, however, suddenly surfaced the problem of the convert. Muslim or not, surely the convert was not due an equal share of the booty? Equal status for those who converted to Islam was perfectly in keeping with the teachings of the Koran, but it was nonetheless strange, and in this case quite costly. The Arabs conceived a compromise. "Any convert who was not a full member by descent of an Arab tribe had to become *mawali*," clients or military apprentices of a true Arab, in order to receive a share of the plunder.[14] To reconcile the theological difficulties caused by this two-tiered form of the *umma*, the Arabs assured the *mawali* that, as the Koran sanctions, they were equal to the "pure" Arabs in the eyes of Allah, but just a little less equal in the view of the state finance ministers. The Koran, unfortunately, is not sufficiently specific on how to divide plunder. Nonetheless, with the passage of time and some political struggle, many *mawali* got as much of the spoils as their Arab brethren.

There were other difficulties with the *mawali*. The caliphs had been diligent in fostering literacy and the reading of the Koran, and the Muslim congregations, Arab and non-Arab alike, were familiar with its passages. However, as any religious organization knows, general education can be dangerous. The *mawali* increasingly felt they were a legitimate part of the imperial Muslim *umma*, but this was not reflected in the estimation of their Arab brothers, nor at first in the distribution of plunder, promotions (the *mawali* were generally confined to the infantry) or other indicators of equal social status.

The number of converts, and, more significantly, the number of imperial soldiers who were converts, had grown very large. The Arabs had suddenly become a minority among Muslims, an upsetting development, but they retained absolute control. Even as the *mawali* felt increasingly alienated and excluded from the aristocratic ruling class of the pure Arabs, the *Shi'a*, similarly ostracized, consistently incited them to revolt—soldiers were essential to the success of an uprising.

The disaffection of the *mawali* and the *Shi'a*, in the milieu of an indolent caliphate supported by an arrogant and self-indulgent *nouveau riche*, led gradually to a breakdown of Umayyad authority. In 749 Abu-al-Abbas exploited this unrest and claimed in a mosque in Kufa to have ascended to the throne. A descendant of an uncle to the Prophet, he announced a restoration of the caliphate to orthodox ways and drew the immediate support of the *Shi'a*.

The meaning of the pretenders's full name, "Shedder of Blood," well foretold the story of his approach to securing Islamic orthodoxy. After defeating and executing the last Umayyad caliph in 750, "a dinner party was held for the males of the defeated house; the guests were murdered before the first course, which was then served to the hosts."[15] With this theological ceremony the Abbasid caliphate was baptized and embarked on two centuries of rule.

The Abbasids had no reluctance to employ violence to achieve their purposes, the most important of which was to preserve their rule. Once in control they confirmed the Sunni orthodoxy of their predecessors, to the surprise and distress of the minority *Shi'a* who had helped bring them to power. Such things mattered little to the Abbasids. "They soon carried out a ruthless extirpation of opposition and even of former allies who might turn sour. Loyalty to the dynasty, rather than the brotherhood of Islam, was increasingly the basis of the empire . . . much was made of religion as a buttress to the dynasty and the Abbasids persecuted religious dissidents."[16]

The new dynasty was no longer that of an enlarged Arab sheikdom defended by its tribal warriors. The tendency of the caliphate to autocracy, restrained by Umayyad roots in provincial rule, came to full flower under Abbasid domination. It ruled through a salaried bureaucracy, mostly Persian, and a standing army, which came to be mostly Turkish. Caliph al-Mansur (ruled 754-75), considered the true founder of the dynasty because he created the power base for the new state with the help of Persian auxiliary troops, moved his capital to Baghdad and introduced a Persian and Byzantine administrative structure to the Islamic empire. The Arabs accordingly lost their dominant position.

The disintegration of the empire was simultaneously begun. In the Abbasid extirpation of the Umayyads, one Abdul Rahman escaped and established his rule in Spain. Al-Mansur sent an army against him, but it was defeated. Under the third Abbasid caliph, Harun al-Rashid (ruled 786-809), both Morocco and a North African province just to its east, Kairwan, established their independence from the caliphate. With Rashid's death the decay of the caliphate was accelerated by protracted struggle for power among his sons. By the tenth century there were two autonomous states in central Asia, Hamnadid families ruled what today are parts of eastern Turkey, northern Syria and northern Iraq, the Tulunids ruled in Egypt, and three other families governed the rest of settled North Africa. What burns bright burns out the more quickly; the Islamic empire needed no invasion of barbarians to cause its demise.

But it was demise only in unity of political rule. Despite a fragmentation of empire much like that which, four hundred years before, had thrown Europe into the cultural abyss of the Dark Ages and from which it would need still another three hundred years to emerge, the various states comprising world Islam were able to flower artistically and scientifically. In Baghdad, Damascus, Cairo, Cordoba, and several other, lesser centers, universities, libraries, medical centers and scores of other forms of civilized intercourse sprang up. Collectively these states formed the finest civilization in the world of that time. Like the Jews of the rabbinical period before them, rendered militarily impotent by Roman domination, and the Christians of the nineteenth century after them, finally stripped of their armies, perhaps the Muslims, free of compulsion to conquer and conquer again, had for a moment time to reflect on more transcendent possibilities of social organization.

This period of tranquility was of course only relative to the feverish period of ever-onward conquest; the Muslim principalities still struggled among themselves, and within themselves as well, since in most cases they were made up of populations from several cultures and languages. But the very need of these Islamic dynasties to consolidate their respective regimes of disparate races and languages, to fuse them together into a societal structure which could mobilize a defense against internal instability and external threat, compelled them to build stable, productive societies. How else can we explain the sudden halt to conquest and the flowering of civilization? The *jihad* was now being supplanted by social organization of the fruits of conquest. Baghdad, the capital of the largest of these states, that which ruled Arabia and most of Iran and Iraq, was called the "city of peace."

Cordoba was especially significant among these centers of culture, because it was the interface of Islam with Europe. A city where Muslims, Berbers, Jews and Christians dwelled peacefully under the control of Islam, Cordoba was mined by all of Europe for scholars, doctors, architects and musicians. Cordoba had seventy libraries, nine hundred public baths and university education unequalled. Muhammad's command to "make war on them until idolatry is no more" was now in eclipse. The Prophet also had said, "The ink of the scholar is more sacred than the blood of the martyr."[17] Like the ancient Hebrews who had created *shalom* in defeat, the fragmented empire of the Muslims now turned to learning and leisure.

The collective achievement of Islamic culture in this period could easily be termed the high tide of civilization to that time, surpassing that of Rome and Greece and making significant, almost formative contributions to the West's eventual emergence from cultural darkness. In this period Islamic societies created medicine and pharmacy as sciences, establishing the first medieval school of pharmacy, introducing the idea of local pharmacies, inventing inhaled anesthesia, introducing the use of animal gut in sutures, and developing the practice of licensing doctors and druggists; an Islamic textbook on human disease, written in ten volumes by a Central Asian genius dubbed Avicenna in the West, was widely used in Europe until the second half of the seventeenth century. Islamic cultures devised the experimental method in alchemy which led to the development of chemistry. Mathematics made significant advances; Islamic cultures invented or embellished from Indian culture algebra, advanced trigonometry (particularly the concept of the sine), the concept of the zero, and the decimal system itself, including the simplicity of Arabic numerals used throughout the West today.

European Crusaders absorbed from their forays in the Middle East countless architectural innovations later used in castles throughout Europe. Islamic commerce was very sophisticated, and it is from Arabic that the word "check" is derived. The guitar, the preeminent form of popular musical expression in the West today, entered Spain from Persia in the twelfth century. Achievements in the crafts and arts and literature, though little observed in the West, were unparalleled—book-binding unrivalled anywhere in the world or any time since, pottery so exquisite that odes were regularly dedicated to its finer examples; and next to the Bible, "itself

Oriental," *A Thousand and One Nights* and the *Fables* of Bidpai (brought from India in the eighth century and translated into forty languages) "are the most widely read books in the world." As Durant summarizes the period, "When scholarship has surveyed more thoroughly this half-forgotten legacy, we shall probably rank the tenth century in Eastern Islam as one of the golden ages in the history of the mind."[18]

Islamic faith had served to plunder other societies, and it had an Eastern Renaissance to show for it. But renaissance is the threat of change if nothing else, anathema to the truly devout, ever lusting after that which does not change. Now it was necessary that the faith of Muhammad put an end to that which it never meant to spawn.

Next to bread and women, in the hierarchy of desire, comes eternal salvation; when the stomach is satisfied, and lust is spent, man spares a little time for God. Despite polygamy, the Moslem found considerable time in Allah, and based his morals, his laws, and his government upon his religion.
—Will Durant, *The Age of Faith*

IV

The Rigor Mortis of Orthodoxy

I slam had achieved much in every realm of human endeavor, but this had strangely little to do with its character as a religion. According to Russell, "The Arabs, although they conquered a great part of the world in the name of religion, were not a very religious race; the motive of their conquests was plunder and wealth rather than religion."[1] As a result, despite the fact that scriptural exhortations had been invoked to inspire martial energies, there was for some time no particular need to refine theology too far beyond its effective use in *Realpolitik*.

The new societies were cauldrons of pluralism, influenced not only by the multiplicity of the empire's races but also by the spread of interest in foreign ideas generated by commerce with the whole of the known world. In order to preserve a cultural identity in this admixture of people and ideas taken from the Jews, various Christian sects and the religions of India, the theoreticians of Islam began to develop orthodoxy. How to remain Muslim in this pluralistic culture?

The same question would be asked by Muslims of the late nineteenth century and to the present day. The Islamic wards of European colonialism wondered how to maintain Muslim cultural identity in the atmosphere of suffocating Western dominance, while at the same time, since the West also had much to offer, loosening the bonds of rigid Islamic orthodoxy. In the twentieth century the answers would run the gamut, from gradual abandonment of much of the Muslim tradition to radical breaks with it, from merely traditionalist reapplication of the laws of the Prophet to revolutionary orthodoxy more fanatical than any before.

The theologians of Islam in the tenth and later centuries suffered less diversity of opinion. They decided that the assertion of an Islamic identity required the adoption of Islam's precepts in the realm of the secular—the application by the state of the sacred laws, the most immutable of Muslim marks of difference, in every sphere of life. But the religious permeation of secular power could not be effected merely by moral suasion, and there were no other means at hand. The theologians were forced to await an opening.

By the time of Eastern cultural achievement in the tenth century, the elements of orthodoxy had been developing for quite some time, although Islamic theology, as all else Islamic, reached a zenith of sophistication in this period. The ascension of the orthodoxy soon to come had two supporting elements. One was the hardening of interpretation of the Koran and Sunna and their derivative laws. The second was the spread of Sufism, a strain of Islam rejecting the trappings of civilization in pursuit of a personal relationship with God.

During the century of conquest, priority had been assigned imperialism. The pace of life did not permit learned leisure, possible only after political consolidation, and in any case theological license could interfere with imperial and dynastic success. But license or no, religious ideology independent of secular power was in embryo.

Theology is called in Arabic *kalam,* meaning "speech," that is, the speech of God, and is understood among Muslims to mean the use of reason to support religious belief. Etymology of course does not necessarily have any relation to meaning. Although its origins date nearly from the moment of Muhammad's death, *kalam* did not begin to flower for more than a century, with Islam's extensive exposure at the court of empire to educated religious peoples from as far away as India.

But the precursors of *kalam* were hardly cosmopolitan, first taking shape in the political disputes of a young society bereft of its founder and inspiration. Islamic religious discourse in this early time was only masked political debate and struggle. This began immediately on Muhammad's death, with the dispute over succession (pitting Muhammad's cousin, Ali, against Muhammad's close associate, Abu Bakr), but attained serious theological significance only with the ascension in 661 of the Umayyad family, headquartered in Damascus. In a debate during this time about whether a person could be determined to have faith (that is, whether one person could decide if another was a Muslim), to decry the possibility of earthly knowledge of such a thing was to support the legitimacy of Umayyad rule. The Umayyads would not countenance the evolution of rationalism; thinking of any kind could eventually lead to questioning of their authority. There was at this time only limited debate over transcendent matters fleshed out for centuries among people who lived only a few hundred miles away. Among Muslims in these early days, "when people spoke of predestination and free will, they were not only seeking clarification of a trenchant and persisting religious problem but were taking a practical stand toward the reigning government of the time. To side with the Qadariya (from *qadr*, or the power to control one's own acts), as the proponents of free will were called, could be an exceedingly dangerous stand."[2]

Nonetheless, an independent *kalam* would eventually assert itself. Greek ideas began to be translated into Arabic; they were not only foreign ideas, but contrary to those held by most of the Islamic community. In response to the intellectual challenge, a group called the Mutazilites emerged in the second century of Islam (the ninth century in the West). Although accused of being freethinkers by their Muslim brothers, they viewed themselves as developing the rational in Islamic thought, purging it of certain grave errors of reason evident in the thinking of their contemporaries. Since Islamic ideas were being formulated even as the Mutazilites considered these matters, it was especially difficult to commingle Greek rationalism, Bedouin mythology, and the range of chameleon Islamic code-ideas, political expedience passing as religious thought. For a while the Mutazilites had the support of the eighth-century Abbasid rulers, but the Mutazilites were more interested in systemizing *kalam*, while their benefactors wished only the tailoring of theology to the exigencies of power. Eventually there was a break, and with the loss of Abbasid support the Mutazilites disappeared as a separate school. To the Muslim world they left a legacy, *kalam*, but its development in the centuries to follow would be profoundly antithetical to the rationalism that was its inspiration.

The most forceful intellectual attack on the "freethinking" Mutazilites eventually came from al-Ashari (died 935), a Mutazilite himself while young but a man with more conservative views in his middle age. The central tenet of al-Ashari's theology was the absolute sovereignty and majesty of God, the inverse of Mutazilite thought in that it promoted unquestioned awe rather than the Mutazilite celebration of inquiry tethered rather than strapped to dogma. Al-Ashari "would allow no compromise at all of God's absolute power, holding that all power and all action come directly from God. Men have no independent ability to act except as God creates the capacity and will in them."[3] Such a theology promotes the acceptance of things as they are, and, of course, a resignation to ruling power as it is.

One would think that so strong a rejection of free will would shortly be modified. Al-Ashari's theological framework has held to this day, however, forming the basis for most religious thought among the overwhelming majority of Muslims who are Sunni. (The relatively small number of

Shiites tend more to Mutazilite rationalism, in their theology if not their politics.) So dominant was al-Ashari's lifework that *kalam* is said to have become the province of mere recapitulationists ever since, pedants content to compile the opinions of their predecessors. "For most of Islamic history, the *kalam* has not played a vital role for the majority of Muslims; of far more importance have been the practical questions raised by the lawyers or the personal spiritual guidance offered by the mystics."[4]

These "practical questions" were of great importance. The Koran offered little that was definitive in the question of social organization, but it was nonetheless necessary to formulate standards of conduct that defined the good Muslim. Already there had been debates over the question of the "relationship between faith, *iman,* and good works, *islam,* and whether the latter are necessary for the former to exist."[5] The Islamic community investigated these questions with gusto in the third and following Islamic centuries, and the resultant guidelines of social conduct were codified into a body of literature called the Sharia.

The Sharia

Sharia is the common Arabic word meaning "the law," although it originally meant "the path in which God wishes men to walk." It established a code of behavior for Muslims much as the Talmud had for the Jews. The Sharia is divided into two parts, *Ibadat,* or duties owed to God by way of worship, and *Muamalat,* or duties of a practical kind toward men and society. Both categories are of equal importance to the Muslims, as distinct from many Christian faiths, which value faith somewhat over works.

The jurist al-Shafii of the third Islamic century (the Christian tenth century) formulated the defining theory of the Sharia, *usulu-l-fiqh,* "roots of the law," or methods to determine the social "path" God has outlined for humanity. *Usulu-l-fiqh* has been almost universally accepted in the world Muslim community, a decisive rejection of the Mutazilite approach to Muslim theology favored by the Shiites, and its rigorous and true application is one of the reasons for world Islam's unique near-solidarity in religious affairs.

There are four such "roots," or sources, and they are to be searched for answers in order, subordinate roots turned to only if search in a previous one proves inconclusive. The first and supreme of the four roots, of course, is the Koran. If answers are not found there, one must proceed to an investigation of the second root, the Sunna. If the Sunna sheds no light on the matter, then *ijma,* or consensus of the community in the whole and in the past (precedent) must be looked to. Finally, if no guidance is obtained from the first three roots, then *giyas*, or analytical reasoning, should be supplied, although it is "closely hedged about by restrictive rules and subject always to the primacy of the other roots."[6] As in other creeds, rationality is strictly subordinated to scriptural incantations. In Islam this principle is most explicit and undiluted by theologians or jurists since its formulation. God's decrees are "based on nothing but his sovereign will; they are not subordinated to rational considerations, nor are they to be judged by the standard of reason. . . . the Sharia is *taabbudi*, to be obeyed as a slave obeys his master."[7]

In a sad pairing, this unquestioned obeisance to the law was soon accompanied by a parallel stricture on changes in its interpretation. "After the emergence of the schools of law, a conviction grew among Muslims that the right of personal exertion (*ijtihad*) in interpreting the sources of the law had ceased to exist. Instead, Muslims hailed to *taqlid*, or submission to authority, according to which men in later centuries must adhere to the opinions of the great jurists of the past."[9]

The Sharia established a number of social norms. Slavery was permitted—Muslim slave-trading would take place on as grand scale and for a longer time than its European counterpart—but fraud and slander against one's fellow man were forbidden. Playing games of chance, imbibing intoxicants, and eating swine's flesh or the flesh of animals that had died of natural causes or been sacrificed to any but the one God, were all prohibited. Similar prohibitions, mostly prophylactic in nature, were designed to arrest illnesses only later eliminated by proper cooking and the eventual development of refrigeration. As in most hot regions of the world, spices were used to flavor meat in order to kill the taste of putrefaction. However, while spices could alter the taste, they did not prevent the stomach problems caused by rotting meat. Religious prohibitions were therefore introduced. This was particularly important on the battlefield, where sick soldiers could jeopardize the military maneuver.

Many social changes pertaining to women had already been made. Muhammad had called a halt to the practice of killing infant girls, certainly a good place to begin. Then he advised his followers to marry slave girls if they could not afford free women, an issue which men in all cultures apparently face. Muhammad encouraged polygamy by taking several wives after his first wife died. This was justified in the Koran (4:2) principally on the basis of the frequency with which widows and their children were left without financial support.

This chapter [of the Koran] was revealed after the battle of Uhud, in which the Muslims were defeated by the Medinans and the Prophet was himself wounded. Some seventy Muslim males out of seven hundred were killed, and there was every likelihood that more would be slain in the future, leaving orphans in the care of widows who would have difficulty in providing for them. In such circumstances polygamy was essential for survival.[9]

Polygamy was declared a duty of the faithful.

Men's and women's rights as outlined in the Koran are quite specifically unequal. Women could inherit only half what men could. They could initiate divorce only at enormous expense, while a man could do so merely by declaring "I divorce you" three times. Women of course could take only one husband. Men were allowed up to four wives, and extramarital sexual relations were expressly permitted, so long as the women concerned were not the property of another man. Infidelity by women was punishable with death by stoning. "Men have authority over women," summarizes *sura* 4, "because Allah has made the one superior to the other, and because they spend their wealth to maintain them."

A man's wives were kept in a separate part of the house called the *harem*, which was sacred and unlawful for other men to enter. Eventually the women who lived there were collectively called by this name. Women origially wore veils to protect themselves from the personal intrusions of a licentious society, but this eventually hardened into a requirement, to protect the husbands from jealousy and to ensure their domination of their wives' lives.

The punishment for murder was execution by the sword. If "plunder" accompanied the crime, crucifixion was the method of execution. Thievery was dealt with very harshly. Conviction on a first offense cost the perpetrator his right hand. A second offense was punished by cutting off the left foot. The general source in the Koran for these punishments is *sura* 5. "Those that make war against Allah and His apostle and spread disorders in the land shall be put to death or crucified or have their hands and feet cut off on alternate sides." To steal, perhaps, is to spread disorder. The right hand was chosen for amputation because it was the one traditionally used to eat with, while the left hand was used to clean oneself after defecation. To cut off someone's right hand was to socially ostracize him—no one could eat at family or other social gatherings with his left hand, since bowls of food were taken from in common.

Loaning money at interest was disallowed, perhaps because Muhammad's original followers were members of the lower classes who had little money. It should not be forgotten that Islam was a social as well as theological revolution; the banning of usury reduced the power of the wealthy.

Prayer, fasting, alms-giving and pilgrimage were all required. Prayer should be said in the mosque, *masjid*, from *sajada*, "to bow down," "to adore," while standing behind an *imam*, an appointed man who leads the movements. At least one pilgrimage to the Sacred Mosque at Mecca is an obligation for every Muslim who has the financial and physical ability to make it, and two-and-a-half percent of one's savings are the prescribed alms to be given to the poor.

In its text the Sharia pays little attention to public law, and its laws and punishments are generally enforced by the communities. But in practice the Sharia clearly influences, and in some cases even determines, the governing of Islamic societies.

As the possible meanings of Islam's scriptures were rigidified, a scathing if usually implicit critique of Islamic society was developing in Sufism. As in other religions, Islam generated mystics who saw only corruption in the material order and sought to escape it by flight to spiritualism more abstract than usual. The fact that material prosperity had replaced poverty because of Islam's secular success did not hinder the mystics' insights. Most Muslim mystics called themselves Sufis, from the simple robe of wool (*suf*) that they wore. Sufism was a meditation- rather than text-based form of worship, and its adherents accordingly "embraced sincere enthusiasts, exalted poets, pantheists, ascetics, charlatans, and men with many wives." Sufi doctrine "varied from time to time, and from street to street."[10] The Sufis were clearly not part of the ruling class establishment.

One of the principal saints of Sufism is Abu-Said Ibn Abi'l Khayr (967–1049), who claimed to have memorized thirty thousand verses of pre-Islamic poetry. One day he heard a lecture discussing the ninth verse of the Koran's *sura* 6: "Say Allah! Then leave them to amuse themselves in their vain discourse." Khayr reflected on the verse deeply. "A door in my breast was opened," he is reported to have said of the experience. Similar to St. Jerome, Kahyr advanced quickly to the conclusion that intellectual pursuits were a form of vanity. Khayr collected all of his books and burned them. In the days of hand-copied books, this was no simple act of self-emasculation. To destroy the product of tens of thousands of man hours of labor, in a society said to have valued calligraphers above all other craftsmen, was a protest against civilization itself. "The first step in Sufism," Khayr proclaimed, "is the breaking of inkpots, the tearing up of books, the forgetting of all kinds of knowledge." Sufism represented "dissatisfaction with the luxury and laxity in which the believers had fallen after the establishment of the Islamic Empire."[11] Religion's intellectual nihilism was once again promoting cultural paralysis.

A flight from the complexities and corruption of contemporary culture through the assertion of an intensely personal relation to God and submission to his will, Sufi attitudes began to permeate Islamic society. Its influence was significant ideologically, as a kind of fundamentalist undercurrent in the thinking of Islam's theologians, but diffuse politically in early centuries of its existence, until the formation of Sufi orders in the twelfth century (the fifth Islamic century). Sufi ideas began to be given more attention and soon Islamic theologians were burning books which could not be "correctly interpreted" and oppressing people whose ideas did not conform to orthodoxy. As such, Sufism came to be an underpinning of the organized drive by Islamic theologians of the twelfth and later centuries to influence the conduct of secular affairs.

With the Sharia in place by the middle of the tenth century, the theologians threatened by Islam's cultural ferment had a base upon which to build a sweeping social and political critique. The fragmentation of the Islamic empire had sparked change—a turn from militarism to social consolidation by the successor dynasties—but the result was still more change, and of a most disturbing type: a blurring of Islamic identity, which had in fact never been fully established. With the pluralism of its culture, Islam seemed to be giving way to anything and everything that was not Islam— or so it appeared to those in charge of thinking about what Islam was. It was an opening to theologians, whose *raison d'etre*, putting everyone on "God's path," had little to do with the happiness or cultural success of society but rather only on their ability to exert influence on it.

Where for some time after the death of Muhammad the theologians had served merely as handmaidens to secular factions, three centuries of pedantry and self-importance in the shadow of power had convinced them that they had a calling to more important doings. Fortunately for Islam's dozens of constituent ethnic parts, Islam did not create an Ezra, the Jewish prophet who had dictated, in somewhat similar circumstances of social reorganization, that all non-Jews should be banned and ostracized. This would have been impossible, since the Arabs were Islam's only "true" race, and they were in the minority. The religion of Muhammad would accordingly seek to establish and maintain identity with less emotional suffering than that mandated by Ezra, but its equally severe codification of intolerance would wreak far more extensive cultural devastation, to the tragic detriment of world civilization.

Just as Khadija's money and social position had freed Muhammad to plot revolution, so the successes of empire had bred a class of learned parasites certain that though they had not constructed the flower of the civilized world, surely they deserved to bring it to heel. The theologians had only one weapon with which to assert their primacy—the dictates of Muhammad. Orthodoxy now came to the Muslims, as it had come to the Christians and Jews before them. And these dictates, this orthodoxy, who but the theologians knew their proper application in the secular world?

The sword of religious tyranny had been sharpened, but the arm to wield it had long lacked strength. But, all praise to Allah, this would change. The years of the eleventh and twelfth centuries saw a decline in the power of Islam's ruling dynasties. At various times they were beset from the east by the Monguls, from the west and north by the Crusades, and in Spain by the progressive encroachment of Christendom. "As political power declined in the Moslem world, it sought more and more the aid of the theologians and lawyers of orthodoxy." But there would be a price. The first step in establishing the primacy of a certain set of ideas is the elimination of all others. And so it began. "That aid was given, but in return for the suppression of independent thought."[12]

In Baghdad, the Caliph Mustanjid gave orders in 1150 that all the philosophical works of Avicenna be burned. By 1194 Emir Abu Yusuf Yaqub al-Mansur of Seville issued instructions to burn the works of Averroes, except certain selected books on natural science. Al-Mansur followed this dictate with an edict prohibiting his subjects from studying philosophy and directing that all books on logic and metaphysics were to be thrown into the flames. An indiscreet idealist named Ibn Habib violated the prohibition on philosophical study and was executed.

War and conquest have always provided an impetus to science and technology, and invading armies have always generated an exchange of ideas with the peoples they overcome; conquerors, of necessity, must attempt to understand the populations they end up ruling. In the process they absorb some of their culture. When the conquests are inspired by religion, however, the intellectual ferment is often quickly curtailed as a threat to religious orthodoxy. This was not the case with Islam, since it had in its first century, the time of its conquests, little orthodoxy to speak of.

But in time Islam developed strict definitions of what it was, and the attempt to impose these definitions was just as inevitable. The once insatiable Islamic appetite for knowledge, originally sparked by conquest, was gradually transformed into an urge to prevent new ideas from contaminating a supposedly immutable and exclusively true Islamic creed. Free thought and learning were slowly replaced by thought and learning exercised only within the parameters of orthodoxy. The Sufis sought to flee from the realities of secular culture into the refuge of mysticism, while other ecclesiastics sought to dominate the intellectual life, and with it the political power, of the Islamic nations. These socially opposite but theologically compatible factions would stimulate each other in an effort to choke the free exchange of ideas by limiting their availability to the theologians, presumably schooled in resisting the lascivious temptations of foreign thought. With study, such thought could be placed in relation to the Koran and categorized as heretical to it, merely odd, or compatible with it.

Supported by the ideology of the Sufis, Islamic theologians and philosophers initiated a repression of those ideas considered outside the narrowing parameters of orthodoxy. A rigid fundamentalism descended upon the Muslim world, and around the thirteenth century, Algazel, a contemporary theologian, wrote a book called *Destruction of the Philosophers*. It put into written form the growing theory that since all truth was in the Koran, there was no need for further speculation on affairs of any sort. It also promoted the contagion of destroying books containing such speculation. This formalized a pattern which would affect the Muslim world down to the twentieth century. Even today one cannot help but notice the lack of books in Muslim homes.

Curiously, Christianity had an identical ideology with respect to independent ideas, but ended up moderating its attitudes in this respect— tainting Christian theology with reason—in order to combat the attractions of Islam! For centuries the Christians had the same attitude as the theologians of Islam regarding the sufficiency of "revealed truths" and denigrated the use of reason and logic. With the rise of Islam, however, the thirteenth-century Dominican scholar Thomas Aquinas challenged the Islamic reliance on revealed truth—how else to deny the truth of a faith clearly less corrupted than Christianity by material encrustations and theological capriciousness, a faith that even in the midst of introversion maintained a civilization vastly superior to the medieval stagnation of Europe?

To make this untenable argument, Aquinas wrote *Summa contra Gentiles* to explain the inherent reasonableness of the Christian faith as opposed to that of Islam, and he amplified his intellectual disquisitions by writing *Summa Theologica*, in which was contained the "Quinque Viae," ("The Five Ways"—to prove the existence of God), in order to demonstrate that Christian revealed truths could be adduced, and affirmed, by the use of reason. To accomplish this apologetic endeavor, however, Aquinas had to resort to the Christian unthinkable: a study of the writings of the secular philosopher, Aristotle, whose works were previously banned by the Church. Thus Islam's superior culture compelled the Christians to introduce some element of reason into their creed.

There is of course a great irony in Aquinas's exertions. Even before the great thinker embarked on his historic task, the flower of Islamic culture which drove him was withering. Repression metastasized in the body of Islam, spreading even to those most hindered by it. Intellectual leaders as prestigious as the fourteenth century's Ibn Khaldon, the greatest Islamic scholar in the Middle Ages, enlisted in the drive to repress thought and inquiry not in conformity with Islamic orthodoxy. "Because Ibn Khaldoun accepted the orthodox view which rejected any rationalist approach to the search for knowledge and truth, he also was hostile to the sciences and philosophy. He argued against the study of natural science unless the student had first been steeped in the religious sciences, and he was violently opposed to the study of alchemy (as chemistry was called in the Middle Ages)."[13] The Arabs had introduced Europe to paper in the eighth century (after learning how to manufacture it from the Chinese in the capture of Samarkans in 704),[14] but nonetheless they came to prefer burning it to writing on it.

A rigor mortis of orthodoxy began to afflict the Muslims, as it had the Hebrews and Christians. Orthodoxy asserts itself in cycles in most creeds, but Islam would have no such luck. By the eighteenth century, when the West invaded the Arab provinces of the Ottoman Empire, the Muslims still had not loosened their theological shackles. Having repressed science, technology and philosophy for centuries in order to protect Koranic purity of thought, the people who had laid or preserved the groundwork for the scientific and industrial rise of Europe were defenseless against its resultant economic and technological power.

Strike terror into the enemies of Allah and the faithful, and others beside them. All that you give for the cause of Allah will be repaid you.

—The Koran, 8:60

V

From Ottoman to Palestinian

I slam had created a cultural legacy that would forever benefit the world, but by the eleventh century the Muslim empire was crumbling in every sense. The rise of orthodoxy had paralyzed its intellectual development, while dynastic and theological-political quarrels had shattered unity irreparably. As an instrument of unified power the creed of the Prophet had nearly disintegrated. Powerful Islam would not disappear, however. A group of pagan invaders called the Seljuks would come to its rescue; with the aid of Islamic ideology they would one day replace decaying Byzantium with the Ottoman Empire.

The Seljuks were a group of the Turks ("Ten Arrows" or "ten tribes"), people who in the sixth and seventh centuries established in Asia the largest nomadic empire known to that time. Some of them migrated west and settled to the north of the Black Sea, becoming known as the Oghuz or Ghuzz. In the ninth century the Ghuzz and other Turkish tribes served as mercenaries for the Muslim armies of the Abbasid caliphate, which ruled for a time northern Egypt and nearly all of what is now considered the Middle East. The caliphate allowed these *mawali* to rise through the ranks of its military and the Ghuzz adopted Islam in the middle of the tenth century.

In 999 the Ghuzz saw an interesting thing. Turks in the employ of the Saminid emirate, Islam's push into what would become southern Russia, revolted and overthrew the Arab ruling class, establishing the Ghaznavid emirate. The Ghuzz found this event most instructive and in 1037 they seized the Ghaznavid lands. It was the first step in the prairie-fire creation of the Seljuk empire, so named after the ninth-century tribal leader who had united a number of Turkish tribes into the Ghuzz. By 1055 the warlike and expansionist Seljuks had conquered the languishing Buwayhid caliphate, which ruled what today is Iraq and Iran. The theology of plunder was back in the saddle.

By 1071 the Seljuk ruler, Alp Arslam, was carrying out forays into Armenia and contiguous provinces, causing the Byzantine co-regent Romanus IV Diogenes to lead a large-scale attack on this sudden threat from what had been the neutralized armies of Islam. Unfortunately, Romanus suffered a catastrophic defeat on the plain of Manzikert, "unimpeachably one of the decisive battles in history," according to historian Colin McEvedy. "There was nothing to oppose the Turkish flood, and only the Bosporus saved the [Eastern Roman] Empire."[1]

The centuries-old defensive system that had protected Asia Minor from the Muslim armies now collapsed. Massive Turkish migration began at once. The Seljuk rulers used Anatolia (modern Turkey) as a resettlement area for migrating tribes from Central Asia not easily absorbed into the Persian economy. Anatolia also became a place of exile for the unsuccessful or fractious elements of the Seljuk dynasty. In 1097 Turks were driven into the hills of central Anatolia by the soldiers of the First Crusade, and they consolidated it into a sub-state of the Seljuk empire.

Seljuk power began to disintegrate in the twelfth century, but the Islamic community established in Anatolia managed nonetheless to survive war with both Byzantium and the Christian crusaders. In 1204 the Fourth Crusade drove the Byzantines out of Constantinople and into western Turkey. The Turks were forced to crowd further east, precipitating a series of internecine wars which seriously weakened Seljuk power. In 1243 the Mongols dealt a deadly blow to the Seljuks at Koesedag and reduced the Seljuk sultan to a Mongol puppet.

One result was that more Turks, these only barely Muslim, streamed into Anatolia. In 1261 the Byzantines expelled their occupying Christian brethren from Constantinople and began a campaign to recover their former territories to the west. In the process the Byzantines began to neglect their possessions to the east; consequently "all but the strongest cities in Anatolia fell by default into the power of the nearest Turkish predators, the Ottomans."[2] The Ottomans were not the Turks of old, the descendants of mercenaries hired by the caliphates and converts of a hundred years to Islam. They were part of the second wave of migrating Turks, which arrived with the Mongol subjugation of the Seljuks, mostly pagans driven west before the Mongol advance.[3]

From this stock a feisty little Turkish state grew up across the water to the southeast of Constantinople. One Osman (Arabic *Uthman*), a leader of a group of warriors, conquered historic Nicaea and by around 1300 had established a small state. Osman's son, Orhan, expanded the territory west and also north, into the peninsula that was the road from the east to Constantinople. But the Ottomans would not need to invade what was left of Byzantium. They would be invited. In 1346 one of the contestants for the imperial throne, John Cantacuzenos, asked the Ottomans for help in his quest for power. On the success of the effort he granted the Ottomans Gallipoli, the peninsula to the southwest of Constantinople that nearly meets the Turkish mainland to form the Dardanelles straits. Things moved very quickly after that. By 1453 the Ottomans had taken Constantinople and established an empire that extended deep into the Balkans to the west and deep into Anatolia to the east. In another hundred years, the Ottoman Empire encompassed what is today Greece, Bulgaria, Romania, and part of Czechoslovakia and the Soviet Union, and stretched around the Mediterranean to the Straits of Gibraltar.

This huge empire grew in large part through the use of Islamic ideology, but the Islamic character of the Ottoman enterprise was as convenient as it may have been sincere. The Ottoman success was really the old story of Eastern hordes invading the West. "[The Ottomans] were a people driven instinctively by an inherited impulse as nomads to move onward, over a deliberately planned westerly route, in search of pastures new. Since their conversion to Islam, this search was sanctified and further inspired by their religious duty as Ghazis, under the holy law, to seek out and fight the infidel in the Abode of War, or *Dar-el-Harb*: to raid and occupy his lands, seize his possessions, kill or carry into captivity his people, and subject their communities to Moslem rule."[4]

Just as Moses had to inspire the pharaoh's slaves with the notion that they had venerable forebears and ancient traditions, so did Osman and his successors unite disparate descendants of the Huns by telling them that they were not simply Turks but part of the tradition dating back to the Prophet. According to historian John Walsh,

> Tradition ... exalted them to the role of *ghazis* (*gazis*), warriors of the holy war (*jihad*) against the infidel, whose only purpose was the spread of Islam and whose only reward was in a life after death. But this theory assumes a view of Islam that it is quite improbable these tribal Turks had yet achieved; their indoctrination and instruction had been mainly from missionaries of the incoherent and extravagant dervish doctrines. Nor is it likely that the founder of the dynasty actually bore the Islamic name Osman (Arabic *Uthman*), which intrudes incongruously in a genealogy almost exclusively Turkish. The year 1300 (corresponding to the Muslim year 699) as the date of the foundation of the new state is arbitrary and was probably selected to endow the event with a millennial portentousness; while the account that Osman was confirmed in his sovereignty in this year by the Seljuk sultan Keybubad III is no more than an attempt to endow the dynasty with a patent of legitimacy.[5]

Merely marauding beginnings or not, the Islamic empire of the Ottomans grew to become one of the largest in history and one of the longest-lived, lasting six hundred years. The empire reached the peak of its vigor under the rule of Suleyman I (reigned 1520 to 1566), when campaigns secured Hungary, Baghdad and Tunisia, but the following two centuries saw a parade of colorless rulers "increasingly exploited by their viziers in competition with the women of the royal harem and their eunuchs."[6]

By the eighteenth century the territorial fortunes of the Muslim were clearly on the wane. Peter the Great resolved to gain access to the Mediterranean and obtained it in 1696 by walking over the Islamic stronghold in Crimea. In 1768 Catherine the Great occupied the whole of Crimea and sent a Russian fleet to attack the Turks from the Mediterranean. The war was brought to a close by the fateful Treaty of Kurchuk Karimarji, after which the Ottoman Empire became merely an arena of European imperial competition. Napoleon invaded the province of Egypt in 1798. During this invasion the French discovered the Rosetta Stone, inscribed in the second century B.C.E. with the same passage in priestly Egyptian hieroglyphics, the demotic script of contemporary spoken Egyptian, and ancient Greek. Already understanding the last of these written languages, scholars could for the first time decode the first two. The writing was on the wall for Islam as well. After peace was concluded with France in 1801 the empire of Allah "was again stretched on the carving board of European ambitions."[7] On French advice the Ottomans treated a limited Serbian uprising as a major revolt, thereby starting a chain of events that would lead to Serbian independence. In 1806 Russia attacked, and the Ottomans lost what is today part of Rumania and the Moldavian province of the Soviet Union.

In 1912 the people of the Balkans thought that together they could wrest control of their land from the Ottomans. They were right. Albania sprang into existence, Serbia and Bulgaria extended their holdings to the south and Greece took most of the rest of the Balkans, leaving the Ottomans control over only a small arc of territory across the Bosporus. The empire foolishly cast its lot with the Germans during World War I, and had to pay the French in the form of Syria, while the British were happy to take Palestine, Jordan and Iraq.

Turkey was all that remained of the Ottoman Empire and soon after the war even that was under Greek invasion, though the Greeks were soon repulsed by Turkish nationalists who had largely displaced the Ottoman sultan's rule in Anatolia. In 1922 the sultanate was abolished and the last sultan, Mehmed VI, fled abroad on a British warship. His successor, Abdulmecid II, was allowed to hold only the semi-religious title of caliph. Once the grandest title in Islam, it was now reduced to a titular religious appellation, never again to obtain its former significance. On March 3, 1924, five months after the proclamation of a Turkish Republic, even the honorary office of caliph was eliminated.

While an Islamic empire in the Middle East would fade from view, the power of Islamic ideology would continue to play an important role in world history. Empire was replaced by colonial and then national states and one day oil was discovered in the Middle East, assuring that however many books it burned or hands it cut off, the region of the birthplace of Islam would not become merely a backwater in world affairs.

Oil was discovered in the Middle East neither by Muslims nor their foreign occupiers, governmental or corporate. Two private entrepreneurs, one Australian, the other Armenian, first discovered and exploited Middle Eastern oil, in Iran and Iraq just before and after World War I. Successful corporate efforts would follow in Bahrain (1932), Saudi Arabia (1936) and Kuwait (1938). These men were able to initiate the flood of oil discoveries because they had developed close relationships with Islamic potentates of the various rival dynasties and as a result were able to receive special privileges. In 1901 Ottoman authorities granted an Australian named William D'Arcy a sixty-year concession on a half million square miles of land—five-sixths of what is now Iran. In 1908 D'Arcy struck oil and established the Anglo-Persian Oil Co., eventually called British Petroleum. In 1904 C.S. Gulbenkian, an Armenian, wrote a report on the possibility of locating oil in Mesopotamia (modern Iraq). Within a decade a company bringing together French investors, British Petroleum and Royal Dutch Shell was formed and in 1925 Gulbenkian secured this Iraq Petroleum Co. a concession for all oil development in northern and central Iraq, on the condition that the company's principals deal with no other Islamic states formed from what had been the Ottoman Empire.[8]

On their own initiative the British and Dutch excluded American companies from any involvement in the burgeoning Middle East petroleum industry, except as distributors. American firms supplied nearly three-fifths of the total foreign demand, however, and used their leverage to intrude themselves into the European monopoly anyway; by 1928 Mobil and Standard Oil of New Jersey (now Exxon) had secured 24 percent of Iraq Petroleum. In 1934 British Petroleum and Gulf Oil set up the Kuwait Oil Co. and got a sixty-five year concession from the government of Kuwait. By 1936 Standard of California (SoCal) moved directly and acquired concessions in Bahrain, following up this coup by entering into a joint venture with Texas Co. (Texaco), "establishing a new jointly owned company, Caltex, under which SoCal received a one-half interest in Texaco's marketing positions east of Suez, and Texaco a one-half interest in the Bahrain concession and facilities."[9] In the meantime, SoCal had also acquired the concessions for Saudi Arabia, and after a decade of maneuvering Caltex entered a joint venture with Jersey Standard and Mobil (SoCal's distributor in the Far East) in order to control production and distribution; an agreement was signed in March 1947 whereby these corporations would share ownership of the Arabian American Oil Co. (Aramco) and the Trans-Arabian Pipe Line Co.[10]

After fifty years of bargaining, the Europeans and Americans had gained what seemed like complete control over Islam's future. But the theology of plunder was not so easily bested. Former animists venerating streams and rocks, the indigenous peoples of the Middle East did not at first realize that the former objects of their worship could provide them with the means to revitalize their culture: oil. Nonetheless, Allah could again serve to unite the various Arabic dynasties for the purpose of using this resource to plunder the world. To do so, however, the control of oil would have to be seized from the neocolonialists. The impetus to indigenous control began in the 1950s, with Iran's nationalization of British Petroleum's Persian properties, followed in 1964 by Iraq's nationalization of parts of the Iraq Petroleum Co.; the rest was taken in 1972. Saudi Arabia pursued a less confrontational course, reaching agreement with Aramco for complete takeover of Aramco's concession by 1976.

But owning production facilities and even primary marketing operations was not enough to influence price, the all-governing factor in the control of a natural resource. For this a cartel was needed, and the Organization of Petroleum-Exporting Countries (OPEC) was dutifully founded in 1960. The unity required for it to be effective was lacking, however, but along came America's strong support for Israel in the 1973 war. Arab fractiousness found reason to dissipate. America's myopic geopolitical analysis, calculated largely in a religious context (inchoate attitudes toward Zionism and Soviet Marxism dominate U.S. foreign policy), blinded Western powers to what was on the economic horizon.

The roots of this oil politics date to World War I. When Turkey entered the war on the side of the Central Powers, the British Arab Bureau sent T.E. Lawrence, popularly known as Lawrence of Arabia, to the Hejaz (modern Saudi Arabia) to assist the sharif of Mecca in the Arab revolt against Turkey. Lawrence soon became a liaison officer of the Arab forces led by the sharif's son, Faisal, and assisted him in obtaining British money and military advice. Together Faisal and Lawrence cut the Hejaz railway, which ran from Damascus to Medina, the Turks' critical means of supplying and reinforcing their troops in the area. The rebels next captured Aqaba, a critical port on the Red Sea. They also succeeded in removing the Turks from Palestine, replacing them with European Jews—one hope was to create a client state useful for protecting access to the Suez Canal—and on October 1, 1918, Lawrence entered Damascus, together with British general Edmund Allenby. The *de facto* creation of Israel began the disaffection between the Arabs and the British, culminating in continued

Arab revolts, now against British rule. The Arab attitude toward the West, for a while most sympathetic, began to sour; by the 1970s ambivalence toward the West turned into rage.

Hatred of Zionism was not the only force at work however. Just as in the twelfth century, when the theologians invented *kalam*, the need to define Islamic identity was felt after the break-up of the Ottoman Empire. In the twentieth century theology was less important than secular government, since managing the revenues of oil was never discussed in the Koran. But amid the changes generated by sudden Western economic penetration—Westernized upper and upper-middle classes and vastly increased disparities between rich and poor—the people of the Middle East were forced to ask what made them special. It was of course Islam that made the people of the Middle East special. But Islam was a facet of Arab and Persian society that seemed fast to be fading in the face of change perpetrated by the West. Another question was necessarily asked: How can we maintain this specialness? The revitalization of Islamic orthodoxy seemed called for. Just as the rapid economic changes of the seventh century had led the people of Arabia to create Islam, the cultural changes wrought by Western penetration generated the desire to fortify it.

The Sunni and Shiite religious hierarchies began a drive for social dominance. Middle Eastern governments had to deal with the issue, and whatever its challenges, an emphasis on Islam had the potential for strengthening social cohesion. Thus the process of putting the various national administrations on a foundation of Islamic law, begun as soon as the Ottoman Empire was dismembered, was accelerated after World War II. Thus also was revived in full strength traditional quarreling over how Islamic law should be interpreted and applied.

The temptation to emulate the West, driven by the impulse to materialism, had to be restrained until an identity could be defined. The theologians could not now decry materialism with the same fervor of the twelfth century, however, because the national economies depended upon Western dollars and the populations had already come to desire the benefits of Western technology at least as much as the piety of ancient scriptures. The acids of modernity had eaten away at the orthodoxy of other religions; Islam would be no exception. Nevertheless, cultural identity had to be established firmly enough to prevent the triumph of Western values. To deviate from Islamic scriptures became not merely heresy but cultural apostasy.

The conspicuous wealth and the general profligacy of those in power spawned a rise in fundamentalism both in Sunni and Shiite circles. According to R. Hrair Dekmejian in his *Islam in Revolution*, Sunni fundamentalism has its roots in the "middle, upper-middle and tribal" classes of Arabs resentful of dynastic wealth and power. Dekmejian also notes an even more pronounced urge to fundamentalism "among non-indigenous Arab and non-Arab Sunni Moslems—Palestinians, Egyptians, Pakistanis, Yemenis, Syrians, Iraqis, and others, most of whom occupy middle- and lower-middle-class positions." Shiite fundamentalism is little different, he says, but particularly observable "among Arabs and Arabized Persians and Iranian citizens working in the Gulf states."[11]

Disparities of wealth and status, haphazard modernization, ethnic pluralism and theological differences have produced regional instability in the Arab world. This condition has been exacerbated by such forces as inter-Arab competition in oil production and pricing, the political ambitions of some Islamic leaders seeking to achieve dominance in the region both overtly and under the guise of pan-Arabism, the global power struggle between the United States and the Soviet Union in which the Arab nations are often pawns, and the multitude of unquantifiable problems caused by the existence and the militant policies of Israel.

Certainly no single event has done so much to polarize the politics and galvanize the societies of Islam in our century than the creation of Israel in 1948. It is reasonable to speculate that without Israel the Muslim nations would have avoided getting into the twentieth century's ideological contest between democracy and communism. What self-respecting Muslim would consort with atheists unless absolutely forced into it by circumstances? The Islamic nations of the Middle East quite likely would have been content to compete economically and militarily with each other, as they have for centuries. Under the sway of Western imperialist interests for more than a century, their rivalries would probably have remained in that context, each nation securing arms and training from its respective Western mentor with no need to turn to the Soviet Union for help. To the Muslims, Western colonialism was a yoke which could gradually be removed, whether through open revolt or the evolution of history. To develop an alliance with the atheists of Marxism for political support and military assistance was theoretically and theologically inconceivable. They did so only when the West chose to favor its surrogate and left the nations of Islam nowhere else to turn. The West, particularly the British and the Americans, had openly espoused the giving of Arab lands to European Jews, and supplied Israel with steadily increasing amounts of money and sophisticated weapons to enable the nascent Jewish state to embark upon its policy of *Lebensraum*, always at the expense of the Arab world.

Israel became for the nations of Islam the single unifying factor, the only issue on which they could all agree. Halting the spread of Zionism became the international theology of the world of Islam. Dynastic disputes were often—but not terribly often, it is true—put aside in order to rally together to fight the common menace of a new form of white imperialism. Able to use ancient theology to justify the Zionist desire for the Holy Land, modern Christian colonialism had a new mantel of morality with which to cloak its geopolitical designs. But the Arab world, while lacking political cohesion, had the riches of oil to fall back upon. With those riches they could purchase weapons from the Soviet Union.

Before the establishment of Israel, the individual Arab ruling classes were opposed to Zionist ambitions but not initially affected by them. Originally the Zionists merely claimed their "small notch of land" in the Middle East. Although tens of thousands of Palestinians were dispossessed of their homes in the decades of Jewish immigration to British-controlled Palestine, the Islamic ruling classes were more concerned with establishing their own national identities after the collapse of the Ottoman Empire, and were preoccupied in no little way with the discovery of oil in their domains. But when Zionist ambitions grew to require both unchallengeable military superiority over contiguous Arab states, as well as territory greater than originally foreseen—enough land to accommodate five million people, as it turned out—general Arab concern grew. With the Israeli war of independence came a flood of Palestinian refugees, hundreds of thousands of whom fled to the neighboring Arab states. These Palestinians sought not only food and shelter but also justice and revenge. They expected the Arab nations to come to their assistance. The Arab populace, and eventually the Islamic ruling classes, began to see Zionism as another form of European colonialism, one whose victims were a serious source of social unrest within the Muslim world.

Defense of Palestinian rights was never high on the agenda of Arab nations, however, except as a geopolitical strategy to check European neocolonialism, or as a factor in the rivalry among the Islamic dynasties. "The Arabs and the Palestinians have always been wary of each other," declares James Adams, a British Middle East specialist. "The Palestinians distrust the Arabs and, in particular, despise the backwardness of the Gulf Arabs who did not begin to develop as nations until the discovery of oil. The Arabs, on the other hand, have reservations about the Palestinians, who they view as a source of potential dissent and disaffection within their own countries, as well as envying their business acumen."[12]

Palestinian distrust of Arabs was hardened during the 1948 war. When the U.N. General Assembly passed its fateful resolution granting nationhood to the Jews in Palestine, the Arab armies joined together to halt what they perceived as blatant colonialism. But with defeat they minimized their losses by agreeing to a partition of the lands of Palestine. Egypt acquired the Gaza Strip in the southwest and Jordan was given hegemony over the West Bank. More than half a million Palestinians were forced to flee from their lands to seek refuge in whatever Arab nations they could, most ending up in permanent refugee camps on the borders of Jordan, Lebanon and Syria. Their Arab hosts provided the sand on which to reside, but little more.

Now without a homeland, the Palestinians set up their own political organizations. In September 1948 the refugees in Gaza set up a provisional government and declared their borders to be "between Syria and Lebanon in the north, Syria and Trans-Jordan in the east, the Mediterranean in the west and Egypt in the south."[13] Official Arab recognition and support was not forthcoming; indeed, Egypt acted immediately to dissolve the provisional government, proclaimed on what it now considered its own territory, the Gaza Strip. From the war and these subsequent events the Palestinian saying arose, "All revolutions conceived in Palestine abort in the Arab capitals."[14] As Palestinian leader Abu Iyad declares in his autobiography, "Experience has shown that, when the chips are down, all the Arab regimes, whether progressive or reactionary, act in the same way, sacrificing the Palestinian cause to their own parochial interests."[15] The Palestinians were confined to their camps or to ghetto areas, denied the opportunity to education, restricted from obtaining executive positions in corporations and generally treated as second-class citizens. The nations of Islam did not perceive it to be in their self-interest to allow these refugees to become part of the *umma*.

An Arab summit meeting led to the creation of the Palestinian Liberation Organization in 1964, and Arab nations provided it with initial financing. The PLO was soon an umbrella organization comprising various factions, including the Palestinian National Liberation Movement (commonly known by its reverse acronym in Arabic, al-Fatah), headed by Yasir Arafat. While alternating between diplomatic initiatives with the West and guerilla raids on Israel, the PLO membership remained fractious. In 1967, however, events propelled the PLO's militant factions to preeminence— Israel launched a full-scale military attack upon Egypt. The 1967 Arab-Israeli war not only devastated the combined forces of Egypt, Syria and Jordan, but permitted Israel to achieve its principal objective, seizure of the West Bank from Jordan. An additional million Palestinians now came under Israeli military rule. Israel's military success spawned a new wave of Palestinian terrorism, soon to be carried out on an international scale. "The war . . . served as an impetus to the Palestinian guerilla organizations. The Palestinian commandos emerged as a new element of major importance on the Middle East scene. They raised the morale of all the Arabs after their humiliating defeat."[16] When Israel launched reprisal raids on PLO strongholds in 1968, it suffered serious losses. The PLO had emerged as an instrument to restore Islamic pride.

In 1969 al-Fatah gained control of the PLO and Arafat became the head of the organization. Terrorism was condoned as a legitimate method of retaliation against Israel and as the most effective way to bring the Palestinian cause to the attention of the West. The organization soon turned to international terrorism, and the PLO became known the world over as a band of bloodthirsty radicals. Although in any given month more innocent people were (and are) killed by Israeli aircraft and armies than by the PLO, the image of terror which the PLO sought to foster backfired. Terrorism had brought the plight of the Palestinians to the front pages of the Western press, but on those same pages the PLO was now indelibly (and justifiably) portrayed as a creature of amoral violence. The origins of the PLO's actions, Israeli military aggression, were soon forgotten. Whether for purposes of public relations or out of genuine belief in the need to alter PLO policies, in 1973 Yasir Arafat began to advocate a halt to international terrorism.[17]

On October 14, 1974, the PLO gained international recognition when the United Nations invited it to participate in a November debate on the Palestinian issue. The PLO called for the creation of a Palestinian state; Israel responded that it would never deal with the PLO. By 1986 the Knesset had gone so far as to make it illegal for Israeli journalists even to talk to members of the PLO. Shades of South Africa. The Jews had long shown themselves little different from the Christians, victims who became persecutors with the acquisition of power. The centuries-old Hebrew desire for a homeland was fulfilled by dispossessing the inhabitants of Palestine, who now had to search for a homeland themselves. Some Palestinians would come to enjoy using the violence that became their only alternative.

Although it received some money and training from the Soviet Union, the PLO obtained most of its initial financing from the more bellicose Arab nations who hoped to avoid direct involvement in the Palestine problem by sending donations. As the PLO became stronger, it extorted money from moderate Arab nations by threatening to create domestic instability in them. Such developments grew more and more credible as PLO-sponsored terrorism became commonplace; anyone who was even moderately supportive of Israel, or, in the case of Arab countries, anyone who was neutral toward the Israeli-Palestinian dispute, was a potential target of PLO terror. Through blackmail the PLO filled its coffers well enough, but it also set up regional administrations so that Palestinians in other countries would donate to the organization. "Every Palestinian is obliged to donate 5 percent of his or her income as taxes to the PLO, and in two places, Libya and Algeria, this amount is deducted at source before the workers receive their salaries."[18] Over the years this accumulation of funds made the PLO less dependent on the Arab nations, so that by 1986 five-sixths of PLO income came from investments. Also by 1986, according to James Adams's

The Financing of Terror, "If finances of all the different groups that fall under the PLO umbrella are taken into account, a total annual income of $1.25 billion and assets of around $5 billion are involved."[19] With investments and assets in the major countries and companies of the world, the PLO has become an economic giant. Financially independent, it is beholden to no nation in the formulation of its policies.

Having acquired such economic power the PLO now seeks to acquire a peaceful image. PLO offices in Western Europe and the United States often promote the PLO's charitable activities, kindergartens, high schools and even a planned PLO open university, a project which has received some support from the U.N. Educational, Scientific and Cultural Organization.[20] The PLO is even known to desire to make investments in the West Bank, but the Israeli government would never permit it. Besides the obvious political challenge such a development would pose for the occupation forces, the creation of a strong Palestinian economy in the West Bank would be a threat to Israeli morale. The Palestinians are clever businessmen and with substantial investments they could very well prosper. A dynamic West Bank economy run by the Palestinians would both limit Israel's access to cheap labor and pose an unflattering contrast to Israel's debtor economy, kept afloat only by foreign subsidies. Accordingly, the West Bank's one million inhabitants are probably condemned to perpetual Israeli military repression played out in a context of economic dependence, a reality which makes PLO terrorism inevitable for the forseeable future.

After oil, terrorism is the principal political tool left to the Muslim world, and, because of Israeli militarism, indiscriminate terrorism is no longer the domain of the PLO. With the Israeli invasion of Lebanon in 1979, the Shiites were at first watchful, waiting to see how Israel would conduct itself. Very quickly they saw. Israeli troops did not come merely to attack the PLO; Israel wanted a "North Bank," and came to take it by force of arms as it had the West Bank in 1967. Israeli troops and armored columns not only attacked military opposition, but killed civilian PLO "sympathizers" at will, destroying homes, sacred places, shops, stores, and civilian food and cooking supplies.[21] The Shiites became aroused, galvanized by Israel's invasion of Lebanon just as the PLO had been galvanized by the Six-Day War. As Israeli Brigadier General Ori Orr, commander of operations for the invasion, put it, "The extremist wing of Shi'ite terrorism will come looking for us . . . We will be involved with terrorism in the north of Israel for a long time to come, for years." And, according to Radio Israel, the head of Israeli military intelligence said, "We are raising the deadliest enemy, and the least predictable."[22] Israeli aggression against Lebanon assured that Israel would have more enemies than ever before. Israeli Defense Minister Yitzhak Rabin summarized the danger: "I believe that among the many surprises, and most of them not for the good, that came out of the war in Lebanon, the most dangerous is that the war let the Shi'ites out of the bottle . . . If as a result of the war in Lebanon, we replace PLO terrorism in southern Lebanon with Shi'ite terrorism, we have done the worst [thing] in our struggle against terrorism In my opinion, the Shi'ites have the potential for a kind of terrorism that we have not yet experienced."[23]

The Lebanon war had a unique effect on many citizens of Israel, not the least of whom were the officers of the Israeli military. As Hirsh Goodman, the military correspondent for the *Jerusalem Post* put it, "Brigadier generals refused to serve in Lebanon . . . Pilots returned with bombs undropped . . . The Army really showed it was separate, and different, from the political echelons."[24] Not all of the army, by any means, but some of the military personnel began to question the morality of the war. Israeli citizens marched by the thousands in protest of their government's policies, but in the most important sense it was too late. Israeli aggression had "let the Shi'ites out of the bottle." Now the PLO would not be alone in the use of terrorism on a worldwide scale to bring attention to, and seek international restraint from, Israeli military repression. The ideology of *jihad*, its modern form one of sporadic terrorism, has again become the expression of Islamic identity.

Dormant *jihad* was also reawakening outside of Palestine. While the ruling classes of the new Arab states were consolidating their power and increasing their wealth, those who did not share equally in the benefits of the new order became increasingly restive. In particular, the religious elements of the Islamic societies were distressed at the emerging secular orientation of their governments, an orientation dictated by the need to deal with the realities of national independence and oil. When their attempts to moderate the expanding secularism were met with government opposition, they began to act. No place was this more dramatic than in Iran.

In the 1920s Reza Khan, the founder of the Pahlevi dynasty, took steps to remove the Islamic clergy from any position of major social or political influence. He secularized laws, adopting European-style legal codes, and established a system of secular courts with the deliberate intention of reducing the judicial functions of the *ulama* (those schooled in Islamic religion and law, the clergy). To solidify secular jurisprudence, he required all judges to hold law degrees, thereby preventing graduates of religious seminaries from becoming judges. He also cancelled the authority of the clergy to notarize and record documents, thereby minimizing even their administrative roles in the emerging secular society—and denying them this lucrative source of revenue. To provide the opportunity for rational scholarship on Muslim history, Reza Khan set up a center of Islamic studies at Teheran University, which the *ulama* saw as a direct challenge on their own intellectual territory. These and similar attempts in other Islamic countries to come to grips with the modern era were viewed by the religious community with divine disdain.

One of the people affected by these acts was a popular and deeply religious teacher at Qom, Iran, the religious center for Islamic studies. His name was Ruhollah Khomeini. With Reza Khan's new rules the certification of seminary graduates was reviewed by the government and the curriculum itself was subjected to revision in order to modernize religious education. This secular intrusion into the schools of theology was anathema to Khomeini's piety. "Khomeini treated Reza Khan as a usurper, the parliaments of the period as lacking in legitimacy, the laws they had approved as harmful, the ministries as corrupt, the police cruel, and the officials as lacking in concern for the poor and downtrodden. He attributed this condition in large part to Reza Shah's deliberate policy of ignoring Islamic precepts and undermining the religious community."[25] One day Khomeini's opportunity would come to restore the nation of Iran to the religious principles of the Prophet.

In 1951 the nationalist Muhammad Mussadegh became prime minister after forcing through the Majlis (parliament) a bill nationalizing the Anglo-Iranian Oil Co. He was granted dictatorial authority by his colleagues in August 1952. The West, particularly Great Britain and the United States, was in shock, since the loss of control over Anglo-Iranian put into question the supply of oil to its consumers. The people of Iran, particularly the mullahs in the coffee shops and bazaars, were also emotionally torn and politically confused. With the dissolution of the Ottoman Empire the Islamic faith had reached a nadir and was in psychological disarray. It could not be easily argued that the fragmented realm of Allah was to be replaced by local dictators whose proclivities were largely secular and whose principal interests were not in the scriptures of the Koran but in the administration of oil. Even the Iranian elite's invocations of the Koran were cynically perceived as the merely self-serving exhortations of a new ruling class. The congregation of the Prophet was befuddled, in search of religious or at least psychological equilibrium. Impulsive notions of independence, while not yet inspired by the twentieth century's concept of democracy in this nation of illiterates, were still instinctive to the plebian and nomadic character, and they were fueled by religious fervor. The mental confusion was exploited by the West, whose need to stabilize its sources of oil engendered an effort to support counter-revolutionary activities against Mussadegh—he was seeking to dislodge Western colonialism! The commercial prerogatives of the West dovetailed with the religious and political frustrations of the

Iranian people. Although its actions could in no sense be equated with the ideals of the American Revolution, the CIA morally justified support for rebellion in Iran by invoking the American ideology of democracy. The fact that American and European consumers would financially benefit from reduced oil prices if Mussadegh were overthrown suggests how Western morality can coincide by merest chance with the philosophy of egalitarianism. Thus popular demonstrations against Mussadegh, largely inspired by the West and orchestrated by the CIA, brought his downfall in August 1953. He was replaced by Reza Khan's son, Shah Muhammad Reza Pahlevi, who spent more than a decade consolidating power by invoking the Koran and gratifying the cupidity of his entourage. On October 26, 1967, an official coronation ceremony took place and Shah Pahlevi received absolute powers. Although the American concept of political equality would not be implemented in Iran for the foreseeable future, the United States and Europe consoled themselves with the realization that oil prices would continue to meet with the favor of equality-minded consumers in the West. So the West viewed the shah's iron control as a positive development. It so happened that the shah's rule would also provide the opportunity for a U.S. military presence in the area. Electronic equipment needed to establish a "listening post" in the Middle East for monitoring Soviet activities was almost immediately installed, and Iran became America's most significant intelligence-gathering center in the region.

But human factors, in this case the ego of the shah, once again intruded into the theories of political science. Put into the position of being a central power in the West's geopolitical strategy, and with enormous wealth and military might at his disposal, the shah's head grew larger than his abilities. The increasingly corrupt members of his political and military hierarchies became ever more assiduous in the preservation of their privilege and power. In short order the Iranian secret police, the Savak, became less a tool of foreign policy than an instrument of ruling class subjugation. Thousands of government opponents were jailed, tortured, or executed. Eventually the shah lost complete touch with reality and publicly ascribed to himself the characteristics of divinity. The mullahs of the coffee shops and bazaars of Iran, however, saw the shah and his Savak not as divine but as increasingly inhumane. Despite the government's vast array of military equipment, by 1978 popular uprisings could not easily be quelled without subjecting the nation to a bloodbath of doubtful outcome. Accordingly, in January 1979 the shah turned over his government to Shapour Bakhtiar, a man he thought capable of restoring order, and left the country for a "vacation" of undetermined duration. After a lengthy battle with political turmoil and poor health, Shah Reza Pahlevi died in exile.

Bakhtiar, also a secularist, dissolved the Savak, initiated freedom of the press and took steps to sever diplomatic relations with Israel and South Africa, the two nations (together with the United States) who had supplied police training and torture equipment to the Savak. But Bakhtiar did not have the support of the mullahs or the people. Within three days of the shah's departure nearly a million demonstrators marched through the streets demanding his resignation. On February 1, 1979, having spent years in exile, Ayatollah Khomeini arrived in Iran to reestablish the rule of Islam in his country. Khomeini's first order of business was to replace secularists with clergy, and to sever relations with the "Great Satan," the United States. To consolidate power "sacred" purges were commenced, somewhat controlled at first while Khomeini sought to form a goverment and reorganize the country. His principal associates in this process were Mehdi Bazargan, whom he appointed prime minister, and Abol-Hasan Bani-Sadr, elected the first president of Iran in January 1980. The nation was in complete turmoil, however, as vying factions of secularists and clergy sought power. Consolidating authority was difficult enough, but what occurred next added to Khomeini's problems, while at the same time providing the solutions for them. Perceiving the chaos in Iran as having weakened it, neighboring Iraq invaded.

Humiliated by Israel's surprise attack on his nuclear facilities in 1979, President Saddam Hussein of Iraq needed fuel for his ego, nuclear or conventional. By invading Iran Hussein "hoped to achieve three aims: to inflict a humiliating and perhaps decisive defeat on the Iranian revolution, which he found troublesome; to secure from Iran territorial and strategic concessions; and to realize his ambition to emerge as the leading figure in the Arab world."[26] The direct result of the Iraq-Iran war so far has been more than two hundred thousand deaths, over a million casualties (military and civilian) and over two million refugees. Hussein failed to achieve any of his objectives, but did prove unintentionally instrumental in helping Khomeini consolidate his authority. The religious factions of Iran united in order to repel the foreign aggressor. With their increasing power the clergy then began a campaign to eliminate all domestic opposition and to implement more fully a legal system based upon Islamic law.

The war did not go well for Iran at first, and President Bani-Sadr was held largely responsible. It was of no moment that hundreds of military officers had been purged for being insufficiently Islamic, with the result that Iran possessed a dismembered military machine. By mid-1981 Bani-Sadr was ousted and had fled to France. Religious passions now had no measure of restraint from within the government. Khomeini sought to rid Iran of anyone who questioned his absolute authority. He "urged parents to turn in their misguided children, students to report on their classmates and teachers, and Islamic committees in factories and offices to purge their fellow employees. Khomeini noted with satisfaction that if the shah had to rely on a secret police, the Islamic Republic could call on a nation of thirty-six million informers."[27] The Ideological Political Bureau of the armed forces maintained two thousand secret agents to spy on the military and report "suspicious movements" in the barracks; some 270 of these agents were clerics in the role of political commissars whose responsibilities included leading communal prayers and delivering sermons at the military bases. In May 1982 the Majlis passed the Law on the Conditions for the Selection of judges, reserving judgeships to the *mojtaheds,* seminary-trained experts in Islamic law. Secular judges were to be given minor clerical posts, retired or dismissed. "The chief justice estimated that 50 percent of the existing civil judges would have to be sacked."[28] The new codes also reinstituted *hadd* punishments for crimes, i.e. the cutting off of hands for theft, death by stoning for adultery, and the law of talion (*diyat*), "an eye for an eye, a life for a life." The reign of terror by which Khomeini consolidated power would cost thousands of lives. Internal documents indicate that in the brief period between June 1981 and September 1983 "7,746 persons . . . lost their lives through execution, in street battles or under torture."[29] The religious terrorism of the new Islamic Republic made the shah's Savak look like an organization of civil libertarians.

Unsated by the domestic bloodshed and brutality, Khomeini called for a worldwide Islamic revolution patterned in principle if not technique after the conquests of the Prophet. To seize the world for Allah was now proclaimed the foreign policy of Iran. The leaders of the world of Islam shuddered as the Shiite revolutionaries challenged their rule and legitimacy, while the West prepared for the long-term instability of its Mideast oil supplies.

Meanwhile the war with Iraq piled up Islamic bodies on both sides of the border and other Muslim nations were quickly drawn into the fray. Iran was supported by Syria and Libya. Iraq found support from Saudi Arabia, Kuwait and Jordan, who provided money and transportation facilities. Iraq began to use chemical warfare, while Iran began to send thousands of teenagers into battle. Both sides marched into carnage to the rhythmic cadences of the Koran.

Nonetheless, Allah's choice for victory has remained in doubt. While the two nations of Islam devastated each others' population and oil facilities, however, the West and Israel sought to determine how to turn Muslim carnage into geopolitical advantage. The United States, no friend of revolutionary Iran, was hardly enamored with the Iraq of socialist rhetoric, bulwark of the "hardline states," the alliance of Arab countries most firm in their hostility toward Israel. To resolve this political dilemma the United States provided limited assistance to both countries, by supplying satellite data and some other forms of assistance to Iraq and at the same time winking while Israel clandestinely supplied Iran with weapons. The CIA also secretly supplied Teheran with a list of hundreds of Iranian Communists and KGB operatives, with the recognition that they would be imprisoned or executed. This "good will" gesture would also serve to insure that post-Khomeini Iran would not face organized Marxist influence internally.

The United States regretted its loss of an intelligence center and a base of operations in the Persian Gulf, but remained indecisive in its policies toward Iraq and Iran. Israel was very clear on its own objectives, however, and seized the opportunity to set its own agenda for the West. As usual, American foreign policy in the Middle East was made in Jerusalem. In 1978, the last full year of the shah's rule, Israel had sold Iran nearly a billion dollars worth of weapons. Such sales have been of great benefit to Israel's perennially troubled economy and an impetus to its expanding military-industrial complex. It was difficult to abandon this source of income, even if Iran had become a nation virulently hostile to Israel and openly supportive of international terrorism. It was highly irrelevant that the United States called for a global boycott of weapons sales to Iran. Israel developed a twofold plan: to prolong the Iran-Iraq war in order to keep Iraq occupied; and to rebuild its annual arms sales to Iran, which had been terminated when Khomeini came to power. Iran proved willing to cooperate. Scandinavian ships entered Israeli ports by night and were loaded with cargos of weapons destined for Iran. Since Iran's military arsenal, like Israel's, is composed of mainly American weapons, Iran welcomed this source of supply. Although Israel denied (and continues to deny) that it ever provided weapons to Iran, some estimates have suggested that by 1987 such sales amounted to more than $200 million annually. This flagrant support of Islamic terrorism was rationalized in Israeli military circles as necessary to protect the tens of thousands of Jews in Iran. America's Mideast policy was caught up in yet another difficulty: the United States could not credibly ask its allies to boycott arms sales to Iran while permitting Israel to do so, yet if Israel did not sell to Iran, its economy would suffer.

To prevent U.S. pressure to limit arms sales to Iran, Israel began to enlist American cooperation in the endeavor, with the rationale that to sell weapons to Iranian "moderate" elements would ensure the United States a relationship with these groups in the post-Khomeini era. Amiran Nir, the former Israeli general who had helped orchestrate the entire matter, was the personal advisor of Shimon Peres, the prime minister of Israel at the time. Acting against the advice of Secretary of State George Shultz and Secretary of Defense Casper Weinberger, President Reagan played into Israeli hands and secretly sanctioned U.S. arms sales to the leading nation of Islamic terror. The result, when leaked by one faction in a power struggle in Iran to a Syrian-influenced Beirut newspaper, and then played up by the American press, came to be the second humiliation of a sitting American president by events in Iran in only a few years. "Unauthorized" actions by members of the U.S. National Security Council staff (said to have been duped by unscrupulous arms dealers of Iran, Saudi Arabia and Israel), was the first in a series of fabricated explanations of the debacle issued by the American government in the ensuing uproar.

The credibility of U.S. policy toward terrorism was irreparably compromised by the affair and the international arms dealers, even of the NATO and SEATO countries, began to flood Iran with arms. For its part Iran took the occasion to further embarrass the United States by participating with its Shiite proxies in kidnapping still more American and European civilians. Shiite terrorism has now taken on even greater dimensions, and the increasingly large number of perpetrators of this modified form of *jihad* can look forward to a confusion of Western policies and a certain supply of Western weapons. Murderous religious militancy has increased its role in Islam's conduct of its affairs of state. The Prophet would be proud.

Bonds between the ancient nomads of the Arabian desert were hammered out on the anvil of nature. Tribal cohesion was essential to assure survival in the competition with other tribes. Tribal-like loyalties of old prevail today, but operate in the context of national entities. The Islamic revolution of the seventh century destroyed the isolationist ethic of nomadic society, but never succeeded in replacing it with any widespread sentiment for pan-Arabic coalition. Even during the century of conquest cohesion was difficult and achieved in limited ways only by the promise of plunder. Today, the fragmented nations of Islam continue in that tradition. Their only common bonds are oil, hatred of Israel and displeasure at the Soviet Union for occupying Afghanistan, an Islamic country. Once again, war is the principal element of Islamic cohesion, surely a fact which reveals much about the religion of the Prophet.

A religion whose principal purpose is conducting wars, holy or not, cannot be good for the world. The beneficent aspects of the Islamic faith, such as alms-giving, are dwarfed by Muslim military conduct through the ages. The charity of Islam has accounted for only a small percentage of the riches obtained through murderous plunder. The heritage the world received from the magnificent era of Islamic science and education is overshadowed by the rigid orthodoxy of Islamic doctrine and the terrorism which current Islamic frustration inspires. Islam was always a political faith, never a religious one; the attempt to place political morality on the Procrustean bed of theology has only served to intensify the intellectual and emotional frustration so rife in the Middle East.

The nations of Islam would do better to forget the puerile passages in the Koran. The Prophet was far smarter than the multitude that have followed his teachings through the ages. For him the theology of Islam achieved secular rule, wealth, and a beautiful youngster named Aisha. If the Muslim world wishes to excel, it should preserve the Koran as merely a relic of the glorious past and buy encyclopedias for their barren bookshelves, emptied because theologians once commanded the breaking of inkpots and burning of all that was best in eclectic, secular Islamic civilization. History has relegated the *jihad* to the realm of barbarian antiquity. The nations of Islam should pursue their tenth-century passion for secular learning, or they will find their cultures assigned to the same ignoble fate.

Part Four

THE THEOLOGY OF HATE

The ruling ideas of each age have ever been the ideas of its ruling class.
—Karl Marx and Friedrich Engels, *The Communist Manifesto*

A single death is a tragedy, a million deaths is a statistic.

—Joseph Stalin

The dictatorship of the communist party is maintained by recourse to every form of violence.

—Leon Trotsky, *Terrorism and Communism*

I

The Philosophy of Violence

M arxism is the philosophical and economic creed based on the writings of a nineteenth-century German named Karl Marx. Many scholars consider him a great economic theoretician and the founder of economic history. While the creed claims to have unique insights into the workings of economics, Marx personally was a financial failure who spent most of his life borrowing money to support himself and his family. Marx's attitudes toward economic theory were doubtless shaped by his experiences with the many newspapers, magazines, and political organizations that went bankrupt once he took charge. These problems were usually caused by political repression, it is true, but the experiences were formative nonetheless. One would feel more comfortable intellectually if an economic sage were financially solvent, hardly the case with Marx.

Marxism has two fundamental components. The first is the theory of "historical materialism," a method of explaining historically the relationship between political and economic change. Known reductively as "economic determinism," the theory asserts that society evolves inexorably through internal economic dynamics, and that such change will, equally inexorably, eventually lead to the development of Marxist socialism. Marxist doctrine maintains that mankind has evolved through several stages of society:

primitive communism, Asiatic society, ancient slave-holding society, feudalism and capitalism. The next stage is said to be "socialism," in which every citizen "gives according to his ability and receives according to his work." The final stage will be "communism," where the operative principle becomes "from each according to his ability, to each according to his needs." At this final stage, there will be a "withering away of the state," since everyone will live in egalitarian harmony and have no need of a centralized government.

The second essential component of Marxism is an exhortation to the working class to carry out violent revolution, in case the first component is not as scientifically inevitable as Marx claims, or as rapid as he might have liked. Marxism was conceived during a time when workers had few rights, were severely exploited, and were widely treated as economic slaves. Rather than peaceful protest, collective bargaining, or other labor techniques fully developed only much later, Marx thought real progress for the working class could only come from violent revolution. Marx himself divided his time between the two conflicting elements of his theories— predicting the inevitable, and acting in the here and now to bring it about— but his successors seem to have decided to concentrate only on the latter.

In the hundred and fifty years since Marx began to write, thousands of thinkers have torn apart the logic of his theories. What had seemed to be unassailable logic during the age of deterministic, science-based social thinking, soon came to be revealed as a muddle. The first repudiation of Marxism, as a philosophy, apparently came from Karl Marx himself, who once said, "I am not a Marxist,"[1] by which he apparently meant that he did not want his followers to turn his writings into theology. Subsequent criticisms have addressed the economic fallacies of this system based on economics, the philosophical contradictions inherent in its metaphysics, its imperative to use violence to achieve its objectives, and the religious character of its fervent, alleged secularism.

The political philosophy of Marxism has come to possess many of the attributes common to most organized religions. The definition of doctrine is reserved for the party theologians, usually a governing organization called the "Central Committee." In this regard Marxism is analogous to the Christian churches or Islam, but particularly to the Catholic church with its Roman Curia. In such institutions adherents have defined limits to what they are allowed to think; they must uphold at least the fundamental tenets of the official dogma. Marxism's "proletariat" is comparable to the "meek," the "elect of God" and the "Chosen People," all in their context scheduled to inherit the earth. Marxist eschatology is akin to Christianity's, although its heaven is a secular one. The passion to proselytize the world is identical to Christianity's evangelism, and the underpinning zeal is inherited from

Judaism. Karl Marx, many of his associates, and many of the founders of the Russian Revolution were Jewish. Marxism has proven to be merely another extension of Judaism and its derivatives, particularly Christianity.

Similarities between Marxist and Christian practice are rife. Like Christianity, Marxism adopted an obsession with centralized control of ideas, and the corollary concept of heresy, called "revisionism" in the Marxist lexicon. The Soviet Union and its satellite countries and Western parties are analogous to the Vatican and its essentially subordinate national Catholic churches. This similarity was greatest when the Western Communist parties followed the Moscow line slavishly, at one time even to the point of their own destruction—they were relatively neutral about fascism in the early thirties and then again during the period of the Hitler-Stalin pact. Like the breakup of Christianity in the schism between Rome and Constantinople, monolithic Communism was shattered by the split between Moscow and Peking; like the countries of the Protestant Reformation that broke with Rome, the Western Communist parties rebelled against Moscow, and also as in the Reformation, did so at first over differences in practices rather than doctrine.

The Marxist saints, Engels, Lenin, Mao and Stalin, are comparable to Saul, Constantine and others; the leaders of Communist parties are nearly as authoritative as the Catholic pontiffs. The officially promulgated Marxist doctrines are similar to Christianity's canons and Marxism even has its apocrypha—the "humanistic" the writings penned by Marx until 1844. The Catholic Inquisition, which tortured and killed suspected heretics, finds its modern counterpart in Stalin's purges of accused apostates; the Vatican's Holy Office of Inquisitors was much like the NKVD and KGB of the Kremlin, while the Soviet Union's purge confessions resembled the church's forced recantations. Soviet control of publishing seems born of the same attitudes as the church's fear of a printed Bible; the *Nihil Obstat* and *Imprimatur* publishing approvals are the censorship predecessors of the USSR's Glavlit oversight. Expulsion from the Communist party corresponds to excommunication, with equivalent social consequences. Socialism claimed to be the Church on earth; its Savior was the state, and its ultimate stage, communism, was the theological equivalent of the Second Coming of Christ, but without the risk of Judgment.

Metaphysically, Marxism has perhaps the most in common with the theology of one of Christianity's sects, Calvinism. John Calvin taught that man was predestined to heaven or hell. Although the "saved" had already been divinely identified, Calvin thought that they were still required to perform good works and engage in piety. To the Marxists the "dictatorship of the proletariat" is inevitable; although already "chosen" for its role in history, the proletariat is nonetheless commanded to foment revolution in order for the the inexorable to manifest itself.

While pretending to be a scientifically based system of metaphysics, Marxism developed into a theologically based political philosophy. It became a creed with anti-rational invocations to scriptures and doctrines, instead of to human reason, and with a passion for political polemics based on history's latest set of written "truths." In short, Marxism became a religion.

The prescription for organized violence inherent in Marxism is both a battle cry and the tacit philosophical assumption that violence is ordained in human affairs. Marx had not only witnessed the political use of violence by the bourgeoisie against the European monarchies; he no doubt also observed the traditional rationalization of violence attributed by the Christians to original sin. For Marx, violence was a philosophical assumption and a political reality; to advocate violence became a simple extension of his education and time. Thus he stipulated that there is a recurrent need for violent revolution—and that it would eventually lead to the establishment of communal living in a classless, communist society.

It is, above all, a utopian vision. The period of violence required to produce economic utopia was viewed as necessary to achieve social and economic harmony and equality. But Marxism's utopian impulses have found themselves impaled on the sword of practical reality; assuming, of course, that a philosophy based upon violence deserves any description as "utopian."

Capitalist production begets, with the inexorability of a law of nature, its own negation.
—Karl Marx and Friedrich Engels, *The Communist Manifesto*

The communists disdain to conceal their views and aims. They openly declare that their ends can be attained only by the forcible overthrow of all existing social relations. Let the ruling classes tremble at a communist revolution. The proletarians have nothing to lose but their chains. They have a world to win. Workers of the world unite!
—Karl Marx and Friedrich Engels, *The Communist Manifesto*

II

Karl Marx: The Prophet of Hatred

A thorough investigation of Marxism's fallacious assumptions requires first a brief look at its founders, Karl Marx and Friedrich Engels. Their lives and times provide some insights into this creed that dominates over one and a half billion people.

Karl Marx was born on May 5, 1818, in the town of Trier in the Prussian Rhineland. Marx's family was Jewish, but in 1824 his father converted to Christianity and the family members were all baptized in the Lutheran church. Karl originally intended to pursue an academic career, studying history, philosophy and law at the universities in Bonn and Berlin, and receiving his doctorate from the University of Jena.

While in Berlin, Marx became absorbed in the study of social and political problems. To participate in their theoretical, if not practical, resolution, he joined a left-wing movement called the Young Hegelians. This group was named after the German philosopher Georg Wilhelm Friedrich Hegel.

Hegel essentially equated metaphysics with logic; indeed, what he calls "logic" is the basis of his philosophical system. Hegel regards the whole, in all of its complexity, as "the absolute"—and as spiritual, i.e. non-physical; hence Hegel is called an "idealist." This "absolute" is the idea of

God in the world; it is the highest stage of evolution of the *Geist* ("spirit"). The *Geist* reveals itself in the world order and acts upon itself until it ultimately achieves the absolute. Hegel's *Geist*, though spiritual, is a force in the world, acting out its intentions through individuals and nations in order to continually achieve a higher stage of development.

Absolute reality for Hegel emerges from self-contradictions: every existing reality or affirmation (thesis) evokes its natural opposite (antithesis); out of the conflict emerges a unified whole (synthesis). This in turn acts as a new thesis, giving birth to a new antithesis, and resulting in another synthesis, until the "absolute idea" is eventually developed. The notion of ideas "debating with each other" is called "dialectic," from the Greek *dialektike*, "the art of debate." (To philosophers, ideas are anthropomorphic and can even argue with one another!)

Hegel's dialectic of the world of ideas was transposed by Marx (together with Engels) into a solely material context, resulting in the creation of a new philosophy, called "dialectical materialism," meaning roughly "the struggle of material realities." The conflict or struggle of ideas, applied to political economy, became "class conflict," or "class struggle."

Hegel's political philosophy was founded on the notion that nations were primary players in the action of a *Weltgeist*, and that they were born to bring the dialectic of ideas to the fruition of the absolute. Thus, for Hegel, nations play the part that Marx would attribute to economic classes. For Hegel the absolute in the political world is the perfect state; for Marx the equivalent is the "withering away of the state" and the development of a "classless society."

Thus, Marx took Hegel's idealist (in the philosophical sense) theories and totally inverted them, transforming them into a philosophy of materialism. He applied Hegel's dialectic to the social world and declared that just as Hegel had maintained that every idea contains its own contradictions, in the world of reality every class contains the seeds of its own destruction— until classes themselves are eventually dissolved.

Hegel also saw fit to account for individuals prominent in world history—their actions and aims embody the dialectical transitions due to take place in their time and place. Hegel saw these men as heroes, the leading players in the action of the *Weltgeist*, the personification of history's forces. (This notion influenced later Germans; Nietzsche and Hitler would not be far behind.)

On meeting Napoleon after the Battle of Jena (1806), Hegel is reported to have said to his colleagues, "I saw the *Weltgeist* riding upon a white horse."[1] The heroes could justifiably contravene ordinary moral rules. While in general Marx denigrated the role of individuals in history, it is one that seems to have appealed to his heirs. The lawless disposition of dictatorial hierarchy dominates Marxist societies.

Karl Marx's liberal political views precluded a teaching appointment by the reactionary educational establishment. So, like many frustrated intellectuals, he turned to journalism. In 1842 he became editor of a liberal Cologne newspaper, the *Rheinische Zeitung*, until it was suppressed in 1843. He then went to Paris with his bride, childhood friend Jenny von Westphalen, who was the daughter of a Prussian aristocrat and government official. Marx was to spend most of the rest of his life in exile, and in penury. Living in poverty while having an aristocratic father-in-law probably did not affect Marx's psychological disposition in any positive manner.

In Paris he edited the radical and short-lived *Deutsch-Französische Jahrbücher*, and then wrote for the magazine *Vorwärts*. During this period he associated with French socialists and developed many of his political ideas. It was also during this time that Marx met Friedrich Engels, who became his lifelong friend, collaborator, and benefactor. Engels's father was a Calvinist, perhaps accounting for the Calvinist logic resident in Marxism, notably that even though the "elect" (the proletariat) had already been saved (by the inexorable laws of history), good works (revolutionary agitation) still needed to be performed. Engels's financial assistance supported the members of the Marx family most of their lives. In 1845 the authorities ordered the staff of *Vorwärts* out of France, and Marx and his family went to Brussels. Engels followed.

A committed socialist and intellectual, Engels was the son of a wealthy textile manufacturer who owned cotton mills in Westphalia, Germany, and Manchester, England. Although he (allegedly) ghosted many writings attributed to Marx,[2] collaborated with him on hundreds of articles, and even finished the last volumes of *Das Kapital* from Marx's notes after Marx died, Engels deferred to him in the public limelight.

Despite his socialist theories, Engels remained the capitalist owner of his family's factory after he inherited it, and on his death willed it to Marx's children rather than his own employees and workers. Bourgeois tendencies die hard, even for a vitriolic socialist.

The two men acquired a local German weekly, the *Brüsseler Deutsche Zeitung*, but Marx spent most of the next several years writing and publishing treatises on philosophy and economics. These included *The Holy Family*, *Theses On Feuerbach* and others, and laid the foundations of his dialectical materialism. It is purported to be a science by its proponents—concerned economically with changes over time of humankind's modes of production and politically with the struggle of classes created by those modes of production. Human beings are social atoms acting according to laws akin to those of physics and biology. Feuerbach, the materialist philosopher whose views Marx sometimes incorporated into his thought but attacked as ahistorical, once stated, "Mann ist was mann isst," that is, "Man is what he eats"—man is above all a material being.

In 1847 Marx and Engels joined the Communist League, an international workers' society, despite the fact that Marx had never been a worker. It was for this organization that, in 1848, they wrote a definitive statement on the league's beliefs and objectives, called *The Communist Manifesto.* This historic document, the first public declaration of international socialism, attacked the state as the primary instrument of oppression of one class by another. The *Manifesto* also set forth an economic, political and social program for the violent overthrow of the capitalist system.

For the remainder of his life, Marx dedicated most of his efforts to the analysis of capitalism and what he viewed as its historically inevitable collapse. The balance of his time was spent in revolutionary activity intended to assist capitalism's inexorable demise, in case history did not rapidly adhere to his theories. He participated in both the French and German revolutions of 1848.

After publication of the *Manifesto,* Marx was expelled from Belgium, went briefly to Paris and then to Germany to participate in revolutionary movements there. In Cologne he revived his first newspaper, creating the *Neue Rheinische Zeitung,* which lasted a year before it was suppressed by the authorities. He was charged with inciting treason and acquitted, then expelled from the Rhineland. Banished soon after from Paris as well, Marx went to London where he remained the rest of his life.

While in London the Marx family lived in poverty and near starvation. Rather than find enough work to feed his family, Marx continued to borrow money from Engels, who by now managed his family's factory. Marx's time was spent day after day in the British Museum where, in order to develop his theories, he read all the available literature on political economics.

To earn some money he became a correspondent for the *New York Herald Tribune.* (The *New York Times* was not founded until 1851 and had no European office.) From 1852 to 1862, with the assistance of Engels, Marx wrote almost five hundred articles on the world politics of the time. He supplemented his income, and added to his influence, by occasionally acting as a correspondent for the *Oder Gazette,* a progressive Breslau paper.

In 1864, after years devoted principally to writing, Marx began again to focus on revolutionary activity, presumably to influence the political events which were not yet conforming to his theories of historic inevitability. In that year he assumed the leadership of the First International Working Men's Association, his principal qualification being that he had never been a workingman. This organization was an international association of revolutionary, reformist, and labor movements. As head of the group's General Council Marx formulated programs and shaped policies until 1873. At that point the organization broke into Marxist and anarchist factions and soon dissolved.

It is significant that all of the organizations and publications headed by Marx eventually collapsed, usually at the hands of government authorities. He had an impatience with evolutionary change, reflected by an intellectual arrogance and intolerance expressed in polemical prose and general demagoguery, thereby inviting the wrath of the authorities. Personal frustration no doubt fueled the fires of his passion to create changes by revolutionary means; personal penury probably contributed to his hatred of the rich and of the capitalism they prospered by. His conscientious intellectual efforts were not matched by similar patience in the world of reality. However, even his theories contained pitfalls and contradictory implications which he conveniently ignored. These included the workings of socialism in practice—a subject he saw fit to neglect. Thus Marx was often impelled to obfuscate ideas with mere political passion. He was better at criticizing than creating; better at destroying than building.

During this period of increased political activity, in 1867, the first volume of Marx's best-known work, *Das Kapital*, was published. In 1885 and 1894 Engels published the second and third volumes posthumously. *Das Kapital* is a detailed exposition of the workings of capitalism, from manufacturing to commerce, from its "iron laws"—of wages, prices, and profit levels—to its cyclical nature. *Das Kapital* is a monumental, systematic critique of capitalism from the viewpoint of Marx's theory that it contains the seeds of its own destruction.

Toward the end of his life, Marx's financial condition improved slightly. His dear wife, Jenny, the daughter of an aristocrat, remained faithful and devoted to him throughout his days. Marx died in London on March 14, 1883, and is buried in Hyde Park cemetery.

In his adult years, "Marx *looked* like a revolutionary. His children called him 'The Moor,' for his skin was dark and his eyes deep-set and flashing."[3] He was a stocky and powerfully built man, with a heavy expression and even heavier beard. He was disorderly too. "His home was a dusty mess of papers piled in careless disarray in the midst of which Marx himself, slovenly dressed, padded about in an eye-stinging haze of tobacco smoke."[4] After twenty years of study and practice, Marx still spoke broken English. He was the stereotypical German scholar, a slow, meticulous and perfectionist pedant. His perfectionism, however, pertained to painstaking attention to the intellectual trees of the written word; his hate-induced emotional myopia did not always allow him to see the forest of physical reality.

One account summarizes Marx's beliefs the most succinctly:

He began and ended his productive life with a few basic assumptions: 1) that religious beliefs channel human energy and hope into another, ethereal world and thereby direct man's efforts [away] from the improvement of his earthly estate; 2) that the capitalist economy, especially in the form of [its] political economy, is unjust and encourages egoism and selfishness, breeding "social atoms" that are only interested in their own welfare; 3) that there are "laws" governing human history, principles of economic evolution and dialectical opposition that derive from the historical patterns of "class conflict"; 4) that a truly human society of communal co-operation toward a common end is possible; 5) that man must overcome both religious and economic alienation if he would attain genuine emancipation; and 6) that the capitalist system of economy entails basic contradictions (especially that engendered by collective production of goods and the unequal benefits of the distribution of these goods) that will eventually lead to its negation.[5]

Certain of these assumptions are based upon observations that have some validity, but Marx's formulation of them either distorts the observations and their realistic implications, or postulates unwarranted conclusions. Marx's philosophy of history is a blend of Hegel and British economics. Like Hegel, Marx claims that the world develops according to a dialectical formula; but whereas Hegel thought the motive force was a mystical entity called "spirit," for Marx the driving force is "matter." Marx does not merely mean the wholly dehumanized matter of the atomists, however. Driven by his preoccupation with the social order, somewhere along the line Marx derived the notion that the driving force of history is really humanity's "relation" to matter.

Since his thoughts were based on materialism, Marx could have claimed that humanity's relationship with matter caused it to alter matter technologically; in that case he would have focused on science and technology as revolutionary tools of materialism. He did not do so, however. Perhaps because of his personal encounters with poverty, Marx gradually developed the assertion that the most important part of humanity's relationship to matter is the mode of production by which it transforms matter into saleable products. By the manufacture and exchange of products, humanity determines its own future. Therefore for Marx the *raison d'etre* of human endeavor is economic; mankind is an economic animal.

In practice, Marx's philosophy of dialectical materialism is a study of economics. The dialectical struggle of an economic society is the struggle between its classes. Among them, the working class and the capitalist class were the two groups which Marx claimed were the dominant adversaries in his era and in the foreseeable future.

Marx may have been the last philosopher to attempt to create a comprehensive system of metaphysics. He dared to call his system scientific, that is, based on material forces, not on spiritual forces or upon the role of human personalities.

Yet Marx personally is either his own system's worst contradiction, or he believed himself to be one of the heroes of Hegel's *Weltgeist,* able to disobey ordinary rules. Throughout his life Marx frequently employed his own personality to assist or accelerate what he claimed to be the inexorable laws of economic progress. The record of his personal behavior often seems to contradict the historical inevitability asserted by his theories. Like many philosophers, Marx failed to account for his own subjectivity, to acknowledge that he was often actuated by bias. "He does not regard his [own doctrines] as . . . an expression of the feelings natural to a rebellious middle-class German Jew in the middle of the nineteenth century."[6]

In Edmund Wilson's *To the Finland Station,* Marx is described as having discounted his Jewishness as a factor in his thought.

> The identification by the Jew of the Jew with the proletariat gives rise to a miscalculation. In Marx's time, both the Jew and the worker had been disfranchised and shut off from society; but there was this difference between them, that the proletarian had been stunted intellectually as well as physically, that the proletarian children, as Engels had said, were not aware that they were unfortunate or unhappy because they had never been anything else; whereas the Jew, though their outlook had been narrow, had been accustomed to intellectual training; through all their migrations and their bondages they had preserved a deep culture of their own; they had behind them a noble past and they looked forward to a national resurrection. Once the enclave of old Jewry was broken open, it was quite natural for a man like Marx to take up the instruments of modern thought like one who was coming into his own. Furthermore, he had inherited from his rabbinical forebears a tradition of spiritual authority.[7]

So, like the ancient Hebrews, Abraham and Moses, and of course Jesus Christ, and like the later Jews who helped lead the Russian Revolution, Marx advocated revolution. "[Marx] disclaimed always all ethical or humanitarian reasons for preferring socialism or taking the side of the wage-earner; he maintained not that this side was ethically better, but that it was the side taken by the dialectic in its wholly deterministic movement."[8]

Marx might also have said that he did not advocate socialism, but prophesied it. He did not say such a thing, because much of his life was spent advocating, but his vigorous exhortation to violent rebellion had within it less the conviction of the scientist and more the passion of a prophet predicting what amounted to a Socialist Coming. "The emotional basis of his ostensibly scientific prognostications is implicit in all he wrote," says Bertrand Russell in *A History of Western Philosophy*.[9] Marx was less the objective philosopher and more the rabid radical who had a cultivated hatred for the capitalist system.

Marx contends that the whole of human history is motivated by economic causes, in particular the class struggle between different economic groups. Such an all-encompassing view is folly on the face of it. Some materialist philosophers have maintained that climate is the predominant influence on human affairs; others say geography. Freud traces everything to sex. There are innumerable materialist ways of viewing history, each with clear elements of validity, which are not purely economic and do not fall within the Marxist formula. Thus Marx's materialist conception of history could be false even if materialism, in the philosophical sense, were true.

On the other hand, it is entirely possible that economic causes might be at the bottom of all political events, even if philosophical materialism were false. Economic forces operate politically through the human desire for possessions and would be supreme if their desires were supreme. This would be true even if desire could not, from a philosophical point of view, be explained in materialist terms.

Consequently, what the Marxists choose to call the materialist conception of history is not a necessary or logical sequitur of philosophical materialism. As Hans Reichenbach writes in *The Rise of Scientific Philosophy*, "We must look for psychological explanations when we wish to understand why Marx did not sever himself clearly from Hegel's metaphysics . . . In regarding a contributing factor (economics) as the exclusive cause (of historical developments), Marx has abandoned the principles of empiricism."[10]

Marxist orthodoxy asserts itself with the same dogmatic certainty that characterizes Catholic theology, and the Marxist theologians restrain their adherents from critical thinking in the same manner as their Christian counterparts. Non-economic motivations of human society are blasphemous to the Marxist theologians, just as materialist philosophies are anathema to Christians. Yet, as with Christian doctrine, certain practical observations undermine Marx's philosophical dogmas.

For example, the Marxist assumes that a man's herd, as in "herd instinct," is his economic class, and that he will politically align with others on the same economic level. This is only partially true. Throughout history religion has been the most decisive factor in determining man's herd. A Catholic workingman is more inclined to vote for a Catholic capitalist than an atheist socialist. In American politics, Catholics, Jews, blacks and other religious and ethnic groups are inclined to vote for their "own," as politicians know. In the social world, people often act for the advancement of their creed, even if such actions entail economic sacrifices. Millions of Catholics, in particular, pay to send their children to parochial schools regardless of the added economic discomfort to the family. Such conduct is contrary to the Marxist notion of an only-economic motivation for working class actions.

In the final analysis, Marx's materialist theory of history requires the assumption that all politically conscious people are governed by one overwhelming desire—to increase their share of commodities—and that this desire extends to helping their economic class as a whole acquire a larger share of those commodities. This assumption is far from the truth. Many people make economic sacrifices to become politicians, political influence and power being far more important to them than money: Lenin, for example. Academics forego financial pursuits in favor of intellectual recognition and people from all walks of life sacrifice their own interests to further social causes. Karl Marx personified both of these impulses. Women do without amenities in order to bear and to provide for their children. People all over the Western world give up lucrative urban jobs in order to move to the rustic simplicity of the countryside. Doctors occasionally enter the medical profession for altruistic reasons. Priests and nuns take the vow of poverty for love of God, and sometimes for love of mankind. Scientists often work for low salaries in order to explore the heavens, or to investigate the earth and oceans. Soldiers enter long-term careers out of patriotism, or to satisfy their love for military pursuits. Police officers earn little in exchange for the psychic rewards of their profession.

In short, Marx's notion that all people are motivated solely, or even mainly, by economic considerations is not an objective observation. Marx extrapolated from certain economic attitudes of one class and applied it to everyone. He did not account for society's diverse groups of human beings and human interests. He also totally ignored the psychological reality— endemic to the whole of humanity, not merely the capitalist class—of greed, jealousy, and opportunism, human characteristics which have come to haunt the parties and states his thought has spawned.

Marx made the remarkably atavistic claim that man lives by bread alone, and that humans are motivated by financial insecurity—not by science, love, or emotional disposition. In his subconscious Marx may have thought that he was advocating an economic system that would enable the proletariat to go to art museums, but even that is questionable; unlike many other philosophers, Marx did not cite artists as exemplars of human achievement.

Despite Marx's antipathy to the loathsome conditions of the working class, he retained a cosmic optimism which could only be justified by either unfettered hope or by theism. He claimed to be an atheist, but his undaunted faith in the future compels us to wonder: his writings and his actions are nothing if not messianic. Yet Marxism has little attraction for people inspired by non-economic goals, apart from their generalized human need to be free from financial worries in order to pursue their desires.

By not taking account of human psychology in the movement of history, indeed, in his own thinking process, Marx could ignore that which would compromise the achievements of his successors: the inevitable evisceration of idealism by ambition. Evading this, thousands of opportunists could, and did, join the Marxist movement for rightful social change, using it not to change the world, but to advance first and and foremost their own interests.

As leaders of the dispossessed in the schema of inevitable revolution, left-wing intellectuals were given Marxist *carte blanche* to cloak the will to power with professions of altruism. What in any other circumstance would have been considered a despicable impulse to tyranny (dictatorship . . .) could be transformed into the purest of moral crusades (. . . of the proletariat).

Until the Soviet purge trials of the 1930s, Marxism had a primitive appeal to intellectuals around the world. How important they could be to the world! Soviet political reality and, more importantly, historical economic compromise (where ruling classes have been willing to negotiate with their subjects, the door to revolutionary opportunism has closed) have since eroded that appeal in the West, but it continues strong in the Third World, where Marx's theoretical fallacies are still an antidote for unrelieved political frustration.

Not all intellectuals drawn to Marxism have been motivated by opportunism. The decline of interest in Marxism in the West can be at least partly attributed to worldwide Marxist practice, clearly antithetical to free thought. Since intellectuals often exhibit imagination and independence, qualities not generally appreciated by Communist regimes, their role in Marxist societies was usually limited. They were often imprisoned, which further dampened their ardor.

Marx's appeal to the underprivileged has been strongest where an improvement in conditions has seemed most remote. In the modern period, where Soviet practice and limited economic achievement are easy to see, intellectual leadership of Marxist movements has fallen mainly to ambitious individuals seeking political power. They join the Marxist revolution to participate in power by seizing it from those who already possess it, namely the capitalists or landed aristocracy. Revolution, for them at least, is also a short-cut to economic opportunity. Throwing grenades and shooting people on behalf of the philosophy of violent revolution can apparently be less frustrating than studying law or accounting.

With idealism subordinated to ambition, transformation of society is finally less important than attaining power. Thus when Communist revolutionaries come to power, they have before them a task that has become a chore rather than an opportunity. The result is predictable: merely bureaucratized societies the mirror image of that which they had purportedly sought to overturn. Two classes, administrators and administered, are (re)created. Look at the new boss. Same as the old boss.

It all goes back to Marx's incomplete analysis. The desire for one's own economic advancement is a reasonable ambition, but does not account for the entire spectrum of human hopes. To Marx, who inherited much eighteenth-century rationalist psychology from the British orthodox economists, self-enrichment seemed to be the natural aim of man's political actions. But he built his philosophical scaffold of hostility to the existing order on the quicksand of rarefied intellectualism rather than on the bedrock of man's daily practical behavior. Sitting for months in the library of the British Museum, Marx neglected to gaze out the window to see the myriad of human desires which have nothing to do with money. How then could he have foreseen that the will to power would disfigure even the absolute fruit of his material *Geist*?

The elimination of economic frustration usually requires tireless work and personal discipline more than hate-filled pyrotechnics. Violent revolution is a crude and unsophisticated substitute for patient progress, or even for peaceful rebellion. Marx was motivated by frustration and hatred; his philosophy is accordingly founded on violence.

The small, battered raft of human reason floats insecurely upon life's ocean of insanity. Marx preferred to swim in the turbulent waters rather than to repair the frail vessel of rationality. As such, he added to man's collective madness. His successors have made that pathology into tradition.

Nothing can have value without being an object of utility.

—Karl Marx, *Das Kapital*

Hurrah for revolution, and more cannon-shot.

—William Butler Yeats, "The Great Day"

III

The Labor Theory of Value

T he "labor theory of value," which many attribute to Karl Marx or David Ricardo, was suggested by economic theories stretching back to the Christian Schoolmen in the era of Thomas Aquinas.[1] It is the doctrine that the value of a product depends upon the labor expended on it.

The labor theory of value has two aspects: ethical, which asserts that the value of a product *ought* to be proportional to the labor expended on it, and economic, which claims that labor *in fact* regulates the price of the product. In modern reality both are erroneous, since the value of a product is a function of: (a) the cost of labor used to produce it; (b) the cost of the materials used to make it; and (c) the costs of marketing and the *pro rata* allocation of expenses such as rent, administration, financing, and other overhead.

Marx asserts that it is a political-economic "law" of capitalism that a laborer's salable energies are worth only that which is necessary to keep the laborer alive. In capitalism according to Marx, a worker was not worth the value of what he produced, but the wage he required merely to stay alive, his "subsistence wage." It happened to be the common case at the time Marx lived, but he described it as one of capitalism's immutable features. Workers would be paid subsistence wages until capitalism was destroyed.

The genus of this idea was in Christian theology, which traditionally taught that to earn more than what was necessary to live was avaricious. Marx removed the Christian mantle of morality from this concept, clothing it instead in economic jackboots. The Christians sought to limit man's economic desires on earth to the bare essentials of life. Marx rightly noticed that the owners of the means of production were profiting from the laborer's willingness to be satisfied with the subsistence wage that Christianity taught was adequate.

The theory of "surplus value" builds on the labor theory of value. According to Marx, since the laborer received only a subsistence wage, and produced the value of that wage in far less time than he or she was required to work, the value of the excess labor was appropriated by the capitalist. It was surplus value. When capitalists sell their products, Marx said, the price reflects a full day's labor, although the worker is paid only for a partial day's labor—the subsistence wage. Hence the worker is being exploited.

According to Marx, the capitalists can deprive workers of this surplus value because they control the means of production, i.e., the industrial machinery, the factory and the real estate on which the factory is built. If the laborers owned the means of production they would not be exploited.

One of the Schoolmen in the fourteenth century, Henry of Langenstein, said that, "He who has enough to satisfy his wants and nevertheless ceaselessly labors to acquire riches, either in order to obtain a higher social position, or that subsequently he may have enough to live without labor, or that his sons may become men of wealth and importance—all such are incited by a damnable avarice, sensuality or pride."[2] The vanguard of the Christian philosophers taught, then as now, that the accumulation of riches was immoral, or led to immorality. The receipt of only a subsistence wage to cover one's daily necessities was prescribed as the moral limit of man's economic desires; to seek or strive for more was to transgress the border between survival and sin.

In the Middle Ages economics was a branch of ethics, and ethics was a branch of theology; all human action was viewed as a temporary occupation preceding man's ultimate spiritual destiny. In the sixteenth century, Martin Luther reemphasized these ideas, often in vitriolic language, reaffirming the moral validity of a subsistence wage.[3] So when Karl Marx, in the nineteenth century, based his theory of surplus value on the widespread practice of paying subsistence wages, he was working in the centuries-old philosophical construct of Christian theology—but inverting it as he had Hegel's idealism. Since the laborer's income in this time was determined by financial need and theological nostrum, the unpardonable sin to both the Schoolmen and Marx was committed by those who profited from the sale of the laborer's effort: the owners of the factories, the money-lenders, and the middlemen. This prompted British economic historian Richard Tawney, a socialist, to conclude that, "The true descendant of the doctrines of Aquinas is the labor theory of value. The last of the Schoolmen was Karl Marx."[4]

The doctrine of subsistence wage tacitly asserted that the laborer, being a fair-minded Christian, should work according to his ability even though he was only receiving enough compensation to satisfy his needs for survival; his rewards would be in heaven. Although he claimed to be an atheist, Marx did not realize to what extent his thinking had been influenced by Christianity. Although he railed against the subsistence wage in his own time, Marx embraced it in his predictions for the future. His eschatology posited a classless society where each "gives according to his ability, and receives according to his needs." This materialist prescription for economic paradise is nothing more than a secular reformulation of Christianity's subsistence wage. Karl Marx was a Christian thinker.

Ironically, Marx's economic utopia of communism inadvertently condones the same surplus value that Marx condemns in his criticism of the workings of capitalism. For if everyone "gives according to his ability" but merely "receives according to his needs," surplus value will still be created by labor, but neither individual capitalists nor the ecclesiastical authorities will receive it. Who benefits from it? It is not hard to imagine that the state, supposed to have withered away after its guardianship during the socialist transition to communism, would be in full flower still, and would be appropriating surplus value as had the capitalist class before it. Despite the Marxist theological mandate, who could resist the temptation to live on with such vast savings lying around waiting to be spent? Fortunately for Marx's theory, and unfortunately for the workers living under its dominance, this problem has not yet arisen in the real world. No Marxist society has reached the supposed final stage of economic development, communism. According to economic statistics of the International Monetary Fund and other international economic agencies, Marxist governments needn't lose any sleep over this potential problem; they are all plagued with another economic term familiar to Marx: scarcity.

Marx goes on in his lengthy analysis to demonstrate that if capitalists compete with each other to produce and sell the same product, the competition will lower prices. In that event laborers will either lose their jobs by the introduction of labor-saving techniques such as improved machinery, or be forced to accept lower than subsistence wages. Either way the laborer is the loser, because the capitalists will look out for themselves in order to avoid bankruptcy. (Marx never evidenced any sympathy for the capitalists who went bankrupt, or for their families.) So while the Christians had once taught that for the weak human character "competition was designed by Providence to provide an automatic substitute for honesty,"[5]

Marx saw competition as the opposite—a spur to greed.

Accordingly, in Marxist analysis, capitalism has only two possible outcomes. First are the alternate evils of the regular increase in the exploitation of workers (due to the continuous reduction of wages as prices are beaten down by competition), and the corollary replacement of workers by more efficient machinery—the structural creation of unemployment. A second theory of capitalist development was postulated by Lenin. He thought that capitalist countries were accumulating excess capital which had to be exported, and so were inexorably compelled to sponsor imperial colonies and exploit the people who lived in them; economic competition in this international arena doomed the capitalists to waging perpetual wars with each other. The principal victims of these wars were naturally the workers, tricked or forced into fighting as soldiers in the opposing capitalist armies. To avoid either of these consequences, Marxism prescribes that the working class must seize the means of production from the capitalists by violent revolution.

His philosophy rooted in Christian thinking, Marx attacked Christian practice. The Calvinists assured the world that financial success on earth reaped eternal bliss. The Church of England was flourishing and the Protestants were prospering—God was on their side. The Vatican owners of a real estate empire had understandably adopted Hegel's view, long before he lived, that private property was the basis for civil society, was in fact a "sacred natural right."[6] The exploitation of child labor was rampant; men worked eighteen-hour days, and women had no time to marry because their entire lives were spent in the textile factories working on the looms and spinning yarn—whence the term "spinster." Capitalism was being incorporated into moral teachings and fast becoming an inalienable element of Christian theology. With an intellectual sleight of hand, Christianity had baptized privilege and power and named them office and duty. While the meek were taught they would inherit the earth, Christian plutocrats were consolidating their own terrestrial possessions. You never knew if Jesus had been mistranslated.

Just as Martin Luther centuries earlier had staged a theological and moral revolt against the corrupt commercialism of the Vatican, so in the nineteenth century Marx wrought a secular challenge against the macroeconomic attitudes of Christian society. In the process he launched an assault against the encroaching idea that private property was a sacred sphere of human affairs. Inverting the Christian economic doctrine regarding a subsistence wage, Marx also believed it wrong that any should fare better than the laborer, who, he contended, was the sole producer of value. One might say he advocated "subsistence profits," but he was unable to articulate how to achieve such a goal in capitalist economic practice.

Instead he opted simply to indict the owners of production as unredeem-
able exploiters, camouflaging the intellectual capitulation with increasingly
hate-filled polemics.

At some point Marx crossed the ethical Rubicon of Christian economic
morality by challenging not simply the practices, but the very existence of
private property. The general rise of anticlericalism, merely most extreme
in Marx, prompted a broad Christian response, particularly in the Catholic
church. Pope Pius IX, originally a liberal reformer, issued the *Syllabus of
Errors*, an attack on secularism and endorsement of monarchy.[7] After the
revolutions of 1848, the First Vatican Council proclaimed papal infallibility
—the most rational of ways to respond to increasingly questioned authority. Less concerned with ethics than economics, Marxists responded with
still louder calls for revolution, while the church continued to ignore the
economic oppression of the faithful. The logic on both sides was unclear,
but the battle lines, while metaphysically obscure, were clearly drawn.

Some current Christian philosophers, primarily Thomists, are engaged
in an attempt to recreate a dialogue with the disciples of their fallen
progeny, Karl Marx. St. Thomas revolutionized Christian thinking by in-
tegrating it with Aristotelian reason. The truth of Christian doctrine could
be rationally apprehended. The Thomists accordingly have common
ground with Marxism in the emphasis on epistemology (the study of
knowledge) and ontology (the understanding of the essence of being).
Perhaps there could be a philosophical synthesis with history's latest army
of self-proclaimed empiricists.

Marxism's claims to be an empirical philosophy are pretentious, however, and Thomism, like Hegelianism, maintains "the priority of Mind and
Spirit to matter. And it was precisely this doctrine which Marx and Engels
were concerned to deny when they affirmed the truth of materialism."[8]
Neither creed is empirical, but both pretend to have a basis in physical
reality.

On the political level, Marx eschewed the non-violent approach to
utopia propounded at the time by Saint-Simon, who preached social ethics
based on Christian love. Marx opted instead for socialized hatred and
organized violence, both of which were inherent in Christian political
conduct. Pope Pius IX in 1875 denounced "all of those who assert that the
Church may not use force."[9] This behavior is still reflected in the Third
World where "liberation theology," albeit rightfully in the service of social
justice, seeks to merge Christian thinking with Marxist revolution, often
citing Christ's exhortation, "I have not come to bring peace, but a sword."[10]

To summarize Marx's overall thinking for purposes of broad outline, one
could say that there are essentially seven Marxist propositions. First, the

political, social and cultural behavior of societies are a function of their economic interests; other considerations are of subordinated importance. Second, history progresses through a series of inevitable struggles between classes of men with conflicting economic interests; in the period of capitalism, the principal class struggle is between labor and the owners of the means of production. Third, feudal societies were destroyed by the emergence of an economic class whose interests depended on trading and manufacturing. Fourth, capitalism generates the seeds of its own destruction by creating an unskilled work force which it exploits, and a pursuit of profit that leads to a competitive struggle for markets; cyclical crises are created since the purchasing power of the exploited workers is inadequate to absorb increased manufacturing production. Fifth, both the exploited and the unemployed workers ("the reserve army of unemployed") will finally realize that the only exit from their despair is the appropriation of the means of production. No class gives up its power willingly; the violent overthrow of capitalist state power is required. Sixth, in order to remain in power the new order must repress the counterrevolutionary activity of dispossessed capitalists; this will require a "dictatorship of the proletariat." Seventh, with time, the capitalist class will fade from the face of history; this will permit the "withering away" of the state needed only to repress it. Communism will be realized and all will live in egalitarian harmony as everyone's economic, emotional, psychological, physical, sexual, aesthetic, cultural and intellectual needs are effortlessly fulfilled.

It is obvious that most of these propositions have proven to be historically erroneous. Let us examine a few facts which Marx overlooked, unintentionally or deliberately, and several developments which he could not have foreseen.

Marx chose to call the working class the "proletariat," an ancient term used to describe the lowest non-slave class in Rome, whose only real function was to produce offspring; they were conspicuously not economically productive. Marx's use of that particular, emotionally laden term to describe the industrial working class was part of his polemical demagoguery. So transmogrified, the working class took on one aspect of the Christian "meek": through the ownership of society's means of production, it was destined to inherit the earth.

When Marx focused on industrial manufacturing, he lost sight of other economic areas of society, which, although small in his day, were destined to grow. These areas produce "products"—services—which do not necessarily fit into the Marxist formula: the medical, legal, information and education professions; the expanding service industries made up of advertising, insurance, entertainment, and management companies; or the city, county, state and federal governments, essentially massive administration and service agencies. Today these and similar groups make up the major part of many economies. Marx did not foresee this, or chose not to focus on it. He also did not foresee, or chose to ignore, the rise in influence of the labor unions, ultimately destined to acquire enormous power in many countries. In short decades they have demolished the capitalist tendency to pay a subsistence wage.

Marx did not anticipate, or at least did not address, industry profit-sharing plans whereby employees participate in final profits, either through bonuses or ownership of stock; indeed he did not foresee the enormous rise of the stock market itself, a serious (potential) vehicle for working-class ownership of the means of production—and a non-violent one. Marx would also be surprised to see that many capitalists have effectively lost control of their companies to a managerial class finally beholden only to the bottom line.

Marx could not forsee the development of capitalist imagination and ingenuity, not only in solving problems but in creating markets which did not, and perhaps even should not, exist. This the capitalists did by invent-ing advertising. Today millions of people buy products they will seldom use, only because the products were advertised cleverly. Often the cost of advertising to create a "need" is several times greater than the manufactur-ing cost of the product itself. The gullible consumer, having never before heard of designer jeans, will pay exorbitant sums of money to acquire them; the same is true for fluoride toothpaste, Perrier, cigarettes, cosmetics, and countless other items. Clearly, as human society develops, it discovers needs it had never before noticed, such as medicines, vitamins, and special foods. Of course, humanity's "needs" expand in direct correlation with its prosperity. Some of these, such as personal cars, are in part required to function economically; others, such as stereos and television sets, are merely social requisites. Marx did not anticipate these developments; he was not aware of modern marketing.

It is a curious irony that the Soviet Union, essentially a non-industrial society at the time of its revolution, became the first country to adopt Marxism. For reasons we will review later, Soviet industry and agriculture suffered under Marxist rule. Two areas in the Soviet Union do thrive, however, although neither was part of Marx's prescription for economic reorganization under a socialist government. The first is the Soviet Union's largest export industry: energy resources such as oil and gas. Energy production in the artificially controlled market of today is hardly sub-ject to any of the supposed rules of the labor theory of value. The other thriving area in the Soviet economy is its second largest export: weapons. Imperialism and the corollary development of military production were supposed to be the salvation of the capitalist system. The dream of socialist society foretold by Marx seems instead to have become the nightmare predicted for capitalism, whereby, in order to survive, many Marxist countries become imperialists.

Marx's adherents officially claim not to be bothered by this anomaly. Unofficially however, the leaders of the major Marxist countries are gradually abandoning their blind belief in Marxian economics. Instead, they have begun to experiment with free enterprise or opted for military prowess. Those who have chosen militarism as a panacea, such as the Soviet Union, invoke the Marxist call for continuous revolution as the justification for domestic repression, exploitation of foreign resources, and the worldwide export of weapons. Karl Marx presumably had none of these developments in mind when he sat in the reading room of the British Museum and postulated socialist economic utopia.

Theoretically, Marx's aim was only to rally the world's exploited laborers. Like most intellectuals, he was capable of painstaking and laborious attention to scholarly details; at the same time he was impatient with the daily grind of practical reality. Since his personality was impetuous, opposed to the fact that progress in the empirical realm is slow and stuttering, Marx developed a theory of fast-track social justice. He came up with a dazzling display of intellectual gymnastics that boiled down simply to a short-cut escape from frustrating reality—violent political revolution.

In ancient times Marx might have invented a religion, but given his secular attitudes and his era he endeavored instead to develop a scientific rather than religious basis for a coherent philosophy of rebellion. Although his philosophy was concerned with social realities, it had an erroneous empirical foundation. One element of human behavior was posited as determinative. Far worse was that Marx's metaphysical system had no empirical basis at all; it was a wholesale appropriation of Hegel's idealist Christianity. Like those of its religious forebears, Marx's metaphysical construction was finally just another call to arms.

Marx's genius, clouded by obsessive and narrow-minded pedantry, discounted numerous economic variables, downplayed non-economic factors and ignored human psychology in the supposed sweep of its analysis. Marx borrowed some of his economic assumptions from traditional Christian theology and his psychology of metaphysics from the Christian philosopher Hegel. Over this framework he draped incongruous, empirically based prognostication. How could such a construction be coherent, much less correct?

Like many of his Christian counterparts, Marx lacked the intellectual integrity to acknowledge the practical cul-de-sac at which his economic analysis had arrived; he had to make a detour and it was a psychological one: hatred for the rich hobbled his creation of an all-encompassing economic analysis. At that point Marx's Christian evangelism and contumacious Judaic zeal combined to create another of history's Hebrew revolutionaries. Economic metaphysics was subordinated to eschatological optimism and revolutionary hopes. Ultimately Marx became a demagogue whose rebellious proclivities and intellectual pyrotechnics produced orgasms of hatred and violence.

No intelligent person in the modern world can take Marx's economic doctrines seriously. The followers of Karl Marx, like those of Moses, Muhammad, and Christ, are another cabal of the disciples of destruction.

And of all plagues with which mankind are curs'd,
Ecclesiastic tyranny's the worst.
　　　　　　　　　—Daniel Defoe, *The True Englishman*

Christians have burnt each other, quite persuaded
That all the Apostles would have done as they did.
　　　　　　　　　—George Noel Gordon, Lord Byron, *Don Juan*

IV

The Marxist Apostles

T he prescriptions for action propounded by Marx were left for his followers to elaborate intellectually and implement practically; as in most religions, the plane of action came to be synonymous with the plains of battle. Like the immediate followers of Moses, Christ and Muhammad, the Marxist disciples would inherit both the task of embellishing and codifying doctrine, and the opportunity to implement their handiwork by developing an organizational structure.

In the history of Marxism Lenin was the intellectual proselyte; like Saul he explicated and expanded theory, and like Constantine he forged a body politic in the crucible of violence. As had the disciples of other religions, Lenin and his fellow apostles, Stalin and Mao, ascribed to themselves the theological authority to define doctrine, and the political mandate to impose it. They took steps to assure that their congregations, that is, their nations, were either theologically captivated or physically captured or slain. A new set of disciples of destruction arrived on the stage of human history.

The scriptures of Karl Marx became the secular bible of the disenfranchised, the fragmented and frustrated multitude who were willing to follow self-appointed apostles. Like the meek who were promised reward in the Christian hereafter, Marxism assured workers a secular salvation in communism; both would inherit the earth. Marx was deified; his writings became canon. He was a Moses whose words came to be viewed as the actual, rather than inspired, word of God.

Lenin played the role of the Christianized Roman centurion Saul, the determined intellectual whose place came to be assured in the pantheon reserved for saints of doctrine; after Marx, Lenin is the second most influential intellectual figure in Communist theology. Like Moses, seeing the chance to gather the slaves of Egypt under his dominion, Lenin seized the opportunity to grab power by leading a similarly disenfranchised constituency, the oppressed peasants and industrial working class of Russia. In historical terms, however, Lenin might best be seen as Marxism's Constantine. He made his theology the creed of a state and enforced adherence to it militarily; like Constantine he formulated much basic doctrine still in force today.

Stalin, less intellectually inclined, the masculine figure in the Marxist hall of church builders, was akin to the Hebrews' Joshua, a man who inherited a military mantel and, like the later Christian popes, loved the fit. Stalin's thirst was for battle in the field rather than in theoretical discourse, even if the field of battle was the Communist party itself. This perhaps makes him most akin to Moses—willing in a flash of anger to massacre the thousands who had lapsed into idolatrous worship of the Golden Calf. With even less pretext of theological heresy, Stalin consolidated power through mass fratricide, all in the name of doctrinal purity. Stalin's Christian counterpart is probably Pope Innocent III (ruled 1198–1216), executor of Crusades and architect of torture chambers, a man who regarded himself a king with absolute power. Called by Bertrand Russell "the first *great* Pope in whom there was no element of sanctity," Innocent III had no reluctance to use whatever violence was warranted to assure his authority.[1] Stalin favored this approach.

Mao was sprawling in his handling of people and ideas, but an innovator. His appeal was mass-oriented, owing largely to the fecundity of the Chinese people, but also, perhaps, to the simplicity and paucity of his ideas. Like Muhammad, Mao had a large and uneducated constituency and ideas that were embraced by hundreds of millions of people. Mao can be considered the third most important figure in the Marxist pantheon of the anointed. Like Lenin and Stalin, Mao has followers around the world, although his influence has waned greatly since his death. Mao's writings, in their time, were treated as canon. Like Constantinople in its schism with Rome, China under Mao separated from Moscow; like the Protestants, Mao created his own bible, *Quotations of Chairman Mao* or "The Little Red Book," which was read to and by the Chinese populace with a religious enthusiasm that would have delighted any Sunday school preacher. Mao's world political influence, while not as great as that of his Russian colleagues, can be seen as just as important—nearly a fourth of the world's population has been shaped by his actions and thoughts. And whatever his direct intentions, Mao left China poised for the greatest experiment in the history of Communism and its theoretical (theological) underpinnings—a sweeping introduction of capitalist practices to a socialist economic system. His cult of personality dominated the stage of the Asian world, and upstaged the other Marxists worldwide. When alive, Mao controlled more people on earth than Christianity or Islam, at a time when the Christian-inspired Americans pretended that Communist China did not politically exist.

Whether by subjugation or example, these Marxist apostles have unalterably affected the entire world. As such, and like their predecessors, the disciples of Moses, Christ and Muhammad, their stories warrant review and analysis.

Lenin: Socialism's Constantine

I think if I had met him without knowing who he was, I should not have guessed that [Lenin] was a great man; he struck me as too opinionated and narrowly orthodox . . . He has as little love of liberty as the Christians who suffered under Diocletian and retaliated when they acquired power.
—Bertrand Russell, *The Practice and Theory of Bolshevism*

It is true that liberty is precious—so precious it must be rationed.
—Vladimir Ilyich Lenin (V. I. Ulyanov)

After Karl Marx, Vladimir Ilyich Lenin (1870-1924) can be considered the most important person in the history of Communism. In testimony to his influence, many Marxist adherents and governments refer to themselves as "Marxist-Leninists." Although Marx was the movement's intellectual originator, Lenin was the first to apply Marx's theories of revolution to a society, namely the nation of Russia and its contiguous nations which, together, came to be called the Union of Soviet Socialist Republics (USSR).

This group of fifteen "republics" was a most unlikely place to introduce the practice of Marx's theories, since Marx concentrated his analysis on nations with an industrial working class. Most of early twentieth-century Russia was non-industrial, being principally agricultural and with an overwhelmingly large peasant population.

When Czar Ivan Nicholas II dropped the reins of power during World War I, through a series of political blunders and due to the disastrous fortunes of the Russian military, Lenin hastily picked them up. Motivated chiefly by the desire to seize control of the Russian government, Lenin used Communist theory as a rallying philosophy to accomplish that objective. While recognizing that Russia was not the ideal society to implement Marxism, he still could not forego the opportunity to seize power there;

dialectical materialism became his rationale for political opportunism. In large measure due to his overthrow of the Russian state and formation of the USSR, Lenin is ranked by all branches of the international Communist movement as second only to Marx and Engels in theoretical inspiration. As a man who first successfully put theory into practice, Lenin is Marxism's Constantine.

Lenin was born in Sinbinsk, now Ulyanovsk (so called after his original surname, Ulyanov), on May 4, 1870. He was one of six children. Lenin's father was a provincial school inspector raised to the ranks of nobility for his government service. Lenin's mother, the daughter of a physician, taught him to read and play the piano.

In 1887, Lenin's eldest brother, Alexander, was executed for leading an unsuccessful attempt to assassinate Czar Alexander III. A few weeks after his brother's execution, Lenin graduated from the Sinbinsk secondary school at the head of his class. Ironically, the director of the school was Fyodor Kerensky, father of Alexander Kerensky, the future prime minister of the provisional government that Lenin and the Bolsheviks would later overthrow.

With the support of Fyodor Kerensky, Lenin successfully applied for admission to Kazan University. A few months later he was expelled for taking part in a student demonstration, whereupon he began to read Karl Marx. He organized a Marxist circle in Samara (now Kuibyshev), where his family had moved.

Lenin successfully passed the law examination at the University of St. Petersburg, although he had not attended classes there. He then set up a law practice in Samara but spent most of his time with his Marxist circle. In 1893 he went to St. Petersburg (now Leningrad) and joined another Marxist group, urging its members to broaden the scope of their agitation.

While abroad for medical treatment in 1895, Lenin met Georgi V. Plekhanov, considered the father of Russian Marxism. Plekhanov is generally regarded as "the first and last of Lenin's contemporaries to whom he deferred in wisdom, and that for only a few years."[2] Lenin shared with Marx an unrestrained intellectual arrogance. At this point Lenin was twenty-five years old, but impressed those around him as mature, intelligent, and a born leader.

In the fall of 1895, Lenin returned to Russia and soon plunged anew into revolutionary activities, recruiting workers in St. Petersburg, organizing unrest, orchestrating rebellion. In December 1895 he was arrested and exiled to eastern Siberia. There he was joined by a comrade from St. Petersburg, Nadezhda Konstantinovna Krupskaya, who became his wife in 1898 and his lifelong co-worker. They conceived many ideas together, but no children.

The Russian Social Democratic Labor Party, forerunner of the Soviet Communist party, was established at a secret congress in Minsk later that year. Although not released from Siberian exile until 1900, Lenin led what would eventually be the majority ("Bolshevik") party faction, which obtained precarious sway in 1907. A close associate in these early affairs was Julian Martov, the future leader of the rival, minority ("Menshevik") faction.

Born of a prosperous Jewish family in Odessa, Martov (before the revolution, Iulii Tsederbaum) developed Bolshevik tendencies largely as a result of Russian anti-Semitism.[3] Jews played a significant role in the revolution for another reason. As one writer noted in 1907, "In the course of the nineteenth century the religious spirit weakened among the [Russian] Jews. They ceased to consider the Talmud as their unique book. The Rabbi was no longer their only oracle. The Jews no longer looked upon their religion as a consolation; they therefore required a new faith." This new faith Jews found in socialism.[4]

While in exile Lenin wrote his first major work, *The Development of Capitalism in Russia*, published in 1899 under the pseudonym Vladimir Ilin. This work analyzes Russian economic life from a Marxist perspective, concluding that as a result of the rise of capitalism a revolution to create socialism and a "dictatorship of the proletariat" to perpetuate it had become possible. Unlike the Mensheviks, Lenin believed (probably correctly) that the Russian bourgeoisie was too weak to carry out a revolution. The intermediate phase of the inevitable historical movement to socialism—the rise of capitalism and bourgeois control of the state—could not be counted on to improve the lot of the people in the near term. Lenin therefore broke new ground in the development of Marxist theology: direct assumption of power by the workers from the feudal aristocracy could be effected. This shift in theory also had the advantage of permitting Lenin himself possibly to acquire state power, otherwise "historically" unlikely.

In 1900 Lenin was freed and went abroad to join Martov, who had been released about the same time. Together with other emigre Marxist leaders they published a newspaper in Geneva called *Iskra* ("The Spark"), principally to counter the influence of "economists" in the party, those who advocated a program of economic reform over other forms of struggle in the belief that this was the best way to win the allegiance of the working class. *Iskra* sought to persuade Social Democrats in Russia to spend more time preparing for the overthrow of the czar and the capture of political power—and less time attempting to improve the general working conditions of the people. Like Marx, Lenin did not aim for evolutionary progress, believing that it was merely patchwork improvement in a system fatally flawed; he sought only revolutionary changes. In fact, Lenin viciously denigrated those who sought progress through compromise. Once he obtained political power, Lenin also killed such people, whom he often referred to as "bourgeois remnants."

In an article entitled "Where to Begin," Lenin and his followers set forth the idea that a viable political organization required a regular newspaper—*Iskra*—to hold it together. In his 1902 pamphlet *What Is To Be Done?* Lenin defends this notion against bitter attacks by critics opposed to wasting energy "propagating armchair ideas . . . [and] bookishness." Lenin called his newspaper a "collective organizer"; it was a concept of the press not dissimilar from the Catholic church's traditional use of it. With *Iskra* Lenin adumbrated his notion that newspapers should have a central role in organizing and controlling the thinking of the people.[5] Newspapers to Lenin were ideological tools to educate the masses—most selectively—rather than to disseminate the news, an authoritarian view of the press shared by monarchies and religions. It was a notion destined to become the model for media in all Marxist societies.

In *What Is To Be Done?* Lenin contended that in order to seize power the party must be led by a group of professional revolutionaries. Only a small group could maintain the conscientious discipline required for the effort. By remaining small and close knit, it could evade infiltration and destabilization by the police, not to mention by liberals willing to compromise revolutionary principles. Lenin contended that the party should avoid the temptation to concentrate on short-term progress or "reformist" compromise. Lenin—by now he was using the pseudonym regularly—wanted total revolution.

On July 30, 1903, the Social Democrats opened a second congress in Brussels and in London. Lenin's dogmatic views and personal intransigence placed him at odds with all the other Marxist leaders except Plekhanov, and even he eventually withdrew his support. Nevertheless, many of the congress's rank and file delegates were captivated by the force of Lenin's ideas and convictions.

Some kind of revolutionary outbreak in Russia was expected by almost everyone. Lenin did not want Marxists to cooperate with liberal groups. He demanded that the party form a tightly organized nucleus which would seize complete power. No coalitions. He was successful in persuading many of those assembled; others differed vehemently. Disagreements over the issue (and the separate matter of forming a new *Iskra* editorial board) split the party into two opposing factions: the Bolsheviks under Lenin and the Mensheviks under Martov and others. Lenin narrowly won his *Iskra* resolution, but only because he called a vote after some delegates had walked out in a dispute over the conditions to be laid down for party membership; his "majority" was not solid. On this shaky ground, Lenin's adherents publicly assumed the name Bolshevik.[6] (The Russian words are ambiguous: *bolshe* means "more," *menshe*, "less." Many people concluded that the Bolsheviks wanted more of a change, the Mensheviks less.)

Power swung between the two groups, and the Mensheviks ultimately had control of the party's Central Committee (what American executives would call an "executive committee") and of the party organ—*Iskra*. Thus the Mensheviks entered the uprising of 1905 at an advantage. In 1906 the Bolsheviks convened a "unification" congress in Stockholm. Lenin continued to insist that the Russian revolution should not end in a liberal bourgeois government, but in a "revolutionary democratic dictatorship of proletariat and peasantry," presumably with himself at the top of the pile. Lenin's interest was not just social reform but supreme power. The "unification" congress apparently said *nyet*, however, and confirmed the Mensheviks as the majority in the party.

Lenin persisted, however, and by the time of the party's fifth congress, held in London on May 13, 1907, the Bolsheviks had a slight majority of actual voting delegates. Wishing makes it so: the Bolsheviks were finally the majority.

From 1907 to 1917 Lenin lived abroad, and in these later years operated from his quarters in Switzerland. The Social Democrats, meanwhile, were in constant internal conflict over policies, including ongoing debate over boycotting the Duma (the legislative assembly), and such other issues as the wisdom of robbing banks to obtain money for the party. More petty squabbles were elevated to full-blown conflicts due to Lenin's uncompromising personality.

To avoid discussion and disagreement, in 1912 Lenin convened a conference in Prague that declared the Bolsheviks a separate party. Shortly thereafter he brought into the Central Committee, as one of his chief aides, a young man called Joseph Stalin.

At the outbreak of World War I, Lenin denounced European socialist leaders who supported the war efforts of their own governments. He regarded them as traitors supporting nationalism at the expense of the welfare of the international working class. He also expounded the notion that the defeat of Russia in the war would be a "lesser evil" than its success, since defeat would lead to a weakening of the monarchy. For like reasons he called for "self-determination" for the national minorities in Russia; it would further weaken the czar. (After the revolution, however, Lenin would violently insist that Russia's national minorities become part of the new Union of Soviet Socialist Republics, under the complete control of the central government.)

In 1916, in *Imperialism, The Highest Stage of Capitalism*, Lenin argued that the developing monopoly character of capitalist monopoly "inevitably gives rise to a tendency to stagnation and decay," and that, "imperialism is an immense accumulation of money capital in a few countries . . . in various securities." This creates "the extraordinary growth of a class . . . of bondholders (rentiers) i.e. people who live by 'clipping coupons,' who take no part whatever in production, whose profession is idleness. The export of capital, one of the most essential economic bases of imperialism, still more completely isolates the 'rentiers' from production and sets the seal of parasitism on the whole country that lives by the exploitation of labor of several overseer countries and colonies."[7]

Lenin goes on to say that an essential feature of imperialism is "the rivalry between a number of great powers in the striving for hegemony, i.e. for the conquest of territory, *not so much directly for themselves as to weaken the adversary and undermine 'his' hegemony*"[8] (emphasis original). One could think Lenin was describing the actions of the modern-day Soviet Union, whose policy is to undermine non-socialist governments. Lenin came to the conclusion that the capitalist powers had temporarily averted "inevitable" economic collapse by the imperialist export of surplus capital, but would undermine each other in rival efforts of expansion— culminating in a conflict such as World War I. The opportunity for the international socialist revolution would then present itself. The analysis, it must be admitted, was insightful.

The Marxist critique of capitalism is twofold: at first it performs a progressive function in history, replacing moribund feudalism and providing for the first time in history the end of material scarcity; but by the nature of its workings, capitalism is subject to periodic crises, and, according to patterns of profit discerned by Marx, these would eventually lead to collapse. Lenin perceived that the "monopoly stage" of capitalism would be the agent of this final collapse. In that it fixed prices and at times restricted innovation, and appeared to grow ever more dominant, monopoly tendencies seemed to forebode long-term capitalist stagnation.

A different form of economic organization, made possible by capitalism as capitalism had been made possible by feudalism, was therefore necessary: "Capitalist monopoly inevitably gives rise to stagnation and decay." Unfortunately, there was little capitalism, let alone capitalist monopoly, in Russia. No matter.

Like Marx, Lenin was unwilling to speculate about the possible solutions capitalism would find to problems he observed. Monopoly, as is abundantly clear in the case of the American automobile and steel industries, *is* a stagnant form of economic organization. Lenin did not foresee, and doubtless was unwilling to in any case, that the integration of the world economy—growing worldwide competition—would chip away at the privileges of national monopolies. Capitalism has dealt with the abuses of Detroit and Youngstown. It is possible that someday world monopolies (more properly, oligopolies) will form, but even that would not inevitably lead to the triumph of stagnating forces in world economic affairs. Despite Marxist shibboleths, few things are inevitable. National governments, for example, could conceivably rise up to confront our theoretical world monopolists, just as political unrest led to the Sherman Anti-Trust Act at the turn of the century.

The possibility of reform or structural adjustment in capitalism was clear in 1916, as perhaps it had not been in the mid-nineteenth century, when Lenin's religion was born. Social and economic reforms to the benefit of the working class had, inch by inch, "inexorably" advanced in capitalist nations. Who was to say where it would end? With the foundation of its creed—the immutability of capitalist injustice—slowly turning to sand, Marxism's religious nature became clearer. Excoriations of capitalism were redoubled. Scientific observations of its workings were twisted, its worrisome features projected as inevitably dominant, its many positive ones ignored entirely. And the need for socialism was extended to nations not remotely prepared for it even in the farthest reaches of Marxist theory. Under Lenin, Marxism was irretrievably lost to theology. It was, however, inevitable. Marx's professions of unique and indisputable insights into the workings of history, with their origins in Christian philosophy, were understandably interpreted by his followers as inspiration near to divine. Moral conviction so derived invariably leads to excesses of doctrine over common sense, of violence over even rudimentary compassion.

In writing the chapter of *Imperialism* entitled "The Parasitism and the Decay of Capitalism," Lenin did not envision that the ranks of the international "parasites" he denounced would come to include the Marxist-Leninist countries themselves; as it has turned out, they too engage in "the exploitation of the labor of several overseer countries and colonies." Lenin should see a contemporary map of Soviet colonies since World War II! The imperialist nations of his time have gradually shed their colonies, while the proletarian Soviets have increased theirs dramatically. This is the only evidence to date of capitalist stagnation and socialist ascension.

In February 1917 an initial revolution struck Russia, producing what Lenin himself called "the most democratic regime on the face of the earth." This of course only recommended the new government to Lenin in the very shortest term. To him it had numerous repugnant features, chief of which was that he did not control it.

Lenin had openly declared that the defeat of Russia would be a "lesser evil" than the survival of the Russian monarchy. The Germans, of all people, took him at his word. On April 16, 1917, just over a month after the abdication of the czar (March 15) and the creation of a moderate bourgeois government, Lenin returned to Russia from Switzerland in a sealed train provided by the Germans. They hoped, correctly, that his arrival would further the turmoil in Russia and thereby hasten the end of Russian resistance on Germany's eastern front. The train which carried Lenin also carried the bloody plans for Russia's turbulent future, the tragic tomorrows of millions of Russian people.

Lenin of course was not satisfied with the reformist government. On April 17 he announced his "April Theses," which called for the overthrow of the provisional government headed by Kerensky. Lenin wanted the transformation of the "imperialist war" into "international civil war," namely a worldwide socialist revolution. It would begin in Russia. Thirsting for power, the Bolsheviks began to attack the new regime, which was primarily concerned with stabilizing Russia, not in promoting international revolution.

Taking a plank from the program of the Social Revolutionary party, Lenin called for dividing the large estates into privately owned farms. This aided him in his fight with the Mensheviks by gaining more supporters for the Bolsheviks in the soviets. (These "councils," or popularly elected, unofficial legislative assemblies, operated on local, regional and national levels—hence, when Russia became socialist, the combined national network of soviets formed the basis for the government; the nation came to be called the Union of Soviet Socialist Republics.)

During the summer of 1917 Lenin converted a fiery and influential radical to his side—Leon Trotsky, who had long vacillated between Marxist factions but in the recent period had attempted to unite them. Together they organized the overthrow of the provisional government on November 7, 1917 (October 27 by the old calendar).

Democracy, even Lenin's socialist variety, was not long lived. "In Russia's only free election, held within a month of the October Revolution [the popular name has been retained even after the Soviet adoption of the twelve-days-advanced Gregorian calendar], 75 percent voted against Lenin's Bolsheviks, whereupon, early in 1918, he dissolved the democratically elected constituent assembly."[9] The Second All-Russian Congress of Workers' and Soldiers' Deputies was convened, and confirmed the establishment of a new government for the Russian Soviet Republic—with Lenin at its head as chairman of the Council of People's Commissars. Lenin's subordination of egalitarian principles to personal power created the mold for Soviet domestic political behavior down to the present day.

Upon obtaining control of the new government, Lenin appointed Trotsky war commissar, giving him the responsibility of organizing the Red Army. At the same time Lenin created the Cheka, a secret police. These were two of his first official decisions. He had wanted to make

Trotsky the minister of the interior (with control of the Cheka), but they agreed it would not be a good idea to have a Jew in that position.[10] The immediate task of these two organizations was to eliminate opposition to the Bolsheviks, gathering quickly in the form of the "Whites," an amalgam of anti-Bolshevik groups with far-right and czarist leanings.

Eventually the Whites were supplied and supported by the Allies, who hoped to draw Russia back into the fighting after the Soviet withdrawal from the war in the March 1918 Treaty of Brest-Litovsk. The Allies sent expeditionary forces against the new regime for the same reason. Lenin's intent was to free time and resources for the consolidation of socialist (and Leninist) power internally. Germany's hope in offering Lenin safe passage to Russia—destabilization of the Russian war effort—had borne fruit. However, the price of peace was high, both for the nation of Russia and for Marxist ideals. With the Brest-Litovsk Treaty, Lenin ceded to the Germans suzerainty over Poland, the Baltic states, and part of the Ukraine. Many of Lenin's fellow Marxists regarded this as a pragmatic betrayal of "international relations"; further challenges to his authority developed. Internecine violence among the Marxist factions increased.

Marx had recognized that the inexorable process of history would experience fits and starts, movement and delay, advances and retreats. The historical dialectic allowed for "two steps forward, one step back" as it progressed to its culmination in the communist society.

Despite the civil war which now raged in Russia, Lenin proceeded with his long-declared purposes. He dissolved the Constituent Assembly, then renamed the Bolshevik Party the "All-Russian Communist Party." On March 2, 1919, he proclaimed the formation of the Third, or Communist, International—the Comintern. The two previous Internationals (International Working Men's Associations) had been organized to unify the causes of workers in different countries. The Second or Socialist International had broken up in the disputes over participation in World War I. The Comintern did not meet with great success; promising revolutionary situations in Germany and elsewhere, already on the defensive following the end of the war, fizzled.

The failure of European workers to launch their own revolutions left Russia isolated as the sole nation where Marxist socialism was becoming dominant. The nations of Europe, democratic and otherwise, viewed the developments in Russia with dismay and alarm. With powerful socialist-inspired insurgencies within their borders, and a far-left socialist government apparently firmly in place in powerful Russia, European governments had much to fear. For his part, Lenin feared the reaction of the capitalist nations which surrounded him. He had long excoriated their warring and imperialist impulses; he had also foretold, and hoped, that the

Bolshevik example would spread to Europe and bring down its governments. He was in error.

Lenin now found himself encircled by nations whose hostility he had
both theoretically proclaimed and politically exacerbated. It was necessary
to retreat in both theory and practice. Lenin undertook a consolidation of
socialism in Russia alone—and a build-up of Soviet armies to defend and,
one day, export it. The "one step back" of the dialectic dictated a contin-
gency plan: the development of Soviet socialism as a prelude to creation
of international communism. Just as the Parousia, the Second Coming of
Christ, was postponed, so too was the international revolution. In both
instances, however, it was not that God or the inexorable process of historical determinism had failed humanity; rather it was imperfect human
perception of the timeliness of these inevitable events which had to be
better honed.

While waiting for their eschatology to effectuate itself, the Marxists,
like their Christian counterparts before them, decided upon a holding
action to maintain the allegiance of their restive followers until Judgment
Day arrived. To do this, in both creeds, meant to consolidate temporal
power. It must be mentioned that since in the process they would be
assuring their personal sovereignty, the leaders of these creeds had no
deep-seated metaphysical objections regarding this unfortunate turn of
events. They rapidly adjusted their attitudes and doctrines in order to
accommodate political reality. When their theological forecasts proved
deficient, their political instincts made the most of it. Revised dogmas
would have to be written in blood.

Lenin originally saw Marxism as the praxis of a revolutionary class
whose concern was not to wrench concessions but to take power. The
Communist party was its principal weapon of struggle. The party was to
be free of all that was ideologically bourgeois, and to be composed only
of class-conscious Marxists. It was to be organizationally separate from the
traditional representatives of the working class, the trade unions, since they
carried the ideological infection of narrow focus on the improvement of
economic conditions. Only revolutionary agitation leading to the proletarian assumption of power could lift the oppression of the capitalist
system; reformist activity could only further entrench it. The trade unions
were to be infiltrated and swayed, or taken over, not used as a base. The
working class itself was the base. As the Bolshevik break with the Social
Democratic party showed, ideological purity was far more important to
Lenin than overall unity of action. That could be attempted, but alliances
with other party organizations purporting to represent the working class
were to be only tactical in nature. Lenin believed (arrogantly, but not, it
seems, without basis) that the Bolsheviks were the only legitimate agents

of the working class in that only they could effectuate class power. This conception, that compromise was more dangerous than unity was valuable, would come to haunt the Bolsheviks.

With the destiny of his party foreordained, Lenin had only to study how to achieve this revolution. That is, what constituted activity that would lead to it? Education. The power of the proletariat was in its numbers. But numbers mean nothing if they are not motivated to act. Workers were aware of their oppression—industrial sabotage and strikes were proof of that—but ignorant of its nature, that it was the oppression of a *system*. Class consciousness was latent, however, inculcated by the conditions in which workers lived; it needed first to be awakened—then to be directed.

The party could be the agent of revolution, Lenin thought, if it brought to the working class the tools of class theory (the awareness that power and oppression were tied to class), revolutionary fervor (the sense that it was possible to participate in one's destiny, and to do so most effectively in class struggle), and political organization (to understand that to struggle with an organized class, one that has set up police and courts and pools of hangmen, it was necessary also to be organized).

Both the movement which carried out this program and the theory it used to do so would have to be pristine in order to prevail. This necessitated a small "vanguard" party of dedicated members, conscientious participants who would be required to exert themselves for the goals of the revolution. It would be an educated organization, each member fully aware of the revolutionary theory behind the party's existence and actions, disciplined, acting always as a member of the party rather than as an outraged (or fearful) individual.

Such a cadre of ideological purists would be dependable and free of the tendency to compromise revolutionary objectives. By remaining small, it would not easily be infiltrated by the police or unexpectedly hamstrung by reform-minded liberals. Lenin's insistence on a small vanguard party facilitated control over party members. But the shortcomings of that insistence would be seen when the party was faced with the administration of a country, and the concomitant control of tens of millions of people. The skills necessary to foment revolution are dramatically different than those of national governance.

Lenin largely subscribed to the idea of two phases of communism, which Marx had best adumbrated in *The Critique of the Gotha Program* (1875). The first phase is the form of society which immediately succeeds capitalism. The workers have put in place the dictatorship of the proletariat, their own state apparatus to protect them from their enemies, and are able to use it to gradually eliminate the bourgeois values and ideas inherited from their capitalist predecessors. Income is derived from the state, not from private ownership of property or factories. During this phase, while plans are prepared for the perfect society, income is disbursed to citizens based on work performed, i.e., "to each according to his work."

When the new society's productive forces develop and the capitalist past is buried, the second phase would be entered, what Marx called "the higher stage of communist society." In this phase the state would gradually "wither away," a different attitude toward work would prevail, and citizens would accept the new philosophy of "From each according to his ability, to each according to his needs."

Lenin recognized that for the proper construction of socialism the realities of non-industrialized Russia required a modification of this two-phase approach. The Russian working class made up only a small part of the population. Lenin saw the need to give a greater role in the revolution to the peasants. Although this was a deviation from classical Marxism, for Lenin all of the "toilers," both workers and peasants, were required to drive the engine of social change, even if the latter, as a class, were undependable. Russia was, after all, a peasant culture. In the process, Lenin began to view peasants worldwide as a useful revolutionary tool, although certainly not as a constituency—their social consciousness was individual rather than collective.

Shaped by the fact of peasant Russia, Lenin's adaptation of Marx's theories led quite naturally to a shift in his international analysis from the focus on capitalist nations alone. Since the industrialized nations could for a while buy off unruly elements of their working classes with the "super-profits" derived from colonialism, Lenin no longer expected these countries to be the first to fall to revolution. The failure of a revolutionary uprising in Europe during or after the war, despite conditions nearly as severe as those experienced in Russia, was incontrovertible evidence of this. The Russian revolutionary experience showed that the colonies and those countries with still-small capitalist enclaves were the most vulnerable targets of revolutionary agitation. Revolutionary success there would deprive the capitalist nations of the most lucrative gains of exploitation, of the bribes they could offer their workers at home, of their protection from a determined revolutionary uprising. Less developed and colonial countries, therefore, began to figure more largely in Lenin's ideas. He regarded them as the "weakest link" of capitalism.[11] This would play largely in Bolshevik strategy for world revolution, as we will see.

Revolutionary success confirmed Lenin's faith in the efficacy of a vanguard party. Now with augmented responsibilities—education of the peasants and, indeed, all the masses of the world, the maintenance of a vanguard, pure-thinking party was only all the more necessary. This led, of course, to the centralization of power in the small cadre which had led the

Bolshevik revolution. How to handle the population was another matter.

Since in Marxist ideology Russia was not ripe for immediate construction of socialism, the Provisional Revolutionary Government could not claim to be a dictatorship of the proletariat. To describe the new regime, Lenin chose the label "a democratic dictatorship of the proletariat and the peasantry." No one knew exactly what this meant, so it served the political purpose of comforting both the working class and the peasants; all could feel that their participation in power was more than vicarious. As Isaac Deutscher puts it, "That cumbrous and self-contradictory formula was never clearly explained either by its author or his disciples, although it was the basis of all Bolshevik propaganda from 1905 until 1917."[12]

The pretense at democracy was more sincere when applied to the party itself. Initially, Lenin genuinely sought to provide the party some semblance of democracy, although there was never any desire to allow democracy to infuse the population. Within the party, Lenin espoused a notion of "democratic centralism," which, at least in theory, provided every member a voice; it was a system in which even Lenin himself was required to submit to the authority of the party, which he initially did.

In practice, the democratic aspects of democratic centralism waned even as they waxed. To ensure the purity of party members in this democratic hierarchy, and, less overtly, to prevent any call for democratic elections, the tenth party congress in 1921, on the demands of the Worker's Opposition, set up the Central Control Commission. Its responsibility was to purge the party of careerists, power-hungry commissars, Communists who had developed a taste for the bourgeois life, deviants from Lenin's pure ideological standards, and others who did not fit the definition of an effective revolutionary.

The original quixotic purpose behind the non-violent purges of the CCC was to enable the people (both inside and outside the party) to keep their rulers in check. Anyone could come to testify regarding the ideological or political transgressions of party members. This participation of non-party members in party affairs, presumably the democratic aspect of the "democratic dictatorship of workers and peasants," reflected two concerns: first, to convey the appearance that the party was responsible to the people; second, to feel the pulse of the population on issues which the party members themselves could not resolve, even with their democratic centralism. But, as Isaac Deutscher observes,

> Since the ruling party was convinced that in all essentials of policy it could not really submit to popular control, these new devices for reviving popular control were *a priori* irrelevant and could not but prove ineffective. They illustrated the party's already familiar dilemma: its grow-

ing divorce from the people, and its anxiety to preserve its popular character; the dilemma that underlay Lenin's pathetic experiments with his
party in the last two years of his political activity. The purges were to
serve as a substitute for real elections; they were to remove corrupted
members, without removing the party, from power.[13]

Thus the Communist party's concept of democracy did not long survive,
even as a chimera. The formation of the CCC, as a ruse to provide the
appearance of popular control, had a deleterious rather than rejuvenating
effect on party democracy. The man who ended up in charge of the
purges was Joseph Stalin, in part because the other members of the party
hierarchy did not want to be bothered by the complaints of the citizen-
critics who would be given a forum. "None of his colleagues grudged
Stalin his assignments," explains Deutscher.[14] As long as Lenin was in
control of the government, Stalin was viewed by all as merely his lieutenant. They did not notice that he was using the purges for his own
purposes, eliminating present and future opponents and setting up the
machinery for more severe purges in the years to come. "Neither [party
members] nor Lenin noticed in time the subtle change by which Stalin
was gradually passing from the role of assistant to that of coadjutor."[15]

The pretense of democracy had ironically set up state organs which
could facilitate the rise of a dictator, one who would not maintain the pretense of democracy, even among fellow members of his ruling class. Hypocrisy, once nurtured, grows uncontrolled; deceit, once spawned, embarks in
its own directions. The parameters of deception are never set by its practi-
tioners; they are defined only by the amorphous circumference of opportunities created by circumstances—the barriers erected by intended victims.
With the Communist concept that democracy was limited to the ruling
party, its monopoly on power properly maintained through deceiving those
outside the party, the cancer of duplicity grew beyond its prescribed limits.
The first victims were those intended, the masses. The next were the
lower-level party members purged by the CCC, their transgressions often
debatable. Finally the hierarchy would begin to savage itself.

Once in power, Lenin devoted his energy and intelligence primarily to running the Soviet government and to building up his army and secret police.
The cause of international communism, of practical necessity, took second
place to consolidating personal power over all of the nations of the USSR.
Lenin justified this course of action by maintaining that the Soviet Union
would become a model for worldwide communism—the "step back"
would allow for another "two steps forward" in more propitious times.

Since Lenin viewed his country as the most important nation in the world by virtue of its Marxist rule, it was only logical for him to believe that worldwide Communism would of course be guided by the Soviet Union. The theoretical borderline between Soviet leadership and Soviet domination was often very vague. It would be only a matter of time before the line did not exist at all, and a brief time at that. Soviet-supported international revolution would gradually be transformed into Russian imperialism of a new type.

Soviet borders were sacrosanct to Lenin, but those of other nations were not—they were only capitalist conveniences. "All borders in nature and society are conditional and mobile," he said.[16] Lenin laid the theoretical base later amplified and fully implemented by Stalin. "The old Bolshevik dream of authentic socialist revolutions was displaced by the commitment to direct military conquest as the only realistic way to spread communism. The goal of decisive control, rather than true socialist revolution, became the highest priority."[17]

To learn how best to carry out his growing theoretical imperialism, Lenin studied the works of Karl von Clausewitz, a nineteenth-century Prussian general. Although not an imperialist, Clausewitz wrote a definitive study, *On War* (1833), which evolved the concept of absolute, unlimited war in which victory depends on total annihilation of the enemy. In such a war, Clausewitz wrote, the manipulation of psychological and moral factors is as important as military skill and resources. Clausewitz also believed that, "Terror, judiciously and consistently directed against non-combatants, could effectively shorten a war."[18]

Lenin did not need much convincing of the merits of this approach, which could be applied both domestically and internationally. The experience of the civil war "gave absolute primacy to the offensive as a means of waging war . . . The doctrine was dominated and directed by Lenin's concept of war, which itself relied heavily on that of Clausewitz. War and strategy were tools of policy, and the aim was political victory—the complete destruction of the enemy's political system, and its replacement with one friendly to the Bolshevik cause."[19]

The "one step backward" in the march to worldwide communism—concentration on the development of socialism in the Soviet Union—accelerated all at the same time the consolidation of power internally, the pace of theological rationalization for Soviet domination of international revolution, and Soviet ability to successfully carry that international struggle out.

Abandonment for a time of the Marxist urge to international revolution in the traditional industrialized nations of Marxist scripture did not preclude trouble-making elsewhere. There were still the colonies, the soft underbelly of the capitalist beast. And with the onset of Allied subversion, third-party harassment became especially convenient. Lenin turned to Asia, initially India, in the hope of inspiring the impoverished illiterates to overthrow the capitalist chains of Great Britain. "The East," he proclaimed, "will help us to conquer the West. Let us turn our faces toward Asia." To set the East ablaze now became the clarion call of the Comintern, with India as the starting point of a conflagration which would destroy imperialism. "England," Lenin declared, "is our greatest enemy. It is in India that we must strike them hardest."[20]

To accomplish this revised objective Lenin sent Grigorii Zinoviev, the head of the Comintern, to lead Muslims in a *jihad* against the British in India. The fact that Muslims are theists did not deter Lenin from assuming that they would embrace Marxist atheism. That India was even less industrialized than Russia—the least likely to revolt for socialism according to Marxist theology—gave him less pause. The effort failed completely.

The Soviets have continued to dabble in Asian subversion, but, with the exception of insignificant Mongolia, were not responsible for a socialist success until the fall of Saigon in 1975.

In May 1922 Lenin suffered his first stroke, aggravating the continuing aftereffects of a wound received in an assassination attempt in August 1918. He remained ill for the rest of his life. Aside from mediating disputes between Trotsky and Stalin, most of Lenin's remaining efforts were devoted to averting the rise of a Communist bureaucracy. He thought idealists rather than paper-pushers were needed to successfully construct socialism. Largely because of Stalin's pernicious influence, Lenin's drive against "bureaucratism" was dramatically unsuccessful.

Lenin died in Gorky, near Moscow, on January 21, 1924. By a decision of the Politburo, Lenin's body was embalmed and placed on permanent exhibition in a glass mausoleum in Moscow's Red Square, where it can be viewed today. Unfortunately for the human race, the corpus of his ideas was similarly preserved by his violent acolytes.

After his stroke and forced retirement, Lenin had finally found the leisure to reflect on what had transpired in Russia. To his own dismay, he was "disturbed that the state apparatus had replicated many of the worst abuses of the tsarist state, that communists were high-handed, incompetent administrators, and increasingly divorced from the people."[22] The state apparatus had swelled into a bureaucracy far larger than its work justified, impelling Lenin to propose massive reductions in its size.

Faced with a gargantuan governmental administration, Lenin began to lose faith. Revolutionaries could effectively use violence against capitalists, but bureaucrats are not so easily vanquished, or inspired. Lenin lost confidence in the party's ability to preserve socialist values in a nation made up of only bureaucracy and peasant mass. The concept of a small cadre of disciplined members, the vanguard party, had to be replaced. In "How

We Should Reorganize the Workers," "Peasants' Inspection," and "Better but Fewer," all written in 1923, Lenin submitted ideas for reorganization. "His final proposals were that the party and state should fuse their best personnel in one exemplary institution which might keep alight a glimmer of socialism in isolated, backward Russia."[23] Lenin wanted the small cadre so dear to his heart to be incorporated into a party/state bureaucracy. This might infuse the bureaucracy with idealism.

But the bureaucracy belonged to Stalin, who had no desire to abridge his own authority. The proposals came to nothing. Before his eyes the revolution Lenin had led was generating another centralized government with a select class at its apex. Since the revolutions predicted in Europe had failed to materialize, Russia retreated into its historic xenophobia. The international revolution once so clearly envisioned was transformed into stumbling efforts to coerce a myriad of foreign parties into following the Soviet example, although the exemplar itself was trapped in an internal quagmire of economic and political disease. In fact, the international revolution itself had become a malaise, claiming brotherhood but operating for Soviet imperial purposes.

Lenin, like Marx, dwelled in the intellectual arena of political panaceas, which, to a Marxist, are synonymous with economic nostrums. Neither Lenin nor Marx paused to look beyond statistics and capitalist abuses, to see the sunset rather than the fires of revolutionary change, to discern that which might be built upon rather than destroyed. Lenin, the first practitioner of state Marxism, cast the template on which future Marxist societies would be patterned, a template of left-wing fascism. Lenin was forced to face his creation in the form of Stalin; in his last days Lenin recognized him for what he was, but it was too late by then.

Lenin passed away into history, forced to view developments which seemed to mutate if not dissolve his life's work. Whatever his original motives, Lenin's actions increasingly subordinated ideals to the preoccupation with personal power. Lenin laid the foundation for Soviet totalitarianism on the corpses of those satisfied with more peaceful reforms. He arrogantly believed he was justifiably the authoritative arbiter of human hopes, and he naively assumed that power would not be abused after he was gone, would not take on a bloody life of its own.

The structure of Soviet government which Lenin built, it is not surprising, was taken over by a man who would make Lenin's violent repression look like a mild exercise in political discipline. Lenin's heir—against his express wishes, according to renowned Soviet historian Roy Medvedev[24]—was his lieutenant, Joseph Stalin.

Stalin: Impersonalism Yields the Personality Cult

Stalin was a totally different type of Bolshevik, both in his psychological makeup and in the character of his party work: a strong, but theoretically and politically primitive, organizer . . . without theoretical viewpoint, without broad political interests and without a knowledge of foreign languages, [he] was inseparable from the Russian soil . . . distinguished among the practicals for energy, persistence and inventiveness in the matter of moves behind the scenes.

—Leon Trotsky, *The Russian Revolution*

By the mid-twentieth century, humanistic socialism found itself totally dominated by adulterated Marxist socialism, which had become perverted in the quest for centralized power. Violent revolution was no longer merely a battle cry; it had become an accepted political philosophy. The brutal decimation of millions of people was regarded as a necessary step to prove that the dialectic of history was not just a theory, but a practical solution to the problem of poverty.

By 1929 the leaders of the Bolshevik party, called the All-Union Communist Party after 1925, sought to entrench their leadership. For the next quarter of a century, their laws and literature would be written in blood. The principal author was Joseph Stalin, who ruled from 1929 to 1953. By the time he died, he had wielded absolute power over the Soviet Union for two-thirds of its history.

Stalin was born on December 21, 1879, in the Caucasian town of Gori, Georgia. He was the only one of four children to survive infancy. His father, a cobbler, became an alcoholic and died of wounds received in a brawl. His mother, Yekaterina, did sewing, housework and washing to earn a living, and was deeply religious, puritanical and ambitious. Since the Russians discriminated against the other nationalities of the empire (a fact that would not change after the revolution), one of the few ways for the Georgian poor to rise in society was to join the priesthood. Yekaterina sought that life for her son. In 1888 Joseph was enrolled in the local Orthodox parochial school in Gori; in 1894 he won a scholarship to the Orthodox theological seminary in Tiflis.

Theology, at least the Russian Orthodox variety, did not seem to satisfy Stalin; so he joined Mesame Dasi, a secret group espousing socialism and Georgian nationalism. (Years later, as head of the USSR, Stalin would violently suppress all Georgian nationalist urges.)

Just before graduating in May 1899, Stalin was expelled from the seminary. He tried tutoring and clerical work at the Tiflis Observatory, but, sought for arrest, abandoned the job in May 1901. Stalin began to reject his ecclesiastical schooling, but the religious psychology instilled in him probably influenced his style for the remainder of his life. Stalin's mind was dogmatic, characterized by categorical assertions. His personality was liturgical, possessed of the intolerance that puritanical training often provides. Stalin's religious mentality remained fixed; he merely replaced the God of guilt with the god of power.

In 1901 the young Dzhugashvili joined the Social Democratic party of Georgia and plunged into revolutionary work, at first in Tiflis and then in Batum, where he helped organize demonstrations and strikes. His life became one of dedicated privation, and he lived and wrote under a succession of pseudonyms. Two favorites were Koba ("Indomitable") and, after 1913, Stalin ("Man of Steel"). Religious humility was clearly in full blossom.

Also in 1901, Stalin's first articles appeared in the clandestine Azerbaidjhan periodical *Brdzola* ("The Struggle"). On April 18, 1902, Stalin was arrested for the first time and exiled to Siberia. He escaped and reappeared in Tiflis in 1904. Arrest and escape would be the pattern of his life until 1917. Although very intelligent, Stalin deviated in one major way from the many of his intellectual revolutionaries: he developed a strong interest in practical problems and party organization. This trait, comparable to Cardinal Thomas Wolsey's under Henry VIII, led Stalin to handle administrative chores which others might not wish to, until, one day, he controlled the party apparatus. Like Wolsey, Stalin was the loyal and subservient lieutenant to his boss, quietly awaiting his moment of power.

Stalin joined a small group of Georgian socialists who supported the Bolshevik faction of the Russian Social Democratic Labor party. Although he propagated Lenin's views in the local underground press, Stalin was not sufficiently prominent to participate in the founding meeting of the Georgian Bolshevik organization in 1904, or the Third National Congress of the Social Democratic party in April 1905.

In June 1904 Stalin married Yekaterina Svanidze, a peasant girl. Her devotion to him seems to have created a happy and conventional marriage, illustrating the conservative and provincial aspect of Stalin's personality. Yekaterina died in 1907, leaving a son, Jacob.

When the Russian revolutionary uprising came in 1905, Stalin served as party organizer in Tiflis, and as co-editor of the *Caucasian Workers' Newsheet*. Not only were Stalin's articles now becoming blatantly Bolshevik, his actions were in true Bolshevik tradition: he began raising funds for the Bolshevik causes by organizing bank robberies, which apparently was less time consuming than soliciting donations. Contemporary revolutionaries worldwide have embellished on this type of economic endeavor.

For several years Stalin either orchestrated revolutionary activities or was in jail for doing so. In 1905 he entered the national arena by attending the first national conference of Bolsheviks, in Tammerfors, Finland, at which he met Lenin for the first time. In 1906 and 1907 he participated in the general congresses of the Russian Social Democratic party, in Stockholm and in London. Almost all of these affairs were held outside of Russia because of the fear of arrest by the Russian authorities.

Stalin was in exile at Vologcha when Lenin went to Prague (January 1912) and formed the ruling body for a separate Bolshevik party. Lenin put Stalin on the committee, even though he had not been elected. Lenin also appointed him one of the leaders of underground work in Russia.

In March 1912, Stalin escaped exile and came to St. Petersburg (modern Leningrad), where he helped set up the new newspaper of the Bolsheviks—*Pravda* ("Truth"), a humble name reflecting the intellectual arrogance of its founders. The first issue appeared on May 5, 1912. Today it is the official newspaper of the Communist Party of the Soviet Union. (The other major Soviet newspaper today is *Izvestia*, the official organ of the government, if such fine distinctions can be made.)

Unlike other leading Bolsheviks, Stalin spent little time abroad, which would later affect his perception of foreign countries and governments. He was relatively unknown outside of Lenin's faction of the party. That was sufficient, however. Lenin was boss, and he wanted a talented organizer and a fanatical activist.

Following the czar's abdication on March 15, 1917, political chaos reigned. While Lenin, Trotsky and other Bolshevik leaders were in public view, Stalin often remained behind the scenes performing administrative and party tasks. On March 25, 1917, after returning from his last period of exile, Stalin joined the editorial board of *Pravda*.

Under the new Soviet regime, established on November 7, 1917, Stalin held a rather minor cabinet position, commissar (minister) of nationalities, which he used to repress dissent in the national areas and to ensure that they would become part of the new country. In 1921 Stalin initiated the brutal conquest of Georgia, which was asserting its nationalist tendencies. He had come full circle. Being in power alters one's perspective. Stalin's experience in dealing with the fifteen republics of Russia gave him insights which enabled him to participate in drafting the first Soviet constitutions of 1918 and 1924.

These military duties provided Stalin with a thirst for blood he was never able to quench. His successes and developing ambitions, however, put him into conflict with the commissar of war, Trotsky. They remained rivals until Stalin ordered Trotsky killed in his exile in Mexico in 1940.

In 1919, at the age of thirty-nine, Stalin married Nadezhda Alliluyeva, the sixteen-year-old daughter of a fellow revolutionary. She provided him with two children (one of them, Svetlana, migrated to the United States after his death, then later returned to the Soviet Union, then later still sought to return to the United States).

That same year Stalin became the head of the Workers' and Peasants' Inspectorate, which had the power to investigate any official in the country, and in 1921 the head of the Organization Bureau (Orgburo), which had the authority to induct or expel party members. Finally, in 1922, Stalin secured the ultimate administrative task, the newly created post of general secretary. Stalin now controlled the administrative machinery of both the Communist party and the Soviet government. Although it had been expected that Trotsky would succeed Lenin, by 1925 Stalin had ousted him.

The civil war of 1918 to 1921 hastened one-party rule and led to brutal repression of all dissent. The bureaucracy, which Lenin had sought to control, was Stalin's ticket to unlimited power. While Lenin and Trotsky were busy ruthlessly crushing various revolts by peasants, workers and sailors, Stalin was working behind the scenes centralizing the bureaucracy with himself at its pivot. Stalin participated only occasionally in the bloodletting; for the most part he quietly bided his time and entrenched his control of the bureaucratic machinery.

The USSR's heroic revolution was over, and the period from 1921 to 1928 saw the need for mundane, day-by-day national administration. Faced with the failure of its initial socialist economic policies, the government was compelled to retreat, or confront ubiquitous revolts and total civil disorder. Lenin fashioned the New Economic Policy, which returned many small industrial concerns to private ownership, but was principally concerned with liberalizing private retail trade. By 1923, "76 percent of retail turnover was in private hands."[25] Some calm was secured.

Before Lenin died he had become increasingly concerned with Stalin's ambitious ruthlessness, and was inclined to remove him from key positions. Lenin even wanted to replace Stalin as the party's general secretary, saying, "I suggest to the comrades that they think of a way of transferring Stalin from this position and assigning another man to it who differs from Comrade Stalin only in one superiority: more tolerant, more loyal, more polite and more considerate of his comrades, less capricious, and so on."[26] In general, Lenin feared (correctly) that if Stalin were to assume greater power he would centralize it in himself—and abuse it. Nonetheless, it was widely assumed at the time that after Lenin passed away Trotsky would take his place as the first among equals in the leadership of his country.

Lenin never acted decisively against Stalin, however. Had he lived longer, scholars believe, Stalin's place in history would have been more limited, possibly even truncated. Lenin's approach, while progressively departing from the freedom to dissent among party leaders enshrined in his original theory of governance by democratic centralism, nonetheless would likely have led the Soviet Union on a course away from the personal absolutism which Stalin would create. At the very least, the Soviet Union's current rule by oligarchical consensus would have evolved long before Brezhnev.

Had Trotsky succeeded Lenin (which many party leaders, including Trotsky himself, assumed would be the case), the character of Soviet socialism would have been dramatically different. Being an internationalist, *par excellence,* Trotsky would undoubtedly have directed his energies to the furtherance of worldwide revolution, and deemphasized the solidification of Soviet nationalism. This would inevitably have resulted in more organized unrest in Europe and elsewhere, and more direct assistance to foreign revolutionary insurgencies—probably with far fewer strings attached. Stalin's preoccupation with Soviet state socialism ultimately led him to concentrate on increasing his own power domestically. In the arena of international revolution, Soviet involvement was less than it would have been had Trotskyist internationalists controlled the party, and Stalin demanded a great deal of Soviet control over the movements he supported. Spontaneous uprisings abroad were viewed by Trotsky as inevitable and deserving on their face of Soviet assistance, whereas Stalin gradually came to regard such movements as anarchical impulses meriting support only if supervised by the Soviet Union. With Stalin's ascension to unchallenged power, the Bolshevik revolution was violently transformed into a socialist monarchy with nakedly imperialist objectives.

When the struggle for power began, Stalin was already in charge of party administration. He was aware of the weariness of the Russian people after years of upheaval. He had a sense of how to manipulate the populace, both through brutality and fear and by occasional sentimental appeals to "Mother Russia." He also knew the Russian people needed a strong leader, a father figure. Russian history had taught him that. Like Lenin before him, Stalin took "one step back" in the Marxist dialectic, and defined it as "socialism in one country." It was essentially the same concept as Lenin's, although more specifically defined.

Stalin's "socialism in one country" was initially an effort to stabilize the Soviet Union's economic and political affairs, an endeavor which possessed the corollary benefit of enabling him to secure personal power. As early as 1925, Stalin and Bukharin had informed a party conference that a new view of the international situation had to be developed. In Europe, they said, the revolutionary impulse had largely come to an end. They believed that "foreign capitalism had achieved a degree of stabilization which made it certain that Soviet Russia would remain isolated for a long time to come."[27] According to Isaac Deutscher, Stalin had concluded in 1927 that, "The capitalist world had recovered from the war and that the prospects of any new revolutionary crisis abroad belonged to a more or less remote future."[28] These prognostications laid down the rationale for forgetting foreign adventures and focusing instead on the solution of Soviet problems.

Since Stalin was already consolidating his power when he promulgated this view, it is difficult to be certain whether these observations were honest evaluations of the international scene, or primarily an ideological justification for state efforts beneficial to Stalin. So early in the revolution, indirect measures for securing personal power were required. Perhaps most threatening to Stalin's ambitions was the eminence of Trotsky and the "internationalists," who sincerely believed in international revolution as essential for the protection of socialism in Russia. "Socialism in one country" was a weapon in the struggle against Trotsky in the theoretical arena. The use of scarce Soviet resources to promote international revolution would of course limit efforts to consolidate state power. This would in turn limit Stalin's influence, which rose in direct proportion with the degree of control—over the state and the people—exercised by the party. The doctrine of "socialism in one country" thus served to secure Stalin's personal power on two fronts at once.

"Socialism in one country" had darker origins still. Stalin identified much of his opposition and its ideology with Jews. Before the revolution, the Mensheviks had such a preponderance of Jews that "Stalin is reported to have said that with one large pogrom there would no longer be a Menshevik movement," write Dennis Prager and Joseph Telushkin in *Why the Jews?*[29] There were fewer Jews among the Bolsheviks, but even so they constituted 15 to 20 percent of the leadership in 1922.[30] After the death of Lenin, the ruling triumvirate for a short time was composed of Stalin, Zinoviev and Kamenev—two-thirds Jewish. Zinoviev and Kamenev quickly conspired with Trotsky (also Jewish) against Stalin.[31] According to Deutscher, "Trotsky, Zinoviev, Kamenev, Redek, were all Jews. (There were, on the other hand, very few Jews among the Stalinists, and still fewer among the Bukharinists). . . . The Jews of the Bolshevik revolution were in a sense the 'rootless cosmopolitans' on whom Stalin was to turn his wrath openly in his old age. Not for them was the ideal of socialism in one country."[32] It could be said that Stalin's "socialism in one country" was, as much as anything else, an expression of ages-old Russian nationalism. Nationalism, of course, goes hand in hand with xenophobia, expressed materially as racism; in Russia, such feelings were especially directed against Jews. "The distrust of the 'alien' was, after all, only a reflex of that Russian self-centeredness, of which socialism in one country was the ideological abstract."[33]

Anti-Semitism was nourished in numerous ways, from "Greek Orthodoxy and the native tradition of pogroms; from the population's war-time contacts with Nazism; from the fact that Jewish traders and artisans, un-adjusted to a publicly owned economy, were conspicuous in the illicit and semi-illicit commerce flourishing amid a scarcity of goods; from the great number of Jews among the early Bolshevik leaders; and from their relative importance, even after the extermination of those leaders, in the middle layers of the Stalinist bureaucracy. The single-minded Communist often looked upon the Jews as the last surviving element of urban capitalism; while the anti-Communist saw them as influential members of the ruling hierarchy."[34]

Stalin was equivocal. On the one hand Jews were quite prominent in his entourage; on the other hand, many of his enemies were Jews. Like many ethnic groups, the Jews did not wish to assimilate into the new Communist culture; some minorities Stalin deported, such as the Volga Germans, the Crimean Tartars, the Ingush-Chechens. He was more indul-gent toward the Jews at first, but as years passed Stalin increasingly re-ferred to Jews as "rootless cosmopolitans" preserving a separate society within the Soviet system. He apparently did not consider them sufficiently threatening as a group to attempt to extirpate them; he allowed them to remain entrenched in the vital spheres of national life, in the management of industry, in nuclear research, in the party machine, in academia, and even in the armed forces. Stalin clearly harbored some animosities toward Jews as a group because he had faced so many as adversaries. But after WWII, Stalin was suddenly to perceive a threat from Jews as a group, a threat that would permit him to make only invidious distinctions between Jews as individuals. Israel had been created.

Israel's first diplomatic envoy to the Soviet Union, Golda Meir, arrived in Moscow in 1948 and received a tumultuous ovation. According to Deutscher,

> The sudden revelation of the depths of feeling that some Soviet Jews had for Israel could not but alarm Stalin. The spontaneity with which they were expressing their sentiment defied the mechanical discipline under which he kept the whole of society. He could not tolerate it. In his monolith the most minute fissure was a danger to the whole structure. If the Jews were to be permitted to vent unlicensed emotions in unauthor-ized demonstrations, how could he forbid the Russians or the Ukrainians to do likewise?[35]

He couldn't. The Jews obviously were not rootless cosmopolitans or "people without a fatherland"; they had empathy for, perhaps even a higher loyalty to, the new-born state of Israel. Stalin could exploit this phenomenon to a certain extent, by sending Russian Jews to Israel as Soviet agents, but at the same time he could not trust them. Their feelings for Israel were unpredictable; their loyalty to Russia was questionable.

Stalin thus began to take action against Jews, not merely to eliminate adversaries, but to prevent the fissiparous developments which could bring down the controlled Soviet system. He used advocacy of "socialism in one country" as a primary weapon to eliminate his Jewish opposition. "In 1953, Joseph Stalin accused a number of doctors, most of them Jews, of a plot to poison the Communist leadership of the Soviet Union. Stalin died three days before their trial was to begin, but we now know that Stalin intended to use the 'doctor's plot' to arouse the Russian public against the Jews, and in the ensuing crisis, exile Russia's Jews to Siberia."[36] For their part, the Jews of Russia began to conclude that if they were required to subscribe to the notion of "socialism in one country," perhaps that country should be Israel. Betrayed by the revolution they had helped to organize, the Jews ultimately would turn to Zion. Today's pattern of conflict for future Soviet Jewry was born in the 1920s.

Stalin's road to unchallenged power took wild turns, but it required only a few years to travel. In brief summary, Stalin first veered politically to the right for the purpose of eliminating his worst enemies on the left. Then he swung left to do battle with his rivals on the right. Achieving complete dominance by the 1930s, Stalin then acted at will, and in the purges of the late thirties wiped out nearly all of his former opposition regardless of their previous factional alliances.

The central ideological issue around which the "right" and "left" factions revolved was agricultural policy. Rapid industrialization was the party's main concern, but its pace was almost entirely determined by the availability and price of food for the urban centers in which industrialization would take place. The question was how peasants could both be induced to accept low prices for their goods, and at the same time be prevented from producing only for their own needs, contradictory aims. The seven-member Politburo of the early 1920s—made up of Stalin, Zinoviev, Kamenev, Trotsky, Bukharin, Rykov and Tomskii—was divided over policy: the "left" (Zinoviev and Kamenev) favored expropriation of agricultural production in the short term and rapid socialist collectivization of agriculture. In theory this would allow faster industrialization. The "right" (Bukharin, Rykov, Tomskii), arguing that national stabilization was of primary importance and that slightly slower industrialization was acceptable, favored incentives for wealthier peasants (called *kulaks*, technically those who employed other peasants), never mind the accompanying higher food prices. Trotsky had long been at ideological odds with Zinoviev and Kamenev, and in any case was not principally concerned with domestic economic affairs. In the struggle between the factions, decided in the forum of the regular party congresses, Stalin acted as a moderator.

Stalin acted decisively only with the election of several of his allies to the Politburo in 1925. The new members, Molotov, Voroshilov, and Kalinin, formed a Stalinist "center," and Stalin's consolidation of personal power began in earnest. He decided on a NEP-like path of accommodation with the kulaks, causing the the fierce opposition of Zinoviev and Kamenev. Bukharin led the theoretical counter-attack. The supporters of what came to be called the "left opposition" began to be removed from party and government positions. Zinoviev and Kamenev successfully appealed to Trotsky for help, but Trotsky's power had waned with his resignation as commissar of the Red Army (in 1925, at the request of the Politburo), and with the death during surgery of his hand-picked successor in what may have been a Stalin-inspired assassination. By late 1926, Zinoviev was removed as president of the Comintern and Trotsky was expelled from the Politburo. By the fall of 1927, members of what had come to be called the "united opposition" began to be arrested for illegal "factional activity." Trotsky was exiled to Alma Alta. Left-wing influence in the party had been decisively defeated.

The failure of the agricultural policies first promoted by Bukharin *et al*—a massive grain shortage had appeared by 1928—prompted a complete reversal of the policy and ideology advocated by the right. Stalin's proposals for solving the grain shortage, soon adopted, "far surpassed the most radical proposals of Zinoviev and Kamenev. He suddenly appropriated Trotskyite conceptions of 'primitive socialist accumulation' and significantly extended them."[37]

Although Bukharin and his associates at first supported some of the measures as necessary, they soon began to urge restraint. This gave Stalin the opportunity to argue the existence of a "right" deviation from the party line, but it was a deviation based more on opposition to Stalin than it was on ideology. "Indeed, in the attack on Bukharin, Rykov, and Tomskii, Stalin pinned the label of 'right deviation' on many other tendencies and groups that had no organizational or ideological connection with Bukharin's faction . . . nothing in common except some disagreement with the basic Stalinist line."[38]

Bukharin was suffering the same fate he had helped bring down on Zinoviev, Kamenev and Trotsky. This he recognized fully by April of 1929, saying, "[Stalin] will strangle us. He is an unprincipled intriguer who subordinates everything to his appetite for power. At any given moment he will change his theories in order to get rid of someone."[39]

Despite their experience of only three years before, Zinoviev and Kamenev, still members of the Politburo, saw conversion rather than opportunism in Stalin's actions. The Bolshevik left wing hoped that Stalin's sudden turn in their direction would enable them to once again share power. Like Bukharin and his associates before them, Zinoviev and Kamenev eagerly abetted Stalin's attack against his enemies of the moment. Within a year Rykov was deposed from his position as premier (in which he had succeeded Lenin), Tomskii was removed from the leadership of the trade unions, his political base, and Bukharin was dismissed as head of the Comintern (where he had replaced Zinoviev), and from the Politburo. All were eventually given less important posts, but none ever dared to speak in opposition to Stalin's policies again.[40]

Stalin now reigned supreme, but his rapid swings in ideology and sudden, fierce campaigns against supposed foes were not to end. The weapons of Stalin's secret police were used first against the idealists of the revolution. While the police apparatus tortured his opposition, Stalin tortured Marxist theory to justify it all. In 1936, in a fit of bloody paranoia that would eventually disillusion Communists around the world, Stalin initiated three years of purges, resulting in show trials and the forced recantations and executions of thousands of party members, many of them Bolsheviks since before the October Revolution. Zinoviev and Kamenev were tried and executed in 1936. Bukharin and Rykov were tried and executed in 1938. Trotsky was assassinated in Mexico City in 1940.

Lenin had been correct—Stalin was too ambitious. Nonetheless, it is naive to suggest that his rule was merely a chance perversion of the ideals of socialist revolution. If not a quintessential product of the Marxist organizational model conceived by Lenin (and therefore of Marxist ideology itself— how else to judge its application in the real world?), Stalin was at least its logical outgrowth. Isaac Deutscher perhaps says it best: "When, on ceremonial occasions, Stalin appeared at the top of the Lenin mausoleum in the Red Square, Lenin's colossal tomb appeared to be only the pedestal for his successor."[41]

Stalin should be seen as the Marxist of fact rather than theory, an only slightly unconventional czar; his theories and policies should be evaluated accordingly. He acted as a statist, not a revolutionary; his actions were riven with opportunism and a willingness to suppress any adversaries, be they individuals or groups, domestic or foreign. Contrary to the traditional mythology fostered by academicians of political science, applied Marxism is a right-wing ideology, manifesting in practice the features of limited monarchism. Stalin, the political practitioner *extraordinaire*, understood this instinctively.

Stalin's essential character as statist rather than revolutionary is clearest in his conduct of foreign policy. His "socialism in one country" amounted to far more than a concentration on the building of socialism in the Soviet

Union. The Soviet-sponsored Comintern, the collective organization of the world's Communist parties, became under Stalin purely a vehicle for the implementation of Soviet foreign policy objectives—which did not always include the success of foreign revolutionary movements. Those whose success would harm Soviet foreign policy interests were sabotaged; those in which Soviet-directed Communist parties were not dominant were either abandoned or suffered merciless internecine struggle fomented by those parties in the pursuit of dominance.

The sad tale begins in 1924, with the adoption of a new strategy for revolution by the fifth congress of the Comintern: reformist socialist parties descended from pre-war Social Democratic parties were to be targeted as primary enemies of the working class. According to Stalin, "Social Democracy is objectively the moderate wing of Fascism . . . These organizations do not negate but supplement each other. They are antipodes, they are twins. Fascism is an informal political bloc of these two chief organizations; a bloc which arose in the circumstances of the post-war crisis of imperialism; and which is intended for combating the proletarian revolution."[42]

The thrust of this analysis was a policy formulated by Stalin in which the "Communist Party must always strike the main blow against the intermediate parties." This was to become "a strategical dogma for the Communist parties down to the turn of 1934-5."[43] It was theoretical idiocy, but with one advantage: the successes of client Communist parties working in such a way would benefit the Soviet Union as much or more than the particular national proletariat. Power won in such scenarios would not have to be shared with either left-wing democrats or "uncontrollable" revolutionaries with other than Soviet interests at heart.

One consequence of this bizarre Comintern strategy, it is frequently argued by socialist historians, was Hitler's ascension to power in 1933 and his immediate, easy liquidation of both the German Communist and Social Democratic parties. The sudden victory of fascism in Germany was a horrifying shock to Comintern leaders and to Stalin. No more determined enemy of the Soviet Union than a Hitlerite Germany could be imagined. The game was up in Germany, but tactics in Britain, France and elsewhere could yet be modified. After a short period of denial (some thought that Hitler would quickly fall from power), the Comintern shifted in May 1934 to a strategy dubbed the "united front"—alliance by Communist parties with other left parties—and in July 1935 to broader collaboration still, called the "popular front," with liberal bourgeois parties as well. In two short years Stalin had travelled a long way from Lenin's original concept of a small cadre, a highly independent and secret vanguard party of the working class.

It would be overzealous to characterize this rapid change in policy as a damning example of Soviet nationalist opportunism acting in the guise of revolutionary theory. No country, however driven by revolutionary idealism, could fail to act other than selfishly in the face of Nazism. It is nonetheless instructive that the Comintern's move to a strategy clearly in the best interest of the various national proletariats—the targeting of fascism as the preeminent danger—was only prompted by the direst of threats to Soviet security. The inexorable overthrow of capitalism gave way to a collaboration with the bourgeoisie in panicky defense against its monstrous progeny.

In less threatening arenas, Comintern opportunism was shown for what it was. Nowhere was this clearer than on the staging field for World War II, the Spanish Civil War. Revolutionary developments in Spain had proceeded steadily for a decade, accelerating with the overthrow of the monarchy by radical democrats in 1931. Socialists, Communists and anarchists permeated a bourgeois government threatened alternately by revolution and reaction. The moment of truth arrived in 1936 with the revolt of General Francisco Franco from garrisons in Morocco. The Republican government was defended by a full spectrum of forces from the center to the far left—liberal capitalists, democrats, socialists, trade unionists, Communists, Trotskyists and anarchists all worked feverishly to supply the troops, weapons, ammunition and organization to fight the fascist danger. Men and women from as far away as the United States banded together into military units to play their part in a defense of liberty correctly seen as the prelude to a dark period in human history.

Some of the actors in this drama, however, were playing their parts with less altruistic aims. The Soviet-directed Communist Party of Spain (PCE) was hardly the most influential of Spain's many leftist groups, at the start of the civil war. The dominant groups were the socialist and anarchist trade unions (the CNT and the UGT) and their corresponding political organizations, the Spanish Socialist Workers' Party (PSOE), and the Iberian Anarchist Federation (FAI).

The threat of fascism prompted a call by the PCE for unity with the socialists, and the parliamentary elections of 1936 "were a victory for the popular front, with 278 deputies, including 88 socialists and 16 communists."[44] The center and right together won only 207 seats.

With Franco's revolt in July, Communist influence would increase dramatically. The Soviet Union immediately provided military advisors and by September had begun to ship arms and ammunition. Within a year the army was under virtually complete Communist control. "According to PCE statistics, in the summer of 1937 60 percent of all army personnel were party members, 5 out of 11 corps commanders, and 56 out of 72 brigade commanders."[45]

However, control of the revolution, not its final success, was the Soviet motivation. During the civil war, the Soviets abstained from providing total support. "Determination to keep the foreign policy of the USSR in line with that of France and Britain, its political allies against the menace of the Fascist powers, was a dominant force in Moscow at this time."[46] Trotsky summarized Soviet policy as preventing the Spanish people "from going beyond the limits of what was acceptable to King George, Chamberlain, President LeBrun, etc."[47]

At the same time Stalin consistently sabotaged the actions of Spanish revolutionaries who would not submit to Soviet supervision of revolutionary objectives. "Security forces . . . under Communist or Soviet control began to arrest individual anarchists; and assassinations of prominent anarchists were also reported."[48] In the words of Trotsky, "The Kremlin intervened in the events in order to restrict the revolution within the limits of the bourgeois regime. . . . The GPU [Soviet secret police] in Spain carried out ruthless oppression against revolutionary wings. . . . Moderate politicians . . . utilized the Moscow police apparatus in order to crush their revolutionary opponents."[49]

In sum, eloquent exhortations substituted for direct help as the USSR merely performed a ritual rain dance of revolutionary rhetoric while trying to gain control of Spain for Soviet imperial purposes. As noted Sovietologist Seweryn Bialer has concluded, "The highest priority in Soviet thinking about revolutions abroad in Stalin's time was not the survival and stabilization of revolutionary power, but rather Soviet control over a new revolutionary government."[50] The Soviet Union under Stalin had become merely another power with nationalist interests as its nearly exclusive motivation. "As expressed in Stalin's own words," notes Bialer, "an internationalist communist revolutionary was whoever supported the Soviet Union above all else. As far as support for the world revolutionary movement was concerned, it had to become subordinate to the national interests of the Soviet Union and its foreign policy."[51]

With himself at the top of the pyramid, Stalin solidifed the permanent power of the dictatorial party and state by ossifying the unequal social hierarchy of officials, technicians, workers and peasants; this was achieved by the permanent reliance on government coercion to accomplish the economic and cultural modernization of the country. Stalin's successors inherited and continued these principles of government, which are less in accord with Marxism than with the elitist state socialism of Saint-Simon and, finally, the outlook of Louis XIV. Even Stalin's Communist contemporary, Mao Zedong, quickly came to regard the Soviet socialist leadership as an elitist, politically privileged class.

To consolidate his power, Stalin physically eliminated both existing and potential adversaries. Through a series of mass purges, usually without publicity, confessions, or trials, Stalin sent tens of thousands to their deaths. Trotsky himself, never known for his weak stomach, wrote that, "Stalin is like a man who wants to quench his thirst with salted water."[52]

Stalin chose instead to slake his thirsts with blood. To quell perpetual rebellion in the Ukraine, and to obtain food for his armies, Stalin in 1932 and 1933 seized grain from that autonomous republic, virtually starving about ten million people.[53]

Unless they were treated leniently and sent to the Gulag, the politicians and bureaucrats targeted by Stalin as counterrevolutionaries (there was only occasional correlation to actual commission of crimes) did not have to suffer the painful death of starvation; they were simply shot, although frequently after being tortured. According to Isaac Deutscher, "He sent thousands to their death and tens and hundreds of thousands into prisons and concentration camps . . . the number of the victims will perhaps never be known. According to some sources, in the army alone about 20,000 officers, 25 percent of the entire officers' corps, were arrested and several thousand shot. The whole structure of the state was shaken."[54]

After his second wife, Nadezhda Alliluyeva, committed suicide and left a note indicting him both politically and personally, Stalin became paranoid and did not spare even his own relatives. Most of the Svanidzes and Alliluyevas came to a tragic end, as did other relations, friends, and even the families of his closest political associates.

Stalin centered his life wholly in his office, and lived either in his Kremlin apartment, which his daughter Svetlana shared with him in the 1930s, or in his new country house at Kuntsovo. Stalin was always surrounded by secret police and trusted no one. He shied away from the public, but permitted national glorification of himself on a scale hardly matched in the twentieth century (except by his fellow Marxist, Mao Zedong, another propounder of the philosophy of impersonalism who thrived on adulation).

Despite his socialist pretensions, in 1939 Stalin once again subordinated Marxist philosophy to Russia's national interest, signing a non-aggression treaty with the archenemy of Communists everywhere, Adolph Hitler. The treaty included an exchange of gifts. Hitler provided "the most up-to-date German military aeroplanes for Stalin (including the top secret ME 109, JU87, JU88, 00217, HE111 and even the ME110) in exchange for the surrender of all German Communists who had taken political asylum in the Soviet Union." To avoid the problem of transporting so many German Communists (and Jews) back to Germany, Stalin allowed Hitler to send

Nazi executioners to the Soviet Union to shoot them in Soviet prisons.[55]

In further exchange for Stalin's neutrality, Germany ceded to the Soviet Union the imperialist right to invade several countries, which, after World War II, the Soviet Union claimed to be in its domain. "This is how the Soviets acquired the Baltic States, Eastern Poland, Southern Finland, and part of Romania."[56] The seizure of these nations and territories was purest imperialism. "There was no revolutionary situation or noticeable revolutionary movement to provide even a fig leaf for Soviet actions . . . By 1941, the Soviet Union had almost entirely restored the borders of the old Tsarist empire by acquisitions that had nothing to do with authentic revolutionary feeling."[57]

Territorial domination was of greater importance than revolutionary legitimacy or even success. Soviet conduct during the Spanish Civil War was only the most grievous example. After World War II, Stalin even went so far as to lay plans to assassinate Yugoslavia's Tito. Perhaps nothing is more illustrative of the subordinate role of socialist ideology in Soviet foreign policy than the fact that, as Bialer has observed, "The Soviet Union could not gain lasting control over any country in which the revolutionary forces came to power as a result of their own strength."[58] Under Stalin, Soviet advocacy and support of external socialist revolution became merely another vehicle for Soviet imperialism.

Apparently not believing his own propaganda against the Western imperialists, and despite months of detailed intelligence received from his own agents in Europe, British and American diplomats, and even the German ambassador to the USSR, Stalin was shocked when Nazi Germany broke the non-aggression treaty and attacked the Soviet Union in the summer of 1941—Operation Barbarossa, two years in the planning. He reacted by getting drunk in his Kremlin apartments, but managed to stumble out once to say for history, "Lenin's work has perished. We were unable to defend it."[59] When he sobered up, Stalin liquidated many of his top military leaders—several of whom had been pleading for permission to draw up defense plans in case of a Nazi invasion. This decimation of the upper echelon of the Soviet military, naturally, aided the Nazi military advance. The behavior was typical of Stalin's reactions in a crisis. About an earlier event Trotsky said of him, "When faced by great problems Stalin always retreats—not through lack of character . . . but through narrowness of horizon and lack of creative imagination. His suspicious caution almost organically compels him at moments of great decision and deep difference to retire into the shadow, to wait, and if possible to insure himself against both outcomes."[60] Inebriation, it seems, was also helpful.

To preserve the socialist system, whose achievements were demonstrably dubious, the Soviet Union once again turned to the capitalist countries for aid, which, as usual, was supplied by the United States. American generosity was unrestrained. The Soviet Union was provided with money, weapons, training and technology. "For the chief of the GRU [Soviet military intelligence] and his colleagues the doors of secret factories and laboratories were opened—the very places Soviet intelligence had been trying for decades to penetrate."[61] American naivete not only helped lay the foundation for modern Soviet military technology, it also provided the Soviets with details of U.S. facilities upon which they built a base for future espionage. Soviet intelligence forces no longer had to work around the clock to locate certain secret American facilities; they were given maps and entry permits.

After the war, in gratitude for Western beneficence, Stalin refocused on traditional imperial objectives. Following Soviet absorption of the Eastern bloc, "the Middle East was the first point of abrasive encounter between the Soviet Union and the West."[61] The desire for unthreatened access to the Mediterranean, and therefore year-round sea access to Europe, had been a driving Russian ambition for more than a thousand years. In the post-war period, the Middle East was dotted with British bases which Stalin regarded as "surrogates for the United States in its global competition with the Soviet Union."[62] Britain was under economic and political pressure to dismantle its worldwide empire. How to assure that it left the Middle East?

Britain had issued the Balfour Declaration in part because it saw a Jewish state in Palestine as a possible client buffer protecting its vital Suez Canal. Perhaps, the Soviets reasoned, Israel could serve as a buffer against a Western presence in the Middle East. The Soviet Union and its satellites began to arm and train Zionists bent on creating a Jewish state in Palestine. "The Soviet Union did not hesitate therefore to reverse and repudiate its long tradition of anti-Zionism in a spectacular campaign of support for the establishment and defense of Israel."[64] The Soviet Union was the first nation to recognize the new Jewish state.

Part of the American Jewish community, ignorant of Soviet ambitions and American interests, joined the campaign to carve Israel out of Palestine. America was finally enlisted in the effort, a decision destined to cause military and political difficulties for the United States for the remainder of the twentieth century.

American Zionists worked hand in hand with Eastern bloc countries to create a Jewish military force in the Middle East, often compromising American military and political interests in the process.[65] Indirect Soviet support for the military creation of Israel was massive, offered in the form of weapons, manpower and intelligence. American help came in the form of money (much of it used to buy Soviet-bloc weapons) and diplomatic support.

The efforts of these two strange bedfellows differed in a more important way, however: while the American commitment, once given, was genuine and firm, Soviet help was provided only with certain ends in mind. "The support of Israel by the Soviet Union lasted for nearly three years, which was long enough to see the British position in Palestine eliminated and the Negev in Israeli hands." Its immediate aim achieved, however, "the USSR turned its back on Israel and began to seek friendships in the Arab countries."[66]

By 1949 the Soviet Union controlled Eastern Europe militarily, had firmly secured the Baltic states under its hegemony, had successfully established its influence in the Middle East, and was directing numerous subversive efforts throughout the world. "The old Bolshevik dream of authentic socialist revolutions was displaced by the commitment to direct military conquest as the only way to spread communism."[67]

However, in the process of military domination, the USSR was repressing bona fide national movements in the countries it came to control. This was especially the case in Hungary and Czechoslovakia, where voters in elections held soon after the war rejected Soviet-supported Communist leadership, only to have it imposed within two years by the machinations of the Soviet secret police and their client movements. Thus eventually the Soviet Union's historic paranoia would be increasingly justified; even its own allies were developing fear and hatred of Soviet suzerainty. The USSR was destined to become the only Communist country surrounded by hostile Communist countries.

Marxist hagiography, for a while, had another saint in Stalin, or perhaps more accurately, the Marxist pantheon had another god. Two levels or "classes" of egalitarianism had arisen under his rule: the priests of the Marxist church of state, surrounded by their henchmen in the military and the secret police, and the workers, the "proletariat," now oppressed by new rulers. Marx had not envisioned that the class struggle would come to be between these two groups in his once-hypothetical transition society. Theoretically they were a unity. A manager class arose in the USSR as it did in the Western world, but from far less meritorious and far more violent (given the list of capitalist abuses, it hadn't seemed possible) origins. In the West professional managers were hired to increase business profits; they eventually came to control corporations and banks which they did not own. In the Soviet Union the leaders appointed Marxist managers to control both the assets and the ideas of their factory workers. Marx had not foreseen either development. The movement of history has not been toward communism, but toward economic rule by proxy. Before Marxist socialism can produce a final "withering away of the state," it is clear, the dialectics of history will have to provide a final class struggle, one between the Marxist rulers and their people.

Marx's view of future historical development, and its endpoint, is clearly just another of his many intellectual miscalculations. Marx's examination of history had revealed to him a pattern: certain classes become dominant, establishing a state used primarily for the purpose of dominating other classes. Monarchical power in Marx's day had rarely been used to oppress the landed aristocracy it represented; bourgeois governments never turned on the merchants and capitalists they represented. Marx failed to consider the possibility that the state machinery established in the interest of the proletariat would do other than act in the interest of that proletariat. If it did, perhaps he thought, such a government would be quickly overthrown, much as the nobility had moved to curb the excesses of England's King John (resulting in the signing of the Magna Carta) and, in France, of Louis XVI (which had the unforeseen consequence of opening the door for other classes to begin the French Revolution).

Marx's economic intellectualism had caused him to ignore the difficulties of applying these historical lessons to a fundamentally new historical proposition: rule by a class not in the minority of the population. Such a class would require rule by proxy to an unprecedented degree. Whereas previous ruling elites stood at the material and educational apex of their cultures and ruled through individuals of their own kind, the workers were impoverished and unlearned and accordingly forced to rule through proxies, individuals of a different class. Lenin had never been a member of the proletariat.

Such differences in historical circumstances required examination of other than historical sciences if predictions were to be accurate—the psychology of rule, for one. The rulers of the Soviet Union, far from acting on behalf of any class, have become a class in themselves, parasitic in nature. Following well-worn historical example, they have also created subsidiary parasitic classes. The development of this structure was far from accidental. It seems as inevitable as the development of classes up to Marx's time. Like "Potomac fever," the power-gathering virus which begins to afflict politicians and bureaucrats who work near the Potomac River in Washington, D.C., the dynamic of rule inspired by Marx has developed independently of the tasks it was designed to fulfill. Human psychology, as it interacts with the structures of political power, is at work here.

It is in this light that Marx's grand scheme is revealed, contrary to its claims, as fundamentally unscientific. State power has always been the ultimate weapon in the armory of class rule, unquestionably. But varying degrees of individual interest in (and skill at) social participation, social-psychological impetuses to hierarchy (visible in all animal societies), and international rivalries all are contributing factors to the existence, ongoing legitimacy, and coloration of that state power, regardless of its class orientation.

With origins and dynamics so multiple, deep-rooted, and complex, how could any man dare venture to predict the "withering away" of state power? Only a man thinking theologically. The state will wither away because dogma, in this case a dogma of inevitable historical thesis, antithesis, and synthesis developing to perfection—Christian-inspired Hegelianism—says that it must. Empirical observation be damned.

After Stalin's death, in a highly publicized secret speech, Khrushchev criticized Stalin's behavior and removed him as an idol from the Soviet pantheon. The Politburo accused Stalin of "excesses," euphemistic reference to the countless millions of gallons of blood he spilled during his reign. Steps were taken to eliminate Stalin's name from history, literature, and the periodical press, and to remove his graven image from all walls and plazas. During his life, Stalin's name was ubiquitous, appearing even in books of science and mathematics, often suggesting that he had written them, or, almost as improbable, understood their contents. In the first fifteen years after his death, Stalin's name, if mentioned at all, appeared only in denigrating contexts usually referring vaguely to the "errors" of the "cult of personality."

On his death in 1953 Stalin had ruled the Soviet Union for two-thirds of its history; afterwards it was pretended that he had never existed. Soviet attempts to rewrite history have the purpose of facilitating the current leadership's change in certain policies, and to moderate the country's image abroad—the only area where moderation is deemed a virtue in Soviet political behavior.

Since the late 1960s Stalin's good name has experienced limited resurrection, but in a tightly controlled way. Visitors to the Soviet Union find conversations quickly become apprehensive when Stalin's name is mentioned. Many Soviets refer to him as a "typical" Soviet Marxist: usually they say it with a sense of fear, often laced with repressed pride.

Stalin, like all other Soviet leaders, apparently misinterpreted a fundamental tenet of Marxist doctrine. Marx maintained that the withering away of the state would be a gradual dismantling of the apparatus of centralized government, giving power to the people in a classless society. Stalin apparently elected to accelerate this inexorable process by decimating millions of people at the bottom of the social and political structure, a physical "withering away" of the population that did not religiously adhere to history's latest brand of madness. Perhaps this approach will in fact hasten the dawn of a truly egalitarian society: there will be fewer people alive with whom to share the economic successes which Marxism continues to predict.

The Soviet economy had recovered somewhat from the devastation of the war by the time of Stalin's death, but was suffering from defense spending kept high despite the peace. Slave labor, a variable not part of the economic model of the West, was long used to help solve economic difficulties, apparently reaching a peak sometime after World War II. It declined substantially and steadily after 1956, but continues to figure in the economy in the forms of prison labor and enforced subsistence wages in some industries.

The West once extended the Soviets political politesse by pretending that the USSR was solvent and respectful, in its own way to be sure, of the condition of its people; this was called statesmanship. It was an exercise in graciousness and self-deception which made sympathetic Westerners feel politically comfortable, partially because it conformed with the Western sense of Christian compassion.

Later, when Leonid Brezhnev became the Soviet emperor, the Western nations created *detente*, also known as the "Marshall Plan for the Eastern Bloc," which provided the Soviet Union and the Eastern European nations with as much technological and financial assistance as was politically possible. There was no effort to halt the illegal hemorrhage of industrial secrets (technology acquired through Soviet espionage), until President Reagan curtailed it by creating the Defense Department's Office of Technology Transfer.

Eventually, through its own efforts and the assistance of the West, the Soviet Union was stronger both economically and militarily. It had secured a designer wardrobe for its international outings, and called it *detente* in order to give it cosmopolitan and diplomatic sophistication. Once the Soviet emperor felt at ease in his new technological attire, he went ahead and took control of Afghanistan, Ethiopia, South Yemen, Vietnam and Cambodia. Despite the economic problems inherent in the Soviet system, or perhaps because of them, the Soviet Union continues a policy of foreign aggrandizement backed by gargantuan military and international intelligence apparatuses. Like the shark, Marxist socialism can survive only if it is on the prowl; otherwise its internal organs would collapse.

Each of the heirs of Stalin, from Nikita Khrushchev to Mikhail Gorbachev, were viewed by ever-forgiving Americans as products of "a new era" in Soviet history. Americans initially regarded Khrushchev as a breath of fresh air, until the invasion of Hungary in 1956. The shared leadership of Leonid Brezhnev and Alexei Kosygin was at first seen as an improvement over the single Soviet dictators of the past—until the invasion of Czechoslovakia in 1968 and Afghanistan in 1979, not to mention the colonization of various sub-continent countries in between. The West saw the ascension of

Yuri Andropov as the rise, finally, of an educated and sophisticated leader to the pinnacle of Soviet power. Noting that he read English literature in the privacy of his apartment, some even saw Andropov as a closet liberal. Hopeful Americans tried to forget that he was previously the head of the KGB, that he had conceived the use of psychiatric hospitals to punish dissidents.

The latest hope of Western liberals is Mikhail Gorbachev, complete with three-hundred-dollar suits and a wife who uses an American Express credit card to buy French designer clothing. These are seen as signs of sophisticated and even liberal tendencies, much different from past Soviet brutishness typified by garrulous old Brezhnev—and a sophistication sure to be longer lasting than Andropov's, since Gorbachev is young. The Gorbachev family is even compared to the Kennedys in the Western press. However, just as Western nations saw fit to forget about Andropov's KGB background, they tend to ignore Gorbachev's past. Although he is the first formally educated Soviet leader since Lenin, Gorbachev obtained his law degree in Moscow during the era of Stalin. As Henry Kissinger once remarked, "It is probably safe to assume that Mr. Gorbachev did not anticipate a career as a public defender." To succeed to ultimate power in the Soviet empire requires a strong stomach and an ideological disposition combining hard-line Marxist theories and Soviet imperial ambitions. As "old sourpuss," Andrei Gromyko, once said of Gorbachev, "He has a nice smile, but iron teeth."

Stalin's political legacy is one of duplicity and repression. He consistently abandoned Communist principles abroad in favor of more proximate priorities: personal power in the USSR. He used ideology primarily to obtain and increase dictatorial authority, while his capricious disposition undercut nominal efforts to carry that ideology out. This was demonstrated in dozens of ways. A very traditional nationalism superseded Marxist internationalism (Stalin even changed the national anthem in 1944, from "L'Internationale" to a patriotic song), economic policy was less the practical application of Marxist principles or response to economic exigencies than a traditional Russian effort to increase state power through centralization for the sake of it, and the rule of the proletariat, in its way supposed to be the purest democracy ever known, was converted to a "cult of personality" that outstripped the excesses of history's vainest and most capricious kings.

In the end, Stalin's totalitarian temperament opted for personal power. The world, particularly the Russian people, would have been better off if he had never been born. Stalin's heirs all learned from him, and came of age in an era when bloodshed was as natural in Soviet culture and political life as on American television. After a while one accepts it as a normal state of affairs. Stalin's practices followed in the tradition of the despots of

Russian history. His special contribution was to enshrine hypocrisy into his country's political life. Rather than the open tyranny of rule by royal whim, Stalin's successors have learned from him that the excesses of old can be dressed up: an officially progressive ideology can mask both the domestic repression and foreign military subjugation used to implement what is only a semblance of that ideology. Ruling class self-aggrandizement moves from naked to clothed. Stalin's disciples have not forgotten their lessons. His reputation, sullied in the Soviet Union only because his "excesses" reached to fellow members of his ruling class, is gradually being resuscitated.

Mao: An Oriental Philosophy of Violence

Political power comes from the barrel of a gun.

—Mao Zedong

The son of a peasant couple whose ancestors for generations were Hunan peasants, Mao was born in 1893, in a village near Hsiangtan in central China. He had two brothers and one sister. While Mao's stern father instilled Confucian thought in the children, his kindly mother was devoted to Buddhism. Mao acquired intellectual discipline from his conscientious parents at an early age, providing him with a primitive but solid desire for education.

Mao went to work in the fields when he was five years old, but by the age of seven he spent much of his free time learning to read and write. Several novels, including *Monkey, All Men are Brothers,* and *The Romance of the Three Kingdoms,* all essentially accounts of revolt against authority, influenced his life and thought profoundly.

By the time he was twelve, Mao was rebelling against his father, most unorthodox in Chinese society. He married at fourteen, but abandoned his wife within the year and enrolled in the Tungshan primary school at Hsianghsiang, his mother's native town. An excellent student noted for the elegance of his essays, Mao entered the Teachers Training School at Changsha in 1913, where he performed well. There he was attracted to the ironical and cynical essays of the brilliant eighth-century philosopher Han Yu. He was to imitate Han Yu's style the rest of his life.

Mao passively watched the famines, turmoil and poverty which afflicted the majority of the Chinese people. During the revolution of 1911 he found himself caught up in events, since Changsha stands at the crossroads of China. He spent a brief time in the revolutionary army. By and large, however, Mao was indistinguishable from thousands of other contemplative students who had little prospect of a successful career.

In 1918 Mao received a small salary as a clerk in the library of Peking University, during which time he had occasion to do a considerable amount of reading. Mao's principal interest was anarchism, and he gradually met others who shared his concern for the plight of the poor. Some of them, Ch'en Tuhsiu, Chang Kuo-t'ao and Li Ta-chao, were impressed by the Russian Revolution and spent much time discussing it with Mao, who listened to them evaluate the prospects for a Communist revolution in China now that the Manchu dynasty had fallen.

In 1921 Mao was invited to attend the first congress of the Chinese Communist party, held in Shanghai. He was apparently impressed by what he learned and observed; from that moment his future was tied to the party, in which he gradually rose to a position of prominence. Mao's chief sympathies remained with the peasant movement in Hunan, however, where he organized local Communist groups and study circles.

In 1925 Mao was made secretary of the propaganda department of the Canton section of the Kuomintang, the official ruling party of the Republic of China set up by Sun Yat-sen in 1911. The boundaries between the Kuomintang and the Communist party were not yet set, and both maintained an anti-imperialist philosophy. Mao also organized Kuomintang-sponsored agricultural and industrial unions, and became the editor of *Political Weekly,* a secret bulletin issued to high members of the Communist party.

Like his revolutionary intellectual counterparts in Europe and Russia, Mao was not satisfied with the evolutionary progress advocated by the Kuomintang. Like Marx and Lenin, he was in a hurry and considered violent revolution the best instrument for rapid and secure change. Also like these forebears, Mao's disposition was to see revolutionary change in his own lifetime, rather than wait through the slow pace of inexorable dialectical laws. The Communist party shared this proclivity, splitting away from the Kuomintang in 1927, and Mao became the head of the party's peasant department with headquarters in Shanghai.

During this period Mao wrote "A Report of an Investigation into the Peasant Movement in Hunan," which called for a peasant insurrection. The report was not inherently Marxist, but espoused the traditional anarchism and violent revolutionary temper of the Hunan peasants who lived a life of degradation and poverty.

In the autumn of 1927 Mao put down his philosophical pen and picked up the sword of revolution. He led what came to be known as the "Autumn Harvest Uprising" in Hunan and Kiangsi, with the goal of capturing Changsha. The results were catastrophic, but in the winter cold of impregnably stark Hunan the Chinese Red Army was born, and the

Communist conquest of China began.

In the spring of 1928, in Chingkanshan, Mao met Chu Teh, whose physical courage and talent for strategy equalled Mao's and forged a bond between the two men which would dominate the Chinese Communist party for twenty years. Four additional attempts were made to capture Changsha. In each case the Red Army was crushed militarily, but with each attempt the army grew in numbers, experience and militarism. The frustration of poverty banished depression from the vacuum created by defeat. The void was instead filled by the politics of desperation, in which the path of least resistance was often the road to violence. Advocacy of violence, or, for some, resignation to it, seem to accompany life on the far side of despair—whether in the French, American or Marxist revolutions. At some point, savagery wreaked on the human spirit warrants tempestuous rage.

Fearing that a fifth campaign might encounter a disastrous defeat, in October 1934 the Red Army army chose flight, breaking through a Kuomintang blockade and beginning what came to be called the "Long March" through southwest China. Bearing the hunger, cold and hardships of travel through unexplored land, the army headed for Shensi province. Nearly a hundred thousand people set out, but after twelve months, covering some six thousand miles through eleven provinces at an average of seventeen miles a day and under almost continuous attack from Nationalist (Kuomintang) forces, only ten percent survived. During the march Mao was elected chairman of the Chinese Communist party.

With the success of the Long March, the prestige of the Chinese Communists grew, even though they failed in attempts to organize Soviet-style councils along the march route itself. At their new base of operations in Yenan, Chu Teh and Mao dominated party strategy and expanded their armies, generating influence out of proportion to their actual strength. They became a formidable force capable of challenging the national government.

In Yenan the pair experimented with guerilla warfare. They tested their techniques against the Japanese, who had invaded China, and against the Kuomintang. Not yet relying much on Karl Marx, Mao personally provided the theoretical justification for violent Communist activities in a series of essays, pamphlets, speeches and handbooks, an approach which he would continue to use once in power.

After World War II the Allies attempted to arrange a truce between the Kuomintang and the Communists. An agreement in principle was even signed between Mao and Chiang Kai-shek in October 1945. The long-awaited civil war erupted anyway, however, and with the fall of Beijing in January 1949 the Communists prepared for a massive attack against the rest of mainland China. By October most of the country had been conquered and Mao was China's undisputed leader. From this point forward, the history of China merged with the history of the Chinese Communist party.

To the rise of godless Communism in China America responded with Christian and Marxist-like anti-intellectualism. While recognizing the exiled Chinese government on the island of Formosa, the United States pretended that mainland China did not exist. Like priests passing judgment on what reality may enter canonical texts, the United States cultivated a theological myopia that wrote China out of its diplomatic bible. For twenty years China was diplomatically apocryphal, until Richard Nixon instituted his version of Vatican II and visited China in 1972.

After the triumph of the Communist revolution, Chu Teh gradually fell into oblivion and Mao rose as "the sun in the east," an appellation of a type not mentioned in the impersonal philosophy of dialectical materialism. Mao's power and abilities as a propagandist enabled him to institute a communal system that abruptly and dramatically altered the structure of China's overwhelmingly peasant society. Many millions died on the road to egalitarian bliss.

While continuing to consolidate power, Mao experimented with different economic reforms, including five-year plans patterned after the Soviet experience. They failed. In an effort to reevaluate his programs, Mao sanctioned in May 1956 a speech by Lu Ting-Yi which promoted the ancient adage, "Let a hundred flowers bloom, and a hundred schools [of thought] contend." This was meant to invite wide participation in the refashioning of government policies, but when the flowers of peasant dissatisfaction "bloomed," they turned out to be cactus thorns pricking the inflated benevolence of Marxist dictatorship. So Mao stopped watering free thought—although it is said he did so only under the duress of widespread party opposition to the Chinese *glasnost*—and put in place a new regime of intellectual drought and repression. During this period, as in former and future times, those who disagreed with Mao often found themselves in the role of fertilizer. Yet, rejecting the Soviet pretension that socialist society is conflict-free, Mao contended that struggle within society is inevitable and stimulates progress.[68]

Centralized bureaucracy, however, so endemic to Communist societies, was shown by the response to the "hundred flowers" speech to have created hostility against the regime which could not be ignored. So Mao attempted to create a decentralized and non-bureaucratic alternative. The first step was a cautious decentralization tied to a reduction in the level of capital accumulation.

Then, in a speech entitled "On the Correct Handling of Contradictions

Among the People," Mao encouraged peasant communities to create their
own industries and to revitalize and modernize their own farms;[69] he also
decided to assist the effort by reducing taxes. In a document not published
at the time, "On the Ten Great Resistances," Mao severely criticized Stalin
and his centralized approach; he was opting for more individual initiative.
This was the beginning of a massive industrialization effort called the
"Great Leap Forward." The communes were given a great deal more
autonomy than those in the Soviet Union, which Mao described as failing
"in thirty years . . . to create a true collective system; all they have done is
to perpetuate the counter-productive exploitation of the landlords."[70] The
Soviet state, of course, was the implied universal landlord.

The Great Leap Forward attempted to expand industry and agriculture by encouraging peasant communities to transform their own lives
by using their own surplus labor, savings and local resources. Donated
labor would be used in water-conservation projects, and to provide consumer goods. The profits would be put back into the communities to
stimulate agricultural productivity. By encouraging local and independent
economic activity, Mao hoped to create a resurgence in the economy and
to avoid falling victim to the trend toward centralized power which
hampered Soviet economic progress and retarded its social development.

The Great Leap Forward failed dramatically. "Its major premise was
that it should be conducted by democratic persuasion, but in spite of
elaborate preparations it was carried on largely by coercion. The authoritarian Communist party inevitably proved to be a poor instrument with
which to conduct a vast democratic movement."[71] The result was a centralized, authoritarian allocation of resources implemented farther down the
economic ladder than ever before. Local cadres were repeatedly compelled to raise production targets and the peasants were coerced into
trying to meet them. In a tragic denouement, just as an exhausted and
demoralized rural labor force was near collapse, bad weather from 1959 to
1961 caused three successive crop failures, bringing the Great Leap Forward to an end.

The experience was nothing new to Marxism: totalitarian central authorities once again inadvertently crushed their own hopes through excessive
coercion. Mao's fears that China would fall into emulation of the Soviet
Union's centralization of power were vindicated, and, as in the Soviet
Union, the economy was in a catastrophic condition. As a result, China's
intellectuals made common cause with the party's right wing; together they
opposed some of Mao's desires. They would pay for their impudence,
however. Mao launched his "Great Proletarian Cultural Revolution" in the
mid-sixties—party leaders were purged and intellectuals were made to
work in the fields to obtain humility and appreciate socialist egalitarianism.

It all came as a surprise, to the West at least. For a while after the disaster of the Great Leap Forward, Mao was subdued. Many Westerners believed him to be ill or in semi-retirement; he was in fact merely evaluating the ideas of the revolution, and in 1966 Mao came back onto center stage. He had renewed his old concern that Chinese socialism would degenerate in the way he believed the Soviet variety had. "In Mao's view, a capitalist restoration had taken place in the Soviet Union . . . Mao dismissed the Soviet leadership not only as revisionist, but also as a right-wing dictatorship."[72] He was particularly upset that the USSR had signed the Nuclear Test Ban Treaty with the United States in 1963, an act which, in Mao's view, was part of a long-term attempt by the "superpowers" to prevent other countries, and particularly China, from developing nuclear capability. To Mao the Soviet leadership had become a revisionist "privileged stratum."

Mao launched the Cultural Revolution to prevent his country from "changing color" too. Increasingly obsessed with a fear of revolutionary degeneration, Mao saw the need for a new wave of revolutionary dynamism. To provide a scriptural inspiration for this theological resurrection he had printed his so-called "Little Red Book," *Quotations of Chairman Mao*, a bible distributed by the army that was reality according to Mao. He then established a gang of young vigilantes, the "Red Guards," who swept across China proclaiming his doctrines—and killing non-believers. Mao's fourth wife, Chiang Ch'ing, a former actress, played the best supporting role of her career by orchestrating much of the repression and bloodshed. The Red Guard movement caused such disruption, however, that by 1967 the government was forced to restrain it.

Disputes with the Soviet Union—over criticism of Stalin, the proper socialist attitude to America, and the nature of Soviet involvement in China (increasingly viewed as "Russian chauvinist")—began in the late 1950s, culminating in a jolting cut-off of Soviet aid in 1960. The full-scale rift was finally revealed to an astonished world when military confrontations flared along the common border. Mao came to consider the Soviets heretical, practicing a perversion of true Marxist doctrine. Perhaps the worst of its supposed sins was that it had grown self-centered; it no longer (in Mao's radical view) adequately fostered international revolution. It was the old debate over "socialism in one country" all over again. In one series of exchanges Mao accused Khrushchev of "kowtowing" to the United States, a charge of strong derision. He thought the United States was only a "paper tiger" to which the Soviet Union was bowing and scraping. Khrushchev responded by pointing out that "unfortunately the U.S. paper tiger has nuclear teeth."

Ironically, by the 1980s it was the Chinese who had revised Marx as never before, embarking on economic programs strongly capitalist in flavor. A front-page story in the foreign-language *China Daily*, published in October 1984 in Beijing, led off with, "Incentives to create new competitive products and improve their quality are to be introduced in China, which is enjoying an industrial boom. The announcement was made by Lu Dong, the country's new Minister in charge of the State Economic Commission."[73] One joke current in China is a proposal to change the name of the Great Wall of China to the Great Mall of China. The Great Wall is increasingly dotted with souvenir shops.

Mao died in 1976, and Chiang Ch'ing was arrested and charged with plotting to overthrow the government. During her defense, Chiang implied that she and Mao *were* the government, an attitude reminiscent of "L'etat, c'est moi." Out of the egalitarian revolution of Marxist socialism was born another class struggle, between the entrenched elements of Marxist authority and the people it claimed to represent. Regardless of where it has been attempted, such struggles have become characteristic of the Marxist experiment.

Following in the footsteps of the Marxist apostles before him, Mao's personal conscience was driven by a belief in the justice of collective control over the nation's resources, natural and man-made. Once obtained, however, collective control led to centralized authority, and ultimately to personal power with Mao at the top of the pyramid. This inevitable accumulation of all-encompassing political and economic power in the hands of a very few seems to be one of the inexorable laws of Marxist governance left unaddressed by its progenitor.

Mao, like other personalities in the history of the impersonal philosophy of Marxism, was enshrined in the pantheon of Marxist gods. However, his ultimate fate was similar to Stalin's. Intra-party struggles, intensified by the need to placate the populace, caused Mao's posthumous decanonization for "excesses," a term we have seen before in reference to the elimination of countless millions of lives on the long march to Marxist nirvana.

In the course of the reading [Pushkin] became more and more melancholy and finally became completely gloomy. When the reading was over he uttered in a voice of sorrow: "Goodness, how sad is our Russia!"
—Nikolai Gogol, *Four Letters Concerning Dead Souls*

V

A Case Study: The Russian National Inferiority Complex

While the metaphysical basis of Karl Marx's philosophy contains irreconcilable contradictions, fallacious historical assumptions and predictions long disproved, its call for violent action appeals to the desperation of the poor, the frustration of emotionally undisciplined intellectuals, and the opportunism of ambitious politicians in need of a convenient, revolutionary ideology. Russia contained many people in each of these categories. So, contrary to Marx's claim that proletarian triumphs could only take place in industrial societies, the agrarian economy of Russia proved to be the first testing ground of his theories. The Russian people would be forced to lay on the Procrustean bed of Marxism, where they would be tortured into conforming to history's latest conception of utopia. (The second place of experiment was agricultural China, similarly nonindustrial. It should thus be irrefutable that Marxism is a political battle cry, not a valid science of history.)

The egalitarian result in Russia (China is a somewhat different case) would be a redistribution, but not of wealth. Instead there was an allocation of poverty, deprivation, torture and death by starvation or firing squad. The Russian experiment would also demonstrate Marx's almost complete misperception of the role of human nature in history. While Christians preached that man did not live by bread alone, the Marxists would see to it that Russian agriculture did not produce enough bread for many of its members to live at all.

Not only was Russian society not suited to Marxist economic principles, the Russian temperament was not receptive to certain aspects of Marxist ideology. The concept of the dictatorship of the proletariat—in the sense of rule by a class as a whole—was alien to Russian psychology, which traditionally evidenced the need for a strong ruler, a "little father," a pope one might say. It was unlikely from the start that Marx's prediction of rule by the working class would be interpreted in a democratic way. The concept of anything other than a steeply angled hierarchy of political power—alive only in societies that possessed a strongly independent nobility or large mercantile and professional classes with (economically based) notions of personal freedom—went against the grain of Russian political history. Russians were long used to near-absolute rule by a single figure, the czar, a tradition which Marxist leaders would hasten to accommodate.

Perhaps the most important trait in the Russian national character— quite specifically not a trait of the other nations that make up the Soviet Union—is its highly developed sense of national inferiority. Early evidence lies in Russia's mythical origins. The people of the land of Rus', it is written, invited foreigners to rule them because they did not feel competent to govern themselves. Indeed, many Russian rulers, such as Polish-born Catherine the Great, were also foreigners. Later, European architects were imported to design many of Russia's most famous buildings. As early as the 1720s Peter the Great considered a "window to the West," access to the world of modern ideas and economic practices, as essential to the development of Russia.

The Russian national inferiority complex is actuated by the country's long-held, ambivalent attitude to the West, its ruling class both wishing to take an active part in the affairs of Europe and its culture, and at the same time zealously protective of the Russian national character and fearful of transformation by Western cultural influences. Economic and cultural inferiority and an intense awareness of it have in Russia alternately stimulated efforts to improve areas of deficiency and prompted mental retreat into national isolation, even paranoia. In the modern period, a curious combination of both responses to the West has arisen, as we shall see.

Compared to the history of Western Europe (and later the United States) Russia has always been scientifically, technologically, and artistically backward. The attempts to remedy these national deficiencies has often impelled it to acquire the knowledge of the West, whether through importing ideas and expertise openly, or, in the modern period, by espionage. When actual inferiority created an "inferiority complex," however, attempts were made to rationalize or camouflage that inferiority. There were turns to paranoia or to condemnations of the values of the West. Peter the Great, Russia's most well-known and most powerful exponent of openness to Europe, faced the strongest domestic challenge to his rule from countrymen opposed to contamination by the decadent nations of the West.

It is a question of the stability of existing power relationships. Those behind in technological or intellectual processes rightfully see in change a threat to the lines of authority with which they are familiar. Observation of areas more advanced leaves no doubt about the character of those changes. However long they may have taken to occur, the threat of change is amplified by its material reality. By the eighteenth century no Russian priest could fail to have noted the erosion of religious power in the West. Likewise the Russian nobility surely noted in the West the rise in influence of classes other than aristocratic. Like religious authority, national ruling classes commonly attempt to maintain "purity"—the status quo of existing lines of social and political power—by denigrating or prohibiting alien ideas.

This is nowhere more the case than in the Soviet Union. It is a nation that is unable to take much advantage from the clear cost-effectiveness of computers, for example, because the accompanying easy dissemination of information (inseparable from the efficiency that makes them valuable) threatens the tight control over information which is the basis of state authority. Because that authority is so pervasive, innovation in industry, academia, art—in nearly any area of human activity—is hindered, even foreclosed. A sense of inferiority (the observation of superiority elsewhere, with a consequent diminishment of sense of self-worth) can infinitely retard what would have been natural improvement, can provoke ever more stubborn retreats into dogma.

Russia is an historical case study of national schizophrenia. On the one hand it has often recognized deficiencies and sought to remedy them. On the other hand, an operative inferiority complex has militated against acknowledgment of Western superiority and the adoption of Western ideas that would solve problems best. This is true of the Soviet Union today, regardless of the fact that its social and political structure, the product of the most sweeping transformation of a society ever known, was born largely of Western ideas.

Like other religions, Marxism provides a rationalization for preserving its purity from foreign contamination; with this theological psychology, the Soviet Union can also assert that it is morally superior to its capitalist rivals. In fact, it is driven to do so: as psychologists tell us, a sense of superiority is often a defensive manifestation of an inferiority complex. The subject feels required to prove superiority.

Perhaps it seems strange to ascribe to governments the psychological characteristics of individuals. There is some evidence for it in this case, however. For example, in initial weapons treaties with the United States, the Soviets curiously demanded provisions indicating a recognition of the USSR as "equal" to America. Somehow the existence of the treaties themselves was not sufficient proof of it.

This sense of inferiority is manifested not only in Soviet foreign policy, but also in various aspects of domestic affairs. The Soviet educational system, for example, is rife with catechizing and mendacity. The Soviets teach that Popov invented the radio, not Marconi; that Yablochkov invented what they call the "edison lamp"—a linguistic irony if ever there was one; that Ivanenko discovered the neutron, not the British scientist Chadwick; that the steam engine was invented by Cherepanov, not Robert Fulton.[1] The Great Soviet Encyclopedia is sometimes more accurate than the Soviet teachers, but sometimes also chauvinistically deceptive.

Clearly part of the Soviet Union's organized mendacity is in accordance with Marxist-Leninist philosophy—that any method can be used to promote the revolution. Mendacity is one of the avowed principles of Marxism. The process is facilitated in the USSR, however, because of what seems to be an inherent need, almost childish, to invent "facts" or create stories to bolster the Soviet ego.

Any visitor to the Soviet Union is struck by constant and needless lies, even pertaining to subjects which are unimportant. Foreign visitors to Peter's palace near Leningrad are told by the Intourist guides that more than 20 percent of the citizens of Leningrad have weekend homes in the surrounding forest. It so happens that the forest is not large enough to accommodate weekend homes for half a million people. Secondly, the citizens of Leningrad are lucky if they have a nice regular home, let alone a weekend one. It goes without saying that in Soviet foreign policy such a tendency to deceit is dangerous, making it difficult to trust the USSR in treaty negotiations.

The character of the Soviet ruling class is foreign to us for reasons more deeply rooted than its different form of government. Its Marxism is colored by a long history of religious and tyrannical experience. Hundreds of years of the religious impulse to aggression and war, conjoined intermittently with equally ages-old state imperialism and abuse of human rights, have like two symbiotic spirals evolved to form a single, indivisible entity in our own time. It is no accident that this unfortunate historical union took root in Russia. Its experience of secular and religious tyranny had been intertwined for almost a thousand years.

Origins

The Russian Primary Chronicle, edited in the twelfth century and one of the earliest of Russian historical texts, begins with the expressed ambition of revealing "the origins of the land of Rus'." Having no documentation on the distant past, the chroniclers proceeded to record what appears to be saga or myth, a tradition continued by Russian historians down to the present.

According to the Chronicle, around 860 some east Slav tribes extended an invitation to three Varangian Scandinavian brothers, Ryurik, Sineus and Truvor, to come to the land of the Rus' to govern them: "Our whole land is great and rich, but there is no order in it. Come to rule and reign over us."[2]

It is unclear whether the brothers came from Denmark or Sweden, or what kind of wealth made the land of the Rus' "great and rich." Archaeology supports the notion of agricultural wealth, whereas literary sources suggest the riches came from trade. The new Varangian overlords apparently imposed order by taxation, assuring in the process their own compensation, of course. They sought to increase prosperity by opening new trade routes and by extending and safeguarding existing ones. The principal route was the Dnieper-Black Sea passage "from the Varangians to the Greeks" that connected Scandinavia with the legendary riches of Constantinople. The significance of the Chronicle is that it claims the need for order as the origin of Russia, order secured by the importation of dictators "to rule and reign over us." Throughout the centuries and down to the present day, Russians have evidenced that need for a strong ruler.

Two of Ryurik's associates, Askol'd and Dir, seized the town of Kiev very early on and used it as a base of operations to launch an attack on Constantinople, the first recorded act of Russian aggression against another territory. In 882 Askol'd and Dir met their death at the instigation of Ryurik, perhaps to curtail their ambitions.

The Byzantines took defensive measures, one of which was to curtail Russia's expansionist impulses by introducing its leaders to Christianity. Many Christians were already in the region, due to the efforts of the Greek missionaries Cyril (died 869) and Methodius (died 885), who are credited with both introducing Christianity to Russia and providing the Slavs with their first written language. The alphabet was patterned after the Greek and called, after its sponsor, the Cyrillic alphabet.

Religion

Man is a pliable animal, a being who gets accustomed to everything.
—Fyodor Mikhailovich Dostoevski, *The House of the Dead*

In 945 a group of local people, the Drevlians, rose in resentment against the ruler of Kiev, Igor, who had levied exceptionally heavy taxes. Igor was slain in the uprising and his wife, Ol'ga, responded by killing the

Drevlian envoys, burning down their town and putting five thousand of its inhabitants to death. Then Ol'ga converted to Christianity, being by disposition obviously attracted to the teachings of the Prince of Peace (and incidentally solidifying trade relations with Constantinople), and was christened under the sponsorship of the Byzantine emperor himself. This laid part of the foundation for what was destined to become the official religion of Russia.

Ol'ga's grandson, Vladimir (died 1015), expanded Christianity's influence in Russia in the tenth century. Although he fostered a pagan revival, Vladimir also recognized that his country's political and economic welfare depended upon conversion to one of the principal faiths: Christianity or Islam. Vladimir chose the former. Islam's proscription against alcohol, which Vladimir called "the joy of the Rus'," was one of the reasons he opted against that faith.

Negotiations with Constantinople, to expand trade and minimize war, led to Vladimir's marriage to the emperor's sister in 989. The precondition of the marriage was his baptism into the Christian faith. Russia's ruling elite quickly followed suit, and in turn forced their new religion of peace on the people they ruled by whatever means necessary. At times these included razing whole villages. Russia absorbed a fully developed Christian tradition from the Byzantine world and accepted the leadership of Constantinople in religious affairs.

Centuries later, when Kiev was sacked by the Mongols, Metropolitan Maksim (died 1305), the head of the church, transferred his residence to the city of Vladimir. For reasons which remain obscure, his successor, Peter (died 1326) moved to the then insignificant town of Moscow in 1325, perhaps to remove the church from government domination. It would prove to be a futile effort. The Mongol invasions encouraged a shift of Russian power to the north, and the government eventually moved to Moscow as well.

The Russian ruling class was growing impatient with Byzantine control over the church. The temporary reunion of the churches of Rome and Constantinople, brought about at the Council of Basel-Ferrara-Florence (1438–39), provided the excuse for a split. Secular power had much to do with this development. Metropolitan Isidor had attended the unification council and agreed with the plan to unite Rome and Constantinople, but on his return to Russia the grand prince of Moscow imprisoned him. The church priesthood, foregoing any consultation with Constantinople, elected one of its own to the metropolitanate. The Russian Orthodox Church became religiously if not politically independent. The Russian government would forever remain a dominating, often determining influence. During the sixteenth century, the church became "ever more closely identified with the State,"³ despite the establishment of the nominally independent church hierarchy. Even that formal independence was not to last long. In his first year of rule (1721) Peter the Great abolished the distinction between the Russian church and state. The merger of the symbiotic spirals of theological and secular imperialism took a giant step forward. This identity became almost cultural in nature, making it easier in the twentieth century for the Communist party, essentially a theological organization, to become indistinguishable from the Soviet government.

Censorship muted the few voices protesting the political subjugation of the church in the nineteenth century. By 1914 the Russian Orthodox Church possessed 73 dioceses, 54,174 churches (and a comparable number of chapels), 1025 monastic foundations, 291 hospitals, and 35,528 parish schools,⁴ but it was unable to achieve the right to govern its own affairs. The czar and the government remained the final authority, evidencing Russia's tradition of centralized power over the totality of Russian life—the distinguishing feature of totalitarian rather than merely authoritarian rule. Throughout Europe czarism was synonymous with tyranny in this period.

During the period of bourgeois revolution in 1917 the church was officially separated from the state. It was, of course, a short-lived change in affairs. The newly independent leadership issued encyclicals maintaining that the new leaders of Russia acted "in a manner contrary to the conscience of the people." Response was swift. While upholding the separation of church and state, a government decree of January 23, 1918, legitimized the confiscation of church property. Bolshevik attempts at destabilization followed. The government sponsored a schism by supporting a reform movement within the church. After a brief period of struggle, the church patriarch was arrested and the reformers put a Bolshevik supporter, Metropolitan Alexander Vvedensky, in his place.

The subjugation of the church by avowed atheists was facilitated by the church's age-old subservience to the state. But what of the response of the mass of devout church-goers? For centuries the Russian church had indoctrinated its congregation with the need for unquestioned theological acceptance of things as they were, in secular as well as spiritual affairs. The priesthood had long served the state, and the landholding class that dominated it, as inculcators of passivity in the face of the direst oppression. In the revolutionary films of Sergei Eisenstein, Orthodox priests are justifiably treated even more viciously than capitalists and the aristocratic officers of the White armies, if such a thing can be conceived. As the church experienced its death throes, the chickens came home to roost, both in terms of the viciousness of those who had long observed its rank hypocrisy and in the passivity of those who might have considered defending it against the Bolshevik onslaught.

The complete merging of religion and state would merely continue, however. The substitution of a new religion, Marxism, and a new church, the Communist party, was merely a slight change in the coloration of a tradition nearly as old as Russia itself.

In 1929 Stalin issued a decree essentially in force to this day that required every religious association to be registered with the secular authorities. In the process, the government would gain some measure of control over the financial affairs and the administrative structure; otherwise the permission to operate would not be granted. The clergy became subject to punitive taxation, through special assessments, faced curtailment of various civil rights such as participating in central government affairs, and were sometimes even deprived of ration cards.[5]

Since the Communist government has a theoretical mandate to provide for the people, it is often considered seditious for other organizations or even individuals to usurp that role by providing "material assistance" such as charity. This government monopoly on welfare is also a tool of control, compelling people to rely upon authorities for aid. Under Stalin's decree, religious associations were expressly prohibited from providing material assistance to their members; the effect was to further weaken church influence.

Repression of church activities was also common. Psychiatric institutions became familiar locations of confinement for religious stalwarts, particularly dissidents, who, it was contended, must have a mental disorder. Although there may be some truth in that contention, the Soviets apparently fail to perceive that believers in Marxism suffer from a similar psychological affliction.

Later in 1929, the right to issue any sort of religious propaganda was tacitly withdrawn: "freedom of religion" was altered to "freedom of worship." This meant that religious associations were no longer allowed to proselytize, or to issue public rebuttals of official anti-religious propaganda. The 1936 constitution restored civil rights to the clergy, but religious propaganda was made officially unconstitutional. (The revised constitution of 1977 continued these restrictions.) In the 1930s monasteries not already confiscated were dissolved and churches were drastically reduced in number. The number of clergy imprisoned is inestimable.

With the outbreak of World War II, the church made a patriotic appeal for its believers to come to the defense of the motherland. Stalin eased some restrictions on the church in order to expand its ability to support the war effort. Throughout the war churches were reopened and many of the clergy were allowed to resume their diocesan duties. By 1944 an Orthodox theological college was inaugurated in Moscow for the first time since the 1920s. It was followed within a few years by nine others.

The church regained influence, but the principal precondition of the concordat achieved under Stalin was the church's steadfast support of Soviet foreign policy.

Under Khrushchev concessions to the church made by Stalin were questioned. This was not because Stalin's early years in the seminary were seen to have influenced his judgment, but because growing church influence was again becoming a social force and increasingly viewed as unacceptable by the authorities. Khrushchev was willing to allow some new freedom in literary expression, but did not want organized religious institutions to experience any similar renaissance. Between 1958 and 1964, under one pretext or another, two-thirds of the Orthodox churches were closed, as well as 70 percent of the theological schools. Most of the monasteries were again dissolved.

The elderly Patriarch Lekay, apart from a protest speech in 1960, remained silent while Soviet authorities instituted the forced contraction of his church and imprisoned and tortured clergy and believers. With Khrushchev's fall in 1964, religious persecution was tempered, but no revival of church institutions was instituted.

The number of traditional religious faithful in the USSR is estimated to be in the tens of millions for the Orthodox church; there is thought to be an inestimable number of believers in other, smaller denominations. Religion remains a potent, albeit repressed force in the Soviet Union. At the bar of history, the religious tradition in Russia will be judged for the servile disposition it fostered in the Russian mentality. The Russian government always kept people hungry, and the Russian church always kept people humble. The resultant subservient psychology paved the way for the acceptance of Marxism.

The Soviet Economy

Ivan Ilych's life had been most simple and most ordinary and therefore most terrible.

—Leo Tolstoi

By the nineteenth century Russia's borders had reached the proportions of an empire. Internally, its economy had remained backward relative to those of Western Europe, which had experienced the Industrial Revolution. Russia's main source of income and wealth came from agriculture and artisan industries.

The seventeenth century had seen the beginning of a business economy in Russia, as industry expanded in response to trade with the Dutch and the British. Although the government officially encouraged these nascent industries and entrepreneurship, it also taxed them heavily. The most lucrative goods in the economy were preempted by the government itself, thereby discouraging steady growth. This is a pattern which continues in our era.

The military ambitions of Peter the Great served as an impetus to Russian economic development, but it had to be sustained. In the eighteenth century Russia was the world's largest single exporter of iron ore and it also had a virtual monopoly on the international trade in flax, hemp and tar.

After several wars, Russia gained access to the Black Sea at the expense of the Ottoman Empire, thereby opening foreign markets to its export of grain. Unable to compete with the industrialized societies of Europe, Russia did not focus on developing its technology. Accordingly, it remained (as it has to this day) technologically backward. It adopted instead the role of supplier of foodstuffs and primary products to the industrial countries. Agricultural output expanded dramatically, but this was due to area expansion rather than improved farming techniques.

In industry Russia was not idle, however. The period between 1799 and 1858 saw manufacturing output grow forty times, becoming about 15 percent of the gross national product.[6] Industries did not continue to expand as rapidly as in Europe, however, and by 1859 only 7 percent of the population lived in cities. In Britain the figure was 50 percent and in France, 25 percent.[7] Agriculture and serfdom remained the face of Russia.

State support stimulated economic growth in the eighteenth century, but also brought excessive government involvement in the economy. This crowded out private enterprise and caused many commercial judgments to be made on non-economic grounds—a problem which would become the hallmark of the Soviet economy as well. Poor-quality soil, the dominance of winter and the distant location of many resources were always central problems for Russian economic development. Military growth, whether under the czars or the Marxists, also continued to drain resources away from domestic savings and capital formation.

With the emancipation of the serfs in 1861 by Alexander II, modern Russia was born. Nearly twenty-two million serfs were freed, approximately 40 percent of the population. In the Marxist view of history, such developments are indicators of a transition from feudalism to capitalism, and indeed, a hope that more rapid industrialization would follow was Alexander's motivation. On the eve of World War I Russian industrial employment and output had more than tripled. The economic development was skewed, however. Large companies accounted for the overwhelming bulk of industry while agriculture and the artisan trades remained small scale.

With the advent of railways, foreign capital was attracted to lay track and construct rail facilities in Russia. The result was substantial Russian management training and the opening of vast areas to the possibilities of a market economy. The railroads then became the collateral for development loans. The transportation and export of grain in particular was facilitated. Spurred by the revolutionary uprising of 1905, government reforms further stimulated agricultural output and allowed the peasants to receive internal passports without the consent of the communes, which after the emancipation had replaced nobles as governors of peasant life. This allowed them to travel more freely and found new farms.

World War I saw an increase in industrial output, primarily due to vastly higher production in the armaments industry. The civilian standard of living continued to improve through 1916,[8] but the war caused withdrawals of labor from farming to the army. As the war dragged on, the effects began to be felt—by 1917 there was a food crisis approaching famine. "Bread!" was the sole shout at numerous revolutionary gatherings. Some historians have called the food shortage the chief economic factor behind the revolution.[9]

Three years of civil war following the Bolshevik overthrow of Nicholas exacerbated an already disastrous situation. Agricultural output did not recover to its pre-war level until 1927,[10] but the country has never again been self-sufficient in agriculture.

Industrial output was in similar straits. Lenin nationalized one company after another; by late 1920 all industry had been expropriated. The result: industrial output stood at less than one-fourth of the pre-war level.[11] The banks were seized as well. The Soviet economic system from June 1918 to March 1921 is known in retrospect as "war communism"—the monetary system was virtually destroyed by monstrous inflation. The number of rubles in 1920 alone multiplied five times, all chasing an ever-declining output of goods. The Bolsheviks were gleeful over this state of affairs. Trotsky's principal economist, E. A. Preobrazhensky, characterized the inflationary pressures as "the machine-gun of the Commissariat of Finance, attacking the bourgeois system in the rear and using the currency laws of that system to destroy it."[12] Rationing, an economy of barter, and trade in "labor units" emerged. The Bolshevik party had demonstrated its revolutionary economic wisdom by destroying the Russian economy.

With the introduction of government confiscations of farm produce, the peasants began to revolt against a centralized economy. Lenin secured a Central Committee resolution criticizing Trotsky (nothing, of course, could be Lenin's fault) and then introduced his New Economic Policy, which included currency reform and most important were a revised banking system to control money supply. Most important were economic decrees of August and December 1921 that handed back "so much property to private owners that only 8.5 percent of industrial enterprises remained nationalized," although they employed more than 80 percent of the work force. As Lenin said, the party continued to control the "commanding heights" of the economy.[13]

The economy was a shambles. The evolutionary gains made in the previous centuries were severely damaged by World War II, and then Marxism's impatient call for violent revolution nearly destroyed them. The economy would never be the same.

Economic equality was the professed political goal of Soviet Marxism. Under Lenin it justified whatever violence was deemed necessary. Under Stalin, economics was subordinated to personal ambitions, becoming simply another tool of oppression to further Stalin's ever-greater concentration of political power and the gratification of his pretensions to intellect. Under post-Stalin Soviet leaders, economics has become the instrument for accelerating the country's military expansion internationally. The Soviet economy was expected by Communist leaders to become a model the world could emulate. Since the Bolsheviks took over in 1917, however, it has been only a model of ineptitude; its survival is based on police repression, its "success" on smoke and mirrors.

The Soviet economy is beset by low labor productivity (ranked twenty-fifth among industrial countries in the 1970s);[14] poor quality products (virtually a joke on the international market as well as the butt of jokes in the Soviet Union itself); management inefficiency (decisions are usually made for ideological rather than business reasons); indecipherable accounting (there are only the most primitive cost vs. profit controls); and unimaginable purchasing practices (materials and goods are often adulterated or stolen, or removed from one plant to another by whichever plant manager has greater influence in the Communist party). To add to this economic stew, the military often commandeers what it needs in total disregard of a factory's quotas. Planning in the USSR is an organizational nightmare. The country's only real gain after a half-century of bloody upheaval has been the creation of an image of equality with the United States at the expense of the reality of poor economic progress.

Soviet Agriculture

During the 1930s the small-peasant structure of Soviet agriculture was transformed into one of large socialized units with slightly varying degrees of state control ("autonomous collectives" are nominally more independent than "state farms"). Like all Marxist-Leninist governments, the Soviet state required farmers to produce food for the urban classes at state-controlled prices. The aim was overt: the appropriation of peasant wealth to provide the capital accumulation necessary for rapid industrialization. It was frank emulation of the practices of early capitalist development, but greatly sped up and consequently carried out at the price of far greater rural misery. The Soviet effort was also less successful. The peasants of early nineteenth-century England were gradually forced into a market economy through the conversion of rent payments from in-kind to cash, and the gradual removal of ages-old privileges (such as the grazing of livestock on lands owned by the nobility) on which many English peasants depended for their margin of subsistence. Once forced to market their produce to survive, the peasants were at the mercy of that market. Unrestrained competition of farm goods, as we know, leads generally to disastrous declines in the price of those products. In England this meant crushing poverty for small producers, but production was high. The free market, in effect, transferred agricultural wealth to the urban centers in ways about as fair as highway robbery and far less socially just.

Soviet forced collectivization and state pricing would not have the same effect. With the revolutionary abolition of rents, Soviet peasants were not at the mercy of market forces. Naturally they had no incentive to produce for anyone but themselves. In the 1920s and 1930s, the state would respond by marching in and seizing production. Many peasants starved as a result, but "surplus" production—that beyond the producer's subsistence which could be given to the cities—was hardly encouraged in the process. The question was how to trick the state, not how to produce enough to survive. The brutality of forced collectivization served as a disincentive to agricultural production, while the brutality of merciless competitive pricing had acted as a spur to it.

Redistribution of wealth to the cities assured a more quiescent working class—the class featured in Marx's economic philosophy—but created disastrous declines in agricultural production. The farmers were made to pay for the social equality Marx predicted for the industrial class. Despite its preoccupation with economic history and an alleged idealism that flowed from studying it, Soviet economic policy in this period emulated the repressive patterns of primitive capitalism. The ruthless force used to implement this conception of economic progress cost millions of lives. Peasant uprisings were frequent.

Because of the accumulated disincentives of Marxist policies and the devastation during World War II of the nation's breadbasket, the Ukraine, Soviet food production took until 1953 to regain the output of 1928[15]—and only with the help of forced labor, which was understandably less efficient than individual initiative. Official statistics published in March 1975 "revealed that 27 percent of the total value of Soviet farm output—about $32.5 billion a year—comes from private plots that occupy less than one percent of the nation's agricultural lands (about 20 million acres). At that rate, private plots are roughly 40 times as efficient as land worked collectively."[16]

The disastrous state of agricultural production in the USSR is usually attributed to the collectivization policies imposed on the farmers and to the delay in the development of agricultural science, which was hampered by the application of Marxist dogma to biology and genetics. T. D. Lysenko (1898–1976) was an agronomist of peasant extraction with political instincts and a fanatical faith in his intuition for agronomic panaceas. In conformance with a general Marxist emphasis on environmental rather than hereditary or psychological determinants in human history, Lysenko attempted to prove that animals and even plants could be trained to take on characteristics that would be passed on genetically. He created the term "vernalization" to describe the process of moistening and chilling seeds before planting. The hope was that wheat seeds so treated, for example, would produce hardier winter wheat. The term eventually referred to any form of seed treatment and for an imaginary period of plant development. The full exploration of ideologically derived "insights" was an essential Soviet tenet, because careful statistical testing was in official disfavor, viewed by the authorities as the "bourgeois specialist's" way of subverting revolutionary enthusiasm. Any scientist who challenged Lysenko's theoretical model was accused of separating Marxist theory from Soviet practice.

By the mid-1930s Soviet authorities were convinced that Lysenko had created a distinct Soviet science, based upon the philosophy of Marx, called "agrobiology." It was also sometimes called Michurinism, after the plant breeder I. V. Michurin (1855–1935). This new "science" was hailed as an advance on "bourgeois" plant physiology and genetics. In 1948, Lysenko's theories were ordained as orthodox by the Central Committee, and the study of other genetic theories was officially curtailed (an approach not dissimilar to the Catholic church's doctrinaire view of evolution).

Although Lysenko's theories and biological innovations may have conformed to a Soviet interpretation of Marxist metaphysics, they suffered one major shortcoming: the plants themselves subscribed to the physical laws of nature. Agricultural production declined.

Lysenko began to encounter opposition in 1956, most importantly from Nikita Khrushchev. Although Khrushchev was unable to curtail all of Lysenko's duties, empirical facts gradually overpowered orthodoxy. After Khrushchev's removal from office, statistical studies of Lysenko's theories were made, such as the carefully monitored training of cows to determine predicted improvement in their meat and milk yields. The results were utterly conclusive: training brought about no measurable changes in later generations of plant and animal life. Although Lysenko was relegated to the status of theologian emeritus, his theories of biology and agriculture were unceremoniously disregarded after 1965.

Soviet agricultural policy thus included collective farms, government usurpation of farm production, and biological genetics based upon Marxist theology. The combined result was that Soviet farm production was set back a quarter of a century.[17] The farmers, disenchanted with Marxist wisdom from its earliest days, declined to completely cooperate with the authorities and often had private sales of part of their harvest; as a result, students and soldiers were conscripted to plant and harvest "collective" crops. This remains government policy today.

The millions of people who died during the Stalinist period, either because of resistance to forced collectivization or by starvation caused by disastrously flawed planning, were merely another statistic in the Marxist experiment. It should be remembered that the application of theology to economic and political life has also killed millions of people under the rule of Christianity, Islam and Judaism. Why should Marxism have operated differently?

Industry

Soviet industry is technologically backward, managerially inept and plagued with labor problems. Some of the difficulties in these areas are attributable to the Russian character, but most are the direct result of the application of Marxist metaphysics to management. The centralized planning system often leads to allocation of resources according to political influence rather than economic value, and generally emphasizes the quantity rather than the quality of output. The wage system lacks incentives to produce quantity or quality (*de facto* job security is so pervasive that employees face little sanction for even the poorest of work), and dispiriting social conditions in and out of the workplace lead to some of the highest rates of alcoholism, absenteeism, and impaired job performance in the industrialized world.

Ironically, under Marxism the workers have not achieved the economic level of members of Western labor unions. Things haven't all come up turnips for workers in Marxist societies, however. In Communist states everyone is entitled to a job, and it is almost impossible to terminate workers unless they are dissidents or Jews hoping to emigrate. This is not the unique advance in human history touted by Marxist propaganda, however. Unemployment safety nets in most of Western Europe provide equal protection (if not, for those who are unemployed, an equal sense of self-worth), and provide it in the context of vastly better living standards for all those who do have jobs.

The toleration of poor job performance and the nearly complete lack of effective work incentives would have less of an impact on industrial productivity if planners regularly invested in more efficient (that is, higher technology) machinery. This is hardly the case. Even agriculture, the most nettlesome hindrance to Soviet economic advance and the sector that would show the most spectacular gains in productivity if sweepingly mechanized, is consistently left in the relative economic dark ages. Soviet economist V. Kirichenko has acknowledged in print that as late as 1970 "more than 80 percent of work in the socialized farm sector was still done by hand."[18] Various estimates indicate that more than 50 percent of Soviet industrial machinery dates back to World War II and before.[19] Travelers to the Soviet Union see the ubiquitous abacus in stores, but seldom, if ever, a cash register. In a speech of June 19, 1986, Soviet Prime Minister Nikolai Ryzhkov was reported to note that "only 29 percent of the engineering products made here are up to international standards."[20] As for the country's other products, visitors to the Soviet Union, economists of both the West and the Eastern bloc, and the poor reception given Soviet products in the international market place all attest that they are of similar or worse quality.

The Marxist-Leninists call their approach to macro-management "centralized planning." They believe they can forecast the needs and desires of the population and produce the manufactured items to fill those needs. For the Marxist the concept of micro-management does not exist in a business sense; what passes for it operates largely as political-ideological supervision intended to control the workers. Hence workers are promoted for party loyalty, not industrial efficiency. Centralized planning, it is believed, enables the state to set priorities, in order to give preference to items deemed essential, such as food, housing and medical care. Other items, including even such basics as clothing and certainly almost all amenities (a word not really found in the Marxist economic dictionary), take second place to necessities. (In the realm of Soviet necessities, one of the most emphasized is weaponry, both to equip the domestic military and police with arms to keep the restless population under control—presumably until the "withering away of the state" comes to pass—and to promote international revolution. So important are weapons to the Soviet economy that they have become the second most important export to the non-Communist world after gas and oil.[21] We will return to this central element of the Soviet economic system.)

One of the main problems with central planning, especially the dictatorial Communist variety, is that it ignores the economic will of the people. The citizenry has no power to choose washing machines over nuclear missiles, less cramped apartments over extra divisions on the Chinese border. Even the inexpensive, small satisfactions in life, a choice of fashions or knickknacks for the coffee table, go unprovided because there is no effective mechanism for determining which such items are wanted. Marx's vision of the full socialist, or communist, society assumed a world in which consumer desires had little range beyond food, housing and medical security, the pressing needs of his day. In the society of Marx's hopes, it is reasonable to presume, there would be no marketing, since everyone would be aware of product availability; sales and purchases might even be replaced by merely satisfying a person's needs—money and wages might be supplanted by official certificates entitling a person to acquire what he needs; material incentives would not exist and there would be no desire for varying kinds of products except those provided. Everything needed (need defined mostly in the terms of material existence rather than social, psychological or aesthetic possibility) would be in abundance.

Unaddressed by centrally planned, as opposed to market, economies is the fact that people have widely varying desires and tastes. Some people may want to have red clothing and black shoes, others may prefer combinations of black and blue. Unlike Marxist ideology, Soviet dress (when available) is unadorned. Should specifically desired items appear in Soviet shops, one must have the good luck to know it, and to buy them before they are sold out. The Soviet system, to date, has created consumer equality largely by having a scarcity of everything. The result is that everyone is unhappy—except the ruling elite and the military.

The Marxist labor theory of value is of little help in a centrally planned economy. On the contrary, it is a contradiction. Labor-value theory relates exchange values to human effort, but exchange value in a planned economy is arbitrary; state-determined prices are set according to relative perceived necessity—and not a little bit according to whim. As a result, labor expended has only an indirect relation to exchange value. Furthermore, goods produced in the Soviet Union, whatever their labor or exchange values, are often of no interest to the consumer because they are poorly constructed or unbearably ugly. The consumer may nonetheless be forced to buy such goods, say, obviously leaky galoshes, because there is a general shortage of them—but only in the rainy season. Their "value" can become a contrived one. The most fundamental Marxist doctrine, the "labor theory of value," has been repressed in Soviet practice—like much in Marxist doctrine that is inconvenient to implement, or at odds with the needs of the ruling elite.

Another contradictory aspect of central planning afflicts the USSR; such planning requires huge inputs of information in order to even hope to operate well. But information is of course a dangerous commodity in the Soviet Union. Information is accordingly so closely held that even the officials who need it are often denied access to it. This causes the most problems in the areas of economic and demographic statistics—the major information needs of central planners. Central planning requires the identification of various social patterns and trends, and statistical analyses of ethnic, religious and economic groups in order to best address their problems and needs.

But dissemination of this kind of information widely enough to put it to best use is threatening to a totalitarian elite. Dissidents could gain valuable knowledge on the location and needs (and therefore discontents) of potential constituencies; they might then use this knowledge to foment social unrest.

Hence such data is kept excessively secret by the Soviet regime, with disastrous implications for social and economic planning. Statistics must be disseminated in order to subject them to continuous critical review for the purpose of verifying and updating them. Without such frequent analysis, central planners are unable to discern growth patterns, changing attitudes, or the evolution of social problems and needs. To attempt to plan an economy without highly developed statistical analysis, particularly in an economy where central planning prevails, is like trying to forecast the weather from the bottom of a well. The Soviet Union has accordingly deprived itself of a fundamental tool of economic planning, exaggerating the already inherent difficulties of centralized economic control. Centralized planning without statistics is almost a logical contradiction—not unlike other logical contradictions in Soviet society.

Soviet paranoia about control of information naturally extends to computers, the area of greatest advance in economic efficiency in the modern period. Although the government naturally desires to use computers as much as possible in the military, it has been very reluctant to introduce them in the areas of business and education where they produce the most economic benefits. Wide access to the easy production and exchange of information is threatening. The economic consequences of such policy are obvious, and they will increase in severity as the West races ahead in the "information age." On the macro-economic level, an unwillingness to fully exploit the power of the computer could be even more debilitating. In the modern age, even wide availability of information can be useless without the ability to process it. How terrible must be the dilemma of lower-level Soviet planners faced with masses of incomplete statistics and machinery little advanced from the abacus to digest them. It is undoubtedly safe to say that Soviet restrictions on information result in tens of billions of dollars in economic inefficiencies.

The Underground Economy

Since in the USSR the government owns all means of production, the state is one giant conglomerate, controlling all processes of manufacturing and distribution. Legislation on "economic crime" prohibits individuals from buying and selling for profit or to employ anyone to make goods for sale. In reality these laws are not obeyed by the population or enforced by the government. There is a large black market which is generally tolerated by the authorities. Any visitor to the USSR will be accosted on the street by Soviet citizens, often youths, offering to buy jeans, shoes, and even pencils produced in the West.

For the most part these buyers will resell the items at a profit. They even buy and sell the ruble, the Soviet currency, for less than a quarter of the official price. Entrepreneurship is so prevalent in the USSR, despite laws against it, that one wonders how strong the economic competition of the Soviet Union would be internationally if it converted to a capitalist system.

Central planning causes inherent labor problems, resulting most significantly in poor workmanship. Plant managers usually fill their production quotas only on paper. Output below quota is explained away by creating fictitious products written off as spoiled and subsequently destroyed. In one such incident, according to *New York Times* reporter Hedrick Smith, a poultry breeder had a daily target of a hundred thousand eggs. If he produced only seventy thousand eggs, he would give the accurate total to his supervisor who would then provide a false report to the regional superior, writing off the non-existent thirty thousand eggs as broken. Over time, the regional superior often lowers the production quota, and a new round of "write-offs" may even begin.[22]

The emphasis in Soviet economic management, according to a report by the prestigious *Morgan Economic Quarterly*, "is on 'more'—to meet quotas—rather than on quality. Obsolete products and processes are retained and progress suffers."[23] Soviet workers generally have the attitude that the products they produce do not have to be of high quality, because they "don't belong to anyone." The quality of workmanship in the Soviet Union is shoddy, whether because of mere lack of worker motivation or because many workers are drunk or hung over. They rarely have wage incentives to produce more or better quality goods, and promotions are mainly a function of party loyalty rather than good job performance.

Even if they were to receive higher wages, Soviet workers have little to spend them on, since the selection and quality of consumer goods is poor and their availability spotty. Only the elite have regular access to high-quality products: they have the money to patronize both the private stores, where only the Soviet hierarchy and tourists are allowed to shop, and the underground economy, where prices are often out of reach for average workers—unless they also trade on the black market.

The underground economy created by this demand, together with massive movements of materials between state enterprises desperate to meet quotas threatened by supply shortages, is enormous. Estimates of the size of the underground economy—categorized as "grey," "brown" and "black" markets according to their degree of illegality—are hampered by a complete lack of reliable data, but the consensus of literature on the topic seems to settle on a figure somewhere above 10 percent of Soviet GNP.[24] According to Hedrick Smith,

> This counter economy has become an integral part of the Soviet system, a built-in, permanent feature of Soviet society. It encompasses everything from petty bribing, black marketing, wholesale thieving from the state, and underground private manufacturing all the way up to a full-fledged *Godfather* operation which was exposed and led to the downfall of a high Communist Party figure, a candidate of the Politburo. It operates on an almost oriental scale and with a brazen normality that would undoubtedly incense the original Bolshevik revolutionaries.[25]

There are two significant implications to the growth of the underground economy, as a leading Soviet dissident, Vladimir Bukovsky, points out. First, where cash is king in the form of a black market, Soviet citizens need fewer favors from the ruling class to obtain coveted consumer items. This reduces people's dependency on the Communist leadership. Secondly, the official Soviet economy continues to experience significant difficulties as a result of the inefficiencies of centralized planning. Factories run short of the raw materials or parts they need to carry on their work, and average citizens can find it impossible to secure the services of state mechanics, plumbers or wall hangers. The underground economy fulfills the needs of everyone from plant managers to housewives.

It is fair to say that the Soviet economy would be crippled without the services of those selling goods and services off the books. The typical government solution to its planning-caused problems, such as the use of students and soldiers to harvest crops rotting because of absenteeism (and the country nevertheless is forced to make up shortfalls in food production with imports), can obviously be applied only to a limited extent.

The underground economy is thus an essential prop for the official economy. At the same time however, dialectically one might say, it debilitates it. Resources are drained from the official economy. Ordinary workers cannot purchase black market products on their salaries; they need an additional source of income, so they begin to buy and sell on the black market. (One Soviet citizen told Smith, "You know, in Odessa, they have a saying that if you get really mad at another person, you put a curse on him—'Let him live on his salary.' It's a terrible fate. No one can imagine it.")[26] Since moonlighting is more lucrative than regular work, workers tend to be absent from their normal employment as much as possible, or to conduct entrepreneurship right in the workplace. The result is a strengthening of the underground economy and a weakening of the official economy, its inefficiencies and low standards, its strangle hold on the daily life of the people.

If the underground economy achieves a sufficient percentage of overall national output (which seems likely, since Soviet economic difficulties have in recent times increased with every year), Soviet leaders may one day no longer be in control of the population. A new, nonviolent revolution may begin to rear its shining visage in the citadel of tyranny, a "cash revolution" irreversibly altering Soviet society and its form of government. If the Communist menace cannot safely be eliminated through a nuclear first strike, perhaps carpet bombing Soviet population centers with Sears catalogues will do the job.

The supreme irony is that although the Soviet leadership may try to control this phenomenon, it cannot afford to be too successful. First, the upper echelons of party and government purchase these products themselves and would never countenance an interruption of their supply of amenities. Secondly, to abruptly halt this major source of consumer satisfaction—both the increased availability of otherwise scarce goods and the lubricating role of the underground economy in Soviet industry—would certainly result in social disorder, possibly even outright rebellion. With the continual decline of credence in the philosophy of Marxism, the authorities must maintain social cohesion by material incentives or police repression. They attempt to use both means of control at once, and if the Soviet economy cannot officially generate material incentives sufficiently rapidly to maintain social stability, the black market must be permitted to do the job. The Soviet system has come to be dependent upon the underground economy.

How could this huge and illegal parallel economy grow and flourish in the shadow of the most frightening police apparatus on the face of the earth? Simply because the Soviet leadership has for seventy years been unable to resolve the central contradiction of Marxist theology: the aim of creating material happiness is forced to labor under the imperative to repress individual initiative. A kind of paralysis set in. Like other aspects of compartmentalized Soviet society, the authorities have long lived in a "numbing isolation," separated from the daily reality of the citizens they rule. The members of the Politburo "lost touch with the reality of the society they directed," writes Arkady N. Shevchenko, a former Soviet official who defected in 1985. "Unwilling to understand it, they were unable to inspire it. They could still generate fear but not sympathy, command obedience but not enthusiasm. And sheltered as they were, they would not venture to change their course."[27]

But they could not endure the limits of its achievements, either. Thus, a blind eye has been turned to incipient Soviet capitalism. Soviet officials can't live with it—undermining as it does all that socialism claims to stand for and be able to deliver—but they also can't live without it.

So the economic satisfactions that Marx taught would be achieved by violent revolution will probably come to realization nonviolently. The principle weapon will be cash rather than guns, freely traded rather than state controlled. As in many of history's societies, there is a bifurcation in the USSR between official theology and the practice of the people. No amount of exhortation or repression of the masses can compel them to conform to doctrines that completely lack common sense—as the liquidation of the kulaks showed. The history of societies of imposed theology is one in which the mass of believers really only accept imposed doctrines as long as they do not interfere too dramatically with personal needs. At that point they either rationalize deviations or begin to reject creed. "If only Stalin knew" was the rationalization of the common people in the 1930s, according to Walter Lippmann. The personal needs that are generally the first to require attention are economic ones. No system of metaphysics, particularly in this age, can persuade most people to endure material hardship if they see a viable alternative. So it is with the Soviet population.

The only way the government can extricate itself from its plodding inertia (if it can) is to stimulate production. To do so it needs, among other things, modern Western technology and financial credit from the West. If it does not obtain such credits, the economy will continue to decline and the underground economy will gradually expand.

There is a paradox in Soviet toleration of the underground economy. Should production expand, Soviet workers will ultimately desire wage increases and a higher standard of living. They will begin to make demands on their government. There have been several instances where Soviet industry and agriculture have permitted experiments in private initiative. When they succeeded, the projects were abandoned, lest private initiative pose too attractive an option, developing a momentum which would dismantle the close control which is the guarantee of domination by the elite. One such instance "demonstrated that labor productivity on [a particular experimental] farm was twenty times higher than on neighboring farms."[28] Eventually the manager of the farm was arrested. The authorities are aware that the bell which summons the workers to increase their productivity could also ring the requiem of the party. So private initiative goes underground, where its tones resound less discordantly in official circles.

Ironically, the black marketeers fall into a category of people most despised by Frederick Engels: the merchants. Engels describes them as

> a class that makes itself the indispensible intermediary between sets of two producers each and exploits them both. On the pretext of saving producers the trouble and risk of exchange, or finding distant markets for their products, and of thus becoming the most useful class in society, a class of parasites arises, genuine social sycophants, who as a reward for very significant real services, skim the cream off production at home and abroad, rapidly amass enormous wealth and corresponding social influence, and for this reason are destined to reap even more honors and gain increasing control over production during the period of civilization, until they at last create a product of their own—periodic commercial crises.[29]

This is a classic socialist diatribe. At the time Engels wrote it, however, he was a factory owner, and certainly must have bitterly resented paying his "parasitic" middlemen. One could say that Engels was observant, but not very prophetic. He thought socialism would eliminate this "class of parasites"; instead, it merely provided them with a different milieu. The Soviet Union's Marxist leaders may believe that their economic philosophy is chiseled in granite, but the persistent waters of human initiative ever erode their inscriptions.

Marx's theory of inexorable historical change was often used as a polemic to espouse violence. He failed to recognize that the only inexorable force in human affairs is humanity's apparently limitless desire to obtain personal liberty, and to satisfy needs with the power of the imagination and the challenge of innovation. The peaceful rebellion exhibited by millions of Soviet participants in the underground economy stands in quiet but stark contrast to the violence Marxism taught was necessary for revolution. Soviet society is daily being transformed, but the means are peaceful rather than violent, characterized by human ingenuity rather than open revolt. Another "class struggle" is underway. It is yet another feature of Marxist utopia not remotely envisioned by Karl Marx.

Soviet Trade

Since the first recorded Russian economic treaty, between Prince Oleg of Kiev and the Byzantine emperor in 911, Russian trade expanded slowly but surely. On the eve of World War I Russia earned one-tenth of its national income from exports. This hard-earned economic advance was demolished with the Bolshevik assumption of power. "The share of exports in the national product in the 1970s was the same as it was in the later 1920s, some 3–4 percent."[30]

The persistently low level of Soviet exports does not reflect a lack of interest in increasing them. In order to stimulate exports to the United States, the Soviet Union is willing to allow high tariffs on its products in exchange for more U.S. credits. It's not much of a trade, for if a government has low-paid labor, or can arbitrarily fix prices, a tariff will not significantly affect the cost of the items. The USSR is not concerned about tariffs; it is concerned about credit. Since the first days of the October Revolution, the only way the Soviet economy has been able to survive is by obtaining external financing from the capitalists. As Jean-Francois Revel puts it, "Capitalist economic assistance in 1921 cushioned the bankruptcy of the Soviets as it has so often since."[31]

The Soviet Union has long borrowed moderately from the West. Its appetite for hard currency has increased greatly in the last decade, however, because it has been able to export oil and natural gas to Europe and reap huge hard currency payments for them. With the recent fall of oil prices, the Soviet Union is negatively affected in two ways: first, the direct loss of export revenue from energy sales, and second, the concomitant deterioration of the market for Soviet arms sales to oil-producing clients, e.g. Libya, Algeria and Iraq. Facing severe revenue shortfalls, these countries are buying fewer weapons, and buying them more often on credit.

For the Soviet Union total exports are down and total hard currency inflow is down even further. Annual plans did not foresee this sudden turn of events; if the plans are to be met, increased borrowing from the West is required. "That is why a non-socialist trade surplus of $1.9 billion in 1986 requires large-scale borrowing in the West . . . Any boost in exports with little or no yield in cash is likely to create additional strains for the Soviet economy rather than helping its external financial picture."[32]

It all revolves around allocation of resources with respect to Soviet investment in the civilian sector of its economy. A substantial percentage of this investment is in the form of imported Western technology. If less hard currency is forthcoming from arms sales to pay for these imports, economic planners are faced with three choices: reduce the level of imports of Western equipment, but make up for it by curtailing arms production and transferring resources to the civilian sector; maintain the level of imports of Western equipment by borrowing more from the West to make up for reduced arms-derived revenues; or reduce the level of investment in the civilian economy.

Reducing arms production has been rejected for two reasons: it would reduce Soviet geopolitical influence; and any transfer of resources to the civilian economy would take years to show results. Reducing the level of investment in the civilian sector has been rejected because improvement in the Soviet quality of life is probably Mikhail Gorbachev's main priority. Increased indebtedness to the West is therefore the only road left to take.

One can say then that increased Western lending is financing Soviet arms sales. Were it unavailable, the Soviets would be forced to choose between arms or reduced allocations to the civilian economy. Given Gorbachev's resolve to increase emphasis on civilian needs, it is unlikely he could tolerate not merely stagnation, but actual deterioration in the Soviet quality of life. Were increased lending from the West foreclosed as an option, he would be forced to reduce cash-draining arms production. So the theory goes. However, it is not wise to underestimate the resolve of the Soviet military-industrial complex to maintain its preeminence in the conduct of Soviet affairs.

Ironically, Western banks not only provide credit to the Soviet Union, they even do so at interest rates lower than the market dictates, often guaranteed by Western governments![33] Western banks and governments lending to the Soviet Union, and the government officials who permit it, should give this some thought.

For various political and economic reasons, the West has safeguarded the Soviet economy since the time of Lenin. Profit is the motive, of course, but in taking this course the West is only financing its own destruction. The Soviet Union is in desperate need of hard currency, primarily to finance its imperial ventures, and to import Western technology to better carry them out. Soviet raw materials such as oil and natural gas can find a market in the West, but Soviet commercial products, at nearly any price, have no appeal to holders of hard currency.

Arms are the one significant exception. Soviet promotion of political unrest around the world has symbiotic purposes: expanding Soviet influence and at the same time assuring a market for Soviet military products. Until recently, the Soviet Union has been able to generate $32 billion per year in hard currency income.[34] With the drop in energy prices during 1986, this figure is believed to have dropped dramatically, increasing the importance of weapons exports, which in 1985 accounted for 16 percent of all Soviet exports to the non-socialist world.[35] It is therefore in the economic as well as political interest of the Soviet Union to bring governments under its influence, particularly those with access to hard currency, such as Libya, and to promote the rise of Marxist leaders who can in turn expand Soviet influence and the Soviet market for military goods—precisely the Leninist charge against capitalism as structurally imperialist.

The Soviet Empire requires hard currency to carry on its business, because it could not advance economically without Western technology. This it obtains either by direct purchase or the financing of industrial espionage. Both require hard currency. Illegal Soviet acquisition of industrial knowledge and goods in the United States alone costs the USSR an estimated $1.5 billion annually.[36] In its efforts to challenge the West, the Soviet military machine would fail as dismally as the Soviet economy has, were it not for voluntary and involuntary help from the West. In the opinion of one Heritage Foundation analyst,

> Each year Moscow obtains thousands of pieces of Western equipment and tens of thousands of documents through a massive campaign to acquire Western technology. Over 5,000 Soviet military research projects benefit from this effort. The result: the U.S. and other Western nations are helping subsidize the Soviet military buildup.
>
> In spite of a massive investment in research and development, it is unlikely that the Soviets can reduce their dependence on Western products and technology, for reasons endemic to the Soviet system. . . Although the Soviets have achieved *adequacy* in nearly all important military technologies, they remain dependent on the West for *innovation*.
>
> Moscow relies on an extensive program of intelligence collection to raise the technical levels of its weapons and military equipment, and to improve its manufacturing processes. This program is managed by the Military Industrial Commission (VPK) of the Presidium of the Council of Ministers. Its goal is to obtain Western documents, product samples and test equipment. . .
>
> The Soviets' most significant acquisitions of Western technology have been achieved through the East European intelligence services, probably because they are perceived in the West as a lesser threat than the Soviets. Their important recent successes include the purchase of documents on the fire-control radars used in the F-14, F-15 and F-18, and missile and air defense data, obtained by Polish intelligence from William H. Bell, a radar specialist at Hughes aircraft, for $110,000. That information served as the technical basis for the look-down/shoot-down radars now being deployed on the newest generation of Soviet fighters.[37]

Lenin declared that capitalist nations always tend to war because capitalist economies were perpetually faced with the accumulation of destabilizing surplus capital—capital which could be destroyed in general by the mass destruction of war and in particular by the process of producing vast quantities of arms and ammunition for immediate waste. Even capitalist alliances, said Lenin, "are *inevitably* nothing more than a 'truce' in periods between wars,"[38] a respite during which capitalist nations can prepare for the next catharsis.

The supposed solution to this structural horror, of course, is the creation of socialism and its spread throughout the world. Things did not go according to plan, however. The West expanded its service sector, creating huge industries in insurance, advertising, and entertainment, industries that created alternative products which could be "continuously replaced." Meanwhile, the first country to implement Marxism has become a nation which can only sustain its needed hard currency reserves by exporting revolution and promoting war. Soviet defense expenditures are variously estimated at between 10 and 20 percent of the nation's GNP. A 1982 CIA estimate put it at 13 percent, projected to rise to 14 percent by 1985. This compares to defense expenditures of 7.2 percent of GNP in the United States and 5.1 percent in the United Kingdom.[39]

Government Service

He shall rule them with an iron rod.

—Revelation 2:27

Because of its seventy-year experience with Marxism, the Soviet Union has developed party and government structures that serve as a model for other Marxist-Leninist governments. It has learned, as have most theological organizations before it, that strict control from the top is the indispensable tool needed to control heresy.

Communist party rules provide the guiding principle of democratic centralism, often referred to as "centralism of a new type," by which is meant that control of all social institutions as well as the state theology is centralized in the leadership. The formal party structure stipulates that a periodic congress is the ultimate governing body of the Communist party.

When the congress convenes, usually every five years, it is an important event. The agenda is determined by the Central Committee, an elite group of party veterans that maintains control in the five-year interims. The Political Bureau of the Central Committe (Politburo), as the most powerful group in the Central Committee, has the responsiblity to direct the work of the party between sessions of the Central Committee. Although the Central Committee nominally elects the Politburo, this power actually rests in the Politburo itself, which meets once or twice a week (most Thursdays and some Tuesdays); the Central Committee as a whole normally meets only twice a year. As a practical matter, therefore, the Politburo is the policy body which controls the entire party, and with it the government of the Soviet Union.

The fourteen-member Politburo is the board of directors of the Soviet Union. It is also comparable to the Curia of the Roman Catholic Church, in that it is the final authority on theology. Politburo members decide upon eight candidate members who stand ready to replace full members who may die or be removed. It is a solemn body of male political chauvinists. Despite Marxist egalitarian pretensions, Ye. A. Furtseva has been the only woman to ever attain Politburo membership (1957-61).[40] All power, whether of party or state, emanates from the Politburo. The general secretary of the Communist party is the most powerful member of the Politburo, and usually also wears the hat of the head of the government. He is the Marxist "pope."

Attached to each of the members of the Politburo is a large retinue of government appointees, party officials and their families and friends. The whole mess collectively forms the Soviet ruling class. They cohere as a class because they all enjoy a wide range of privileges obtained at the expense of the population at large. By strict material comparison, this structure of exploiter and exploited does not differ terribly from that in Western countries. The system by which this structure is enforced, however, and the degree of mobility within it, vary dramatically from the Western model.

Thought Control

To tell the truth is a petty bourgeois habit.
                            —Vladimir Ilyich Lenin (Ulyanov)

Censorship and repression of free thought in Russia existed long before Marxists took control and set up the Soviet Union. The Bolsheviks developed censorship into a science, however. For centuries emperors, kings, czars, and particularly popes have censored or controlled the press to one extent or another. Even in the country with the freest press of all, the United States, news blackouts are occasionally imposed during which facts are given an official interpretation before being independently confirmed.

In Russia, the government always held tight reins on the peasant population. For the most part there was no need for censorship, for very practical reasons—few peasants could read or write, and in any case were so controlled that they were not a political threat.

When literacy and printing began to develop, Russian leaders assiduously monitored the activities of news journals and literature, a relatively easy task given their paucity. The government also imposed restraint, and often outright censorship, on the Russian Orthodox Church, which could wield enormous power. To avoid any potential threat from the church, the government usually maintained a large measure of control over its policies.

Peter the Great, the inaugurator of Russia's modern age, developed a sophisticated process of censorship (for the time), which included opening mail. Peter also organized the first domestic newspaper, which, of course, he supervised. Later czars expanded these practices, regularly improving the reach and power of the censors, whether by mechanical methods or the application of imprisonment and torture. So by the time the Marxists arrived on the scene, the Russian public had come to take censorship for granted.

The Bolsheviks had relied heavily on an underground press. As a result, when Lenin attained power he realized that he might not have succeeded if the czar had been more successful in suppressing subversive newspapers and pamphleteering. He would not make the same mistake.

Just as the Roman Catholic Church once subscribed to an authoritarian view of the press as the best defense of orthodoxy, so Marxist societies see any uncontrolled discussion as harmful to the state. Traditional censorship, however, is a passive affair. Its agents regulate only material generated independently. It would accordingly be inaccurate merely to say that the USSR employs censorship. Its policies go far beyond that. Soviet authorities control the press completely. It is an overt instrument of propaganda, persuasion, and a form of education to create the "new Soviet man."

In the tradition of the Catholic church's *Nihil Obstat* and *Imprimatur* permissions to publish, the Soviet press cannot publish anything unless it conforms to the theological policies of Marxism. "A newspaper," Lenin observed, "is not only a collective propagandist and collective agitator; it is also a collective organizer."[41] Since the use of print media was critical in the Bolshevik rise to power, Soviet authorities never underestimate the power of the press either to control the population or to undermine the government.

Soviet newspaper circulation was estimated in 1979 at more than thirty-nine billion copies per year. The publication of periodicals totalled more than three billion copies annually.[42] All are controlled by the Communist party or the Soviet government.

Newspapers in the Soviet Union are also a practical and inexpensive commodity for public use, as wrapping paper, table cloths and insulation in walls. In a penurious society, these functions are important and taken quite seriously by the citizenry. As previously in Western Europe, newspapers in the Soviet Union are frequently used for toilet paper. This is generally the best use for the editorial section of a Soviet newspaper, that is, nearly its entirety, since one of the distinguishing features of Soviet journalism is that even the blandest of news is editorialized.

The official Communist party daily, *Pravda*, usually contains six pages, apparently all the truth that the authorities believe a population of 270 million can handle in one day. The front page usually contains an "agitational editorial," and various reports on production achievements. The Soviet population, nurtured in cynicism, has learned how to interpret these official views and statistics. The classical Soviet comment is that if *Pravda* says the farmers have had a "bumper year" in cabbages, it usually means the potato crop has failed, and everyone will be eating cabbage next year.

The other five pages are devoted, in the main, to party affairs, correspondence and foreign news supplied by TASS (Telegraphic Agency of the Soviet Union), the official Soviet news agency. The 1978 daily circulation was estimated to be 10.7 million copies, but the readership is larger because copies are posted for public perusal and many copies change hands several times.

The second most significant newspaper in the USSR is probably *Izvestia* ("News"), the official government newspaper. It was founded in 1917 and has an estimated daily circulation of eight to nine million. Other papers include *Komsomol' skaya pravda,* the paper of the Komsomal youth organization, founded in 1925 to educate future generations (its circulation is approximately ten million copies), and *Sel'skayhizn* ("Rural Life"), produced for the rural readership, at about 8.5 million copies daily.

In a society starved for news, the press is read avidly. Polls conducted in Leningrad showed that 75 percent of those polled read the newspapers every day, and an additional 19 percent read them three or four times a week.[43] The people also discuss articles with relatives, friends and co-workers. In 1979 approximately half a million Soviet citizens wrote letters to *Pravda*, although only a small percentage could be published. All such letters are supposed to be answered and followed up. They often are, and suggestions are frequently acted upon.

Soviet readers are thought to be less interested in party politics than in international, cultural and sports topics. They do evince interest in party affairs when a leader has a minor illness, such as Andropov's "cold" of five months, which cleared up only with his death. The political or physical well-being of Soviet leaders is not discussed in the media, unless the official involved is on his way out. Perceptive Soviet readers get most of their information by reading between the lines.

Television in the USSR began experimentally in 1931. Although only an estimated 8 percent of families owned a television in 1960, by 1980 there were an estimated sixty-four million television sets in use. This provided TV reception to approximately 85 percent of Soviet families, since there are frequently two, three, or more families living in the same house or apartment. (The shortage of housing is a critical problem in the Soviet Union.)

On the eight main channels, the majority of the population prefer to watch variety programs, feature films and documentaries, particularly pertaining to foreign events or people. One study in Leningrad indicated that only 4 percent of viewers were interested in more programs on economic matters.[44] Such information could not please the authorities of a country claiming undisputed economic superiority over the rest of the world. The statistic does not necessarily suggest a general lack of interest in economic affairs. It may also reflect the combination of widespread distrust of economic forecasts, and the fact that to Soviet citizens the more interesting aspects of the economic life concern the unreported underground economy.

Official censorship of the press began very early in the USSR, on October 24, 1917, with the confiscation and burning of the latest issue of the liberal newspaper *Russkaya volya* ("Russian Freedom"), on the grounds of its "libelous concoctions." The next day the paper's printing press began to produce copies of the Bolshevik *Rabochy put* ("Workers' Way"). On October 27, 1917, a "Decree on the Press" was issued to suppress all non-Bolshevik publications, as a "temporary measure to stop the flood of filth and slander." The decree is still in force today. By July 1918 the Bolshevik Military Revolutionary Committee had halted the regular appearance of almost all non-Bolshevik newspapers in Communist-held areas.

In 1918 the Extraordinary Commission for Combating Counterrevolution and Sabotage, or Cheka, the security police (it was reorganized successively as the GPU, OGPU, NKVD and MVD; in 1954 it acquired ministry level structure and the designation KGB), was assigned the task of arresting anyone involved in the publication of materials regarded as "counterrevolutionary," as determined by the authorities. In 1922 the official organ of censorship, Glavlit, was set up, and soon censorship of even Bolshevik publications was in place. Such agencies are integral parts of Marxist-Leninist governments, equal in importance to departments of education in enforcing ideology, but with virtually unlimited police powers.

On June 6, 1931, Glavlit was given the authority of pre- and postpublication control over any form of public information activity. It was a broad mandate; included were movies, lectures, ballets, pictures, exhibitions, "handkerchiefs with pictures on them, book jackets, bus tickets and matchbox labels."[45] Even social gatherings and the use of the mail fell under the jurisdiction of Glavlit. To prevent evasion of postal censorship, in 1939 the government began to strangle carrier pigeons, yet another class of victims on the road to economic equality and social utopia.

When foreign radio and TV broadcasts began to reach the USSR, Glavlit set up jamming facilities—not carried out wholeheartedly, or at least very effectively—to assure that the Soviet population would not be corrupted by the bourgeois media of the West. It has not been able to stem the flood of American and European records and tapes, however, nor of video cassettes of Western films, an actively traded part of the underground economy with individual units sometimes selling for hundreds of dollars. When in 1984 *Pravda* officially condemned the American comedy film *Moscow on the Hudson*, the cassette price rose from sixty-five to three hundred dollars on the black market[46]—a price, ironically, which many Soviet officials may have had to pay.

Whenever the party decides that certain parts of history are inconvenient to present-day conceptions, books are recalled and burned, or, in the case of periodicals, new issues are printed. In one comical example, the authorities resolved to alter an entry in the third edition of the *Great Soviet Encyclopedia*. At the time it contained a lengthy article concerning Laurenti Beria, Stalin's police chief. Khrushchev had him executed in a power struggle, but, not content to bury only his body, the authorities resolved to entomb Beria's memory as well. The editors of the encyclopedia produced an article on the Bering Strait with the same number of words used to describe Beria, and mailed it to encyclopedia owners with instructions to paste it directly over the article on Beria.[47] The paste, presumably, had to be supplied by the reader.

Soviet censorship abounds with such incidents, not the least concerning Soviet leaders themselves. In one official history of the country up to the beginning of the February Revolution, Stalin appears only as an appendage, mentioned as having attended a meeting in 1909, years before his influence was significant; Trotsky also appears once (in a pejorative way, despite having been one of the most inspiring speakers and leaders of the revolution), and he is omitted from the index.[48] Lately, however, there is a gradual tendency to rehabilitate at least some aspects of Stalin's life.

The production of "truth" in Marxist societies requires enormous editorial staffs. This provides employment for the intellectuals, and keeps the population free of the "filthy" facts to which Lenin had so strenuously objected. Inducing tortured intellects to fabricate "truth" is evidently a small price for all Marxists to pay for the promised social idyll.

Foreign literature, books and magazines are officially and unashamed-ly confiscated at the border, as any visitor to the Soviet Union will discover. The attitude is akin to classical theological tendencies of Christianity and other religions—protect the population of believers from contamination by alien ideas. Confiscated material is not destroyed, however; it is a prized source of reading material for the ruling elite. How else could they know about the latest Western fashions and electronic appliances available through their private retail stores?

Soviet Foreign Policy

Rus', whither are you speeding so? Answer me. No answer. The middle bell trills out in a dream its liquid soliloquy; the roaring air is torn to pieces and becomes wind; all things on earth fly by and other nations and states gaze askance as they step aside and give her the right of way.

—Nikolai Gogol, *Dead Souls*

About the capitalist states, it doesn't depend on you whether or not we exist . . . whether you like it or not, history is on our side. We will bury you.

—Nikita Sergeyevich Khrushchev

The foreign policy of the Soviet Union is simple to define; its motivations are considerably more complex. The grand strategy of the Soviet Union is to control the world, but, ironically, it is schizophrenic about its desire to do so.

The paramount Soviet political motivations are to expand the Russian Empire and protect the USSR from external threats, real or imagined, to placate its active inferiority complex. This it accomplishes by achieving parity with, if not superiority over, the United States, and developing its economy through control of foreign markets and resources. To achieve these ends, the Soviet Union promotes international revolution on every continent in the world.

The contemporary leadership of the country is intelligent, sophisticated and pragmatic. It is accordingly difficult to imagine that any of its members truly believe in Marxism. Among American leaders personally acquainted with the Soviet hierarchy, it is generally thought that there are few, if any, orthodox Marxists in the upper echelons of the Soviet government. Conservative American Republicans, ultra-liberal Democrats, Christian fundamentalists, young intellectuals and the oppressed of the world are probably the only people who take Marxist philosophy seriously. It is enough. Demonstrated appeal to the world's poor makes Marxist-Leninist ideology a potent tool of Soviet foreign policy. Equally important, however, is the fact that it capitalizes on the opportunism of ambitious politicians around the globe.

The first concern of Soviet foreign policy is to defend and expand the nation's geographical perimeters. Throughout history, from the Romans to the Russians, the imperial imperative has been to defend borders. For the Soviet Union, which lost twenty to thirty million people in World War II (called in the USSR the "Great Patriotic War"), defending national boundaries is a matter of historical experience. All empires view their expanding borders also as expanding vulnerabilities. The Russians are no exception, and to a degree, understandably so.

The psychology of defense sometimes makes a transition to a psychology of offense. The simplest way to defend a national boundary is to "neutralize" contiguous neighbors, particularly if they are of a different theological persuasion, that is, potentially hostile. Aggression takes on the character of defense. Attack can appear warranted if conceived in terms drawn from history's highly developed encyclopedia of national rationalizations. What to a foreign observer appears to be aggression to the paranoid country is only national defense.

This principal is not only operative in border disputes with China and Soviet forays into Afghanistan and Eastern Europe. It also inspires the United States to invade Grenada, and Israel to attack Egypt, Jordan, Syria, Lebanon, Iraq and Tunisia. There are a host of other historical examples. The Soviet Union's military assaults on adjacent nations should therefore be viewed in the peculiar perspective of political paranoia; while not justifiable, they are at least more understandable. Soviet adventures beyond its fluid border regions, into South Yemen, Cuba, Ethiopia, Nicaragua and other countries are also inversions of a defensive mindset—they are at least partly attempts to disrupt U.S. sources of supply and preempt or displace U.S. influence through the acquisition of geographically strategic bases of operation. Defense through offense.

Such ventures entail commitments and structural risks. Popular militancy rises with foreign domination, particularly in a time when concepts of civil rights and nationalism continue to spread into the lower reaches of social hierarchies everywhere. That in turn generates further, countering repression.

With the acquisition of territory, whether through occupation or influence, there are additional borders to defend, and the empire acquires further vulnerabilities. It is a cycle of paranoia and aggression that has afflicted empires throughout history; their aggrandizement was often checked only by practical rather than moral limits. "But, until the rise of the Soviet Empire," says Jean-Francois Revel in *How Democracies Perish*, "none had concluded that it had a right to appropriate the entire planet before it could set its mind at rest."[49]

The second motivation of Soviet foreign policy is its constant attempt to gratify its inferiority complex. A quotation from a typical Russian writer may illustrate the point:

> At present the most advanced states are fervently disseminating perfect absurdities about Russia . . . Their most serious political publications herald as an accurate truth [allegations of serious domestic turmoil led by dissidents] . . . let them in their blind wrath say all these things. For it goes without saying that they would be eager to incite hatred against us everywhere abroad as dangerous enemies of their civilization.
>
> They already visualize us in a defeated condition, in disgraceful impotence as a ridiculous military power and a state organism. But he who is so weak and insignificant—how can he arouse the fear of the [Western] coalition?
>
> And yet they feel it necessary to incite their societies against us. But why this hatred of us? Why cannot they all, once and for all, start trusting us?
>
> No, they cannot place trust in us. The main reason is that they are altogether unable to recognize us as theirs. Under no circumstances will they believe that we can in truth, *on an equal footing with them*, participate in the future destinies of their civilization.
>
> They consider us aliens to their civilization; they regard us as strangers and impostors, as Asiatics and barbarians.[50] (emphasis added)

One would suppose this polemic was written by a Central Committee propagandist attacking a current U.S. president. In fact, the author was a journalist writing during the so-called Eastern Crisis of 1876–78. His name was Fyodor Dostoevski.

Similar attitudes are expressed repeatedly throughout Russian history, as we have seen. The desire to be treated as equals by Western society is an obsession which seems to have afflicted the Russian psyche for centuries. The United States is the contemporary focus of that preoccupation. A worldwide belief that the Soviet Union is equal to the United States enables it to achieve more credibility with the Third World in the global pursuit of power. Apparently the Soviet Union believes that one method to achieve this goal is to demand the incorporation into Soviet-American treaties the acknowledgment that the USSR is an equal party, no matter whether the treaty concerns military weapons, fishing rights or scientific collaboration. This enhances the Soviet position at the United Nations, and in its international propaganda, which is more highly developed than that of the United States.

The Soviet sense of inferiority, developed through centuries of Russian history, should be viewed as one of the most significant components of the Soviet state personality. It impels the USSR to act as individuals do, overcompensating by exhibiting a superiority complex. The resultant obnoxious and aggressive behavior cannot be tolerated by others, or they will suffer the consequences of Munich; it must be restrained. The principal restraint is the military prowess of the United States.

To achieve "equality" with the West, particularly the United States, the Soviets abandoned their efforts to create an economic idol for the world to worship. Instead, they have turned their attention to building another kind of altar at which foreign nations could venerate Soviet achievements—they have embarked upon the creation of the largest military establishment in history. "If the Soviet Union could no longer hope to conquer the world by the novel method of becoming its irresistibly successful economic and social model, it could instead pursue the lesser but still grandiose aim of becoming the world's leading military power." It is a phenomenon Edward Luttwak calls the "last stage of Soviet optimism."[51]

If the USSR could not inspire the respect of the world as a co-equal with the United States economically, it would engender the world's fear of its military prowess. Wonderfully enough, this was also theologically justified by Marxism's philosophy of violence. Creating a Communist utopia became subordinated to promoting the international revolution.

The Soviet Union will avoid battles which it cannot win, however, such as a nuclear war. Since they are restrained from directly engaging the United States militarily, the Soviets resort to other weapons. The principal ones are propaganda and, the same thing by another name, "disinformation," so integral a part of Soviet governmental structure that there are numerous special government departments for the purpose. "Disinformation" is a term used to describe the planting of false information, favorable to Marxist objectives, in the Western press. Marxist-Leninist countries have "active measures" departments whose function is to forge press releases, plant phony stories in the Western media, slander the integrity of Western journalists who are anti-Soviet, and pressure the Western media into omitting items critical of Communist countries. The USSR even objected officially when the Wendy's fast-food chain ran commercials ridiculing Soviet fashions. The war of words is one the Soviets are winning, especially in the Third World.

The priority given to civil rights by Western democracies affords the Soviets untold opportunities to exploit Western jurisprudence to their advantage. Protest movements are funded by the KGB, local terrorist groups are supplied training and arms, and covertly Soviet-controlled media outlets are created. In Marxist societies, on the other hand, even local nationals do not enjoy the civil rights taken for granted by the West; foreigners in a Marxist nation fare even less well. "The idea that an authoritarian political system must collapse because it cannot provide a decent life for its citizenry can only occur to a democrat," writes Jean-Francois Revel.[52] Relative

Western permissiveness hardly engenders Soviet respect; on the contrary, it induces Soviet leaders to perceive the West as naive.

The third motivation of Soviet foreign policy is to develop the Soviet economy. In a very real sense this may be the most important Soviet foreign policy goal, since without an economy to support military production and equally important, keep most of the population under control, the Communist party and its elite would not be able to rule.

The dangers of too poor an economy were amply demonstrated in Poland: *Solidarinosc* ("Solidarity") was formed, valiantly representing the working class in that nation far more genuinely than the Communist party. The consequences of direct Soviet intervention in Poland would have been high, badly damaging the Soviet image throughout the world and doubtless prompting a wide range of retaliation by the West. Solidarity's claim to the allegiance of the proletariat is blasphemy in Marxist theology, contesting as it does the underpinning of Soviet control of the entire Eastern bloc.

If unrest in Communist countries is to be avoided, the economy must perform at a certain basic level. Not that it need be too high. Food lines in the Soviet Union and other Eastern bloc countries have become part of Communist culture. They are caused by the scarcity of agricultural products, but the food lines also serve a political purpose: if people must stand and wait three or four hours a day for food, and must do so every day, they do not have time to revolt.

Liquor serves a similar function. If a major part of the population is drunk or hung-over, it will not revolt. Clearly the government has the power to severely limit liquor sales, and at times demonstrates the desire to do so (by raising prices and decreasing availability) in order to reduce alcoholism and raise labor productivity. It does not do so consistently, however. The consequences—sustained mass outrage—would be too severe. Also, since alcohol accounts for 18 percent of Soviet retail sales[53] and is heavily taxed (providing a significant part of the subsidy for necessities such as food), any serious strictures on the consumption of alcohol create major government revenue shortfalls.

The primary control of the restive Soviet population lies with the military and police forces, which employ over 5 percent of the population. Officially, the military is dominant because it is required for the defense of the revolution. In fact, a large military and police force is required to control those for whom the revolution was supposedly carried out. But the military is not a profit-oriented operation. It requires subsidies. By nature, military establishments do not generate income. They must make some money back by foreign adventures, either by selling military products abroad or by acquiring control over foreign nations' resources.

Soviet priorities require, first, to create a military-industrial complex to provide the military with the means to control the people and to protect the borders; and second, to convert that military-industrial complex into a profit-making entity. To do so necessarily entails the export of arms. But, to export arms requires a market. If the market does not exist, it must be created.

This leads us to the fourth motivation of Soviet foreign policy: the international revolution. It might more aptly be called international colonialism, for its purposes are to sell weapons and to obtain national resources (which can be exploited by local nationals who are not perpetually drunk, hung-over, lethargic or absent from work). Any map showing Soviet aggrandizement since World War II illustrates how the Soviet Empire has expanded and obtained control over foreign resources worldwide. Any similar map shows how the Western democracies have given their colonies independence and significantly retreated from colonialism—often being replaced by the Soviet Union. "At a time, then, when territorial annexation, once considered a legitimate reward for military superiority, has given way to peoples' right to self-determination and national status, only the Soviet Union continues to grow by means of armed conquest."[54] As Arkady Shevchenko, former Soviet official and undersecretary general of the United Nations, notes, "The idea of expanding Soviet power to the point of world domination is a fundamental long-range aspiration."[55]

Marxist revolution promises an amelioration of the problems of the poor. Like all Marxist promises, it is a subterfuge. When the poor of the world wish to improve their condition, they obviously desire to advance economically. They are unable to rely on the wages of their employment to provide for their families, particularly if they live in a Catholic country where birth control is either taught to be immoral—or in those desperately poor nations where children are an insurance policy to provide for parents in their old age. Since these poor people cannot secure higher wages, the Marxist prospect of "controlling the means of production" owned by the company or landlord for whom the poor work is an ideal solution, the ideological perfectly complementing the emotional.

The Soviet Union exploits the plight of the world's poor by inspiring them to rebellion against their governments. To do so, the rebels require arms the Soviets are more than willing to supply. Sometimes they even donate weapons—an investment that they know will pay future dividends. If a country's revolution achieves success, the people who come to power by such violent means generally fall into the pattern of history's revolutionaries: they are trained in shooting and bombing, but are deficient in the skills required to operate and administer a government. Historically, it takes less effort to learn how to use grenades or machine guns than to study accounting and business administration.

Once in control, and despite all of their previously expressed idealism, Marxist revolutionary leaders refuse to create a government of economists and administrators, who would soon assume the power which the revolutionaries had struggled long to achieve. Instead, they usually solidify their own position. In order to do so they need strong military and police forces. The place to go to help build the arsenal to equip them is, of course, their old friends, the Soviets, whose weapons they will purchase. The Soviet investment begins to pay off. However, given the structure of Soviet industry, including inefficiency and bizarre accounting practices, even the Soviets cannot determine (in a business sense) how profitable their arms sales are.

The profitability of Soviet economic involvement in subjugated satellites is easier to quantify. In the case of Afghanistan, the Soviets are exploiting copper and natural gas resources, and refuse to share output statistics with their Afghan hosts. All such information is kept secret by the Soviet military. Indeed, "Several former Afghan officials complained that, in building the [natural gas] pipeline, the Soviets had installed the meters on their own side of the border, preventing the Afghans from monitoring how much gas they pumped to the Soviet Union."[56]

A parallel situation in the United States illustrates the two sides of the same coin of death. Military sales are also rapidly becoming the predominant U.S. export. The Soviets create revolutions to sell weapons, and the United States also sells weapons to create stability so it can sell its other products. In this manner both sides assure each other a continued and expanding market, but for different reasons. Since the quality of Soviet products is so abysmally poor that it cannot compete in the economic sphere, the arms race and resultant military products alone act as a stimulus to the Soviet economy.

Looking at matters cynically, it may be fortunate for Americans that the USSR exists. For if the United States were the modern-day empire of the earth, everyone would hate America. Now only half the world hates the United States; the other half hates the USSR. These international fears and hatreds serve as a stimulus to both economies.

Marxist profits do not derive only from these initial military sales, however. Occasionally they experience wind-fall profits from a revolution. Just as the USSR must export arms and revolutions to remain in power, so do new-born Marxist-Leninist governments. Creating a foreign enemy, or espousing international revolutions provides the excuse to create an arms buildup, threatening neighboring states, promoting instability in them and setting new stages for subversion. The expanded requirement for weapons thereby enlarges the Soviet international market for arms sales. The new

Soviet client is rewarded with economic or military aid, the sales commission for selling arms in new markets.

This process has led the Soviet economy into the position where armaments and weapons are its second largest export, after energy. The USSR has become a manufacturing plant and warehouse for weapons to such a degree that noted Soviet expert Edward Luttwak refers to the USSR as "a vast international supply depot for arms."[57] All of this is made possible by espousing violent international revolution to help the world's poor.

Soviet Theology

Cuius regio eius religio (Whosoever's kingdom, also his religion)
—Roman proverb

Marxism, like Christianity, began its earthly existence with one set of principles, and, like Christianity, broke into various sects which still fight each other in the struggle to defeat and convert non-believers.

Like Christianity, Marxism has scriptures, such as the *Communist Manifesto*. Like Christianity, Marxism has evangelical zeal. Like Christianity, Marxist societies traditionally persecute Jews. Like Roman Catholic Christianity, Marxism has repressed the development of science when it contradicted scriptural truths. Also like Roman Catholicism, Marxism has a hierarchy of theologians who define doctrine, doctrine based upon scriptures and invested with moral imperative and the sanction of law. Marxism's holy writings were initially the words of the founder; but, like Christianity, eventually the words of disciples were included. The Matthew, Mark, Luke, John, Peter, and Paul of Marxism are Engels and Lenin, Stalin, Mao and their succeeding party chairmen.

Like Christianity, Marxism seeks a utopian paradise ("the classless society"), and has an eschatology of evolution to perfection. Replicating Judaism and Christianity, Marxism has an equivalent of the Chosen People and the elect of God in its concept of the proletariat.

As Christianity has, Marxism represses literature and condemns ideas which are antithetical to its own, and like historic Christianity, Marxism imprisons and tortures people who read or write such literature. Like Christianity, Marxism has a pope, called the general secretary of the Communist party, a Roman Curia, called the Politburo, and a clergy, the members of the Communist party, the vanguard of the proletariat, who make up a mere 5 percent of the people in Marxist society. As in Christianity, Marxist leaders believe that theirs is the one true faith, and wish to spread it across the world by whatever means necessary and possible. In both creeds, violence is philosophically justified by moral imperatives.

When behavior and ethics are based upon a scripture, philosophy dies and theology is born. For all of the above reasons, Marxism after Marx ceased being a philosophy and became a religion.

Marxism was a primitive and barbaric attempt to mobilize the masses to obtain social and economic justice. But when violence is the avowed weapon of change, it is difficult to refashion it into a tool for constructing a better society. When a theology is based upon hatred, even hatred of injustice, it is not easily transformed into a philosophy of love. When deceit is an ordained field tool of progress, honesty becomes difficult to unearth; when mendacity is the currency of communication, noble words become the short change of deception.

From its inception, Marxism was a philosophy of intolerance and impatience. The slow growth of human society and its institutions was supplanted by the impatient call for violent change. Marx never recognized that when one rides the tiger of violence, he is quite likely to become its victim.

Political and economic experience has relegated the doctrines of historical materialism to the dustbin of religious history; Marxist economic assumptions have been impaled upon the sword of Soviet experience. Human psychology was so ignored by the original Marxist-Leninist theologians that their descendants find themselves unable to subscribe to Marxist doctrines. Like their religious counterparts, the Marxists know that their philosophy is not practiced for the benefit of the poor, but for the pursuit of world power to the benefit of the elite. That psychology is well understood by all theologians, regardless of creed.

However, like all creeds, Marxism is losing its credibility as a philosophy. The acids of modernity eat away at all orthodoxies; Marxism is no exception. Added to this general erosion of beliefs in our era, Marxism has had the difficulty of being an economic philosophy that has failed wherever it has been strictly applied, and only marginally successful when accompanied by its companion—violence, midwife to whatever successes Marxism has achieved. Without the most vicious of coercion, Marxism would not have been able to achieve any economic gains, which may be why violence is a Marxist tenet.

The only long-term beneficiaries of Marxist economic wisdom, to date, have been the military-industrial complex of the Marxist-Leninist nations, and those of their adversaries who must defend themselves against Marxist aggrandizement. The principal short-term beneficiaries of Marxist commercial sagacity are those in power in Communist societies, and their families and friends. As a result, although many people in Marxist societies may have absorbed its dogmas as a set of pieties and conventions, Marxism is clearly disintegrating as a viable philosophy. "Whatever we know of the new privileged class of the sons and daughters suggests that the assiduous study of the writings of Marx, Engels and Lenin would not fascinate them nearly as much as the pursuit of privilege; as for the *jeunesse doree* of the third generation, it seems that among them an attitude of ideological indifference is a social norm and at least fashion, and even loud contempt is not rare."[58]

Because Marxism fails to account for the psychological motives for human behavior, Marxist-Leninist societies are guilty of abuses found in the most reactionary of nations. One of the most notable is the tendency of Marxist leaders, once in positions of authority, to retain power as long as possible. The "withering away" of the state in Marxist eschatology apparently refers only to the physical bodies of the state's leaders. Like the elites of most nations, Marxist leaders enrich themselves by appropriating the best apartments, the best educations for their children, and the best consumer items and other accouterments of power and influence. This elitist disposition on the part of Marxist leaders is understandably abhorred by the populace.

Soviet leaders are imbued with a psychology of defense, manifested aggressively. In reality, the defense needed by the Marxists is one against ideas, not against military weapons. That is why there is no free speech in the Marxist-Leninist societies, and why, in most of them, disallowed books and magazines are not produced within the country, and are confiscated from tourists at the border. That is also why Marxist nations must sabotage or conquer free-enterprise countries. As Revel says, "For communism, incapable of engendering a viable society, cannot tolerate the continued existence of other societies to bear witness against it; each such society would by its very existence be an indictment of socialism, a point of comparison by which to judge unrelieved failure in terms of human happiness. . . . The only way to convince oneself and the rest of humanity that the socialist system is best is to see to it that there are no other systems."[59]

Although this observation describes Marxist geopolitical behavior, it masks a paradox. If there were no free-enterprise societies left in existence, the Marxist nations would have no one to turn to, as they traditionally have, to extricate them—by technology and credits—from economic catastrophe.

Men from the dawn of time to the present era, and boys from the cradle to the grave, all love weapons. Various military considerations seem to be an adequate rationalization for men to continue stockpiling and refining arms, claiming to do so in order to preserve that which is optimistically called civilization. In reality, the male "hunter instinct" has not yet been supplanted by the spirit of peace. To ignore this obvious fact is to court disaster.

The Marxist-Leninists have a weapon more potent than a nuclear missile with which to fight, however. It is disinformation, the spreading of falsehoods in the Western press, and the use of democratic laws and freedoms to undermine Western democracies. Western societies would like to hope that Marxists are mellow human beings, and so they fall victim to Marxist mendacity. While Marxist governments manipulate the Western press, and their leaders even appear on television talk shows, Western figures are generally not allowed to speak in the Soviet Union, and Western literature is banned and confiscated. It is in this arena of information that the war will be won or lost. The Marxists are winning it every day.

Denouement

It is those who advise you to defend yourselves who are said to press for war.

—Demosthenes

The more destruction there is everywhere, the more it shows the activity of town authorities.

—Nikolai Gogol

When the age of the Reformation began, economics was still a branch of ethics, and ethics was a branch of theology; all human activity was regarded as part of the spiritual destiny of mankind. Economic thought was subordinated to the theories of the theologian, and was not yet forged in the crucible of social utility. Since then, man asserted his intellectual independence; rather than accepting the economic penury of a Christian "subsistence wage," and the cultural and mental poverty to which he was thereby condemned, man raised his economic awareness and prudently relegated religion to the realm of the hereafter. Instead of keeping economic reality on the Procrustean bed of theological orthodoxy, man placed economics at the center of his physical existence; in the process religion was subordinated to secular concerns, and was left as the ambiguous arbiter of ethics—a role made even more vague due to the developing influence of jurisprudence, which grew in tandem with commerce.

Like the scientific experiments of Galileo once anathema to the ecclesiastics, economic experience ignored theological fiat and began to fashion man's political and social behavior. Marx was in the forefront of this intellectual revolution; but, ever the theoretical theologian, he remained with the Christian Schoolmen in a vain attempt to superimpose a metaphysical scheme on a society about which too little is known to even begin the task. It is only in the last forty years, with the spread of so-called structuralist inquiry (originating in linguistics, but spurred to a gallop by the anthropology of Claude Levi-Strauss) that even the list of areas of inquiry has begun to seem complete. Like the churches, Marx and his followers were reluctant to accept the obvious and to refashion theory to accommodate ever-augmented knowledge of social forces; they chose, instead, to model themselves after Procrustes, ruthlessly imposing an only rudimentarily deduced structural conformity on an oddly shaped world. Although the Marxists pretend to be scientists, socio-economic analysts, they act as theologians, retaining the traditional metaphysical disposition to ignore human desires and human psychology—important if not determining elements of any social analysis, surely. The Marxists are atavistic remnants of the lengthy period in human history, only just past, when it was thought a moral imperative to impose social and religious theories on humanity by force of arms.

The brutal road to the social mirage predicted by Marx is paved with the tombstones of abandoned hopes. The fields have literally been watered with the blood of the peasants, farmers and other opponents of Marxist hatred. The hillsides are populated with the grave-markers of the ungrateful dead; only in the cemetery has Marxism created social equality.

Marxism and its philosophical justification of violence represent a retreat to man's most barbarous instincts. Marxism not only openly sanctifies terror, it viciously condemns the patient discipline required by peaceful progress. Without shame Marxism demands that peace-loving people be executed or imprisoned as remnants of bourgeois culture. The fact that so many millions of people could subscribe to such an ideology tells us a great deal about mankind's basic instincts.

Society's silent progress, enshrined in mankind's delicately constructed cathedrals of human achievement, is demolished by the philosophical wrecking balls of economic determinism. Personal love and humane compassion are replaced by state-supported hate. Man's arduous and passionate pursuit of dignity is crushed by the impersonal philosophy of materialism.

In short, Marxism repudiates most of what is good and holy in human civilization, and substitutes organized savagery. Marxism is the latest human regression into barbarism. Mankind should be ashamed that the human spirit has allowed such a philosophy even to be born, let alone to dominate the lives of a fourth of humanity.

CONCLUSION

To tame the savageness of man, and to make gentle the life of the world.
—Aeschylus

E volved from man's primal, animal origins, human psychology has clearly retained instincts of violence as a necessary tool of survival. Rather than channel these instincts into constructive social purposes, religion has used them as its sustenance, cultivating them in the loam of higher purpose but directing them to aggression and manipulating them for the maintenance of illegitimate rule.

While most religions preach desirable attitudes such as love, compassion and almsgiving, it must be observed that this multitude of little kindness has not remotely offset the savagery condoned and often incited by religion in the name of these same beatitudes. For every morsel of bread given to a stranger in need, hundreds have died from diseases whose cures were thwarted by organized religion's traditional opposition to science. For every word soothing the tempers of men, there have been calls to arms resulting in the death and maiming of thousands. The United Nation's Children's Emergency Fund estimates that forty thousand children die each day even as religious organizations obstruct the distribution of birth control devices in poor countries. The resultant daily pain and torturous deaths by starvation far outstrip the almsgiving and generosity religion has always claimed to espouse. Whatever percentage of this toll is attributable to church practices, surely it has added up to far more accrued pain and death over the centuries than the atrocities of Stalin and Hitler combined. Perhaps religion could devote less attention to its inspiring liturgies and arrays of beautiful vestments and examine the real-world effects of its abstract theological fiats.

Historians can recount the evils humanity has inflicted upon itself, and the theologians can justify them with divine excuses, but the poets provide the balm of hope to sustain humankind through its history of horrors. That is why, as Russell says, tragedy is probably the most triumphant of the arts, for it constructs a cathedral of unvarnished understanding in the heart of the hostile territory of superstition and sorrow. Within this cathedral dwell the dauntless, whose willingness to accept the pain of reality can inspire those without. Its walls of ideals are built of stones cut from the granite of renounced fear and held in place by the mortar of stoic wisdom, protecting the inhabitants from the forces of despair and agony, preserving the priceless heritage of free thought and keeping undefiled the sanctuary of the unsubdued. Its citizens water the flowers of human creativity with tears of determination and hope rooted in this world.

Most religions posit an eternal war between the forces of good and evil, and usually claim that human society is merely a microcosm of that grand conflict. The theological conclusion is generally that all of us should take up the fight against evil, which even today often means killing people who do not agree with us. Marxism in particular, permeated with the conception of absolute good (the masses) and absolute evil (the capitalists) locked in historical battle, preaches this religious doctrine. The world is not so simple, and the road to a betterment of our collective lot only rarely required to be so confrontational. The religious spirit of old, a contentious spirit eclipsed for the moment but certainly not emasculated, will only perpetuate hostilities on our planet.

Religion teaches that man is wicked and that each person should purge this wickedness from his own soul; soon after the development of this useful idea, the ecclesiastical rulers undertook the delectable task of purging everyone's soul for them. Ezra sought to limit social impurity by exiling "foreign wives," the Muslims quickly transformed the inner *jihad* into a holy war, the Christians developed the Crusades and the Inquisition, and the Marxists sought to eliminate "bourgeois values" by exterminating those who maintained them. The prophets perceived flaws in human character and sought to remedy them by sacrifice and renunciation, but theirs was an incomplete wisdom; they failed to say when renunciation should cease and joys be realized. Thus a preoccupation with sacrifice created persecution masquerading as morality.

The human struggle to liberate the mind from religion's physical and psychological tyranny proceeds in different ways under various systems of belief. Restraints on religious excesses have usually been achieved as a consequence of the influence of a religion's adversaries, not by any interior urge to rationality or compassion. Ancient Judaic militarism was transformed into the psychology of *shalom* only by decimation at the hands of the Romans. The cessation of Muslim hostilities after the ninth century was the result of external forces, geography or successful foreign resistance. The amelioration of Catholic abuses was prompted by the Protestant challenge. Marxist retreats have resulted from external opposition, or the abject failure of doctrine to function effectively in the real world.

There is an old story of a statute built to honor a dead general. The monument was placed in a large park, situated in a corner for passers-by to observe as they strolled through the trees. A soldier was assigned to stand guard over the statue to prevent damage by vandals. Eventually the monument was moved to another park on the far side of town, but someone forgot to advise the army, which continued to assign a soldier to keep vigil over a monument no longer there. Day after day, night after night, year after year, the guards kept watch over the corner where the monument had stood, never bothering to learn the purpose of their quiet labors.

We all guard monuments and beliefs that have long lost their place in the world. Yet, year after year, most of us maintain a dutiful vigilence lest someone attack one or another of these phantasms, though the reason for our vigilance may have disappeared centuries, even millennia before. Many of the beliefs we cherish are nostalgic relics of a bygone age, inappropriate to our present circumstances. Like holding on to old clothes that bring back memories of a past fantasized as lovelier than it likely was, we cling to certain myths. But, unlike worn-out clothing, outmoded beliefs can possess the owner. They can stultify our growth. Unaware of this effect, we are often powerless to prevent it. Growing up means putting away the things of our childhood, and living in the world of today means putting into storage the beliefs once held dear but now only a hindrance to our functioning.

Somewhere between the poles of religious theory, between the spirituality of the traditional theologians and the materialism of the Marxists, there exists a realm of the spirit which may have little to do with either. The deposit of wisdom in the world's holy texts can provide us with a number of insights, but it is incapable of prescribing definitive moral solutions to concrete, daily problems. Whoever seeks specific guidance from these texts is doomed to disappointment, for their rules of conduct are imprecise, often inexplicit even in their generalities. Were they not so, were they based on criteria any rational person could invoke, many of the violent wars and poisonous hatreds of the world would not have come to exist.

Morality is not an obligation imposed by ecclesiastics; it is the natural opportunity of every human, a way of acting that may be demanded of all by each. The nuclear age compels us to accept the ultimate burden of our own conduct, since magnificent hopes and awful fears are equally justified by the possibilities. We have the power to play God, the benevolent and tyrannical deity of the main religions, or to be part of the eternal being that some call God. Whether or not there is a traditional, anthropomorphic God, collectively we make up a creature nearly as magnificent and awful. We have the capability to abolish all forms of human suffering, or all of human life. "How is it possible to be a saint, if there is no God?" asks Camus. It is the most significant moral question of our technological age. We are better advised to place our daily faith in constitutional texts, guides to conduct we have the power to amend, rather than follow the prescriptions of the various religious manuals, the Torah, the Bible, the Koran, the *Communist Manifesto,* and all their versions and derivatives. If we truly do believe in the basic goodness of people, we will not be disappointed. If we do not cherish such a belief, no religious manual or doctrine will bring about our happiness or our goodness.

The tale of the Sword of Damocles contains the essential truth of our times. According to Cicero, in the fourth century B.C.E. the tyrant of Syracuse overheard a messenger describe in extravagant terms the happiness of his ruler. Struck by an instructive urgce, the tyrant forced the young man, Damocles by name, to sit at a banquet table beneath a sword suspended by a single thread. The tyrant wished to impress on Damocles how precarious were the fortunes of men in power. Humanity's power in the nuclear age is greater than it has ever known, but this nuclear power is a sword suspended over its head by the mere thread of human judgment. Even a false start by any of a dozen of the world's leaders can release the sword, and humanity will be destroyed. There would be less need for fear if our geometric advances in technology and science were not accompanied by a rise in religious fundamentalism. Some among the Christians in the United States, the Marxists in the Kremlin, the Muslims in the far-flung world of Islam and the Jews in Israel are quite willing to fence with the nuclear broadsword. A return to religious fundamentalism and a resurgence of orthodox passions are growing side by side with the world's nuclear proliferation. In long-term retreat though they are, the world's religious fanatics may have the last word: "Armageddon," perhaps the easiest prophecy to fulfill. Perhaps it can be avoided, perhaps not. In our era the prophesied "wars and threats of war" remain a daily occurrence, and the gods of war maintain their sadistic leers. It is incumbent upon us all to see that these gods do not have the last laugh.

By now mankind should have learned the price of suffering that theology has forced us to pay. We will continue to pay with sorrow until we learn the lesson taught so many centuries ago by Aeschylus: "Even in our sleep, pain that we cannot forget, falls drop by drop upon the heart, until in our own despair, against our will, comes wisdom through the awful grace of God."

Three passions, simple but overwhelmingly strong, have governed my life . . . Love and knowledge, so far as they were possible, led upward to the heavens. But always pity brought me back to earth.

—Bertrand Russell, *Autobiography*

NOTES

The Theology of Conquest

I

1. Bernard R. Youngman, *The Lands and People of the Living Bible*, (New York: Bell Publishing, 1982), 68.
2. *The Holy Bible*, (New York: Hawthorne, 1958), 12.
3. Youngman, *Living Bible*, 13.
4. Charles J. Adams, *Encyclopedia Americana*, (Danbury, Conn.: Americana Corporation, 1980), vol. 15, 493.
5. *The Koran*, translated by N. J. Dawood, (London: Penguin, 1974), *sura* 14, pages 100-104. Dawood chose to organize his version of the Koran according to the likely chronological order of its writing, rather than the traditional arrangement of *suras* from longer to shorter. Page numbers for this version of the Koran are given in these notes for clarity.
6. Theophile James Meek, *Hebrew Origins*, (New York: Harper & Row, 1960), 10.
7. *Holy Bible*, Genesis 15:18-21.

II

1. Moshe Dayan, *Living with the Bible*, (New York: William Morrow, 1978), 40.

III

1. Meek, *Hebrew Origins*, 31.
2. Ibid., 30.
3. Youngman, *Living Bible*, 56.
4. Dayan, *Living with the Bible*, 71.
5. Meek, *Hebrew Origins*, 37.
6. Ibid.
7. Ibid.
8. Sigmund Freud, *Moses and Monotheism*, (New York: Vintage, 1967), 33.
9. Ibid., 34.
10. Ibid., 34-35.
11. Ibid., 156.
12. Edward S. Gifford, Jr., *The Evil Eye*, (New York: Macmillan, 1958), 42.

IV

1. Freud, *Monotheism*, 55.
2. Ibid., 142.
3. Ibid., 164.

V

1. Solomon Grayzel, *A History of the Jews*, (New York: New American Library, 1968), 43.

2. *Holy Bible,* Deuteronomy 20:1-5.
3. Ibid., Isaiah 37:5-8.
4. Freud, *Monotheism,* 42-43, 57-59.
5. *Holy Bible,* Deuteronomy 28:64-67.
6. Salo Whittmayer Baron, *Encyclopedia Americana,* vol. 16, 67.
7. Ibid.

VI

1. Henry A. Halley, *Halley's Bible Handbook,* (Grand Rapids, Mich.: Zondervan, 1984), 403.
2. Halley, *Bible Handbook,* 404.
3. Bertrand Russell, *A History of Western Philosophy,* (New York: Simon and Schuster, 1972), 316.
4. Ibid., 317-18.

VII

1. Barbara W. Tuchman, *Bible and Sword,* (New York: Funk & Wagnalls, 1956), 330-33.
2. Ibid., 333.
3. Ibid., 329.
4. Ibid., 337.
5. Richard P. Stevens, *Weizman & Smuts,* (Beirut, Lebanon: Institute for Palestine Studies, 1975), 35.
6. Tuchman, *Sword,* 337.
7. Ibid., 346.
8. Francis R. Nicosia, *The Third Reich and the Palestinian Question,* (Austin, Tex.: University of Texas Press, 1985), 100.
9. Ibid., 127.
10. Frederic Morton, *The Rothschilds,* (Great Britain: Penguin, 1961), 181.
11. Ibid., 182.
12. Ibid., 248.
13. Nicosia, *Palestinian Question,* 127.
14. Ibid., 74.
15. Ibid., 69.
16. Ibid., 74.
17. Ibid., 82.
18. Ibid., 79.
19. Ibid., 72.
20. Ibid., 82.
21. Ibid., 91.
22. Ibid., 83.
23. Morton, *Rothschilds,* 222.
24. Nicosia, *Palestinian Question,* 59-60.
25. Ibid., 50-54.
26. Ibid., 62-63.
27. Edwin Black, *The Transfer Agreement,* (New York: Macmillan, 1984), 175.
28. Nicosia, *Palestinian Question,* 41-42.
29. Ibid., 42.
30. Black, *Agreement,* 253.
31. Ibid., 258.

32. Ibid., 373.
33. Ibid., 318.
34. Ibid., 226.
35. Ibid., 88.
36. Ibid., 226.
37. Ibid., 379.
38. Ibid., 78.
39. Ibid., 382.
40. Ibid., 374.
41. Ibid., 74.
42. Ibid., 34-35.
43. Stephen Green, *Taking Sides,* (New York: William Morrow, 1984), 50.
44. Ibid.
45. Ibid.
46. Abba Eban, *The New York Diplomacy: International Affairs in the Modern Age,* (New York: Random House, 1983), 204.
47. Green, *Taking Sides,* 59.
48. Ibid., 60.
49. Ibid., 62.
50. Ibid., 63.
51. Ibid., 52-54.
52. Isaac Deutscher, *Stalin: A Political Biography,* (New York: Oxford University Press, 1949), 591.
53. Ibid., 607.
54. Arkady N. Shevchenko, *Breaking with Moscow,* (New York: Knopf, 1985), 135.
55. John G. Stoessinger, *Why Nations Go to War,* (New York: St. Martin's, 1982), 144.
56. Green, *Taking Sides,* 72.
57. Ibid., 36.
58. Ibid., 38.
59. Ibid., 39-40.
60. Ibid., 37.
61. Ibid., 100.
62. Ibid., 105-6.
63. Ibid., 107-14.
64. Viktor Suvorov, *Inside Soviet Military Intelligence,* (New York: Berkeley, 1984), 63.
65. Green, *Taking Sides,* 130.
66. Ibid.
67. Moshe Dayan, *The Story of My Life,* (Jerusalem: Steimatzky, 1976), 150.
68. Ritchie Ovendale, *Origins of the Arab-Israeli Wars,* (New York: Longman, 1984), 163.
69. Abba Eban, *An Autobiography,* (New York: Random House, 1977), 211.
70. Ovendale, *Arab-Israeli Wars,* 176-77.
71. Ibid., 178.
72. Ibid.
73. Stewart Steven, *The Spymasters of Israel,* (New York: Ballantine, 1980), 234.
74. Paul Findley, *They Dare to Speak Out,* (Westport, Conn.: Lawrence Hill, 1985), 176.
75. Ibid.
76. Green, *Taking Sides,* 23.
77. Findley, *Speak Out,* 179.
78. I. L. Kenen, *Israel's Defense Line,* (Buffalo, NY: Prometheus, 1981), 223.
79. "Israeli Economy Depends on No-Questions-Asked Arms Sale," *Washington Post,*

12/12/86, A-1. The *Post* says that Israel's "defense industry employs between 140,000 and 200,000 people to make and sell arms." The Israeli labor force in 1986 was estimated to be 1,476,000 people, according to the Israeli embassy in Washington, D.C. Thus, between 10 percent and 14 percent of the work force manufactures or sells arms. However, since an estimated 500,000 Israelis do not live in Israel, the active work force in Israel is closer to 1 million people. This means between 14 percent and 20 percent of Israeli residents are employed by the arms industry. A similar number work for the Israeli military. Altogether, between 25 percent and 35 percent of the resident members of the Israeli work force are employed by the military-industrial complex.

80. Ibid. The *Post* cites the Stockholm International Peace Research Institute, a center for defense information, as concluding that Israel was the ninth-largest arms supplier in the world between 1981 and 1985. In 1980 Israel sold in excess of $1 billion worth of arms. Clients included South Africa, Iran, the People's Republic of China, and several countries in Latin America. Sales for 1986, assuming an Israeli population of 4.1 million people (including non-residents) was pegged at an astounding $244 per capita, a figure that would be much higher if non-resident Israelis and Palestinians in the annexed territories were subtracted from the calculations.

81. Connor Cruise O'Brien, *The Siege*, (New York: Simon and Schuster, 1986), 624-25.

82. "Israel as Public Works Project," *Washington Post*, 12/15/85, C-1.

83. "Pro-Israel PACs Giving More to GOP," *Washington Post*, 11/4/85, A-1.

84. Findley, *Speak Out*, 80.

85. "Israel Builds and U.S. Funds Lavi Jet Fighter," *Washington Post*, 8/6/86, A-22.

86. "Pro-Israel PACs," *Washington Post*, A-1.

87. Findley, *Speak Out*, 161.

88. Michael Saba, *The Armageddon Network*, (Vermont: Amana, 1984), 18.

89. "U.S. an Intelligence Target of the Israelis, Officials Say," *Washington Post*, 6/5/86, A-1.

90. Seymour M. Hersh, *The Price of Power*, (New York: Summit, 1983), 85.

91. *Washington Post*, 10/27/86, A-18.

92. *Washington Post*, 10/25/86.

93. Saba, *Network*, 175-76.

94. "Intelligence Target," *Washington Post*, 6/5/86, A-1.

95. "Many Soviet Jews Face Problems Adapting to Israel," *Washington Post*, 10/11/86, A-1.

96. "1986 Report Demographic, Economic, Legal, Social, and Political Developments in the West Bank," (Jerusalem: American Enterprise Institute, The West Bank Data Project, and the *Jerusalem Post*, 1986), 7.

97. Ibid., 10.

98. Ibid., 21.

99. Ibid., 28.

100. Ibid., 30.

101. Ibid., 11-12.

102. Ibid., 13.

103. Ibid., 38.

104. Ibid., 44.

105. Ibid., 17.

106. Ibid., 18-19.

107. Ibid., 17.

108. A. P. Thornton, *The Imperial Idea & Its Enemies*, (New York: St. Martin's, 1959), 154.

109. Stevens, *Smuts*, 2.

110. Ibid., 3.

111. Ibid., 11.

112. Howard A. Sachar, *A History of Israel*, (New York: Knopf, 1985), 107.

113. Stevens, *Smuts*, 30.

114. Ibid., 10-11.

115. Ibid., 113.

116. Regina Sharif, *Non-Jewish Zionism*, (London: Zed, 1983), 128.

The Theology of Power

I

1. William Shakespeare, *The Riverside Shakespeare*, (Boston: Houghton Mifflin, 1974), 1766.

2. David Estes, *Encyclopedia Americana*, vol. 16, 165.

3. Ibid.; 43.

4. Ibid., 44.

5. Michael Baigent, Richard Leigh, and Henry Lincoln, *The Holy Blood and the Holy Grail*, (London: Corgi, 1982), 367.

6. Ibid., 368.

7. Ibid., 366-67.

8. Ibid., 364.

9. Ibid., 366.

10. Ibid.

11. Ibid., 375-76.

12. *The Holy Bible*, Romans 5:12-14.

13. Hugh Schonfield, *The Passover Plot*, (Lonmead, England: Element, 1985), 34.

14. Halley, *Bible Handbook*, 609.

15. Will Durant, *Caesar and Christ*, (New York: Simon and Schuster, 1972), 585.

16. Ibid.

17. *Encyclopedia Americana*, vol. 21, 413.

18. Durant, *Christ*, 583.

19. Josephus, *Complete Works*, William Whiston, A. M., trans., (Grand Rapids, Mich.: Kregel, 1985), chap. 3, 3-6.

20. Michael Grant, *The Jews in the Roman World*, (New York: Dorset, 1984), 203.

21. Ibid., 214.

22. Ibid., 215.

23. Ibid., 214.

24. Ibid., 215.

25. Ibid., 217.

26. Ibid., 221.

27. Ibid., 219.

28. Ibid., 211.

29. Ibid., 213.

30. Bertrand Russell, *Western Philosophy*, 326.

31. Ibid., 327.

32. Ibid., 329.

33. John T. MacNeil, *Encyclopedia Americana*, vol. 6, 652.

34. Ibid., 652.

35. J. J. Fox, S.T.D., *Encyclopedia Americana*, vol. 21, 252.

36. Russell, *Western Philosophy*, 368, citing Edward Gibbon, *Decline and Fall of the Roman Empire*, chap. 15.

II

1. Baigent, Leigh, and Lincoln, *Holy Grail*, 386.
2. Ibid., 387.
3. Ibid., 388.
4. Ibid., 387.
5. Ibid., 389.
6. Malachi Martin, *The Decline and Fall of the Roman Church*, (New York: G. P. Putnam's Sons, 1981), 37.
7. J. N. D. Kelly, *The Oxford Dictionary of Popes*, (Oxford: Oxford University Press, 1986), 28.
8. Edward Gibbon, *Roman Empire*, (New York: Random House), vol. 1, 511.
9. *Encyclopedia Americana*, vol. 2, 297.
10. Russell, *Western Philosophy*, 362.
11. Ibid., 362-63.
12. *Encyclopedia Americana*, vol. 2, 687.
13. Frederick C. Grant, *Encyclopedia Americana*, vol. 13, 101-2.
14. Schonfield, *Plot*, 228.
15. Ibid., 238-39.
16. R. A. F. MacKenzie, S.J., *Encyclopedia Americana*, vol. 28, 245.
17. Ibid., 246.
18. Russell, *Western Philosophy*, 368, citing Gibbon, *Roman Empire*, chap. 47.
19. Ibid.
20. Ibid.
21. Michael P. Carroll, *The Cult of the Virgin Mary*, Princeton, NJ: Princeton University Press, 1986), 85.
22. Schonfield, *Plot*, 50, citing Matyr, *First Apology*, xxi-xxii.
23. Carroll, *Virgin Mary*, 92.
24. Ibid., 32.
25. Ibid., 79-83.
26. Ibid., 99.
27. Ibid., 111.
28. Ibid., 88.
29. Ibid.
30. Schonfield, *Plot*, 57.
31. Charles Sheedy, E.C.S.C., *Encyclopedia Americana*, vol. 14, 802.
32. "Sixty Minutes," CBS News broadcast, 12/28/86.
33. Will Durant, *The Age of Faith*, (New York: Simon and Schuster, 1950), 742.
34. Ibid., 742-43.
35. Ibid., 743.
36. Ibid., 744.
37. Ibid.
38. Ibid.

III

1. Russell, *Western Philosophy*, 378, citing Gibbon, *Roman Empire*, chap. 37, note 57.
2. Karlfreid Froehlich, *Encyclopedia Americana*, vol. 13, 468.
3. Hermann Kinder and Werner Hilgemann, *Anchor Atlas of World History*, (Garden

City, NY: Anchor/Doubleday, 1974), 140.

4. Russell, *Western Philosophy*, 385-86.

5. Ibid., 46y.

6. Ibid., 389.

7. Ibid., 388.

8. Ibid., 389.

9. Ibid., 392.

10. Ibid., 390.

11. Ibid., 392.

12. Martin, *Roman Church*, 121.

13. Ibid., 119.

14. Ibid., 125.

15. Ibid., 126.

16. Kelly, *Popes*, 127.

17. Martin, *Roman Church*, 126.

18. Ibid.

19. Ibid., 120.

20. Ibid., 129.

21. Ibid., 130.

22. Ibid., 132.

23. Ibid., 131.

24. Russell, *Western Philosophy*, 409, citing *Cambridge Medieval History*, vol. 5, chap. 10.

25. Kelly, *Popes*, 148.

IV

1. Steven Runciman, *The First Crusade*, (Cambridge, England: Cambridge University Press, 1980), 15.

2. Jean Canu, *Encyclopedia Americana*, vol. 27, 165.

3. Runciman, *Crusade*, 48.

4. Ibid.

5. Ibid.

6. Ibid., 61.

7. John Saunders Jr., *Encyclopedia Americana*, vol. 8, 264-65.

8. Ibid.

9. Runciman, *Crusade*, 66.

10. Ibid., 62.

11. Hugh Trevor-Roper, *The Rise of Christian Europe*, (London: Thames and Hudson, 1978), 101.

12. Ibid., 101-2.

13. John J. Saunders, *Encyclopedia Americana*, vol. 8, 265.

14. Russell, *Western Philosophy*, 443.

15. Ibid., 442.

16. Trevor-Roper, *Christian Europe*, 110.

17. Russell, *Western Philosophy*, 442.

18. *New Columbia Encyclopedia*, (New York: Columbia University Press, 1975), 691.

19. Russell, *Western Philosophy*, 443.

20. Ibid., 446.

21. Ibid., 444-45.

22. Steven Runciman, *The Sicilian Vespers*, (London: Penguin, 1960), 32.

23. Ibid.

24. Joseph F. O'Callaghan, *Encyclopedia Americana*, vol. 13, 472.
25. Barbara W. Tuchman, *The March of Folly*, (New York: Knopf, 1984), 72.
26. Ibid., 73.
27. Ibid.
28. Trevor-Roper, *Christian Europe*, 124-25.
29. Trevor-Roper, *Christian Europe*, 129.
30. J. G. Rowe, *Encyclopedia Americana*, vol. 15, 192.
31. Ibid.
32. Durant, *Faith*, 781-82.
33. Ibid.
34. John Charles Nelson, *Encyclopedia Americana*, vol. 4, 655.
35. "Rehabilitating Galileo's Image," *Time*, 3/12/84, 72.
36. Colin A. Ronan, *Galileo*, (New York: G. P. Putnam's Sons, 1974), 217.
37. Stillman Drake, *Encyclopedia Americana*, vol. 12, 243.
38. Ronan, *Galileo*, 221.
39. Ibid., 243.

V

1. Martin, *Roman Church*, 154.
2. Ibid., 158.
3. Ibid., 153.
4. Ibid., 159.
5. Ibid.
6. Ibid., 161.
7. Ibid., 164.
8. Ibid., 163.
9. Russell, *Western Philosophy*, 480.
10. Ibid., 482.
11. Fernand Braudel, *The Structures of Everyday Life*, vol. 1 of *Capitalism & Civilization, 15th to 18th Centuries*, (New York: Harper & Row, 1981), 399.
12. Tuchman, *Folly*, 75.
13. Ibid.
14. Ibid., 83.
15. Ibid., 88.
16. Ibid., 89.
17. Ibid.
18. Ibid., 95.
19. Ibid., 96.
20. Ibid., 97.
21. Ibid.
22. Ibid., 114.
23. Ibid., 110.
24. Will Durant, *The Renaissance*, (New York: Simon and Schuster, 1953), 688.
25. James G. Frazer, *The Golden Bough*, (New York: Avenel, 1981), 89-90.
26. Clyde L. Manschreck, ed., *A History of Christianity*, (Grand Rapids, Mich.: Baker Book House, 1984), vol. 2, 38, citing Martin Luther, "Against the Thievish, Murderous Hordes of Peasants."
27. John T. McNeill, *Encyclopedia Americana*, vol. 5, 239.
28. Will Durant, *The Age of Reformation*, (New York: Simon and Schuster, 1957), 490.
29. Robert M. Kingdon, *Encyclopedia Americana*, vol. 14, 539.

30. Edmund Dickerson, *Encyclopedia Americana*, vol. 11, 757-58.

31. Robert M. Kingdon, *Encyclopedia Americana*, vol. 14, 539.

32. William Montgomery McGovern, *From Luther to Hitler*, (Boston: Houghton Mifflin, 1941), 36.

33. Ibid., 50.

VI

1. Martin, *Roman Church*, 254.

2. Ibid., 255.

3. Ibid., 248.

4. David A. Yallop, *In God's Name*, (New York: Bantam, 1984), 10.

5. Hans Küng, *Infallible? An Inquiry*, (New York: Doubleday, 1983), 37-38.

6. Yallop, *God's Name*, 93.

7. Ibid.

8. Ibid., 94.

9. Ibid., 95.

10. Ibid., 96.

11. Lorraine Boettner, *Roman Catholicism*, (New Jersey: Presbyterian and Reformed Publishing, 1986), 435.

12. Ibid., 436.

13. Ibid., 437.

14. Yallop, *In God's Name*, 156.

15. Ibid., 97-98.

16. Ibid., 31.

17. Ibid., 98.

18. Ibid., 299.

19. Ibid., 289.

20. Ibid., 321.

21. Ibid., 324.

22. Ibid.

23. Ibid., 100-102.

24. Ibid., 171.

25. Ibid., 171-72.

26. Ibid., 169.

27. Ibid., 320.

28. Ibid., 220.

29. Ibid., 222-54.

30. Ibid., 254.

31. Ibid., 255.

32. Ibid., 222.

33. Ibid., 223.

34. Ibid., 232.

35. Ibid., 239.

36. Ibid., 294.

37. Ibid., 321.

38. Ibid., 294.

39. *Washington Post*, 1/10/87, D-3.

40. Ibid.

41. James Randi, Paul Kurtz, Joseph N. Barnhart, and Paul Singer, "An Investigation of Faith-Healers," *Free Inquiry*, Spring 1986, 43.

42. Conversation between the author and a former employee of the Moral Majority, who wishes not to be identified.

The Theology of Plunder

I

1. N. J. Dawood, trans., *The Koran*, (England: Penguin, 1981), *sura* 93:6, page 24.
2. J. M. Roberts, *The Pelican History of the World*, (England: Penguin, 1985), 318.
3. Will Durant, *The Age of Faith*, (New York: Simon and Schuster, 1950), 162.
4. *The Koran*, page 9.
5. Philip K. Hitti, *Encyclopedia Americana*, vol. 19, 315.
6. Durant, *Faith*, 164.
7. Ibid.
8. *The Koran*, page 10.
9. Philip K. Hitti, *Encyclopedia Americana*, 315.
10. Durant, *Faith*, 165.
11. Ibid., 172.
12. Ibid., 172-73.
13. Philip K. Hitti, *Encyclopedia Americana*, 316.
14. Charles J. Adams, *Encyclopedia Americana*, vol. 15, 493.

II

1. Durant, *Faith*, 175.
2. Adams, *Encyclopedia Americana*, 495.
3. Malise Ruthven, *Islam in the World*, (New York: Oxford University Press, 1984), 102.
4. Ibid., 82.
5. William H. McNeil, *A World History*, (New York: Oxford University Press, 1979), 217.
6. Adams, *Encyclopedia Americana*, 496.
7. Ibid.
8. Ibid.
9. Ibid., 496-97.
10. Ruthven, *World*, 98.
11. V. S. Naipaul, *Among the Believers*, (New York: Vintage, 1981), 132.
12. Ibid.
13. Steven Runciman, *The First Crusade*, (Cambridge, England: Cambridge University Press, 1980), 15.
14. *The Koran*, *sura* 3:13, pages 408-9.
15. Ibid., *sura* 3:14-141, page 419.
16. Ibid., *sura* 3:111, page 417.

III

1. Ruthven, *World*, 96.
2. Ibid., 90.
3. Ibid., 92.
4. Colin McEvedy, *The Penguin Atlas of Medieval History*, (New York: Penguin, 1967), 36.

5. Roberts, *History of the World*, 322.
6. Ibid.
7. Durant, *Faith*, 191.
8. Ibid.
9. Ibid., 192.
10. Ibid., 191-92.
11. *New Columbia Encyclopedia*, 1371.
12. Ibid.
13. Bertrand Russell, *Western Philosophy*, 420-21.
14. Peter Mansfield, *The Arabs*, (England: Penguin, 1980), 40.
15 J. M. Roberts, *History of the World*, 329.
16. Ibid.
17. *The Koran, sura* 8:37, page 317.
18. Durant, *Faith*, 235-80.

IV

1. Russell, *Western Philosophy*, 421.
2. Adams, *Encyclopedia Americana*, 498.
3. Ibid., 499.
4. Ibid.
5. Ibid., 498.
6. Ibid., 500.
7. Ibid., 499.
8. Ibid., 500.
9. Mansfield, *The Arabs*, 28.
10. Durant, *Faith*, 258.
11. *Encyclopedia Americana*, vol. 25, 849.
12. Durant, *Faith*, 338.
13. Mansfield, *The Arabs*, 115.
14. Ibid., 117.

V

1. McEvedy, *Atlas Medieval*, 62.
2. John R. Walsh, *Encyclopedia Americana*, vol. 27, 253.
3. John P. D. B. Kinross Baron, *The Ottoman Centuries*, (New York: Morrow Quill, 1977), 24.
4. Ibid., 34.
5. Walsh, *Encyclopedia Americana*, 252-53.
6. Ibid., 258.
7. Ibid., 259.
8. John M. Blair, *The Control of Oil*, (New York: Pantheon, 1976), 31.
9. Ibid., 36.
10. Ibid., 41.
11. R. Hrair Dekmejian, *Islam in Revolution*, (New York: Syracuse University Press, 1986), 150.
12. James Adams, *The Financing of Terror*, (New York: Simon and Schuster, 1986), 54.
13. Ibid., 54-55.
14. Ibid., 55.
15. Ibid.
16. *Encyclopaedia Britannica*, (Chicago: Encyclopaedia Britannica, 1986), vol. 25, 418.

17. *Encyclopaedia Britannica*, vol. 9, 82.
18. Adams, *Terror*, 117.
19. Ibid., 234.
20. Ibid., 113.
21. Robin Wright, *Sacred Rage*, (New York: Linden/Simon and Schuster, 1985), 230.
22. Ibid., 237.
23. Ibid., 233.
24. Ibid., 239.
25. Shaul Bakhash, *The Reign of the Ayatollahs*, (New York: Basic, 1984), 23.
26. Ibid., 125.
27. Ibid., 226.
28. Ibid., 227.
29. Ibid., 221.

The Theology of Hate

I

1. Robert L. Heilbroner, *The Worldly Philosophers*, (New York: Simon and Schuster, 1972), 135.

II

1. Carl Joachim Friedrich, *Encyclopedia Americana*, vol. 14, 49.
2. Ellsworth, Raymond, *Encyclopedia Americana*, vol. 10, 349-50.
3. Heilbroner, *Worldly Philosophers*, 135.
4. Ibid.
5. Gordon Stein, Ph.D., ed., *Encyclopedia of Unbelief*, (Buffalo, NY: Prometheus, 1985), vol. 2, 443.
6. Bertrand Russell, *Western Philosophy*, 785.
7. Edmund Wilson, *To The Finland Station*, London: Fontana, 1966, 323-324.
8. Russell, *Western Philosophy*, 788.
9. Ibid.
10. Hans Reichenbach, *The Rise of Scientific Philosophy*, (Berkeley, Calif.: University of California Press, 1963), 71-72.

III

1. Russell, *Western Philosophy*, 635.
2. R. H. Tawney, *Religion and the Rise of Capitalism*, (Gloucester, Mass.: Peter Smith, 1962), 36, citing Henry of Langenstein, *Tracticus Bipartibus de Contractibus Emptionis et Verditioris*.
3. Tawney, *Rise of Capitalism*, 79-102.
4. Ibid.
5. Ibid., 36.
6. Ibid., 25.
7. Yallop, *In God's Name*, 10.
8. Frederick Coplestone, S.J., *History of Philosophy*, vol. 7, 334.
9. Yallop, *In God's Name*, 10.
10. *The New Oxford Annotated Bible*, (New York: Oxford University Press, 1977), Matthew 10:34.

IV

1. Russell, *Western Philosophy*, 444.

2. Donald W. Treadgold, *Encyclopedia Americana*, vol. 17, 204.

3. W. Bruce Lincoln, *Passage Through Armageddon*, (New York: Simon and Schuster, 1986), 231.

4. Angelo S. Rappaport, *Pioneers of the Russian Revolution*, (New York: Brentano's, 1919), 231-32.

5. V. I. Lenin, *What Is to Be Done?*, (New York: International, 1969), 156-67.

6. Donald W. Treadgold, *Encyclopedia Americana*, vol. 4, 178.

7. V. I. Lenin, *Imperialism: The Highest Stage of Capitalism*, (New York: International, 1984), 99-100.

8. Ibid., 91-92.

9. Arkady N. Shevchenko, *Breaking with Moscow*, (New York: Knopf, 1985), 175.

10. Martin McCauley, *The Soviet Union Since 1917*, (England: Longman, 1981), 17.

11. Tom Bottomore, *A Dictionary of Marxist Thought*, (Cambridge, Mass.: Harvard University Press, 1983), 280.

12. Isaac Deutscher, *Stalin*, (New York: Oxford University Press, 1949), 72.

13. Ibid., 234.

14. Ibid.

15. Ibid.

16. Derek Leebaert, *Soviet Military Thinking*, (London: George Allen & Unwin, 1981), 32.

17. Seweryn Bialer, *The Soviet Paradox*, (New York: Knopf, 1986), 184.

18. Lincoln, *Armegeddon*, 50.

19. *Cambridge Encyclopedia of Russia*, (Cambridge, England: Cambridge University Press, 1982), 435.

20. Peter Hopkirk, *Setting the East Ablaze*, (New York: W. W. Norton, 1985), 102.

21. Ibid., 228.

22. Bottomore, *Marxist Thought*, 278.

23. Ibid., 279.

24. Roy A. Medvedev, *Let History Judge*, (New York: Vintage, 1973), 24-26.

25. *Cambridge Encyclopedia of Russia*, 332.

26. Medvedev, *Let History Judge*, 25.

27. Deutscher, *Stalin*, 304.

28. Ibid., 305.

29. Dennis Prager and Joseph Telushkin, *Why the Jews?*, (New York: Simon and Schuster, 1983), 62.

30. Ibid.

31. *Encyclopedia Americana*, vol. 29, 782.

32. Isaac Deutscher, *The Prophet Unarmed*, (New York: Oxford University Press, 1980), 259.

33. Ibid., 258.

34. Deutscher, *Stalin*, 605.

35. Ibid., 607.

36. Prager, *Why the Jews?*, 102-3.

37. Medvedev, *Let History Judge*, 66.

38. Ibid., 67.

39. Deutscher, *Stalin*, 314.

40. Medvedev, *Let History Judge*, 68.

41. Deutscher, *Stalin*, 318.

42. Fernando Claudin, *The Communist Movement*, (New York: Monthly Review, 1975), 153.

43. Ibid., 154.
44. E. H. Carr, *The Comintern & the Spanish Civil War*, (New York: Pantheon, 1984), 3.
45. Ibid., 45.
46. Ibid., 15.
47. Leon Trotsky, *The Spanish Revolution*, (New York: Pathfinder, 1973), 329.
48. Carr, *Comintern*, 36.
49. Trotsky, *Revolution*, 350.
50. Bialer, *Paradox*, 185.
51. Ibid., 180.
52. Deutscher, *Stalin*, 377.
53. William F. Buckley, Jr., "Harvest of Despair," *Washington Post*, 9/9/86, A-25.
54. Deutscher, *Stalin*, 377.
55. Viktor Suvorov, *Inside Soviet Military Intelligence*, (New York: Macmillan, 1984), 20.
56. Jean-Francois Revel, *How Democracies Perish*, (New York: Harper & Row, 1985), 56-57.
57. Bialer, *Paradox*, 183.
58. Ibid., 185.
59. Vitaly Rappaport and Yuri Alexeev, *High Treason*, (Durham, NC: Duke University Press, 1985), 349.
60. Trotsky, *Revolution*, 301.
61. Suvorov, *Soviet Intelligence*, 25.
62. Abba Eban, *The New Diplomacy*, (New York: Random House, 1983), 203.
63. Ibid., 204.
64. Ibid.
65. Stephen Green, *Taking Sides*, (New York: William Morrow, 1984), 16-75.
66. Eban, *Diplomacy*, 204.
67. Bialer, *Paradox*, 184.
68. *Cambridge Encyclopedia of China*, (Cambridge, England: Cambridge University Press, 1982), 285.
69. Ibid., 286.
70. Ibid.
71. Ibid.
72. Ibid., 290.
73. "Rewards to Create Better Products," *China Daily*, 10/3/84, 1.

V

1. Author's conversations with citizens of the Soviet Union during various visits.
2. *Cambridge Encyclopedia of Russia*, 80.
3. Ibid., 128.
4. Ibid., 130.
5. Ibid., 131.
6. Ibid., 329.
7. Ibid.
8. Ibid., 331.
9. Ibid.
10. *Encyclopedia Americana*, vol. 27, 428.
11. Ibid.
12. *Cambridge Encyclopedia of Russia*, 332.
13. Ibid.
14. Hedrick Smith, *The Russians*, (New York Times Books, 1983), 238.

15. *Cambridge Encyclopedia of Russia*, 337.

16. Smith, *Russians*, 205.

17. *Cambridge Encyclopedia of Russia*, 338.

18. "Soviets Solicit New Economic Ties," *Washington Post*, 6/9/86, A-33.

19. Ibid. This does not apply to machinery directly related to the Soviet Union's military-industrial complex which, owing to Soviet priorities, is the recipient of the latest domestic technology.

20. Ibid.

21. *PlanEcon Report*, 10/2/86, 18.

22. Smith, *Russians*, 233.

23. *Morgan Economic Quarterly*, June 1986.

24. Smith, *Russians*, 90.

25. Ibid.

26. Ibid., 93.

27. Schevchenko, *Moscow*, 320.

28. Smith, *Russians*, 217.

29. Karl Marx and Frederick Engels, *Selected Works*, (New York: International, 1984), 582-83.

30. *Cambridge Encyclopedia of Russia*, 370.

31. Revel, *Democracies Perish*, 90.

32. *PlanEcon Report*, 5/4/86, 3-4.

33. "Controls on the Export of Capital from the United States," Committee on Banking, Housing and Urban Affairs, 9/26–12/4/85, 3.

34. Roger W. Robinson, Jr., "East-West Trade and National Security," speech, 2/11/86.

35. *PlanEcon Report*, 10/2/86, 18.

36. "Controls on the Export of Capital," 3.

37. Congress and National Security Affairs, *National Security Record*, April 1986, 5.

38. Lenin, *Capitalism*, 119.

39. David Lane, *Soviet Economy & Society*, (New York: New York University Press, 1985), 56.

40. *Cambridge Encyclopedia of Russia*, 298.

41. Ibid., 406.

42. Ibid., 407-8.

43. Ibid., 407.

44. Ibid., 409.

45. Ibid., 411.

46. Conversation between the author and a Soviet black market operator, July 1984.

47. *Cambridge Encyclopedia of Russia*, 262.

48. George A. Hanna, trans., *History of the USSR*, (Moscow: Progress, 1977).

49. Ravel, *Democracies Perish*, 90.

50. *Washington Post*, 7/27/84, A-25.

51. Edward N. Luttwak, *The Grand Strategy of the Soviet Union*, (New York: St. Martin's, 1983), 25.

52. Ravel, *Democracies Perish*, 17.

53. *PlanEcon Report*, 8/14/86, 16.

54. Ravel, *Democracies Perish*, 56.

55. Shevchenko, *Moscow*, 285.

56. Buckley, "Despair."

57. Conversation between the author and Edward N. Luttwak.

58. Luttwak, *Grand Strategy*, 67.

59. Ravel, *Democracies Perish*, 92.

INDEX